Cultural Competence

A PRIMER FOR EDUCATORS

JERRY V. DILLER
The Wright Institute, Berkeley, California

JEAN MOULE
Oregon State University

THOMSON
WADSWORTH

Australia • Canada • Mexico • Singapore • Spain • United Kingdom • United States

THOMSON
✳ ™
WADSWORTH

Publisher/Executive Editor: Vicki L. Knight
Acquisitions Editor: Dan Alpert
Development Editor: Tangelique Williams
Editorial Assistant: Erin Worley
Marketing Manager: Dory Schaeffer
Advertising Project Manager: Tami Strang
Project Manager, Editorial Production:
  Rita Jaramillo
Art Director: Rob Hugel

Print/Media Buyer: Emma Claydon
Permissions Editor: Stephanie Lee
Production Service: Shepherd, Inc.
Copy Editor: Sybil Sosin
Cover Designer: Brenda Duke Design
Cover Printer: Transcontinental
Compositor: Shepherd, Inc.
Printer: Transcontinental

For more information about our products,
contact us at:
**Thomson Learning Academic
Resource Center
1-800-423-0563**
For permission to use material from this
text or product, submit a request online at
http://www.thomsonrights.com
Any additional questions about permissions
can be submitted by email to
thomsonrights@thomson.com

Library of Congress Control Number:
2003116984

ISBN 0-534-58416-0

Thomson Wadsworth
10 Davis Drive
Belmont, CA 94002-3098
USA

Asia
Thomson Learning
5 Shenton Way #01-01
UIC Building
Singapore 068808

Australia/New Zealand
Thomson Learning
102 Dodds Street
Southbank, Victoria 3006
Australia

Canada
Nelson
1120 Birchmount Road
Toronto, Ontario M1K 5G4
Canada

Europe/Middle East/Africa
Thomson Learning
High Holborn House
50/51 Bedford Row
London WC1R 4LR
United Kingdom

Latin America
Thomson Learning
Seneca, 53
Colonia Polanco
11560 Mexico D.F.
Mexico

Spain/Portugal
Paraninfo
Calle Magallanes, 25
28015 Madrid, Spain

Contents

Chapter 3

Understanding Racism and Prejudice   28

Chapter 4

Understanding Privilege and Racial Consciousness among Whites   52

Chapter 5

Understanding Culture and Cultural Differences   65

Chapter 9

Critical Issues in Working with Culturally Different Students   169

Chapter 10

Working with Latino/a Students: An Interview with Aurora Cedillo   190

Chapter 11

Working with Native American Students: An Interview with Jack Lawson   208

Preface

Cultural Competence: A Primer for Educators is a basic textbook for students in education. It is about how to most effectively and competently provide services cross-culturally. It presents a clear understanding of how a complex variety of social and psychological factors come together to shape a teacher's ability to work with students who are culturally different. Included are chapters on cultural competence; racism; culture, ethnocentricity, and privilege; ethnic children, parenting, and families; multicultural issues in education; bias in curriculum delivery; and the practical dynamics of getting started. There are, in addition, chapters focusing specifically on working with African Americans, Latinos/as, Asian Americans, and Native Americans written by expert educators from those communities, as well as a final chapter on White ethnics.

The book can be used as a primary text for multicultural issues and cultural diversity courses in education as well as for student services programs in community colleges, four-year colleges, and beginning graduate programs. It can also be used as a supplementary text in basic education and field experiences courses where the intent is to sensitize students to the cultural dimensions of teaching and learning. Finally, it can be a valuable asset in the continuing education of teachers interested in broadening their theoretical and practical knowledge of what has become the fastest growing content area in the field of education.

The book is unique in its breadth of coverage as well as its organization and style. It integrates theory with hands-on practical knowledge and does so from the perspective of asking what kinds of information a student needs to grasp the essentials of culturally competent teaching. Its treatment of topics is comprehensive. For example, racism, a vital issue summarily addressed in most multicultural texts, is explored from a variety of perspectives. What is it? How does it operate in the individual and in society's institutions to oppress people? Why do many mainstream individuals find it so hard to acknowledge racism and their own privilege? How do teachers' prejudices compromise the learning process? How does one become aware of and alter negative racial attitudes? What are the psychological consequences of racism and oppression on People of Color, especially the developing child? And how does racism operate within schools and the teaching professions? To assist the reader in personalizing these questions, self-awareness exercises are provided at the end of Chapter 3. Other chapters end with questions related to the steps of creative problem solving that allow the reader to engage with the chapter material while learning a practical problem-solving technique.

A second unique feature of the book is its accessibility. Though it is rich in theoretical and practical material, it is not overly academic. For example, rather than exhaustively reviewing all studies within a given subject area, it succinctly surveys critical questions and issues and supports them with detailed descriptions of exemplary research. In addition, anecdotes, personal practical experiences, and real-world examples are generously included. It is easy to read and written for and to the student educator, anticipating questions, concerns, and anxieties that the topic has regularly elicited from course participants during over forty years of our joint teaching experiences. For most students, cultural diversity is a loaded topic, and the more roadblocks that can be removed, making it more accessible, the more likely significant learning will occur. It is important, for example, to acknowledge White students' concerns over being called racists and to normalize their anxieties over cultural differences as well as to acknowledge the enormous frustration People of Color feel at the denial of racism by Whites. Part of the motivation for writing this text comes from our experience of seldom having found a textbook on cultural diversity that truly engaged students while educating them. The vast majority of books on the topic are overly academic and hard for the average student to wade through. Such engagement is imperative, however, if students are not only to grasp a body of knowledge, but also to become sensitized to their own biases and discomfort with difference. All efforts to define cultural competence to date begin with acknowledging the importance of self-awareness in the teacher.

A third unique feature of the book is its treatment of Students of Color and White ethnics and the presentation of specific cultural knowledge about working with African Americans, Latinos/as, Asian Americans, Native Americans, and Jews as an example of White ethnics. Five educators, each with extensive practical experience working with students from their respective groups, were interviewed and asked to discuss the following topics: professional and ethnic autobiographical material, demographics and shared characteristics of their community, group names, history in a nutshell, learning styles, family and community characteristics, cultural style, values and worldview, common school-based problems, socioeconomic issues, subpopulations at risk, tips for developing rapport, effective teaching strategies, and a short classroom example. The result is five highly informative and engaging chapters, each filled with rich cultural material and practical hands-on suggestions and cautions, relayed with passion by five educators strongly committed to working with students from their communities. While we are aware of the dangers of assuming major similarities within groups, these interviews allow us to go more deeply below the surface and become aware of subtle differences that can help teachers widen their perspectives and improve their pedagogical skills when working with specific groups. The interviews are only lightly edited to retain their personal and cultural flavor.

Acknowledgments

A book such as this requires much work and support. We would first like to make the following personal acknowledgments.

I would like to thank my daughters, Rachel and Becca, for their continual support, advice and encouragement as I have proceeded with the writing and development of this work. I am also grateful to my friend, Jack Lawson, and my colleague, Rachel Israel for their willingess to share their time and knowledge as teachers for their interviews that appear later in the test. Finally, I would especially like to express appreciation to Dan Alpert, Acquisition Editor at Wadsworth who encouraged my initial idea for this book, brought Jean and I together to work on it, and has provided direction, advise and support throughout the process. It would not have happened without his wise guidance.

Jerry V. Diller

On the home front, I would like to thank my husband Rob, who fed me encouragement and many meals. My three children gave me life experiences and stories that I have shared and my daughter Mary edited early draft chapters. My friend Bonnie Morihara never fails to give my written work serious attention, close editing and useful insights. I thank my colleagues and students for feedback that has helped me to better understand what I should and shouldn1t do in this often challenging field of education.

Among colleagues in the field, I am especially grateful to Christine Sleeter, Valerie Ooka Pang, William Cross, Aurora Cedilo, and Eileen Waldschmidt for sharing their stories and their hearts with me in person, by phone or email. We are in this together, and I value you immensely.

At the technical level, I appreciate the transcription work of Sarah Parish and Jon Opfer and the entire front office staff at the School of Education at Oregon State University.

Jean Moule

Together, we would like to thank the following individuals at Wadsworth for their contributions to the development and production of this text: Dan Alpert, Acquisitions Editor; Trudy Brown, Project Editor; Rita Jaramillo, Project Editor; and Dory Schaeffer, Marketing Editor, as well as Peggy Francomb who served as Project Editor and Sybil Sosin who served as copy editor at Shepherd, Inc. Finally, special thanks to the following people who served as readers and reviewers of the text: Patrick Coggins, Stetson University; Winston Vaughn, Xavier University; David Bishop, NKU College of Education; David Whitenack, San Jose State University; Kimberly Higdon, Southwest Texas State University; and Deborah Estell, San Francisco State University.

About the Authors

JERRY V. DILLER   I bring to this text both my own perspective on ethnicity and my experience as an American Jew and White ethnic. These are not merely academic issues for me. Like so many other racial and ethnic-group members, I have struggled personally with group belonging and identity. This has taught me both the complexity of the kinds of issues that are the focus of this book and the fact that becoming culturally competent is indeed a lifelong process that needs constant monitoring. It is important for you to know, as someone beginning to learn in this field, that even those of us who have gained some competence in working cross-culturally never stop struggling with these issues. They are part and parcel of the process of becoming culturally competent.

I have worked in intergroup relations for over twenty years: teaching courses on multicultural issues in counseling, consulting with various public and private agencies and institutions, and doing clinical work with a wide range of ethnic populations. Yet I still grow uneasy when I am put in the position of speaking about those who are culturally different from me. To this end, Jean and I have written the chapters dealing with the broader conceptual issues, drawing on research as well as examples from our own experience, and have invited experts from the four Communities of Color and a White ethnic educator to speak about working with students from their respective groups. I am still learning about my own culture and heritage. How can I presume to speak authoritatively about the culture of others? Finally, I take very seriously the proposition put forth by many Professionals of Color regarding the role of Whites in teaching about multiculturalism. It involves educating and transforming the consciousness of other Whites about issues of race and ethnicity. This is one of the goals I have for this text.

JEAN MOULE   I am a wife and the mother of three biracial children. I work ski patrol in the winter and jump, run, and throw in master's track-and-field events in the summer. My teaching experiences have ranged from prekindergarten to doctorate level, from talented and gifted students to people in prisons.

As an isolated Person of Color on the faculty of Oregon State University, I have a unique perspective and unique challenges. My research is among preservice teachers of primarily European descent, who themselves will be teaching primarily European American students and a few isolated Students of Color. Many of the preservice teachers in my courses react to their simultaneous introduction to multicultural issues and their first African American professor. It is my goal to provide a margin of safety for those who undertake the difficult journey to prepare themselves to teach culturally diverse students. In meeting this goal, I hope to find and share opportunities to more closely connect theory and practice in the area of cultural competency.

I am a link between the institution as it is and the institution as it wishes to become: more welcoming and diverse in its faculty and students, with greater multicultural awareness. The institution is changing. Over the past seven years, we have been able to place our students in more culturally diverse classrooms in Portland and Salem, Oregon, with the assistance of an Eisenhower Professional Development Grant. This book has presented an opportunity to disseminate much that we have learned in this project, and has allowed me to further understand my role within teacher education as I help diversify the teacher force and prepare the teacher force for diversity.

<hr />

Together, we bring to this writing project a richness of diversity: of race, gender, ethnicity, and scholarly discipline. We have both lived these realities as well as having studied them. Our dialogues, disagreements, and debates, which we both thoroughly enjoyed, could have filled another entire volume. Of special value is the fact that one of us is a teacher and teacher educator and the other a psychologist and professional counselor. Bringing these two perspectives together in a book on culturally different students and what happens to them in the classroom offers unique insights into the psychology of multicultural education. The task of becoming culturally competent is usually viewed from one perspective or the other, as an educational challenge or as a psychological one. Neither, however, is sufficient by itself to provide the richness of analysis necessary to truly appreciate the psychoeducational factors that define the experience of culturally different students and the classrooms and worlds they face. By bringing together knowledge and insights from both disciplines, we feel we have created a unique text that is best suited to teaching you about becoming culturally competent. The needs of children, especially the needs of culturally diverse children, are not limited by the confines of the classroom. Children are privy to and defined by cultural and social forces that have deep emotional impacts on their psyches and shape the very essence of what and how they learn. As teachers of culturally diverse students, you will be called upon to interact with and enter the lives of not only your students, but also their parents, siblings, families, and communities. At times you may find yourself acting as babysitter, confidant, culture broker, social worker, or counselor as well as teacher. The broader your knowledge and insights, the better you will be able to perform and meet the needs of these children.

INTRODUCTION

As an Anglo teacher, I struggle to quiet voices from my own farm family, echoing as always from some unstated standard. . . . How can we untangle our own deeply entrenched assumptions?

—Finders

Dresser (1996) offers the following example of cross-cultural misunderstanding in the classroom.

> Mrs. Gussman is one of the best English teachers in the school. She spends every weekend reading her immigrant students' compositions and making careful comments in red ink. To soften her criticisms, she says something positive before writing suggestions for improvement, using the students' names to make the comments more personable. "Jae Lee, these are fine ideas." These red-inked notes send shock waves through the families of her Korean students, but Mrs. Gussman is unaware of this until the principal calls her into the office. She is told that—Koreans, particularly those who are Buddhists, only write a person's name in red at the time of death or at the anniversary of a death. Therefore, to see the names of their children in red terrified the Korean parents. (pp. 38–39)

Contained in this simple scenario is the crux of a serious problem currently facing teachers and educators. How can we hope to teach cross-culturally when we lack basic knowledge about the students we hope to educate?

The mission statements of most school districts advocate educating all students to reach their fullest potential regardless of race and ethnicity. However, our schools are only now beginning to define what culturally competent teaching is and to ask questions about how to insure that those who provide it have the requisite abilities.

Consider, for example, the diversity standards individual states set for teacher licensure. In a recent survey of twenty-four states in the U.S. only seven had specific standards for cultural competence (Oregon University System, 2001). The majority either had no standard at all or merely a generic statement about diversity. Even the seven with specific standards were

1

lacking in specific ways. Some had standards that were not defined according to performance or outcome-based criteria. Others had distributed their standards for diversity across a series of different educational categories. In all cases the determination of cultural competence was left to the teacher-training institutions themselves which in turn usually required only a course or two. None of the states surveyed had developed a test for measuring cultural competence or other means of assessing it. The survey concludes with the following: "implementation of outcome-based standards is a time-consuming and complex process often plagued with political and racial tensions" (p. 6). In addition, funding is all but non-existent for such purposes, and while some public educational institutions may have mission statements supporting diversity and cultural competence, all too often the impact of these statements is not apparent in practice.

What is cultural competence? Put most simply, it is the ability to successfully teach students who come from cultures other than your own. It entails developing certain personal and interpersonal awarenesses and sensitivities, learning specific bodies of cultural knowledge, and mastering a set of skills that, taken together, underlie effective cross-cultural teaching. We will define cultural competence in much greater detail in Chapter 2. The objective of this text is to initiate a process of learning that will ultimately lead you toward greater cultural competence as a teacher.

Most teachers regularly, though unknowingly, discriminate against culturally different students by lacking the sensitivity, knowledge, and skills necessary to teach them properly. Research consistently shows that schools are not welcoming places for culturally different students, especially those of Color. For example, these students drop out earlier and achieve at lower educational levels than their mainstream counterparts (Garcia, 2001; Taylor & Whittaker, 2003). There are a number of reasons for this. Schools, as in the opening scenario, may inadvertently make students feel uncomfortable or unwelcome. Students and parents may not trust the motives or abilities of educators because of past experiences with the system. They may believe they will not be understood culturally or have their needs met. Students from culturally different backgrounds and home environments may require more support in order to succeed in the mainstream school settings.

The purpose of this book is to sensitize preservice teachers and those already in classrooms to the complex issues involved in cross-cultural education. Only when culturally competent teaching is routinely available will culturally different students be able to reach their full potentials. Educators, as professionals, are expected to demonstrate expertise in transmitting curriculum and structuring the classroom for optimal learning. Cross-cultural teaching should be no less an area to be mastered. Only by gaining the requisite awarenesses, knowledge, and skills necessary to become culturally competent can teachers hope to actualize their professional commitment to insure the academic success of all students.

Discrimination in education involves more than merely ignoring the contributions of ethnically and racially different people in the curriculum. It also includes being unaware of one's own prejudices and how they may inadvertently be communicated to students; being unaware of differences in cultural style, interactive patterns, and values, and how these can lead to miscommunication; being unaware that many of the theories taught during training are culture-bound; being unaware of differences in cultural definitions of success as well as the existence of traditional cultural learning styles; and being unaware of the necessity of matching learning modalities to the cultural styles of students or of adapting teaching to the specific cultural needs of culturally diverse students.

Of equal importance to effective cross-cultural teaching is developing empathy and an appreciation for the life experiences of those who are culturally different. Why do so many culturally different students and parents harbor fears about and mistrust those who represent the system? Why are so many angry and frustrated? Why do many culturally different people tend to feel tenuous and conflicted about schools? Why is parenting these students such a challenge? What is the source of the stress felt by many culturally different students and their parents? Why do they so often feel that majority group members have little awareness of or concern for the often harsh realities of their daily lives? Without keen insight into the complex answers to these questions, educators cannot hope to teach their students sensitively and successfully.

The life experiences and training of educators have made them familiar with the inner workings of the educational system. Therefore, teachers need to take special care to recognize their own strong assumptions about schooling. As a result of interacting with teachers and the system, culturally different students may be unintentionally socialized into the ways of the dominant culture. For example, Latino/a students may be inadvertently encouraged to be competitive or self-assertive, or Asian students to be informal in relations with authority, characteristics that are devalued in their home cultures. A second danger is overdependence on teachers. Culturally different students are especially susceptible because their knowledge of mainstream culture is limited. Teachers may inadvertently perpetuate dependence rather than help students learn to function independently. Often, for example, it is easier and more expedient to expose students to dominant paradigms than to teach them to negotiate a parallel course that works better for them culturally. Teaching is most useful, however, when it facilitates students' interaction with the system on their own terms and in light of their own cultural values and needs. In the literature, this is called "empowerment." It involves supporting and encouraging students to become self-directed lifelong learners.

Teachers and students from culturally different backgrounds do not come together in a vacuum. Rather, each brings preconceived ideas about the ethnicity of the other. A student, for example, may initially feel mistrust, anger, fear, suspicion, or deference in the presence of teachers. A teacher, in turn, may respond with feelings of superiority, condescension, discomfort, fear, or inadequacy. Each may also perceive the other in terms of cultural stereotypes. Such reactions may be subtle or covered up, but they are there and, for a time at least, will get in the way of forming a successful learning environment.

The least helpful thing a teacher can do is to take these reactions personally and respond defensively. A much better strategy is to acknowledge the different perspectives and raise them as topics of discussion. Although students may initially be more comfortable with teachers from their own culture, the truly successful learning environment is based on the sensitivity, caring, and commitment of the teacher, regardless of race or ethnicity. Because of the serious shortage of non-White teachers, Students of Color will likely find themselves working with dominant group teachers. This is where cultural competence comes in. Basic trust can develop cross-culturally. But it is not easy. It requires the right skills, a sincere desire to help, a willingness to openly acknowledge and discuss racial and ethnic differences, and a healthy tolerance for being tested. Projections will fade with time as the student and the teacher come to know each other as individuals instead of stereotypes.

THE PURPOSE OF THIS TEXT

There are many forms of human diversity: race and ethnicity, gender, socioeconomic class, age, sexual preference, religion, ability and disability, and more. Each affects the individual differently and operates by its own unique set of rules and dynamics. It is our belief that no single text can adequately and comprehensively cover all forms of diversity. For this reason, we have chosen to focus on teaching students from different racial and ethnic groups. The decision to highlight only race and ethnicity is pragmatic and in no way minimizes the importance of gender, class, age, sexual preference, and so on. Rather, it underlines the fact that each deserves its own separate text. Some writers even argue that coverage of too many forms of diversity in a single treatment tends to be superficial and minimizes the importance of each.

We do focus extensively on the diversity within racial and ethnic groups. Differences in class, gender, age, geography, and social and political leanings, among others factors, can lead to such diverse life experiences that members of the same ethnic or racial group may feel they have little in common. A lower-class White teacher, for example, who grew up in a major city may experience difficulties when working with middle-class White students from a rural mountain setting. On the other hand, teachers and students from different cultural backgrounds who share similar demographics of class, gender, geography, and so forth may feel that they have much in common on which to build a teaching–learning relationship.

We have deliberately used a number of different terms to refer to culturally different students. Anyone familiar with this field is aware of the power of such terms. They possess, first of all, subtle connotations and at times implicit value judgments. They have often been used to oppress and demean devalued groups. They are also powerful sources of empowerment and pride. It is not surprising that ethnic group members pay serious attention to the ways in which they label themselves and are labeled by others. Finding out what term is preferable is a matter of respect, and teachers who are in doubt should ask students and parents what name they prefer. We have seldom seen anyone offended by that question. We have, however, repeatedly watched educators unintentionally alienate students and parents through their use of outdated and demeaning terms like "Orientals" or insensitive general references to "you people."

The following terms will be used in this text.

- *Cultural diversity* refers to the array of differences that exist among groups of people with definable and unique cultural backgrounds.
- *Culturally different* is used synonymously with *cross-cultural* or *ethnic* and implies that the student comes from a different culture than the teacher. It includes no value judgment about the superiority of one culture over the other, only that the people have been socialized in very different ways and may find communication problematic.
- *Culture* is viewed as a lens through which life is perceived. Each culture, through its differences (in language, values, personality and family patterns, worldview, sense of time and space, and rules of interaction), generates a phenomenologically different experience of reality. Thus, the same situation (such as the first day of school in a kindergarten classroom) may be experienced and interpreted very differently, depending on the cultural backgrounds of individual students and teachers.
- *Cultural competence*, as stated earlier, is the ability to successfully teach students who come from cultures other than your own. It entails mastering complex awarenesses and sensitivities, various bodies of knowledge, and a set of skills that, taken together, underlie effective cross-cultural teaching.
- An *ethnic group* is any distinguishable group of people who share a common culture and see themselves as separate and different from the majority culture. Their observable differences—whether physical, racial, cultural, or geographic—frequently serve as a basis for discrimination and unequal treatment within the larger society.
- A *racial group* or *race* is a biologically isolated, inbreeding population with a distinctive genetic heritage. Socially, the concept of race has created many difficulties. In general, we avoid using the concept as a definer of group differences (with the exception of talking about the development of racial awareness and consciousness in People of Color).

The distinction between race as a social and biological category is made in Chapter 4.

- *People of Color* and *Students of Color* are terms used to refer to non-White students and their families.
- *Communities of Color* are collectives of ethnic groups that share certain physical (racial), cultural, language, or geographic origins features. In naming specific Communities of Color, we try to use the term or referent that is most current and acceptable to members of that group (although there is always some debate within communities about what names are most acceptable). In relation to students, parents, and Communities of Color, the following terms are generally used: *African American, Latina/o, Native American* or *Native People,* and *Asian American* or *Asian.* In quotations and in references to research, terms are used as they appear in the original texts.
- *Whites* are members of the dominant or majority group of Northern European origin.
- *White ethnics* are dominant or majority group members whose origins are not Northern Europe.

This book assumes that all ethnic and culturally different students share certain psychological characteristics and experiences. First is the experience of belonging to a group that is socially stigmatized and the object of regular discrimination and derision. Second is the stress and harm this causes to the psyche and the resulting adaptations, some healthy and empowering and others unhealthy and dysfunctional, that ethnic individuals and families must make in order to survive. Third is the stress and harm that result from problems regularly associated with prejudice and racism (poverty, insufficient health care, crime, drug abuse). Fourth is that problems in ethnic identification and racial consciousness are often evident in ethnic students. *Ethnic identification* refers to the attachment that individuals feel to their cultural group of origin. *Racial or ethnic consciousness* refers to people's awareness of the impact of race or ethnicity on their lives. In one form or another, most ethnic students exhibit some modicum of these four factors and thus share in their impact.

Not all cultures or individuals within cultures, however, experience these factors with equal intensity. Each society, in its inner workings, designates certain groups as primary scapegoats and others as secondary. In the United States, for example, People of Color have traditionally been the primary objects of derision. In Europe, on the other hand, it has been Jews and the Rom (gypsies). There, religion, that is, being non-Christian, rather than race or skin color often defined minority status.

Teachers need to be aware of the diversity that exists both across and within ethnic groups. Each group, first of all, has its own unique history in

America. As a result, somewhat different problems have emerged for each. People of Color, for example, are set apart primarily by skin color and other physical features. As a consequence, they may struggle with concerns over body image, passing for White, or peer group identity versus achieving in the mainstream White school culture. Many Latinas/os and Asians have immigrated from traditional homelands and face ongoing dilemmas around assimilation, bilingualism, and the destruction of traditional family roles and values. Native Americans, as victims of colonization in their own land, have struggled with the representation of their histories in traditional mainstream curricula. African Americans have faced a similar psychological dislocation due to slavery and its enduring effects. White ethnics, in turn, find themselves suspended between worlds: they are culturally different, yet are perceived and often wish to be perceived as part of the majority. These ethnically specific circumstances shape and determine the kinds of problems diverse children bring to the classroom.

Differences among students from the same ethnic group (class, age, gender, ableness, language) can also be extensive, as suggested earlier. Collins (1990), for example, teases out such differences in relation to Black women.

> All African-American women share the common experience of being Black women in a society that denigrates women of African descent. This commonality of experience suggests that certain characteristic themes will be prominent in a Black women's standpoint. For example, one core theme is a legacy of struggle. . . . The existence of core themes does not mean that African-American women respond to these themes in the same way. Diversity among Black women produces different concrete experiences that in turn shape various reactions to the core themes. . . . A variety of factors explain the diversity of responses. For example, although all African-American women encounter racism, social class differences among African-American women influence how racism is experienced. (pp. 22–24)

The surest indicator of cultural insensitivity is the belief that all members of a group share similar characteristics and circumstances. A recently arrived child of a migrant worker from central Mexico, poor and barely able to speak English, faces very different life challenges than a similarly aged U.S.-born child from a wealthy Chilean family whose parents are professionals. The first task of any cross-cultural teacher is to carefully assess students' demographic and cultural situations. Some of the following information may be critical in determining the learning needs of a culturally different student: place of birth, number of generations in America, family roles and structure, language spoken at home, English fluency, economic situation and status, amount and type of preschool education, amount of acculturation, traditions still practiced in the home, familiarity and comfort with Northern European lifestyle, religious affiliation, and community and friendship patterns.

The culturally competent teacher not only seeks such information, but is also aware of its possible meaning. The child of the migrant worker may need material assistance, such as meals and clothes. The parents may be unfamiliar with the school system and fearful of authorities. The Chilean child is more likely to be concerned with cultural as opposed to economic survival: how ethnicity is impacting him or her in school, parental concern over acculturation, changing roles with the peer group, and balancing success in school with retaining traditional ways.

We have called this work a primer. According to Webster, a *primer* is a book of elementary or basic principles. Our intention in writing the book is to provide you with basic principles, sensitivities, and knowledge that will lay a foundation for becoming a culturally competent educator. The chapters that follow explore different aspects of cultural competence. Chapter 2, What It Means to Be Culturally Competent, discusses the need for cultural competence, the skill areas cultural competences comprise, and the benefits gained by educators who choose to pursue it. In Chapter 3, Understanding Racism and Prejudice, we describe the dynamics of racism and prejudice as they operate at individual, institutional, and cultural levels and how they may impinge on the classroom. In Chapter 4, Understanding Privilege and Racial Consciousness among Whites, we highlight the ways racial attitudes are structured among Whites and how Whites unconsciously protect the privilege their racial identity affords them in our society. Chapter 5, Understanding Culture and Cultural Differences, focuses on the elusive concept of culture and its various dimensions, how to make sense of and deal with cultural differences, and the meaning of multiculturalism.

With Chapter 6, Children, Parents, and Families of Color, we begin exploring issues involved in the psychology of the cross-cultural classroom. This chapter discusses developmental issues peculiar to children from racial and ethnic backgrounds, the challenges to parenting these children, differences in family structure across cultures, and issues related to biracial and bicultural families. Chapter 7, Psychological and Educational Issues, explores a variety of psychological issues as they affect the classroom that have particular relevance for culturally different students. Included are discussions of racial and ethnic identity development, stress, acculturation, and assimilation. In Chapter 8, Bias in the Curriculum and in the Classroom, we explore various issues that lead to bias in classroom management, student–teacher interaction, and curriculum development and discuss ways of adapting educational principles to varied cultural needs. Chapter 9, Critical Issues in Working with Culturally Different Students, directs attention to the process of actually working in the classroom with culturally different students and provides guidelines, specific hands-on information, and solutions to frequently occurring problems.

The next four chapters focus specifically on working with Students of Color. We have chosen a unique way of presenting this group-specific information. In each chapter, an expert teacher from one of the four Communities of Color in America—Latinos/as (Chapter 10), Native Americans (Chapter 11), African Americans (Chapter 12), and Asian Americans (Chapter 13)—highlights key issues and differences of which teachers working with students and parents from their communities should be aware. Chapter 14, Working with White Ethnic Students, focuses attention on teaching White ethnic students, with American Jews as a case in point, using a similar interview format. Through these interviews, you will experience the words and passions of real teachers who are culturally competent experts, deeply dedicated to meeting the educational needs of students from their respective cultures.

What It Means to Be Culturally Competent

They just understand some things outside, but they cannot understand some things in our hearts.

—Hoang Vinh

Hoang's parents immigrated to the United States in hope of a better lifestyle and a sound education for their children. Noella, a Latina classmate, likewise has parents who prepare her for school physically and with encouragement and who count on her teachers to help her reach her potential. Will their teachers be well-prepared? Will you be their teacher? How deep and wide are the new demographics in our country, and what does it mean to become culturally competent to meet the needs of Hoang and Noella?

DEMOGRAPHICS

The demographics of the United States are dramatically changing, and central to these changes is a significant increase in non-White populations. Atkinson, Morten, and Sue (1993) refer to this trend, which began in the 1980s, as the "diversification" of America. The statistics speak for themselves. Between 1980 and 1992, the relative percentages of population increase for ethnic groups were as follows: Asians and Pacific Islanders 123.5 percent, Hispanics 65.3 percent, Native Americans/Eskimos/Aleuts 30.7 percent, African Americans 16.4 percent, and non-Hispanic Whites 5.5 percent. These percentages represented not only a sizable increase in the actual numbers of People of Color in the United States, but also a significant decline in the relative percentage of Whites from almost 80 percent to less than 75 percent. Healey (1995) suggests that "If this trend continues, it will not take many generations before 'non-Hispanic whites' are a numerical minority of the population" (p. 12).

Estimates bear out Healey's prediction. Riche (2000) reports the following projections based on the U.S. census data: In 1999 the relative population percentages for ethnic groups were as follows: non-Hispanic White 72 percent, African American 12 percent, Hispanic 12 percent, and Asian 4 percent. In 2020, for example, it is estimated that the relative percentages will be non-Hispanic White 64 percent, Hispanic 17 percent, African American 13 percent, and Asian 6 percent. And by the year 2050, population estimates will be non-Hispanic White 53 percent, Hispanic 24 percent, African American 13 percent, and Asian 9 percent. While Native Americans are projected to remain below 1 percent of the population, actual numbers will triple during this period. By 2060 it is estimated that non-Hispanic Whites will represent less than 50 percent of the population, and by 2100 Hispanics alone will represent 33 percent of the U.S. population and non-Whites 60 percent of the population.

Such changes are even more dramatic for certain subpopulations and regions of the United States. By 2030, for example, half of all U.S. elementary schoolchildren will be Children of Color. In California (a clear pacesetter for diversity), such parity was reached in 1990, when one school-aged child out of every four came from a home where English was not the primary language, and one out of every six was born outside the United States. By 2020 four states—New Mexico, Hawaii, California, and Texas—and Washington, D.C., will have "minority majority" populations.

These changes are largely due to two factors: immigration and birthrates. The last thirty years have seen an unprecedented wave of immigration to the United States, with yearly numbers rising to 1 million. The new arrivals are primarily non-European: approximately a third come from Asia, and a third from South and Central America. In 1998, for example, while 9 percent of all U.S. citizens were foreign born, 63 percent of Asian Americans and 35 percent of Hispanics were foreign born. Differential birthrates of ethnic groups in the United States are equally skewed. Birthrates of Hispanic populations tend to be approximately 1.7 times those of Whites, and Asian Americans' birthrates are between three and seven times greater, depending on the specific subpopulation.

In the 2000 census, for the first time, there was an attempt to identify multiracial individuals, and 6.8 million people or 2.4 percent of the population reported multiracial backgrounds. Of these, 93 percent reported being biracial. Thirty-two percent of this group reported being White and "some other group"; 16 percent White and American Indian or Alaska Native; 13 percent White and Asian; and 11 percent White and Black or African American (Grieco & Cassidy, 2001).

REACTIONS TO THE CHANGING DEMOGRAPHICS

What has been the reaction to this growing diversification? First, many Americans have clearly felt threatened by the changes. The sheer increase in numbers has stimulated a widespread political backlash. Most prominent has been a rise in anti-immigrant sentiment and legislation and a strong push to repeal affirmative action practices, which were instituted over the last several decades to level the economic and social playing fields for oppressed peoples. As economic times have worsened for working-class and middle-class Whites, frustration has increasingly been directed at non-White newcomers, who have been blamed for "taking our jobs" and told to "go back to where you came from if you're not willing to speak English." In a similar vein, White supremacist, militia, and antigovernment groups, playing on racial hatred and a return to "traditional values" and "law and order," have attracted growing numbers. The result has been even greater polarization along Color lines. People of Color, in turn, have sensed in their growing numbers an ultimatum to White America: "Soon you won't even be the numerical majority. How can you possibly continue to justify the enormous injustice and disparity?"

For those in the teaching professions, a major implication of these new demographics is a radically different student base. More and more, educators will be called on to teach students from diverse cultures. Job announcements will increasingly state: "experience with diverse student populations required" and "fluency in a second language preferred." There is, at the same time, a growing awareness that it is not sufficient to merely channel new students into the same old structures and programs or to hire a few token Teachers of Color. Rather, a radical reconceptualization of effective teaching of those who are culturally different is needed. At the center of such a renewed vision is the notion of cultural competence.

A MODEL OF CULTURAL COMPETENCE

In its broadest context, cultural competence is the ability to effectively teach cross-culturally. According to Cross (1988), it is a "set of congruent behaviors, attitudes, and policies that come together in a system, agency, or among professionals and enable that system, agency, or those professionals to work effectively in cross-cultural situations" (p. 13). It is not a new idea. It has been called "ethnic sensitive practice" (Devore & Schlesinger, 1981), "crosscultural awareness practice" and "ethnic competence" (Green, 1982), and "ethnic minority practice" (Lum, 1986) by human service providers. It has been referred to as "intercultural communication" (Hoopes, 1972) by those working in international relations and as "cross-cultural counseling" (Petersen, Draguns, Lonner, & Trimble, 1989) and "multicultural counseling" (Ponterotto, Casas, Suzuki, & Alexander, 1995) in the field of counseling psychology. In education, early efforts at preparing for cultural competence were labeled "ethnic studies" and then "multiethnic education" (Banks & Banks, 1995). Other early terms included "education of the culturally different" and "education for cultural pluralism" (Gibson, 1976). Today, "cultural diversity" (Marshall, 2002) and "multicultural education" are most frequently used (Banks & Banks, 1995) as umbrella terms for approaches and strategies undergirding culturally competent teaching.

What is new, however, is the projected demand for such teaching and the urgent need for a comprehensive model of effective educational strategy. The work of Cross, Bazron, Dennis, and Isaac (1989) offers such an evolving model. The lead author, Terry Cross, is executive director of the National Indian Child Welfare Association in Portland, Oregon. For over a decade, he and his associates have attempted to articulate an effective and comprehensive real-life model of cross-cultural service delivery in the helping professions. In the material that follows, we have drawn on Cross's work, adapting the model for use in the field of education.

BASIC ASSUMPTIONS

Cultural competence, whether in a school system or an individual, is an ideal toward which to strive. It does not occur as the result of a single day of training, a few consultations with experts, reading a book, or even taking a course. Rather, it is a developmental process that depends on the continual acquisition of knowledge, the development of new and more advanced skills, and ongoing reflective self-evaluation of progress.

An effective and culturally competent education system must begin with a set of unifying values, or what might be called assumptions, about how to best educate diverse communities. These values share the notions that being culturally different is positive, that education must be responsive to specific cultural needs, and that teaching must be offered in a manner that empowers students. According to Cross et al. (1989), a culturally competent system

- Respects the unique, culturally defined needs of various student populations.
- Acknowledges culture as a predominant force in shaping behaviors, values, and institutions and that culture has an impact on education.
- Views natural systems (family, community, church, healers) as primary mechanisms of support for minority populations.

- Recognizes that the concepts of family, community, and the like are different for various cultures and even for subgroups within cultures.
- Understands that minority students are usually best served by persons who are part of or in tune with their cultures.
- Educates students in the context of their minority status, which creates unique educational issues for them, including issues related to self-esteem, identity formation, isolation, and assumptions about the role of schooling.
- Recognizes that the thought patterns of non-Western peoples, though different, are equally valid and influence how students view problems and solutions.
- Respects cultural preferences that value process rather than product and harmony or balance within one's life rather than achievement.
- Recognizes that taking the best of both worlds enhances the capacity of all.
- Recognizes that minority people have to be at least bicultural, which in turn creates educational and mental health issues such as identity conflicts resulting from assimilation.
- Understands when values of minority groups are in conflict with dominant society values. (Cross et al., 1989, pp. 22–24)

Taken together, these assumptions provide the psychological underpinnings for a truly cross-cultural model of education. First, they are based on the experiences of People of Color and those who have worked intimately with them. Second, they take seriously notions that are not typically included in dominant-culture educational models. These include the impact of cultural differences on education, the family and community as a beginning point for teaching, school accountability to the constituent community, and biculturalism as an ongoing life experience for People of Color. Third, they provide a yardstick against which existing educational institutions can measure their own philosophies and assumptions.

INDIVIDUAL CULTURAL COMPETENCE SKILL AREAS

Related to these basic assumptions about cultural competence are individual skill areas associated with the development of cultural competence in individual teachers. Cross et al. (1989) define five basic skill areas necessary for effective cross-cultural teaching: (1) awareness and acceptance of differences, (2) self-awareness, (3) dynamics of difference, (4) knowledge of the student's culture, and (5) adaptation of skills. Each can be assessed on its own continuum, although growth in one tends to support positive movement in the others. It is believed that these skills must infuse not only a teacher's work, but also the general climate of the school and the educational system as a whole. These skill areas must be taught, supported, and, even more basically, introduced as underlying dimensions of everyday functioning within schools. One skill area, for example, involves being aware of and accepting differences. For teachers, this means respecting differences in students. At a school level, however, a similar commitment to accepting and valuing diversity must also be evident in the educational practices that are adopted, in the philosophy that is shared, and in the relationship between colleagues and with parents.

Awareness and Acceptance of Differences

A first step toward cultural competence involves developing an awareness of the ways in which cultures differ and realizing that these differences may affect the learning process. While all people strive to meet the same basic educational needs, they differ greatly in how they have learned to do so. Cultural differences exist in values, styles of communication, the perception of time, the meaning of success, community, and so on. In attuning one's educational efforts to work with students from other cultures, acknowledging and looking at differences are as important as highlighting similarities. The discovery of exactly what dimensions of living vary with culture is an ever-evolving drama. Each individual begins life with a singular experience of culture, which is taken as reality. Only with exposure to additional and differing cultural realities does one begin to develop an appreciation for the diversity that is possible in human behavior.

Equally critical to becoming aware of differences is accepting them. Rokeach (1960), in his analysis of the sources of prejudice, goes so far as to suggest that differences in beliefs and cultural views, rather than a reaction to race per se, are at the heart of racial antipathy. Most difficult is accepting cultural ways and values that are at odds with our own. For instance, a success-oriented, hyperpunctual individual of Northern European ancestry might find it difficult to accept the perpetual "lateness" of those whose cultures view time as flexible and fluid. What eventually emerges in educators who are moving toward cultural competence, however, is a broadening of perspective that acknowledges the simultaneous existence of differing realities and requires neither comparison nor judgment. All exist in their own right and are different. Farther along the continuum, differences are not merely accepted or tolerated, but are truly valued for the richness, perspective, and complexity they offer. A culturally competent educator actively and creatively uses these differences in the service of teaching and learning.

Self-Awareness

It is impossible to appreciate the impact of culture on the lives of others, particularly students, if one is out of touch with his or her own cultural background. Culture is a glue that gives shape to life experience, promotes certain values and experiences as optimal, and defines what is possible. As a skill area, self-awareness involves understanding the myriad ways culture impacts human behavior. "Many people never acknowledge how their day-to-day behaviors have been shaped by cultural norms and values and reinforced by families, peers, and social institutions. How one defines 'family,' identifies desirable life goals, views problems, and even says hello are all influenced by the culture in which one functions" (Cross, 1988, p. 2).

In addition, the skill of self-awareness requires sufficient self-knowledge to anticipate when one's own cultural limits are likely to be pushed, foreseeing potential areas of tension and conflict with specific student groups, and accommodating them. Cultural self-awareness is an especially difficult task for many White teachers who grew up in households where intact cultural pasts have been lost. What remains instead are bits and pieces of cultural identity and personal history that were long ago cut loose from extended family, traditions, and community, and as a result lack meaning. Without such a felt sense of the role of culture in the lives of People of Color, certain areas of student experience become difficult to empathize with and understand.

Dynamics of Difference

Related to self-awareness is what Cross et al. (1989) call the "dynamics of difference." When students and teachers come from different cultures, there is a strong likelihood that sooner or later they will miscommunicate by misinterpreting or misjudging the behavior of others (Fox, 1993). An awareness of the dynamics of difference involves knowing what can go wrong in cross-cultural communication and knowing how to set it right. Cultural miscommunication has two general sources. The first relates to past experiences of students, their parents, and teachers with members of the other's group or to the nature of current political relations between groups. Mexican immigrants, for example, tend to be hypervigilant in relation to anyone who is perceived as either White or authoritative. Dynamics of difference also involve differences in cultural style. If a teacher from a culture that interprets direct eye contact as a sign of respect works with a student who has been taught to avert eyes as a sign of deference, there is a good chance that the teacher will come away from the interaction with erroneous impressions of the student. If educators are prepared for the possibility of such cross-cultural miscommunication, they are better able to immediately respond to a potential problem.

Knowledge of the Student's Culture

It is also critical for teachers to familiarize themselves with a student's culture so that behavior may be understood within its own cultural context. Many serious mistakes can be avoided if the teacher prefaces each attempt at motivating students and encouraging academic success by considering what it might mean within the context of the student's cultural group. Similarly, other kinds of cultural information can be educationally useful. Interpreting the learning behavior of someone who is culturally different without considering cultural context or ethnocentricity (that is, from one's own cultural perspective) is fraught with danger, as the following anecdote amply demonstrates.

Several years ago, during a period of particularly heavy immigration from Southeast Asia, Children's Protective Services received a rash of abuse reports on Vietnamese parents whose children had come to school with red marks all over their bodies. A bit of cultural detective work quickly turned up the fact that the children had been given an ancient remedy for colds called "cupping," which involves placing heated glass cups on the skin, leaving harmless red marks for about a day. The result was a group of irate Vietnamese parents, always hyperattentive to the needs of their children, who were deeply insulted by accusations of bad parenting, and several teachers who felt foolish about their cultural ignorance.

Given the variety of populations that must be taught and the diversity that exists within each, it is not reasonable to expect a single teacher to be conversant in the ways of all cultures and subcultures. However, it is possible to learn to identify the kind of information that is required to understand what is going on in the teaching–learning situation and to have cultural experts and resources to consult.

Adaptation of Skills

The fifth skill area involves adapting and adjusting generic teaching practices (that in reality, as we shall see, have their roots in the dominant cultural paradigm) to accommodate cultural differences. Such adaptations can take a variety of forms. Learning goals can be altered to better fit cultural values. For example, a Korean family may not feel comfortable about being involved in conflict resolution in the classroom. The style of interaction in which the learning process is carried out can be adjusted to be more familiar to the student. In many cultures, for instance, teaching practices are highly authoritative, with advice freely given by experts. Asian students may tend to respond to teachers by showing deference. African American students, for their part, may not even believe a teacher cares unless he or she is highly authoritative (Delpit, 1995).

The definition of who is a family member, and thus should be included in parent–teacher conferences, can also vary greatly from culture to culture. Meeting with families of African American students, for instance, may involve the inclusion of multiple generations as well as nonbiological family members, such as good friends and neighbors. Time and place of meetings can be modified to fit the needs of those who could not ordinarily be available during traditional hours or would find it difficult or threatening to come to school.

DEFINING PROFESSIONAL STANDARDS

Banks et al. (2001) offer a somewhat different approach to defining cultural competence in an educational system. According to the authors, the goal of multicultural education is two-fold: to prepare all students for the responsibility of citizenship, and to do so by valuing and considering the cultural background of all students in the learning process. In the authors' words, "to forge a common destiny, educators must respect and build upon the cultural strengths and characteristics that students from diverse groups bring to school" (p. 5). To this end, they have titled their model "Diversity Within Unity."

Based on research related to diversity, Banks et al. (2001) begin by asking what we currently know about culture and education, and then proceed to define a comprehensive set of principles of culturally competent teaching and educational delivery. They group these principles into five categories: teachers, students, cross-cultural relations, school structure and equity, and evaluation. Consider for a moment a school system with which you are familiar. Are teachers, for example, knowledgeable about the cultural dynamics that might occur within the classroom? Are all students afforded access to all aspects of the curriculum and school resources? Do school personnel actively promote positive interaction between students of different cultural backgrounds? These are the kinds of questions that their work directs you to ask. Their joined research and theorizing provide a comprehensive model for current thinking as to what a culturally competent school looks like. For a complete copy of their document—*Diversity Within Unity: Essential Principles for Teaching and Learning in a Multicultural Society*—contact the Center for Multicultural Education, College of Education, University of Washington, Seattle (see the Bibliography for mailing and e-mail addresses).

WHY BECOME CULTURALLY COMPETENT?

In the past, gaining what is now called cultural competence was an ethical decision by educators with a particularly strong moral sense of what was right and fair. Usually, such individuals sought cultural knowledge with the express purpose of working with specific cultural groups, and gravitated toward urban schools. Mainstream teachers with a predominantly White student base had little reason to pursue cultural competence. But today, the picture is quite different. For example, preservice teachers in Oregon are surprised by the steady increase in recent years of minority students from perhaps 1 percent to 4 percent of the student bodies in the "all-White" rural communities from which they come. All schools especially those in urban settings are seeing more culturally diverse students walking through their doors, and it may not be long before cultural competence becomes a professional imperative. In time, cultural competence may be a routine requirement for all jobs, not just those in the teaching professions. If projections are correct, most Americans will find themselves in close working relationships with colleagues who are culturally different. Whether it is a matter of working under a superior who is a Person of Color, supervising others from different backgrounds, or just retaining good relations with colleagues who are culturally different, being skilled in cross-cultural communication will increasingly be an asset.

Given the dramatic diversification that is currently underway in the United States, cultural competence may someday reach a status comparable to computer literacy. Twenty-five years ago, computer skills were an isolated novelty. Today, it is difficult to compete successfully in any job market without them. The same may eventually be true of cultural competence in teaching.

THE FEAR AND PAIN ASSOCIATED WITH MOVING TOWARD CULTURAL COMPETENCE

It is our experience that most people are rather apprehensive of learning about race and ethnicity and that they approach the topic with reluctance and even dread. The same may be true for readers of this book. When we start a new class, the tension in the room is palpable. Students don't know what to expect. Race is a dangerous subject for everyone. People can come unglued when discussing it. White students wonder if they will be attacked, called racists, and made to feel guilty. Students of Color wonder if the class is "going to be for real" or just another "exercise in political correctness." All students wonder whether they will really be able to speak their minds, whether things might get out of control, and whether we will be able to handle what happens. Their concerns are understandable. Few Whites have had the experience of talking openly about race and ethnicity, especially cross-racially. Society has evolved strong taboos against it.

What is more familiar are accusations and attacks, name-calling, and long, endless diatribes. Consider people's views about racial profiling, affirmative action, anti-immigrant legislation, and what constitutes terrorism. What one doesn't hear about or talk about, and what must become a focus of attention if there is ever going to be positive change, is the pain and suffering caused by racism and the ways in which everyone is touched by it. We cannot help but think of past students and their stories: the young White woman who was traumatized as a young child when her mother found her innocently touching the face of their Black maid; the Latina girl who was never the same after being accused of stealing the new bike that her parents had scrimped and saved to buy her; the man who discovered at the age of twenty-five that his parents had been hiding from him the fact that they were Jews; the Asian woman, adopted at birth by White parents, who could not talk to them about how difficult she found living in an all-White world; and the White woman consumed by guilt because of what she felt to be an irrational fear of African American and Latino men. There is clearly as much fear and nervousness about expressing such feelings as there is about working with students from other cultures.

We try to alleviate some of the anxiety by reviewing the ground rules and assumptions that define how we will interact in our college classrooms.

1. There will be no name-calling, labeling, or blaming each other. There are no heroes or villains in this drama; no good people or bad. We all harbor our own negative reactions toward those who are different. It is nearly impossible to grow up in a society and not take on its prejudices. So it is not a matter of whether one is a racist or not. We all are. Rather, it is a question of what negative racial attitudes one has learned so far and what, from this moment on, one is willing to do about them.
2. Everything that is said and divulged in this classroom is confidential and is not to be talked about with anyone outside. Students often censure, measure their words, and are less than honest in what they say out of fear of looking bad or of having their personal disclosures treated insensitively or as gossip.
3. As much as possible, students will personalize their discussion and talk about their own experiences. There is much denial around racism that serves as a mechanism for avoiding responsibility. Only by personalizing the subject and speaking in the first, rather than the third, person can this be avoided.
4. Students can say whatever they believe. This may, in turn, lead to conflict with others. That is okay. But they must be willing to look at what they say, take responsibility for their words, and learn from what ensues. Anything that happens during class is a learning opportunity. It can and may be analyzed as part of the process. The class is a microcosm of the outer racial world, with all of its problems, and honest interaction in class can shed valuable light on the dynamics of intergroup conflict.
5. The intention of this class is to create a safety zone where students can talk about race in ways that they cannot talk about race in most parts of the real world.

As teachers, we also try to lessen anxiety in the classroom by modeling transparency and openness. We try to talk openly and honestly about ourselves and our personal experiences with race and ethnicity, and to react to students in the same open and honest manner. Such modeling will hopefully, in time, be mirrored by students in their conversations and writings. This process is particularly encouraged by certain classroom activities and practices we have developed. We ask students to self-evaluate their reactions and progress throughout the course. In some courses, they are asked to keep journals of their reactions and experiences related to the course and the topic of race and ethnicity. For comfort, students are allow to propose their own reading lists (beyond certain basic requirements) and also selectively participate in a choice of various discussion venues. For example, they can choose to avoid class presentations and do more introspective activities, such as interactive journal writing with the instructor, or they can choose small discussion groups or participate in online discussion forums. We try to respond to all remarks and sharing in an affirming manner and let students resolve for themselves any dissonance from conflicting facts and other voices in the classroom. We may also use nonverbal affirmations or gentle challenges that do not raise defenses.

Most students have serious questions about race and ethnicity that need to be answered or experiences that must be processed and better understood. Significant learning and unlearning about race and ethnicity cannot proceed without this happening. Opportunities to do so are rare in most people's lives, but only through such occasions can growth and healing begin. Once some safety has been established, the floodgates open, and students become emboldened by others' frank comments to share what is really on their minds. The following are the kind of concerns that emerge.

- "Why do so many immigrants refuse to learn English? If they want to live here and reap the benefits, the least they should be willing to do is learn our language. My parents came over from Italy. They were dirt poor, but they made successful lives for themselves. They didn't have all this help. I really don't understand why it should be any different for People of Color."
- "This is all really new to me. I grew up in a small town in rural Oregon. There was one Black family, but they stayed to themselves mostly. It's confusing and, to be perfectly honest, it is also pretty scary. There's just so much anger. If I had a Friend of Color, I'm not sure I would know what to say or do."
- "My biggest issues are with Black men. I try to be supportive of them and understand the difficulties they face. But when I see them always with White women, overlooking me and my sisters and all we have to offer, I get really angry."
- "To be perfectly honest, I hate being White. I feel extremely guilty about what we have done to People of Color and don't know how to make up for it. I don't feel I have any culture of my own. We used to joke about being Heinz 57 variety Americans. And I envy People of Color for all of their culture and togetherness. We tried practicing some Native

American ways, but that didn't seem exactly right, and besides we were never made to feel very welcome."

- "I've come to realize how much racial hatred there was in my family while I was growing up, and this disturbs me greatly. I find it very hard to see my parents in this negative light and don't know what to do with all of this."
- "It's gotten pretty hard being a White male these days. You've always got to watch what you say, and as far as getting a job, forget it. There's a whole line of women and minorities and disabled in front of you. I guess I sort of understand the idea of affirmative action, but just because I'm White doesn't mean I have it made. I find it very difficult just getting by financially. I don't see where all of this privilege is."
- "I just can't buy all this cultural stuff. People are just people, and I treat everyone the same. I grew up in an integrated neighborhood. I always had a lot of Black and Latino friends and never saw them as different. Frankly, I think all of this focus on differences is creating the problem."
- "I'm Jewish, but am finding it hard to discover where I fit in all of this. I don't feel White, but everyone treats me and classifies Jews as White. I was very involved in the civil rights movement a number of years ago; even worked down in the South for a summer registering voters. But that seems so far away, and now Blacks hate Jews. What did we do?"
- "I'm in this class because I have to be. I don't need to take a class on racism. I've lived it all my life. White people don't get it. They just don't want to see, and no class is going to open their eyes. What I'm not willing to do is be a token Person of Color in here."

Moving toward cultural competence is hard emotional work. Personal issues such as those just described have to be given voice and worked through. Students need good answers to their questions and support in finding solutions to personal conflicts. Each of the five skill areas described by Cross et al. (1989) earlier in the chapter represents a new set of developmental challenges. It is as if a whole new dimension of reality—that of culture—has been introduced into a student's phenomenological world. Old beliefs about oneself, others, and what one does and does not have in common must be examined and adjusted where necessary. There are, in addition, vast amounts of information to learn and new cultural worlds to explore. Perhaps most exciting, however, are the ways in which one's mind has to stretch and grow to incorporate all of this new material. Students who have progressed in their learning about cultural matters often speak of a transformation that occurs in the ways they think about themselves and the world.

Bennett (1993) has tried to describe these cognitive changes. Of particular interest is the qualitative shift that occurs in a person's frame of reference; what he describes as movement from "ethnocentrism" to "ethnorelativism." In typical ethnocentric thinking, culturally different behavior is assessed in relation to one's own cultural standards; it is good or bad in terms of its similarity to how things are done in one's own culture. In ethnorelative thinking, "cultures can only be understood relative to one another and . . . particular behavior can only be understood within a cultural context . . . cultural difference is neither good nor bad, it is just different" (Bennett, 1993, p. 26). People who make this shift increase their empathic ability and experience greater ease in adopting a process orientation toward living. When the actions of others are not assessed or judged, but just allowed to exist, it is far easier to enter into their felt experience and thereby empathize with them. Similarly, realizing that behavior, values, and identity itself are not absolute, but rather are constructed by culture, frees one to more fully appreciate the ongoing process of living life, instead of focusing entirely on its content or where one is going or has been. These skills not only transform how people think, but also prepare them for working more effectively with culturally different students.

In our increasingly global and diverse world, the ability to work with people whose backgrounds and lived experiences are different from our own has become a necessary skill. Perhaps you have worked in a diverse placement. You may have learned valuable lessons about how to work with African American students or how to teach children with dual languages. Cross-cultural knowledge is a natural by-product of such placements. Equally important are other kinds of cultural learning: how to listen, how to value different experiences, how to call into question the norms with which you were raised. Such skills transcend the specific knowledge gained in individual placements and are highly transferable. This process has been called "post holing" and reflects the fact that going deeply into a single aspect of curriculum content permits one to expand knowledge laterally. For example, a person grows in relation to cultural competence along racial and ethnic lines and discovers that he or she has also developed insights and sensitivities to gender diversity and so on. The result is growing competence in being more sensitive and just when working with an increasing array of diverse populations and issues.

A WORD TO THE READER

In closing this chapter, we wish to address the reader in a more direct way regarding the pursuit of cultural competence and this book. The old adage is still true; you get as much out of reading as you put in. There is much useful information in the following pages that cannot help but contribute to your growth as culturally competent educators. And that certainly is worth the price of admission. But it can also be the beginning of a journey that may change you in deep and unpredictable ways. As suggested earlier, engaging in the serious pursuit of cultural competence can be transformational, not so much in a religious sense, but rather in a perceptual one. You may in time think very differently than you do now. We can also guarantee that at times, if you take this latter course, you will be disturbed or disoriented or find yourself feeling very lost and alone. One of the authors reports the following: "I can remember the first time I had the experience of cultural relativity and realized that what I had for my entire life taken to be absolute reality, the underpinnings of my world, was merely relative. It came from reading the books of Alan Watts on Zen Buddhism, and what I found so disturbing and unsettling was the realization that there was more than one way to understand reality. I was never quite the same person again, as if the center of my consciousness had shifted slightly, and everything looked a little different." This was an unhinging experience, to say the least. But it has been repeated over and over again for both of us as we continue to delve into cultural material.

Two things will make a difference in how you relate to this book and ultimately in your pursuit of cultural competence. The first is self-honesty. There is an aspect of ethnocentrism that is delusional. It seeks to hide the fact that human experience can be relative—that there might be another show in town. As shall become evident in Chapter 3, there is also a strong tendency to deny and hide from consciousness many of the negative feelings about race, ethnicity, and cultural differences that one has learned over the years. Together, the two conspire to keep one in the dark. Only by pushing oneself to critically engage the concepts and material of this book and discovering precisely how they play themselves out in the confines of individual lives can one truly begin to understand what it is about. Second is a sustained commitment to gaining cultural competence. The kind of learning that has been the topic of this chapter is long-term. It is as much process as content, tends to be cumulative in nature, and—as Cross et al. (1989), Sue, Arredondo, and McDavis (1992), and Bennett (1993) point out—is highly developmental, meaning that the learner goes through various predictable stages of growth, emotion, and change. This book is only a beginning. What happens next—what additional cultural learning experiences you seek and the extent to which you seriously engage in providing culturally competent teaching—is up to you.

DISCUSSION QUESTIONS

How personally ready are you to engage in the needed introspection to become culturally competent? What obstacles or consequences do you foresee as you undertake this task?

ACTIVITY: TAKING THE CULTURAL COMPETENCY SURVEY

This survey, developed by one of the authors, is for your personal reflection and growth. You may revisit it after reading this text and as your journey continues. Reflecting on educational practice and perspectives improves them. Teaching others provides a continuing set of experiences and opportunities to reflect on the educational process. Each day in the classroom, you will be challenged by ideas, interactions, and experiences. What will you make of them? How will they affect your growth as a teacher?

The present survey focuses on race and ethnicity. It is, however, most useful to think of it as an index of your growth in learning about differences that reflects an ever-widening perspective. Many educators believe that active and ongoing growth of this kind is the hallmark of a well-educated teacher. The survey is also developmental. It asks you to assess your cross-cultural knowledge as it currently exists and your ultimate goal for yourself in relation to each dimension of cultural competence.

Self-Assessment for Cultural Competence

Use the following key to assess your level of competence for each of the statements.

U	Unfamiliar	The information is totally new to me.
AW	Awareness	I have heard about it, but I don't know its full scope, such as its principle components, applications, and modifications.
K	Knowledge	I know enough about this to write or talk about it. I know what it is, but I'm not ready to use it. I need practice and feedback.
AP	Application	I am ready to apply or have applied this information in my own work and/or life.
F	Facilitation	I am ready to work with other people to help them learn this. I feel confident enough to demonstrate and/or teach this to others, yet I know that my learning is a lifelong process.

Where I Am Now	Where I Want to Be	Competencies
U AW K AP F	U AW K AP F	I am aware of the problem of language, images, and situations that suggest that most members of a racial or ethnic group are the same (e.g., "All Asians are good at math").
U AW K AP F	U AW K AP F	I substitute factual and meaningful information for ethnic cliches. For instance, I avoid using terms and adjectives that reinforce racial and ethnic stereotypes.
U AW K AP F	U AW K AP F	I try to address stereotypical statements when I hear them used by others.
U AW K AP F	U AW K AP F	I avoid patronizing and tokenism of any racial or ethnic group (e.g., "One of my best friends is Black").

(continued)

Where I Am Now	Where I Want to Be	Competencies
U AW K AP F	U AW K AP F	I understand the histories of oppressed groups (Native American, African American, Latino/Chicano, Asian/Pacific American) in the United States.
U AW K AP F	U AW K AP F	I thoughtfully view books and films to see if all groups are fairly represented.
U AW K AP F	U AW K AP F	I am aware of how my membership in different groups influences the power that I possess, and I am aware of how to constructively use that power.
U AW K AP F	U AW K AP F	I understand racial identity development. I know how to evaluate personal attitudes, emotions, and actions around my own racism and prejudices.
U AW K AP F	U AW K AP F	For White individuals: I am conscious of my White racial identity and its relationship to racial oppression in the United States. I think critically about what it means to be White in this country.
U AW K AP F	U AW K AP F	For Individuals of Color: I am conscious of my racial identity development and its relationship to racial oppression in the United States. I think critically about what it means to be of Color in this country.
U AW K AP F	U AW K AP F	I understand the concept of levels of curriculum reform (contributions/additive, transformation, social action, see Banks & Banks, 2001).

Summary

We are currently experiencing a diversification of American society. This includes both a sizable increase in the actual numbers of People of Color in the United States and a decline in the relative percentages of Whites. Projections suggest that these trends will only increase. By 2060, for example, non-Hispanic Whites will represent less than 50 percent of the population. Two factors are primarily responsible for these changes in demographics: immigration rates and birthrates. The implication for our educational system and classrooms is staggering. Increasingly, schools will be asked to teach Children of Color and other pupils from nonmajority cultures, students born outside of the United States, and students for whom English is not the primary language. Adequately serving this new student base requires more than merely color-coding and applying bandages to a system designed for a monocultural White student population. In its place, we must establish a new vision of education and teaching based on the notion of cultural competence.

Cultural competence is the ability to effectively teach students from different cultures. It can reside in an individual teacher as well as in a school or education system, and it is generally defined by an integrated series of awarenesses and attitudes, knowledge areas, and skills. We have presented two models of cultural competence in this chapter: a skills approach developed by Cross et al. (1989) and an attempt to define professional teacher standards by Banks et al. (2001). Cross et al., for example, point to five skill areas that teachers must develop in moving toward cultural competence. These include the awareness and acceptance of difference, self-awareness, understanding the dynamics of difference, knowledge of the student's culture, and the ability to adapt skills to changing cultural needs and demands.

Becoming a culturally competent teacher is quickly becoming a professional imperative and will increasingly become a basis for hiring. Increasingly, teachers will find themselves working with colleagues and students who are culturally different.

Moving toward cultural competence is an emotionally demanding process that does not occur overnight or with a single course or workshop. There are few places in which it is safe to speak openly and honestly about ethnicity and race. Everyone has been personally hurt by prejudice and racism, Whites as well as People of Color. Developing cultural competence requires looking at the pain and suffering racism has caused as well as looking at one's own attitudes and beliefs. Gaining cultural competence can also provide enormous personal growth in the form of increased self-awareness, cultural sensitivity, nonjudgmental thinking, and broadened consciousness. The chapter ends with a personal word to the reader and a cultural competence survey to be used as an assessment tool.

UNDERSTANDING RACISM AND PREJUDICE

The greatest education comes from action.
The greatest action is the struggle for justice.

—Myles Horton

Ron Takaki (1993) begins his book *A Different Mirror* by recounting a simple but powerful incident. In a taxi from the airport to a hotel in a large Eastern city on his way to a conference on multiculturalism, Takaki and the cab driver engaged in casual conversation. After the usual discussion of weather and tourism, the driver asked, "How long have you been in this country?" Takaki winced and then answered, "All my life . . . I was born in the United States . . . My grandfather came here from Japan in the 1880s. My family has been here, in America, for over a hundred years." The cab driver, obviously feeling uncomfortable, explained, "I was wondering because your English is excellent!" (p. 1).

Encapsulated in this incident are the basic feelings that fuel racial tensions in the United States. The cab driver was giving voice to a belief shared by the majority of White Americans that this country is European in ancestry and White in identity, and that only those who share these characteristics truly belong. All others, no matter how long they have resided here, are viewed and treated with suspicion and considered outsiders. Takaki's wince tells the other side of the story. People of Color who call the United States home are deeply disturbed by their second-class citizenry. Being reminded of their unequal and unwanted status is a daily occurrence. This country, they argue, has grown rich on the labor of successive generations of immigrants and refugees, and their reward should be the same as Whites: full citizenship and equal access to resources as guaranteed in the Constitution. The situation is further exacerbated by White America's seeming indifference to the enormous injustice in the system.

Culturally competent teaching is most usefully viewed against this backdrop. The educational system is, after all, a microcosm of broader society and is susceptible to the same racial tensions and dynamics. It was suggested in Chapter 2 that cultural competence depends on self-awareness, which includes, above all, awareness of the attitudes and prejudices that teachers bring to their work. Neither teacher nor student exists in a vacuum. Both carry into the classroom prejudices and stereotypes about the ethnicity of the other, and these, if unaddressed, cannot help but interfere with learning.

This chapter explores the dynamics of racism: its structure and meaning, the functions it serves for the individual and for society, how it operates psychologically, and why it is so resistant to change. The chapter ends with a series of exercises intended to help readers explore personal prejudices, stereotypes, and attitudes toward specific ethnic groups, issues of race and ethnicity in familiar institutions, and their own cultural backgrounds.

DEFINING AND CONTEXTUALIZING RACISM

According to Wijeyesinghe, Griffin, and Love (1997), racism is "the systematic subordination of members of targeted racial groups who have relatively little social power . . . by members of the agent racial group who have relatively more social power" (p. 88). Racism is supported simultaneously by individuals, the institutional practices of society, and dominant cultural values and norms.

Racism is a universal phenomenon, exists across cultures, and tends to emerge wherever ethnic diversity and differences in perceived group characteristics become part of a struggle for social power. In the United States, African Americans, Asian Americans, Latinos/as, and Native Americans— groups we have been referring to as People of Color—have been systematically subordinated by the White majority.

There are three important initial points to be made about racism. The first is the distinction between prejudice and racism. Allport (1954) defines prejudice as an "antipathy," that is, a negative feeling, either expressed or not expressed, "based upon a faulty and inflexible generalization which places [a group of people] at some disadvantage not merited by their actions" (p. 10).

Thus, prejudice is a negative, inaccurate, rigid, and unfair way of thinking about members of another group. All human beings hold prejudices. This is true for People of Color as well as for majority-group members. But there is a crucial difference between the prejudices held by Whites and those held by People of Color. Whites have more power to enact their prejudices, and therefore negatively impact the lives of People of Color, than vice versa. It is not that members of one group can garner more animosity than the other. Rather, it is the fact that one group (in this case, Americans of Northern European descent), because of its position of power, can more fully translate negative feelings into educational, social, political, economic, and psychological consequences for the targeted group. Because of this difference, the term *racism* is used in relation to the racial attitudes and behavior of majority-group members. Similar attitudes and behaviors on the part of People of Color are referred to as *prejudice* and *discrimination* (a term commonly used to mean actions taken on the basis of prejudice). Another way of describing this relationship is that "prejudice plus power equals racism."

Second, racism is a broad and all-pervasive social phenomenon that is mutually reinforced at all levels of society. In this regard, J. M. Jones (1972) distinguishes three levels of racism: individual, institutional, and cultural. *Individual racism* refers to "the beliefs, attitudes and actions of individuals that support or perpetuate racism" (Wijeyesinghe, Griffin, & Love, 1997, p. 89). *Institutional racism* involves the manipulation of societal institutions to give preferences and advantages to Whites and restrict the choices, rights, mobility, and access of People of Color. While individual racism resides within the person, the institutional variety is wired into the very fabric of social institutions: into their rules, practices, and procedures. Some forms of institutional racism are subtle and hidden; others are overt and obvious. All, however, serve to deny and limit access to those who are culturally different. *Cultural racism* is the belief that the cultural ways of one group are superior to those of another. In the United States, it takes the form of practices that "attribute value and normality to White People and Whiteness, and devalue, stereotype, and label People of Color as 'other,' different, less than, or render them invisible" (Wijeyesinghe, Griffin, & Love, 1997, p. 93). Cultural racism can be found in both individuals and institutions. In the former, it is often referred to as *ethnocentrism.* Each level of racism supports and reinforces the others, and together they contribute to its general resistance to change. Later sections of this chapter explore the workings of each in depth as well as inquire into the relevance for teachers working with culturally different students.

The third point is that people tend to deny, rationalize, and avoid discussing their feelings and beliefs about race and ethnicity. Often, these feelings remain unconscious and are brought to awareness only with great difficulty. It is hard to look at and talk about race because there is so much pain and hurt involved. Children's natural curiosity about human differences is quickly tainted and turned into negative judgments and discomfort. They, often imperceptibly, pick up parental prejudices with little awareness (at least at first) that the racial slurs and remarks that come so easily cut to the very core of their victim's self-esteem.

In a society so riddled with racial tensions, everyone is eventually hurt by racism. Accompanying the pain is always enormous anger, and anger, whether held inside or directed toward someone else, is hard to deal with. When such emotions become overwhelming, people defensively turn off or distance themselves from the source of the feelings. Such defenses become habitual, and by adulthood they are usually firmly in place, effectively blocking emotion around the topic of race.

There is an interesting dynamic that exists around empathizing with those who have been the target of racism. When young children hear the stories of People of Color, they tend to deeply and sincerely share the feelings of the storyteller, for they are able to connect with the lived experiences of others. "We are really sorry that you had to go through that" is the most common reaction of children. By the time they reach adulthood, however, the empathy is often gone. Reactions instead tend to involve minimizing, justifying, rationalizing, or otherwise blocking the emotions. Teachers are no less susceptible to such defensive behavior, but they must force themselves to look inward if they are sincere in their commitment to effectively teach cross-culturally. For this reason, the present chapter concludes with a set of activities and exercises aimed at stimulating self-awareness.

An Example

By way of example, consider the following experience of a teacher-in-the-making as she struggles to understand her racial awareness. She is discovering the prejudices that reside within herself and the young child she cares for.

> Since the beginning of this class a situation that I encountered recently has continually been popping in to my mind. I figure that this situation has been surfacing for a reason, so I decided that this class presents a good opportunity for me to discuss it. Throughout the past two years I have babysat for a young girl on a regular basis. Throughout this time we have shared a lot of quality time together, and I feel I have played a fairly significant role in her first three years of life.
>
> About six months ago I was watching her on a beautiful sunny day and I asked her if she would like to go outside and play. She looked at me very seriously and replied "no." I thought this was unusual so I asked her why she did not want to play outside. She responded by saying, "I don't want to play out there when it's sunny because I'm afraid my skin will turn dark like yours." She continued on and explained to me that she wants to keep her light white skin and she is afraid that if she goes outside on sunny days she will become dark. She said that she does not think that dark skin is pretty like her white skin. I have to say that I was pretty taken back by the fact that this child was only three years old and she was expressing this concern to me. I know her parents very well and they both value diversity and show respect for individual differences. I was struggling to decipher just what this child's words meant and how I should respond to her. I could not believe that at such a young age this child had somehow developed the notion that a dark skin tone was not as pretty as a light skin tone.
>
> I bring this situation up mainly because I want to talk about how I felt when she talked this way. I have a very olive tone complexion, and in the summer my skin gets fairly dark. I noticed that I began to become very defensive when she talked this way. In a sense I became offended. She continued to state her concern about going outside in the summer because she did not want to be dark like myself. I decided that I should talk to her about how everyone has different skin tones and that no one color is better than the next. I explained to her that even her skin tone was slightly different than her mother's and brothers'. I told her that I thought my skin color as well as hers was beautiful in many ways.

I would like to hear your response to this particular situation. Specifically, I want to know if you feel that this young child was actually forming some biases that a parent should be concerned about, or if you think this was just common curiosity. I also would like to know how you would like to start to discover why I felt hurt and defensive when she was talking about my skin color in the manner she did. What do you think about all of this? (Moule, 2003b)

The child's reactions provided an opening for the preservice teacher to examine both her charge's and her own biases about skin color with increasing sensitivity and clarity.

INDIVIDUAL RACISM AND PREJUDICE

The burning question that arises when one tries to understand the dynamics of individual racism is, Why is it so easy for individuals to develop and then retain racial prejudices? As suggested earlier, racism seems to be a universal phenomenon that transcends geography and culture. Human groups have always exhibited it and, if human history is any lesson, always will. The answer, according to Allport (1954), lies in the fact that racial prejudice has its roots in the "normal and natural tendencies" of how human beings think, feel, and process information. For instance, people tend to feel more comfortable with those who are like them and to be suspicious of those who are different. They tend to think categorically, to generalize, and to oversimplify their views of others. They tend to develop beliefs that support their values and basic feelings and avoid those that contradict or challenge them. And they tend to scapegoat people who are most vulnerable and subsequently rationalize their behavior. In short, racism grows out of these simple human traits and tendencies.

Traits and Tendencies Supporting Racism and Prejudice

The idea of in-group and out-group behavior is a good place to begin. There seems to be a natural tendency for human beings to stick to their own kind and separate themselves from those who are different. One need not attribute this to any nefarious motives; it is just easier and more comfortable to do so. Ironically, inherent in this tendency to love and be most comfortable with one's own are the very seeds of racial hatred. As Allport (1954) suggests, "We prize our mode of existence and correspondingly underprize or actively attack what seems to us to threaten it" (p. 26). Thus, what is different can always be, and often is, perceived as a threat. The tendency to separate oneself from those who are different intensifies the threat because separation limits communication and thus heightens the possibility of misunderstanding. With separation, knowledge of the other becomes more limited, and this limited knowledge seems to invite distortion, the creation of myths about members of other groups, and the attribution of negative characteristics and intent to them.

Prejudice is also stimulated by the human proclivity for categorical thinking. Organizing perceptions into cognitive categories and experiencing life through these categories is a basic and necessary part of the way people think. As one grows and matures, certain categories become detailed and complex; others remain simple. Some become charged with emotions; others remain factual. Individuals and groups are also sorted into categories. These categories can become charged with emotion and vary greatly in complexity and accuracy. On the basis of the content of these categories, human beings make decisions about how they will act toward others. For example, one of the authors reported the following experience.

> I have the category "Mexican." As a child, I remember seeing brown-skinned people in an old car at a stoplight and being curious about who and what they were. As we drove by, my father mumbled, "Dirty, lazy Mexicans," and my mother rolled up the window and locked her door. This and a variety of subsequent experiences, both direct and indirect (such as comments of others, the media, what I read), are filed away as part of my Mexican category and shape the way I think about, feel, and act toward those I place in the category Mexicans.

It is even more complicated than this, however, for categorical thinking by its very nature leads to oversimplification and prejudging. Once a person has been identified as a member of an ethnic group, he or she is experienced as possessing all the traits and emotions internally associated with that group. One may believe, for instance, that Asian Americans are very good at mathematics and hate them because of it. A person who meets and identifies individuals as Asian American, will assume that they are good at mathematics and dislike them. Consider the African American student whose classmates were shocked by her "unexpected" top-of-the-class test score. The "usual" top performers were all Asian American and male.

Related is the concept of stereotype. Weinstein and Mellen (1997) define *stereotype* as "an undifferentiated, simplistic attribution that involves a judgement of habits, traits, abilities, or expectations . . . assigned as a characteristic of all members of a group" (p. 175). For instance, Jews are short, smart, and money-hungry; Native Americans are stoic and violent and abuse alcohol. What is implied in these stereotypes is that all Jews are the same and all Native Americans are the same (in other words, share the same characteristics). Ethnic stereotypes are learned as part of normal socialization and are amazingly consistent in their content. As a classroom exercise, one of the authors asks students to list the traits they associate with a given ethnic group. Consistently, the lists contain the same characteristics down to minute details and are overwhelmingly negative.

One cannot help but marvel at society's ability to transmit the subtlety and detail of these distorted ethnic caricatures. Not only does stereotyping lead to oversimplification in thinking about ethnic group members, but it also provides justification for the exploitation and ill treatment of those who are racially and culturally different. Because of their negative traits, "they deserve what they get." Because they are seen as less than human, it is easy to rationalize ill treatment of "them." Categorical thinking and stereotyping also tend to be inflexible, self-perpetuating, and highly resistant to change.

Human beings go to great lengths to avoid new evidence that is contrary to existing beliefs and prejudices. First, they avoid situations in which old beliefs may be challenged or contrary information found. In a similar manner, people holding like views are sought out to reinforce existing beliefs. That is why segregated housing and neighborhoods are such an effective means of perpetuating the racial status quo. Often, when contrary information is encountered, it is unconsciously manipulated so as to leave ethnic categories unaffected. Say, for instance, that an office worker believes that African Americans are lazy. One day, a new employee, an African American, is hired, and no one works harder or more diligently than this person. So how does the person make sense of this fact, given his or her beliefs about African American laziness? What the person does is to treat the African American worker as an exception; that is, he is not like other African Americans. Allport (1954) calls this "re-fensing." Contrary information is, thus, briefly acknowledged. But by excluding this exception to a general stereotype ("He is really not like other African Americans"), one may retain beliefs about African Americans in light of seemingly contradictory evidence.

A similar phenomenon involves the actual distortion of perceptions. Social psychologists have demonstrated that individuals perceive and remember material that is consonant with their attitudes and beliefs. They have even shown that perceptions can be distorted to avoid the introduction of contrary information. A classic example is the recall of ambiguous pictures. Pictures are shown to subjects at such high speeds that they can barely perceive the content. The more ambiguous the exposure, the easier it is for the subject to distort perception to support existing prejudices. Thus, when shown a drawing of an African American man being followed by a White man who is carrying a sticklike object in one hand, an individual with extremely negative attitudes about African Americans may report seeing an African American with a knife or club chasing a White man. One of the authors, in reviewing a film containing fleeting images of people of different races with a class, listened as a preservice teacher not only turned the action around, but then castigated the filmmaker for perpetrating a stereotype that existed only in the student's mind.

Psychological Theories of Prejudice

Psychologists, like Allport, suggest that in-group and out-group behavior, categorical thinking and stereotyping, avoidance, and selective perception together set the stage for the emergence of racism. But without some form of internal motivation, an individual's potential for racism remains largely dormant. In a similar manner, Wijeyesinghe, Griffin, & Love (1997) distinguish between active and passive racism: the extent to which an individual actively engages in or advocates violence and oppression against People of Color, in contrast to taking a more covert and passive stand. Various theories have been offered about the psychological motivation behind prejudice and racism. In reality, there does not seem to be a single theory that can adequately explain the impetus toward racism in all individuals. More likely, there is some truth in all of the theories, and, in the case of a given individual, one or more may be actively at work.

Probably the most widely held theory of prejudice is known as the frustration-aggression-displacement hypothesis. This theory holds that as people move through life, they do not always get what they want or need and, as a result, experience varying amounts of frustration. Frustration, in turn, creates aggression and hostility, which can be alternately directed at the original cause of frustration, directed inward, or displaced onto a more accessible target. Thus, if my boss reprimands me, I go home and take it out on my spouse, who in turn yells at the kids, who then kick the dog. Such displacement, according to the theory, is the source of racism.

How does one choose an appropriate target for displacement? There are a number of competing theories. Williams (1947) believes that the target must be "visible and vulnerable." Dollard (1938) sees any group with which one is in competition as a potential target. Still others believe that the target often symbolizes certain attributes that the individual detests. Another theory holds that societal norms dictate the acceptable targets for displacement. Finally, there is the belief that the choice of targets depends on the "analytic" mechanism of projection. Individuals displace their hostility on groups who possess "bad" attributes, which are in reality similar to attributes they unconsciously detest in themselves. The irrationality of displacement requires the person to find justification for the hatred. This is often done by creating myths about why the group being discriminated against really deserves such treatment or by drawing on existing stereotypes, negative traits, and theories of inferiority. During the period of American slavery, for example, many slave owners asserted that African Americans were subhuman and incapable of caring for themselves, and because of this, slavery was actually a benign and kindly institution.

A second theory holds that prejudice is part of a broader, global personality type. The classic example is the work of Adorno, Frankel-Brunswik, Levinson, and Sanford (1950) on what has become known as the authoritarian personality. Growing out of the horrors of World War II and the willingness of so many to collaborate and "merely follow orders," Adorno and his colleagues postulated the existence of a bigoted personality type that manifested a variety of traits revolving around personal insecurity and a basic fear of everything and everyone different. Such individuals are believed to be highly repressed and insecure, and to experience low self-esteem and high alienation. In addition, they tend to be highly moralistic, nationalistic, and authoritarian, to think in terms of black and white, to have a high need for order and structure, to view problems as external rather than as psychological, and to feel anger and resentment against members of all ethnic groups.

Other theories suggest that racial prejudice is manipulated within a society to promote certain economic and political objectives; that it is a means of buoying up self-esteem by viewing members of other groups as inferior; that it is socially sanctioned in certain geographical areas against specific ethnic groups and that many people who discriminate are adjusting to a social norm; and that it is based not on racial differences as much as on perceived dissimilarities in belief systems (that is, people tend to dislike those who think differently than they do).

What all of these theories share is the idea that racist beliefs and actions help individuals meet important psychological and emotional needs. To the extent that this process is successful, their hatred remains energized and reinforced. Within such a model, the reduction of prejudice and racism can occur only when alternative ways of meeting emotional needs are found.

Implications for Teachers

What does this information about individual racism have to do with teachers? Put most directly, it is the source of, or at least a contributing factor to, many of the problems that culturally different students face in schools. Some students experience academic difficulties related to dealing with racism. They live with it on a daily basis. Dealing with racism in a healthy and non–self-destructive manner is, therefore, a major life challenge for many students. To be the continual object of a person's hatred as well as the hatred of an entire social system is a source of enormous stress, and such stress often produces educational problems. It is no accident, for example, that disproportionate numbers of African American males are often referred to special education programs.

Other educational problems are more indirect consequences of racism. Many Students of Color are poor and have limited resources and skills for competing in a White-dominated school system. More-affluent Students of Color are no less susceptible to the far-reaching consequences of racism. Life goals and aspirations are likely blocked or at least made more difficult because of the color of their skin. There is a saying among People of Color that one has to be twice as good as a White to succeed. This, too, is a source of inner tension, as are the doubts a Person of Color may have about whether he or she earned a grade, either higher or lower, because of ability or skin color.

It is equally important for teachers to become aware of the prejudices they hold as individuals. There are a number of exercises at the end of this chapter. If undertaken with honesty and seriousness, they can provide valuable insight into feelings and beliefs about other racial and ethnic groups. Without such awareness, it is all too easy for teachers to confound their teaching with their own prejudicial reactions. For example, if I think stereotypically about Students of Color, it is very likely that I will too narrowly define their potential, miss important aspects of their individuality, and even unwittingly guide them in the direction of taking on the stereotyped characteristics I hold about them. My own narrowness of thought will limit my success in teaching culturally different students. It is critical to remember that prejudice often works at an unconscious level and that educators are susceptible to its dynamics. It is also important to be aware that, after a lifetime of experience in a racist world, Students of Color are highly sensitized to the nuances of prejudice and racism and can identify such attitudes very quickly. Finally, it is important to reemphasize that schools are places where one must put aside personal values and beliefs in order to hold a position of wholesome neutrality in areas of difference. Prejudice and racism are considered value conflicts.

INSTITUTIONAL RACISM

Consider the following statistics from Hacker (1992) about African Americans in the United States.

- The infant mortality rate for African American babies is twice that of White babies.
- Of African American children, 44.8 percent live below the poverty level.
- In Illinois, 83.2 percent of African American children attend segregated schools.
- The income of African American families is 58 percent that of White families.
- Unemployment among African Americans is 2.76 times that of Whites.
- African Americans are overrepresented in low-paying service occupations (for example, they make up 30.7 percent of nursing aides and orderlies) and underrepresented among professionals.
- Whites are 1.92 times more likely to have attended college for four or more years than are African Americans.
- African Americans comprise 45.3 percent of the prisoners behind bars in the United States.
- Life expectancy of African Americans is 93 percent that of Whites.

These are examples of the consequences of institutional racism: the manipulation of societal institutions to give preferences and advantages to Whites and to restrict the choices, rights, mobility, and access of People of Color. In each instance, African Americans are at a decided disadvantage or at greater risk compared to Whites. The term *institutions* refers to "established societal networks that covertly or overtly control the allocation of resources to individuals and social groups" (Wijeyesinghe, Griffin, & Love, 1997, p. 93). Included are the media, police, courts, jails, banks, schools, organizations that deal with employment and education, health system, and religious, family, civil, and governmental organizations.

Something within the fabric of these institutions causes discrepancies such as those listed to occur on a regular and systematic basis. In many ways, institutional racism is far more insidious than individual racism because it exists beyond the attitudes and behaviors of the individual in the bylaws, rules, practices, procedures, and culture of organizations. Thus, it appears to have a life of its own, and those involved in the daily running of such institutions can more easily disavow responsibility for it.

Determining Institutional Racism

How does one go about determining the existence of institutional racism? The most obvious manner is through the reports of victims: those who regularly feel its effects, encounter differential treatment, and are given only limited access to resources. But such firsthand reports are often considered suspect, and people who may not, for a variety of reasons, want to look too closely at the workings of institutional racism can try to explain them away as "sour grapes" or claim "they just need to pull themselves up by their own bootstraps."

A more objective strategy is to compare the frequency or incidence of a phenomenon within a group to the frequency within the general population. One would expect, for example, that a group that comprises 10 percent of this country's population would provide 10 percent of its doctors or be responsible for 10 percent of its crimes. When there is a sizable disparity between these two numbers (when the expected percentages don't line up, especially when they are very discrepant), it is likely that some broader social force, such as institutional racism, is intervening.

One might alternatively argue that something about members of the group, rather than institutional racism, is responsible for the statistical discrepancy. Such explanations, however, with the one exception of cultural differences (to be described), must be assessed very carefully, for they are frequently based on prejudicial and stereotypical thinking. For instance, members of Group X consistently score lower on intelligence tests than do dominant-group members. One explanation may be that members of Group X are intellectually inferior. But there is a long history of debate over the scientific merit of taking such a position. An alternative and more scientifically compelling explanation is that intelligence tests are culturally biased and, in addition, favor individuals whose first language is English.

There are indeed aspects of a group's collective experience that do predispose members to behave or exhibit characteristics in a manner different from what would be expected statistically. For instance, because of ritualistic practices, Jews tend to experience relatively low rates of alcoholism. Therefore, it is not surprising to find that the percentage of Jews suffering from alcohol abuse is disproportionately lower than their representation in the general population. Such differences, however, tend to be cultural rather than biological.

Consciousness, Intent, and Denial

Institutional racist practices can be conscious or unconscious and intended or unintended. "Conscious or unconscious" refers to the fact that those working within a system may or may not be aware of the practices' existence and impact. "Intended or unintended" means that the practices may or may not have been purposely created, but they nevertheless exist and substantially affect the lives of People of Color. A similar distinction was made early in the civil rights movement between *de jure* and *de facto* segregation. The former refers to segregation that was legally sanctioned and the existence of actual laws dictating racial separation. De jure segregation was, thus, both conscious and intended. De facto segregation, on the other hand, implies separation that exists in actuality or after the fact, but may not have been consciously created for racial purposes.

It is important to distinguish among consciousness, intent, and accountability. A person may have been unaware that telling an ethnic joke could be hurtful and may not have intended such harm. But the person is still responsible for the consequences of the action. Similarly, a school may unintentionally track Students of Color into low-level classes. It was never the school's intention to concentrate Students of Color into these classes and thereby resegregate the school, yet the policies had this effect. Intention does not justify consequences, and teachers in that school should be aware of the racist effects of its policies. Lack of intent or awareness should never be regarded as justification for the existence of institutional or individual racism.

Although denial is an essential part of all forms of racism, it seems especially difficult for individuals to take personal responsibility for institutional racism. Acknowledging one's own prejudicial thoughts or stereotypes is far easier than feeling that one has played an active role in the creation of a racist institution, organization, or school.

First, institutional practices tend to have a history of their own that may precede the individual's own tenure in the system. To challenge or question such practices may seem presumptuous and beyond the person's power or status. Or the individual might feel that he or she is merely following the prescribed practices expected of an employee or the dictates of an administrator or school district and, thus, cannot be held responsible for them. Similar logic is offered in discussions of slavery and White responsibility: "I never owned slaves; neither did my ancestors. That happened hundreds of years ago. Why should I be expected to make sacrifices in my life for injustices that happened long ago and were not of my making?"

Second, people tend to feel powerless in relation to schools and school districts. Sentiments such as "You can't fight central administration" and "What can one person do?" seem to prevail. The distribution of power and the perception that decisions about curriculum and school functioning are made "above" contribute further to feelings of powerlessness and alienation.

Third, schools are by nature conservative and oriented toward maintaining the status quo. Change requires energy and is generally considered only during times of serious crisis and challenge. Specific procedures for effecting change are seldom spelled out, and important practices tend to be subtly, yet powerfully, protected.

Fourth, the practices of a school district that support institutional racism (that cause underachievement for some students) are multiple, complicated, mutually reinforcing, and therefore all the more insidious. Even if one were to undertake such efforts sincerely, it is often difficult to know exactly where to begin.

A Case Study

The following case study provides a better sense of the complexity with which institutional racism asserts itself. It is an excerpt from a report and evaluation describing a five-year partnership with an inner-city school, focusing on multicultural teaching, staff and community interactions, and staff racial proportions. The purpose of this partnership was to increase the pedagogical strength of the school faculty, particularly in math and science. Cultural competency was an additional goal of the partnership. Although the report does not directly point to instances of institutional racism in staffing practices, they become obvious as one reads through the material and separates the "heart intent" of the individuals involved and the net result of unintentional institutional racism.

> Currently, 15 of the 35 teachers at School X are People of Color. At present it has a minority population of 650 students. In the front office one office worker is White and one is African American. Both administrators are White and among other staff members who are not classroom teachers but could be seen in influential or leadership roles, two are African American and six are White.
>
> When parents enter the school for the first time, unless their child's teacher is one of those that is of Color, they are faced with a staff that is overwhelmingly White. While there is no question that the majority of White faculty and staff at the school are caring and unusually competent in matters of cultural understanding and knowledge, the "face validity" is poor. For instance, African Americans who come to the school as parents or in other roles may not know the competency of the staff, and it may take more effort on both the parts of the parents and the staff to connect or bridge over a racial divide, even one that is merely

perceived. The net result has been that, even with extraordinary efforts by the administration, parental involvement has dropped as a result of the lack of connection that may occur on the basis of similarity of race alone. For example, the former principal, an African American male, had natural connections to community members that increased initial trust and natural connections to community resources that are not available to White administrators without extraordinary efforts.

An often-cited problem is the fact that there are few minority candidates on the list from which hiring is done. What is required to compensate is special and proactive recruitment efforts to get People of Color on the lists as well as the creation of special positions and other strategies for circumventing such lists. At a systems level attention must be given to screening practices that may inadvertently and unfairly reject qualified minority candidates, even at the level of admissions to teacher education programs.

While at least parity in numbers of Staff of Color to population demographics should be an important goal, holding to strict quotas misses the point of cultural competence. The idea is to strive for making the entire organization—all leadership positions and staff—more culturally competent, that is, able to effectively work with students who are culturally different. Nor is it reasonable to assume that all Staff of Color will be culturally competent. While attempting to add more Staff of Color, it is highly useful to fill the vacuum through the use of community resources and educators hired specifically to provide cultural expertise.

In this study, staff interactions, conversations, and journal reflections during courses held on-site revealed major previously unseen and unacknowledged differences in perspective. This would include: awareness of broader issues of culture and cross-cultural communication, history and cultural patterns of specific minority cultures and implications of cultural differences for the provision of student services. Especially relevant was knowledge of interactional patterns as they differ across cultural groups, so that culturally sensitive and appropriate classroom teaching strategies might be carried out. In moving toward a more supportive and culturally sensitive model within the school as was indicated by several staff members during our coursework and casual conversations, it is critical to understand the dynamics between students and students and teachers from the perspective of the culture of origin as opposed to a singular, monocultural Euro-American perspective. Also evident was a basic conflict within the organization on methods of providing educational services. Many staff adhered to a model that tended to devalue the importance of cultural differences in working with Students of Color. In addition several staff viewed Youth of Color as using racism and cultural differences as an excuse for not taking responsibility for their own behavior.

White staff members report the following needs and concerns in regard to working with Children of Color: need help in identifying culturally appropriate resources for teaching; some avoidance of issues dealing directly with race; recognition that silence often hid unacknowledged racism; the need for more and better training; lack of knowledge about biracial children; and need for a better understanding of the role of culture in the teaching model they use.

Staff of Color did not report any experiences of overt discrimination and felt respected by their colleagues. They felt that School X was in fact trying to deal with the problem of cultural diversity. They also felt that the liberal climate of the school did much to justify a pervasive attitude that "we treat everyone with respect" and "I know good teaching when I see it and can deal with any student no matter what their background." Together, such attitudes can serve as an excuse for not dealing directly with cultural differences in students. Staff of Color also believed that cultural diversity was experienced by some coworkers as an extra burden and merely more work to do. Often teachers who participated in volunteer training were already the most motivated to make a difference. As in most work situations, the Staff of Color did experience some distance from coworkers, for instance, lunchtime was often highly segregated by race. The onus of keeping up good relations was sometimes felt to be on the Person of Color to put their White coworkers at ease.

It is likely that School X will continue to be faced with the need to hire additional bicultural staff to meet the growing need. In this regard two caveats should be offered. First, culturally sensitive workers and those assigned to work with students from non–Euro-American cultures tend to work most effectively and creatively when they are allowed maximum flexibility, leeway, and discretion in how they carry out their duties. Rules and policies established within the context of serving Euro-American students may be of little help and possibly obstructive to working with culturally different groups. Second, the existence of several competent cultural experts within an organization should not be viewed in any way as a justification for not actively pursuing the cultural competence of the school in general and its staff.

Implications for Teachers

What, then, are the implications of institutional racism for teachers? First and foremost, the vast majority of teachers work in schools and school districts that may suffer in varying degrees from institutional racism. To the extent that the general structure, practices, and climate of a school make it impossible for Students of Color to receive culturally competent teaching, the efforts of individual teachers, no matter how skilled, are drastically compromised.

It is not possible to divorce what happens between a teacher and students from the larger context of the school. Culturally different students may have their achievement incentive affected if they sense racist or biased practices. (Such information travels very quickly within a community.) Even though they must attend school, their willingness to engage in the learning process with the teacher to whom they are assigned may be seriously compromised. Again, their work with an individual staff member is affected by how they perceive and experience the school as a whole. In their eyes, the teacher is always part of the school and responsible for what happens within it.

Finally, the ability to do what is necessary to meet the needs of a culturally different student may be limited by the rules and atmosphere of the school. Does the school provide support, resources, and knowledgeable supervision for working with culturally different students? Is the teacher afforded enough flexibility so as to be able to adapt teaching to the cultural demands of students from various cultural groups? If the answer to either of these questions is no, then the teacher must be willing to try to initiate changes in how the classroom, and even the school, functions—in its structure, practices, and climate—so that it can be more supportive of efforts to provide more culturally competent education.

CULTURAL RACISM

Closely intertwined with institutional racism is cultural racism: the belief that the cultural ways of one group are superior to those of another. Whenever we think of cultural racism, we remember a Latino student once telling a class about painful early experiences in predominantly White schools.

> One day a teacher was giving us a lesson on nutrition. She asked us to tell the class what we had eaten for dinner the night before. When it was my turn, I proudly listed beans, rice, tortillas. Her response was that my dinner had not included all of the four major food groups and, therefore, was not sufficiently nutritious. The students giggled. How could she say that? Those foods were nutritious to me.

Schools, like ethnic groups, have their own cultures: languages, ways of doing things, values, attitudes toward time, standards of appropriate behavior, and so on. As participants in schools, students are expected to adopt, share, and exhibit these cultural patterns. If they don't or can't, they are likely to be censured and made to feel uncomfortable in a variety of ways. In the United States, White Northern European culture has been adopted by and dominates most social institutions. The established norms on how things are done are dictated by the various dimensions of this dominant culture. Behavior outside its parameters is judged as bad, inappropriate, different, or abnormal. Thus, the Latino family's eating habits, to the extent that they differed from what White culture considers nutritious, were judged to be unhealthy, and the student was made to feel bad and ashamed.

Herein lies the real insidiousness of cultural racism: those who are culturally different must either give up their own ways, and thus a part of themselves, and take on the ways of majority culture or remain perpetual outsiders. (Some people believe it is possible to be bicultural, that is, learn the ways of and function comfortably in two very different cultures. This idea is discussed in Chapter 7.) Institutional and cultural racism are thus two sides of the same coin. Institutional racism keeps People of Color on the outside of society's institutions by structurally limiting their access. Cultural racism makes them uncomfortable if they do manage to gain entry. White society's ways are foreign to them, and they know that their own cultural traits are judged harshly.

Wijeyesinghe, Griffin, & Love (1997) offer the following examples of cultural racism.

- Personal traits: Characteristics such as independence, assertiveness, and modesty are valued differently in different cultures.
- Language: "Standard English" usage is expected in most institutions in the United States. Other languages are sometimes expressly prohibited or tacitly disapproved of.
- Standards of dress: If a student or faculty member dresses in clothing or hairstyles unique to their culture, they are described as "being ethnic," whereas the clothing or hairstyles of Europeans are viewed as "normal."
- Standards of beauty: Eye color, hair color, hair texture, body size, and shape ideals exclude most People of Color. For instance, Black women who have won the Miss America beauty pageant have closely approximated White European looks. . . .
- Cultural icons: Jesus, Mary, Santa Claus, for example, are portrayed as White. The devil and Judas Iscariot, however, are often portrayed as Black. (p. 94)

Implications for Teachers

Cultural racism has relevance for teachers in several ways. First, teachers need to be aware of the cultural values they bring to the classroom and acknowledge that these values may be different from and even at odds with those of their students. This is especially true for White teachers working with Students of Color. It is not unusual for Students of Color to react to White teachers as symbols of the dominant culture and to initially act out their frustrations with a society that so systematically negates their cultural ways.

Second, teaching across cultures must involve some degree of negotiation around the values that define the learning environment. Most important, educational goals and the general style of interaction must make sense to the student. Yet, at the same time, they must fall within the broad parameters of what the teacher conceives as sound education. Most likely, the teacher will have to make significant adaptations to standard methods of teaching to fit the needs of the culturally different student.

Third is the realization that traditional training as teachers and the models that inform preservice education are themselves culture-bound and have their roots in dominant Northern European culture. What exactly are the values and cultural imperatives that teachers bring to the classroom? What relevance do these have for students whose cultural worldviews might be very different?

Cultures differ greatly in how they view success and how they conceive of the role of teacher. The notion of sacrificing peer approval for the sake of academic achievement in a seemingly racist system makes little sense to many students. Similarly, what success is and how one measures it vary greatly across cultures. Given all of this cultural variation and the ethnocentricity of traditional teaching and learning methods, teachers must answer a number of very knotty questions. Is it possible, for example, to expand present culture-bound teaching methods so they can become universally applicable (appropriately applied multiculturally)? If so, what would such teaching look like? Or is there, perhaps, some truth to the contention of many minority educators that something in the Northern European dominant paradigm is inherently destructive to traditional culture, and that radically different approaches to teaching must be forged for ethnic populations? These questions are addressed in Chapter 5.

DISCUSSION QUESTIONS AND ACTIVITIES

A theme that has reverberated throughout this chapter is the critical nature of self-awareness. Again, it is not just a question of whether one holds racist attitudes and stereotypes or if one is involved with practices of institutional or cultural racism. We all do and are. Rather, the issue is discovering the ways a teacher's thinking is slanted racially, how this will affect his or her role as an educator, and what can be done to change it. The exercises that follow are meant to stimulate increased self-awareness. They are necessary in counteracting natural tendencies toward denial, avoidance, and rationalization in matters of race and ethnicity. They are useful to the extent that the reader takes them seriously, allows sufficient time to adequately process and complete them, and approaches them with candor.

Exercise 1

This exercise involves a series of questions about your experiences with ethnicity and cultural differences. Several ask you to identify a time or event in the past. Allow yourself to relax and visualize the time or event you have identified. Try to reexperience it as much as possible. When you are finished, describe the experience in writing. Include how you felt at the time, how you now feel about it, how it has affected you today, and any other associations, images, or strong feelings that may come up. Use as much time and detail as you need.

1. When did you first become aware that people were different racially or ethnically?
2. When did you first become aware of yourself as a member of a racial or ethnic group?
3. When were you first made aware of people being treated differently because of their race or ethnicity?

4. When did you first become aware of being treated differently yourself because of your own race or ethnicity?
5. Are there things about you as a person that make you feel that you are different from other people? Describe them and describe how having these qualities makes you feel and has affected you over time.
6. When were you proudest being a member of the group to which you belong?
7. When were you least proud of being a member of the group to which you belong?
8. How do you identify yourself racially/ethnically? Culturally? How has your sense of race/ethnicity or culture changed over time?
9. How would you describe the extent of your contact with people who are racially/ethnically different from you? How has this changed over time?

You can increase the intensity and learning value of this exercise by sharing your answers with someone else. After you have shared each answer, use it as a springboard for further soul-searching and personal discussion of each topic.

Exercise 2

This exercise involves writing a detailed autobiography focusing on issues of race and ethnicity. You might find it helpful to do this chronologically. With the experience of Exercise 1 as a stimulus, write a personal history of your experiences with prejudice and racism and how your own ethnic background has impacted these, contact with those who are culturally different from you, and the general experience of being different.

You can increase the power of this exercise by getting together with another person or in a small group and taking turns reading your autobiographies. Have the other person or people respond to various aspects of your writing, and follow this up with a discussion of their reactions.

Exercise 3

This exercise gives you an opportunity to verbalize and identify your experiences with, attitudes toward, and beliefs about members of different racial and ethnic groups. Answer the following questions in relation to each of the following groups: (a) African Americans, (b) Latinos/as, (c) Asian Americans, (d) Native Americans, (e) White Northern Europeans, (f) White ethnic groups (Jews, Irish, Italians, etc.).

1. Describe in detail experiences you have had with members of this group.
2. At present, how do you feel about members of this group (describe your reactions in detail and, if possible, relate them to specific experiences), and how has that changed over time?

3. Are there any characteristics, traits, or other things about members of this group that make it difficult for you to approach them?
4. Without censoring yourself, generate a list of characteristics—one-word adjectives—that describe your beliefs and perceptions about members of this group.
5. What reactions, feelings, thoughts, or concerns come to mind when you think about working professionally with members of this group?
6. What kinds of answers, information, learning experiences, contacts, and so forth do you need to become more comfortable with members of this group?

Exercise 4

This exercise is intended to help you identify dynamics and aspects of institutional and cultural racism in schools. Choose a particular school or organization with which you are familiar. It may be one in which you are currently teaching or volunteering or one from your past. Answer the following questions about it. Some of the questions may require you to do research or seek additional information.

How many People of Color or other ethnic group members work and teach in this school, and what positions do they hold? How are people hired or brought into the school? Is there anything about this process or the job requirements that could differentially affect People of Color or other ethnic-group members?

Does the school take any position on promoting cultural diversity within its ranks? Do any mission statements, plans, or projections in this direction exist? Can you discern any unwritten feelings or attitudes that prevail around race and ethnicity within the school? Has the school done anything specific to promote greater diversity?

How would you describe the school culture? Do you feel that members of various Communities of Color would be comfortable entering and being a part of it? Specify your answers by group and explain in detail. How do you feel various segments of the school would react to the entry of a Person of Color? How does the school function? Who has the power? Who makes decisions? Is there anything about the school's structure that makes it accessible or inaccessible to People of Color?

What does it feel like to teach or volunteer in this organization? Are there any rules, policies, and styles of working that are unique or unusual? Would you say that the school's culture is predominately Euro-American? Explain.

If it is a school, who are its students? Are any efforts being made (or have there ever been any efforts) to broaden or narrow the racial and ethnic composition of the student body?

You may find it particularly informative to have other teachers or volunteers answer these same questions and then compare answers or use the questions as stimuli for discussing the cultural competence of the school.

Exercise 5

This last exercise is intended to help you become more aware of your own cultural roots and identity as well as prepare you to better understand the material in Chapter 5, Understanding Culture and Cultural Differences. The following is a detailed list of questions to be answered in relation to each ethnic group constituting your culture of origin. The questions were developed by Hardy and Laszloffy (1995). In answering them, you are encouraged to seek additional information from your parents or other relatives.

1. What were the migration patterns of the group?
2. If other than Native American, under what conditions did your family (or their descendants) enter the United States (immigrants, political refugee, slave, etc.)?
3. What were/are the group's experiences with oppression? What were/are the markers of oppression?
4. What issues divide members within the same group?
5. Describe the relationship between the group's identity and your national ancestry (if the group is defined in terms of nationality, please skip this question).
6. What significance does race, skin color, and hair play within the group?
7. What is/are the dominant religion(s) of the group? What role does religion and spirituality play in the everyday lives of members of the group?
8. What role does regionality and geography play in the group?
9. How are gender roles defined within the group? How is sexual orientation regarded?
10. (a) What prejudices or stereotypes does this group have about itself? (b) What prejudices or stereotypes do other groups have about this group? (c) What prejudices or stereotypes does this group have about other groups?
11. What role (if any) do names play in the group? Are there rules, mores, or rituals governing the assignment of names?
12. How is social class defined in the group?
13. What occupational roles are valued and devalued by the group?
14. What is the relationship between age and values of the group?
15. How is family defined in the group?
16. How does this group view outsiders in general and educators specifically?

17. How have the organizing principles of this group shaped your family and its members? What effect have they had on you? (Organizing principles are "fundamental constructs which shape the perceptions, beliefs, and behaviors of members of the group." For example, for Jews an organizing principle is "fear of persecution.")
18. What are the ways in which pride/shame issues of the group are manifested in your family system? (Pride/shame issues are "aspects of a culture that are sanctioned as distinctively negative or positive." For example, for Jews a pride/shame issue is "educational achievement.")
19. What impact will these pride/shame issues have on your work with students from both similar and dissimilar cultural backgrounds?
20. If more than one group comprises your culture of origin, how are the differences negotiated in your family? What are the intergenerational consequences? How has this impacted you personally and as a teacher? (p. 232)

As a second part of this exercise, and as a way of focusing more specifically on cultural content, carry on an inner dialogue while reading Chapter 5. As different dimensions of culture are introduced and discussed (such as experiencing time), ask yourself where you fit on each dimension and from where in your cultural past this characteristic is likely to have derived.

Summary

A dynamic that fuels racial tensions in the United States is the belief that the United States is European in ancestry and White in identity and culture. Those who do not share these characteristics are viewed with suspicion, are not seen as truly belonging here, and are often relegated to second-class citizenship. Educational systems are merely a microcosm of broader society and susceptible to the same racial tensions and dynamics. As we saw in the previous chapter, self-awareness of one's own prejudices and stereotypes about ethnicity and race is a crucial component of cultural competence. In this chapter we explored the dynamics of prejudice and racism, especially as they impact classrooms, teachers, and their schools.

Racism is "the systematic subordination of members of targeted racial groups who have relatively little social power . . . by members of the agent racial group who have relatively more social power" (Wijeyesingne, Griffin, & Love, 1997, p. 88). Prejudice is a negative, inaccurate, rigid, and unfair way of thinking about members of another group. Racism equals prejudice plus power and exists on three different levels: individual racism, institutional racism, and cultural racism. In general, people deny, rationalize, and avoid discussing feelings and beliefs about race and ethnicity.

Individual racism emerges out of the normal and natural tendencies of how people think, feel, and process information. In-group and out-group behavior, categorical thinking and stereotyping, avoidance, and selective perception set the stage for the emergence of racism. There are a variety of theories about the psychological motivation behind racist behavior. The frustration-aggression-displacement hypothesis, the idea of a global bigoted personality type, prejudice as a political and economic tool, and prejudice as a means of buoying up self-esteem are examples.

Students of Color face racism on a daily basis and are stressed by it, and such stress often leads to educational problems. There are also more indirect costs of racism: the impact of poverty, blocked aspirations, the role of racism in hiring and advancement. Teachers must become aware of their own prejudices and stereotypes so they do not interfere in their educational interactions with Students of Color.

Institutional racism involves the manipulation of societal institutions to give preferences and advantages to White people and at the same time restrict the choices, rights, mobility, and access of People of Color. One method of identifying institutional racism involves comparing the frequency or incidence of a phenomenon within a group with the group's general frequency in the population. If, for example, a group comprises 10 percent of the population, one would expect the group to provide 10 percent of a population's doctors. If not, institutional racism may be at work. Lack of intent or consciousness should never be regarded as a justification for institutional racism. Although denial is typically at work in all forms of racism, it is especially difficult for individuals to take personal responsibility for the existence of institutional racism.

Like all organizations, schools and school districts suffer from institutional racism. To the extent that such rules and practices put Students of Color at a disadvantage, they compromise the educational process. Similarly, a culturally competent teacher is compromised by having to function within a broader educational context that undermines her or his efforts. Students perceive the teacher as responsible for all events and practices that occur within a school. If the structure, practices, and climate of the school limits a teacher's ability to meet the needs of culturally different students, it is the teacher's responsibility to initiate change in the necessary direction.

Cultural racism is the belief that the cultural ways of one group are superior to those of another. Schools, like ethnic groups, have their own cultures: languages, ways of doing things, values, attitudes toward time, standards of behavior, and so on. In most schools, as in most institutions in our country, White Northern European culture has been adopted and dominates. Behavior outside its parameters is judged as bad or inappropriate. To succeed in such a school environment, students who are culturally different must give up their own ways, and thus a part of themselves, and take on the ways of majority culture, or they remain perpetual outsiders.

Teachers must be aware of the cultural values that inform their teaching and recognize that these may be at odds with the cultural styles of their students. Teaching across cultures typically involves some degree of negotiation around the values that define the learning process. Goals and interaction style must make sense to both the student and the teacher.

The chapter ends with a series of assessment exercises that help identify personal patterns of prejudice, stereotyping, and cultural insensitivity. Their goal is to help you discover ways your thinking is slanted racially, how these will affect your role as a teacher, and what can be done to change them.

Understanding Privilege and Racial Consciousness Among Whites

I'm not asking you to apologize or pay for what others have done in the past. I'm only asking you to realize that we wake up in different worlds each day, with different challenges based on the color of our skin alone. As long as you can acknowledge that reality, we're okay.

—Overheard by a Student, Source Unknown

As discussed in Chapter 3, racism exists on three levels: within the individual, within institutions, such as our schools, and within the culture of those institutions. Each aspect reinforces the others, making them all the more difficult to change. Most schools and the teaching styles that define them are Eurocentric and, as such, put Students of Color at an educational disadvantage. These students often feel unwelcome and unwanted: they feel that they do not belong, do not understand the rules of classroom interaction, are not valued, and must give up their cultural identities to succeed. The realities are disproportionate failure and dropout rates, depressed achievement scores, negative attitudes toward education and schooling, and differential funding and educational spending vis-à-vis the ethnicity of the students being taught. Kivel (1996) offers the following analysis of racial disparity and institutional racism within our schools.

> Most students in the United States are still attending segregated schools. Within schools, students are segregated by race and tracked by class. . . . Segregation and tracking destine most students from a very early age for a particular socio-economic role in their adult life. There is a vast disparity in what is spent per student. White suburban schools have approximately twice the funds per student as compared with urban schools where students of color are congregated. . . . When this is multiplied by the number of students in a classroom or school, the disparity is enormous. That money buys fewer students per teacher, classroom necessities like books, pencils and paper, not to mention computers, art and music classes, recreational equipment, teacher's aides, special events and field trips, and in the long run, the best teachers. Students are given a direct measure of their social worth and future chances by the amount of money they see being

spent on their education. When we look at the disparities in educational expenditures we have to acknowledge that most white students have tremendous educational advantages over students of color. . . . Education is more than money. It includes teachers, curricula, school buildings, safety to learn and many other factors. Racism affects the quality and quantity of each of these resources. Teachers in the United States are disproportionately white, far beyond their representation in the general population, and this disparity is increasing. Few students of color have role models of their own ethnicity, and few white students have contact with people of color in positions of authority. In addition, challenges to white culture-based curriculum are harder to organize because there aren't sufficient numbers of teachers of color to counter traditional curricula. (pp. 186–187)

In order to better understand how such dynamics of inequality have evolved, we must first understand how majority group members, that is, White Americans, perceive and understand race and ethnicity. To this end we begin this chapter by looking at the concept of White privilege, ways in which European Americans are afforded certain benefits and rights based solely on the color of their skin. As will become obvious, Whites have great difficulty acknowledging the existence of such privilege.

Next we will explore racial consciousness in European Americans: how Whites think about race and racial difference and how White racial identity develops and can evolve and mature over time. This material is especially important to White teachers as they move toward cultural competence and a self-understanding of how they perceive, understand, and react to the ethnicity of their students.

White Privilege

In a very heated classroom discussion of diversity, several White male students complained bitterly, "It has gotten to a point where there's no place we can just be ourselves and not have to watch what we say or do all the time." The rest of the class—women and ethnic minorities—responded in unison, "Hey, welcome to the world. The rest of us have been doing that kind of self-monitoring all of our lives." What these men were feeling was a threat to their privilege as men and as Whites, and they did not like it one bit. Put simply, White privilege is the benefits that are automatically accrued to European Americans just on the basis of the color of their skin. What is most insidious is that, to most Whites, it is all but invisible. It is so basic a part of their daily experience and existence, and so available to everyone in their "world," that it is never acknowledged or even given a second thought. Or, at least, so it seems.

If one digs a little deeper, however, there is a strong element of defensiveness and denial. Whites tend to see themselves as individuals, just "regular people," part of the human race, but not as members of a racial group.

They are, in fact, shocked when others relate to them racially (that is, as "White"). In a society that speaks so seriously about equality and equal access to resources ("With enough hard work, anyone can succeed in America"; "Any child can nurture the dream of someday being president"), it is difficult to acknowledge one's "unearned power," to borrow McIntosh's (1989) description.

It is also easier to deny one's White racial heritage and see oneself as colorless than to experience the full brunt of what has been done to People of Color in this country in the name of White superiority. Such an awareness demands some kind of personal responsibility. If I am White and truly understand what White privilege means socially, economically, and politically, I cannot help but bear some of the guilt for what has happened historically and what continues to occur. If I were to truly "get it," then I would have no choice but to give up my complacency, to try to do something about it, and ultimately to find myself with the same kind of discomfort and feelings as the men mentioned above. No one easily gives up power and privilege.

It is easy for Whites to perceive themselves as relatively powerless in relation to people who garner power because of gender, class, age, and so forth and thereby to deny holding any privilege. As Kendall (1997) points out, one need only look at statistics regarding managers in American industry. While White males constitute 43 percent of the workforce, they hold 95 percent of senior management jobs. White women hold 40 percent of middle management positions, compared to Black women and men who hold 5 percent and 4 percent, respectively. Having said this, it is equally important to acknowledge that as invisible as White privilege is to most European Americans, that is how clearly visible it is to People of Color. To those of Color, Whites are clearly racial beings and obviously in possession of privilege in this society. That Whites do not see it is, in fact, mind-boggling to most People of Color, for those of Color, race and racial inequity are ever-present realities. To deny having these privileges must seem either deeply cunning or bordering on psychotic.

At a broader level, White privilege is infused into the very fabric of American society, and even if individuals wish to deny it, Whites cannot really give it up. Kendall (1997, pp. 1–5) enumerates several reasons why this is so. First, it is "an institutional (rather than personal) set of benefits." Second, it belongs to "all of us, who are white, by race." Third, it bears no relationship to whether we are "good people" or not. Fourth, it tends to be both "intentional" and "malicious." Fifth, it is "bestowed prenatally." Sixth, it allows us to believe "that we do not have to take the issues of racism seriously." Seventh, it involves the "ability to make decisions that affect everyone without taking others into account." Eighth, it allows us to overlook race in ourselves and to be angry at those who do not. And, finally, it lets me "decide whether I am going to listen or hear others or neither."

Peggy McIntosh (1989) offers a number of examples of the kind of life experiences Whites, as people of privilege, can count on in their daily existence. Consider the following.

- If I should need to move, I can be pretty sure of renting or purchasing housing in an area which I can afford and in which I would want to live.
- I can be pretty sure that my neighbors in such a location will be neutral or pleasant to me.
- I can go shopping alone most of the time, pretty well assured that I will not be followed or harassed.
- I can turn on the television or open to the front page of the paper and see people of my race widely represented.
- When I am told about our national heritage or about "civilization," I am shown that people of my color made it what it is.
- I can be sure that my children will be given materials that testify to the existence of their race.
- I can go into a music shop and count on finding the music of my race represented, into a supermarket and find the staple foods which fit with my cultural traditions, into a hairdresser's shop and find someone who can cut my hair.
- Whether I use checks, credit cards, or cash, I can count on my skin color not to work against the appearance of financial responsibility.
- I am never asked to speak for all the people of my racial group.
- I can be pretty sure that if I ask to talk to "the person in charge," I will be facing a person of my race.
- I can take a job with an affirmative action employer without having coworkers on the job suspect that I got it because of race.
- If my day, week, or year is going badly, I need not ask of each negative episode or situation whether it has racial overtones.
- I can choose blemish color or bandages in "flesh" color and have them more or less match my skin. (pp. 10–12)

The opposite of each of these is the experience of People of Color in the United States. What can be done about White privilege? Mainly, individuals can become aware of its existence and the role it plays in their lives. It cannot be given away. Denying its reality or refusing to identify as White, according to Kendall (1997), merely leave us "all the more blind to our silencing of people of color" (p. 6). By remaining self-aware and challenging its insidiousness within oneself, in others, and in societal institutions, it is possible to begin to address the denial and invisibility that are its most powerful foundation. Like becoming culturally competent, fighting racism and White privilege, both internally and externally, is a lifelong developmental task.

A MODEL OF RACIAL ATTITUDE TYPES

Two groups of authors have developed frameworks for understanding how European Americans think about race and racial differences. Rowe, Behrens, and Leach (1995) enumerate seven different attitudes that Whites can adopt vis-à-vis race and People of Color. They first distinguish between achieved and unachieved racial consciousness. What this refers to is the extent to which racial attitude is "securely integrated" into the person's general belief structure—in other words, how firmly it is held and how easily it can change.

Unachieved racial consciousness can have one or both of two sources. It can reflect the fact that individuals have not thought about or explored matters related to race and ethnicity or that they have no real commitment to a position or set of attitudes. Rowe et al. (1995) begin by describing three attitude types that are unachieved: avoidant, dissonant, and dependent. Avoidant types tend to ignore, minimize, or deny the importance of the issue both in relation to their own ethnicity and that of non-Whites. Whether out of fear or just convenience, they merely avoid the topic. The following sample statement typifies such a position: "Minority issues just aren't all that important to me. We just don't get involved in that sort of thing. I really am not interested in thinking about those things" (p. 228).

Dependent types hold some position, unlike the avoidant, but merely have adopted it from significant others (often as far back as during childhood). Therefore, it remains unreflected, superficial, and easily changeable. The following is a typical dependent response: "My thinking about minorities is mainly influenced by my (friends, family, husband or wife), so you could say I mainly learned about minorities from (them, him or her). That's why my opinion about minorities is pretty much the same as (theirs, his or hers)" (p. 228).

The final unachieved type of attitude is dissonant. Such individuals are clearly uncertain about what they believe. They lack commitment to the position they are currently holding and are, in fact, open to new information even if it is dissonant. Their position may result from a lack of experience or knowledge or from an incongruity between a previously held position and some new information or personal experience. It may also reflect a transition period between different positions. The following is typical: "I used to feel I knew what I thought about minorities. But now my feelings are really mixed. I'm having to change my thinking. I'm not sure, so I'm trying to find some answers to questions I have about minorities" (p. 229).

Rowe et al. (1995) next define four types of racial attitudes that they consider as having reached an achieved status—one that is sufficiently explored, committed to, and integrated into the individual's general belief system. Dominative attitudes involve the belief that majority group members should be allowed to dominate those who are culturally different. They tend to be held by people who are ethnocentric, use European American culture as a standard for judging the rightness of others' behavior, and devalue and are uncomfortable with non-Whites, especially in close personal relationships. These are the classic bigots. The following statement is exemplary: "The truth about minorities is that they are kind of dumb, their customs are crude, and they are pretty backward compared to what Whites have accomplished. Besides that, they are sort of lazy. I guess they just aren't up to what Whites are. I wouldn't want a family member, or even a friend of mine, to have a close relationship with a minority. You may have to work near them, but you don't have to live close to one" (p. 229).

A slight variation on this theme is the conflictive attitude type. Such individuals, though they wouldn't support outright racism or discrimination, oppose efforts to ameliorate the effects of discrimination such as affirmative action. Where they are conflicted is around competing values: that of fairness, which requires significant change, versus retaining the status quo, which says that they are content with the way things are: "There should be equal chances to better yourself for everyone, but minorities are way too demanding. The media are always finding something they say is unfair and making a big deal out of it. And the government is always coming up with some kind of program that lets them get more than they deserve. We shouldn't discriminate against minorities, but tilting things in their favor just isn't fair. White ethnic groups didn't get a lot of government help, and the minorities of today shouldn't expect it either" (pp. 229–230).

Individuals who possess integrative attitudes tend to be pragmatic in their approach to race relations. They have a sense of their own identity as Whites and at the same time favor interracial contact and harmony. They further believe that racism can be eradicated through goodwill and rationality. The following reflects an integrative attitude: "Integration is a desirable goal for our society, and it could significantly improve problems relating to prejudice and discrimination if people would keep an open mind and allow it to work. Race and culture is not a factor when I choose my personal friends. I'm comfortable around minority people and don't mind being one of a few Whites in a group. In fact, I wouldn't mind living next to minority people if their social class were similar to mine. I think we will need racial harmony for democracy to be able to function" (p. 230).

The final attitude type delineated by Rowe et al. is called reactive and involves a rather militant stand against racism. Such individuals tend to identify with People of Color, may feel guilty about being White, and may romanticize the racial drama. They are, in addition, very sensitive to situations involving discrimination and react strongly to the inequities that exist in society. "Our society is quite racist. It is really difficult for minority people to get a fair deal. There may be some tokenism, but businesses won't put minorities in the top positions. Actually, qualified minority people should be given preference at all levels of education and employment to make up for the effects of past discrimination. But they don't have enough power to influence the government, even though it's the government's responsibility to help minority people. It's enough sometimes to make you feel guilty about being White" (p. 230).

According to the authors, these are the most frequently observed White attitudes toward race and race relations. The unachieved types are most changeable, by definition, not having been truly integrated into the person's worldview. The four achieved forms are more difficult to change, but under sufficient contrary information or experience, they can be altered. When that does occur, the individual looks a lot like those who are in the dissonant mode.

A MODEL OF WHITE RACIAL-IDENTITY DEVELOPMENT

Helms (1995) offers a somewhat different model of White racial-identity development. Rather than suggesting a series of independent attitudes, as do Rowe et al., she envisions a developmental process (defined by a series of stages or statuses) through which Whites can move to recognize and abandon their privilege. According to Helms's model, each status or stage is supported by a unique pattern of psychological defense and means of processing racial experience.

The first stage, contact status, begins with the individual's internalization of the majority culture's view of People of Color as well as the advantages of privilege. Whites at this level of awareness have developed a defense Helms calls "obliviousness" to keep the issues out of consciousness. Bollin and Finkel (1995) describe another aspect of contact status as a "naive belief that race does not really make a difference" (p. 25).

The second stage, disintegration status, involves "disorientation and anxiety provoked by unresolved racial moral dilemmas that force one to choose between own-group loyalty and humanism" (Helms, 1995, p. 185). It is supported by the defenses of suppression and ambivalence. At this stage, the person has encountered information or has had experiences that lead to the realization that race does in fact make a difference. The result is a growing awareness of and discomfort with privilege.

Reintegration status, the third stage, is defined by an idealization of one's racial group and a concurrent rejection and intolerance for other groups. It depends on the defenses of selective perception and negative out-group distortion for its evolution. Here, the White individual attempts to deal with the discomfort by emphasizing the superiority of White culture and the natural deficits in Cultures of Color.

The fourth stage, or pseudo-independence status, involves an "intellectualized commitment to one's own socioracial group and deceptive tolerance of other groups" (p. 185). It is grounded in the reshaping of reality and selective perception. The individual has developed an intellectual acceptance of racial differences, espouses a liberal ideology of social justice, but has not emotionally integrated either.

A person functioning in the immersion/emersion status, fifth along the continuum, is searching for a personal understanding of racism as well as insight into how he or she benefits from it. As a part of this process, which has its psychological base in hypervigilance and reshaping, there is an effort to redefine one's Whiteness. Entry into this stage may have been precipitated by being rejected by Individuals of Color and often includes isolation within one's own group in order to work through the powerful feelings that have been stimulated.

The final stage, autonomy status, involves "informed positive socioracial-group commitment, use of internal standards for self-definition, capacity to relinquish the privileges of racism" (p. 185). It is supported by the psychological processes of flexibility and complexity. Here, the person has come to peace with his or her own Whiteness, separating it from a sense of privilege, and is able to approach those who are culturally different without prejudice.

Helms's model of White identity development parallels models of racial-identity development for People of Color that are introduced in Chapter 7. All involve consciousness-raising—that is, becoming aware of and working through unconscious feelings and beliefs about one's connection to race and ethnicity. The goal of identity development in each group is, however, different. For People of Color, it involves a cumulative process of "surmounting internalized racism in its various manifestations," while for Whites, it has to do with the "abandonment of entitlement" (p. 184). What the two models share is a process wherein the Person of Color or the White person sheds internalized racial attitudes and social conditioning and replaces them with greater openness and appreciation for racial and cultural identity as well as cultural differences.

IDENTITY DEVELOPMENT IN THE COLLEGE CLASSROOM

Ponterotto (1988), drawing parallels with the earlier work of both Helms (1985) and W. E. Cross (1971), describes "the racial identity and consciousness development process" of White participants in a multicultural learning environment, an educational setting similar to that in which many readers may find themselves. Ponterotto identifies four stages through which most students proceed: (1) preexposure, (2) exposure, (3) zealot-defensive, and (4) integration. In the preexposure stage, the student "has given little thought to multicultural issues or to his or her role as a White person in a racist and oppressive society" (p. 151).

In the second stage, exposure, students are routinely confronted with minority individuals and issues. They are exposed to the realities of racism and the mistreatment of People of Color, examine their own cultural values and how they pervade society, and discover how interaction often "is ethnocentrically biased and subtly racist" (p. 152). These realizations tend to stimulate both anger and guilt: anger because they had been taught that teaching was "value free and truly fair and objective," and guilt because holding such assumptions probably led them to perpetuate this subtle racism in their own right.

In the zealot-defensive stage, students tend to react in one of two ways: either overidentifying with ethnic minorities and the issues they are studying or distancing themselves from them. The former tend to develop a strong "prominority perspective" (p. 152) and use it to manage and resolve some of the guilt feelings. The latter, on the other hand, tend to take the criticism very personally and, by way of defense, withdraw from the topic, becoming "passive recipients" (p. 153) of multicultural information. In the real world, such a reaction leads to avoidance of interracial contact and escape into same-race associations. In classes, however, where students are a "captive audience," there is greater likelihood that the defensive feelings will be processed and worked through.

In the last stage, integration, the extreme reactions of the previous stage tend to decrease in intensity. Zealous reactions subside, and students' views become more balanced. Defensiveness is slowly transformed, and students tend to acquire a "renewed interest, respect, and appreciation for cultural differences" (p. 153). Ponterotto is, however, quick to point out that there is no guarantee that all students will pass through all four stages, and some can remain stuck in an earlier stage.

IMPLICATIONS FOR WHITE TEACHERS

White teachers are encouraged to assess their own reactions to the concept of privilege and to locate their current level of development in each of the models. To what extent is one aware of the existence of White privilege in his or her life? This is an important question because culturally different non-White students view and relate to a White teacher in light of his or her having that privilege. As suggested in earlier chapters, one cannot help but be a magnet for the feelings of culturally different students about White dominant culture and how it has treated them and those they love. What a teacher can do is struggle to fully grasp the meaning and ramifications of White privilege and then communicate that awareness to non-White students.

Trust is more difficult when two people live in perceptually different worlds. A key aspect of unacknowledged White privilege is its invisibility to Whites and its very obvious visibility to People of Color. To the extent that

White teachers can acknowledge the centrality of race to a non-White student and at the same time grasp the nature of their own attitudes about racial differences, the cultural distance between them can be dramatically reduced.

REFLECTION QUESTIONS AND A TECHNIQUE FOR SOLVING PROBLEMS

At the conclusion of most chapters, we ask you to consider a series of questions and activities based on creative problem solving (Parnes, 1967). This practical tool will help you incorporate the concepts and specifics in the chapter as well as give you practice in the technique.

The first step in the process is to recognize that there is a problem that needs solving. So before going farther, jot down any conflict, controversy, or question that comes to mind on the material in this chapter. This step is sometimes called "the mess."

Next, list three to five facts that have been established about the material covered. Either think of things that particularly moved or surprised you, or scan the pages again for a few details.

Based on the facts and your original concern, complete the statement "In what ways might we ———?" We will refer to this sentence with the initials "IWWMW" in subsequent chapters. This restating of the problem helps us get beyond complaint into an active and collective consideration of a specific problem. You may need to generate two or three IWWMW sentences before you have one that you would like to take through the remaining steps of the process.

Use an open-ended brainstorming technique that includes the following specifics to generate ten to twelve ideas to answer your IWWMW statement:

- Don't make judgments. At this point all ideas have value. This strategy allows you to generate rather than defend or critique your ideas.
- Come up with multiple ideas, as many as you can generate in two minutes, for instance. The more creative ideas you have to choose from, the better. Having many ideas increases the likelihood of coming to a great idea.
- Build on ideas you or others have. Piggybacking and looking over each others' shoulders are allowed at this point. Perhaps ask others to help you think of or modify an idea.
- The wilder an idea, the better, for a wild idea often leads to an unexpected and viable solution. Encouraging far-out ideas expands the imagination.

Your list could contain ideas that were included in or suggested by the material in the chapter.

Now that you have generated a free-flowing and perhaps wild-eyed list, apply criteria to see which ideas are worth pursuing. Choose criteria that you believe are appropriate for evaluating your ideas from the following:

acceptance by others? adaptable to situation? advantageous? agreement of those concerned? appealing; attractive? assistance available? attitudes (positive) about idea? behavior (positive) toward idea? beneficial? commitment: long term? commitment: short term? consistent? cooperation available? cost-effective? cost-efficient? cost for start-up reasonable? challenging; holds interest? creative solution? creative enhancement? (not) dangerous? deadline can be met? (not) distracting? materials and cost? measurable results? needs met? organizational acceptance? operational? performs well? performance over time? policies fit? practical? predictable? prevents _____? price? produces desired result? profitable? reasonable or logical? resources available? results immediately given? ease in doing? effect: immediate? effect: long term? effect: short term? efficient? economical? endorsement from key people? explainable to others? financing available? fits situation? flexible to situation? functional? imaginative? improve a condition? improvement: long term? improvement: now? improvement: short term? interest will expand? lasting effect? manageable? markets available? materials available? results: short term? rewarding to others? rewarding to self? rewards? risks: low? safety? socially acceptable? success likely? time? time: efficient use of? timely? transfer? transferable to other situations? useful? values intact? valuable?

Evaluate your brainstormed list using three to five criteria you have chosen. Give 0 to 3 points for each generated idea for each criterion you have selected. When one or two ideas have the most points, go to the next step.

Plan to implement your idea either as an actual event if you have the opportunity to do so in your current situation, or in a future classroom or other community setting you may encounter.

For example, I am concerned that children in a racially homogenous classroom may not have an opportunity to develop realistic perceptions of People of Color. I know

- That such attitudes develop early
- That prejudices are deeply embedded in our culture
- That well-intentioned teachers may unknowingly perpetrate stereotypes

My IWWMW statement is: In what way might we bring children to a more realistic view of those who are not like themselves? My brainstormed list of ideas includes: experiences in diverse cultures, diverse books written by people from the cultures, first-person stories of children their own ages if possible, role-playing to help them move beyond their own perspectives, actively pursuing appropriate resources in the family, school, or neighborhood.

Two of these ideas did not occur to me until I was writing my list. One is to read a first-person story and then get the children involved in reflecting on it by acting parts out. The other is to gently ask the children if anyone in their family has an additional language or represents ethnic or racial diversity. The criteria I choose to evaluate all my ideas, particularly these two, include: Will it work? Is it low cost? Do I like the idea of carrying my idea out? Would the parents like it? Working with just those criteria, I think I would start with the story-reading and role-playing idea and perhaps use it as a springboard for my other valuable idea.

Lastly, in planning to carry out my idea, my list might look like this:

1. Think about stories I have read. Would one work? Or ask around for good stories to read.
2. Plan a time to read the story, and think how to present acting it out.
3. Consider how this reading would fit into my classroom curriculum and the state benchmarks. Is there anything I can do to increase the saliency of the reading and role-playing?

In this example, I have used creative problem solving (CPS) to help me glean a practical plan for improving my classroom. While we will focus on ways to provide sound multicultural curricula in Chapter 8, CPS may help us apply material in each chapter to our particular educational roles.

SUMMARY

It is well established that White students have significant educational advantages over Students of Color. One need only look at differences in the amount of money and resources available in White suburban schools as compared with inner-city schools. In order to better understand how such inequality evolves, one must first understand how majority-group members, that is, White Americans, perceive and understand race and ethnicity, both in relation to themselves and to those who are culturally different.

White privilege refers to the benefits that are automatically accrued to European Americans merely on the basis of skin color. What is most insidious and surprising about such privilege is that it is largely invisible to the people involved. Most Whites tend to see themselves not as racial beings but as individuals. As such, they tend to deny or play down the import of race and ethnicity as a social force. One reason may be that it is difficult to acknowledge "unearned power" in a society that gives such powerful lip service to equality and equal access to resources. A second reason is that acknowledging the import of race and the obvious racial inequity that exists in our society would lead to strong feelings of guilt and responsibility, and a need to make amends. It is also easy for many European Americans to experience themselves as powerless in relation to class, gender, age, and so on, thereby downplaying the power they accrue in relation to their Whiteness.

Rowe, Behrens, and Leach (1995) offer a model of racial attitude types by way of explaining how European Americans think about race and racial differences. They identify seven different types. Three are considered unachieved and four achieved—that is, three are easily changeable, and four are securely integrated into people's belief systems. They include avoidant (ignore, minimize, or deny race); dissonant (lack commitment and change positions easily); dependent (adopt positions of significant others); conflictive (oppose efforts at social justice); dominative (classic bigot); integrative (militant stand against racism); and reactive (open to change through goodwill and rationality). Helms (1995) offers a model of White racial-identity development that assumes the existence of five stages that White individuals progress through toward self-awareness and the abandonment of privilege. Based on teaching diversity in the college classroom, Ponterotto (1988) identifies a progression of four stages that most students pass through as they become more culturally sensitive and competent. These are preexposure, exposure, zealot-defensive, and integration.

What are the implications of research for White teachers? First, they should carry out a self-assessment, looking at their own racial attitudes, awareness of privilege, and where they rank themselves according to the three models just reviewed. Students of Color react to White teachers in relation to their privilege. They may also relate to the teachers as symbols of White culture and its treatment of them and their families. Only through an awareness and acknowledgement of privilege can a teacher begin to narrow the gap that usually exists between White teachers and Students of Color.

UNDERSTANDING CULTURE AND CULTURAL DIFFERENCES

The real voyage of discovery consists not in seeking new landscapes, but in having new eyes.

—Marcel Provost

A Zen story tells of a millipede that is stopped by an earthworm and asked how it can possibly manage to walk with so many legs to coordinate. The next moment the millipede is lying on its back in a ditch, trying to figure out which leg to put in front of the next. Many Americans have become like that millipede vis-à-vis culture. Our White students often complain that they have no culture; they know nothing and feel nothing about where they came from. What they mean is that they lack the kind of connection to a cultural heritage and community that they see among People of Color and White ethnics. And they are jealous. When culture is alive and vibrant, it provides the kind of inner programming that keeps the millipede walking. It's always there, much of the time beyond awareness. It gives life structure and meaning. When it becomes fragmented, however, a central part of what it is and can offer gets lost.

This chapter discusses a number of issues related to culture. What exactly is it, and how does it function in the life of a person? Why do we today find it preferable to describe group differences in terms of culture rather than in terms of race? Along what cultural dimensions do groups differ, and in what ways do the cultures of Euro-Americans and People of Color clash? How does all this affect our schools? Are the theories that inform teaching culture-bound, as some educators have suggested? Finally, is there such a thing as multicultural education (a single approach that can adjust itself to the needs of all cultural groups)? Answers to these questions provide a better understanding of the ways culture affects teaching and education in general and what happens in our classrooms when teachers and students from different cultures meet.

WHAT IS CULTURE?

Culture is a difficult concept. It is so basic to human societies and so inter-twined with our natures that its workings are seldom acknowledged or thought about by those who have internalized it. It is so all-encompassing, like water to a fish, that it remains largely preconscious and is obvious only when it is gone or has been seriously disturbed. Anthropological definitions point to certain aspects. Culture is composed of traditional ideas and related values, and it is the product of actions (Kroeber & Kluckhohn, 1952); it is learned, shared, and transmitted from one generation to the next (Linton, 1945); and it organizes and helps interpret life (Gordon, 1964). Culture is also defined as the ways in which a people have learned to respond to life's problems. For instance, all human groups must deal with death. But there is great variation from culture to culture in the rituals and practices that have developed around death. What these definitions lack, however, and what would be particularly helpful for the present purposes, is a better sense of how culture functions within the individ-ual. To get at this, the concept of paradigm is most useful.

Kuhn (1970) introduced the term *paradigm* in his book *The Structure of Scientific Revolutions* to describe the totality of the way a science conceives of the phenomena it studies. He argued that sciences change over time, not through the slow accumulation of knowledge (as taught in high school physics), but rather through paradigm shifts. A paradigm is a set of shared assumptions and beliefs about how the world works, and it structures the per-ception and understanding of the scientists in a discipline. For example, when Newton's theory of the way physical matter operated no longer fit the accumulating evidence, physicists eventually replaced it with Einstein's the-ory of relativity, which was a qualitative shift in thinking. The new paradigm was a radical departure from its predecessor and gave physicists a totally dif-ferent way of thinking about their work. What is so engaging about Kuhn's idea is that it suggests that our beliefs (paradigms) define what we perceive and experience as real.

The notion of paradigm was quickly appropriated by educators to describe the cognitive worldviews through which teachers and students expe-rience their lives. Our paradigms, without our being very aware of them, tell us how the world works and tell us our place in it: what is possible and impos-sible, what the rules are, how things are done. In short, they shape our expe-rience of reality and the worldview each of us brings into the classroom.

People think through their paradigms, not about them. "I'll see it when I believe it" is a more accurate description of how beliefs can give form to what is experienced as "real." People also grow emotionally attached to their para-digms and give up or change them only with great difficulty and discomfort. A challenge to one's paradigm is experienced as a personal threat, for ego gets invested in the portrayal of how things should be. Having one's paradigm shattered is somewhat akin to the chaos of psychosis. When the world no longer operates as it "should," people feel cut adrift from familiar moorings, no longer sure where they stand or who they are.

Culture is the stuff that human paradigms are made of. It provides their content: identity, beliefs, values, and behavior. It is learned as part of the natural process of growing up in a family and community, and from participating in schools and other societal institutions. These are the purveyors of culture. In short, one's culture becomes one's paradigm, defining what is real and right for each of us. Different cultures generate different paradigms of reality, and each is protected and defended as if a threat to it is a threat to a group member's existence. From this perspective, it is easy to understand why the imposition of one group's cultural paradigm upon members of another cultural group—as occurs in most classrooms, where the Northern European cultural paradigm is the standard against which Students of Color, who view their world through different cultural paradigms, are measured—is experienced so negatively.

RACE AND CULTURE IN THE DEFINITION OF GROUP DIFFERENCES

Before describing the dimensions along which cultures differ, it is useful to make a short digression to discuss difficulties with the concept of race. Increasingly of late, educators and social scientists have found it more useful to distinguish between human groups on the basis of culture rather than race. For example, when they refer to tribal subgroupings within the broader racial category of Native Americans as separate ethnic groups, they are emphasizing cultural differences in defining group identity as opposed to biological or physical ones. We have followed a similar practice in this text by using terms such as *ethnic group* and *culturally different students* to describe human diversity. *Ethnic group* was defined in Chapter 1 as any distinguishable people whose members share a common culture and see themselves as separate and different from the majority culture. The emphasis is on shared cultural material as a basis for identification. It is not likely that the concept of race and its usual breakdown into five distinct human groupings will ever completely disappear. It is too deeply ingrained in the fabric of American society. Rather, its importance as a social as opposed to a biological concept will increasingly be emphasized.

There are many serious problems with the concept of race. First, physical anthropologists have shown quite conclusively that what were assumed to be clear and distinct differences between the races are not clear or distinct at all. In fact, there is as much variability in physical characteristics within racial groups as there is between them. It is not uncommon, for example, to see a wide array of skin colors and physical features among individuals who are all considered members of the same racial group. There has been so much racial

mixing throughout history that many groups that may have once been genetically distinct are no longer distinguishable.

Second, the term *race* has become so emotionally charged and politicized
that it can no longer serve a useful role in scientific discussion.

Third, racial categories have been consistently used throughout U.S. his-
tory to simultaneously oppress People of Color and justify White privilege.
For example, U.S. census classifications of race and color have changed over
time to reflect changing racial attitudes. In 1890 they included "White, Black,
Mulatto, Quadroon, Octoroon, Chinese, Japanese, and Indian." In 1998 they
included "White, Black, Indian, Eskimo, Aleut, Asian or Pacific Islander,
Chinese, Filipino, Hawaiian, Korean, Vietnamese, Japanese, Asian Indian,
Samoan, Guamanian, Other." What is particularly interesting about the redef-
inition of racial groups every ten years is that the list closely parallels
increased immigration restrictions. An increased demand for entry into the
United States from groups that are perceived as threats by the White establishment results in reduced immigration quotas.

Fourth, defining *race* biologically and genetically opens the door to pseu-
doscientific arguments about intellectual and other types of inferiority among
People of Color.

Fifth, the social reality of race in the United States does not conform to five
distinct groups. Rather, only two bear any real social meaning: White and of
Color. The notion of the great melting pot, for instance, was in actuality only
about melting White ethnics. The myth was never intended to apply to People of
Color. For White ethnics, upward mobility involved discovering and asserting
their group's Whiteness to set themselves apart from and above the groups of
Color that perpetually resided at the bottom of America's social hierarchy. When
they first arrived in America, various White ethnic groups were met with prejudice and scorn and were merely tolerated because they represented a source of
much needed cheap labor. In time, however, as they acculturated into the system, they discovered that they could progress most quickly by identifying themselves as White and by taking on prejudices against People of Color that were an
intrinsic part of White culture. Even though many individuals experience a world
more defined by skin color than by culture, for the reasons listed we turn to cultural differences as a more useful and less controversial yardstick than race.

THE DIMENSIONS OF CULTURE

Cultural paradigms define and dictate how human beings live and experience
life. Brown and Lundrum-Brown (1995) describe the dimensions along which
cultures can differ. The content and specifics of each dimension vary from
culture to culture. Because of these differences, and because of the natural

tendency to ethnocentrically assume that everyone else views the world the same way we do, cross-cultural misunderstanding occurs. Brown and Lundrum-Brown enumerated the following dimensions of culture: psychobehavioral modalities, axiology (values), ethos (guiding beliefs), epistemology (how one knows), logic (reasoning process), ontology (nature of reality), concept of time, and concept of self. They are summarized and defined in Box 5.1.

To support these dimensions, each culture evolves a set of cultural forms—ritual practices, behavioral prescriptions, and symbols. For example, a culture stresses the doing mode on the first dimension. Certain kinds of child-rearing techniques tend to encourage directed activity. Parents differentially reinforce activity over passivity and also model such behavior. Cultural myths portray figures high on this trait, and moral teachings stress its importance. The group's language likely favors active over passive voice. What makes a culture unique, then, is the particular profile of where it stands on each dimension combined with the specific cultural forms it has evolved.

The dimensions of culture are not totally independent. Rather, some tend to cluster with each other. In relation to ethos, for instance, beliefs concerning independence, individual rights, egalitarianism, and control and dominance tend to occur together in the belief system of a culture, as do interdependence, honor and family protection, authoritarianism, and harmony and deference. This is because such clusters tend to be mutually reinforcing. Certain cultures share a number of dimensions. The Cultures of Color in the United States, for example, have many dimensional similarities, and as a group differ considerably from Northern European culture.

Finally, it is important to note that each culture generates a unique experience of living. The quality of life differs in tone, mood, and intensity. So too do educational and learning issues and the emotional strengths members develop. A most dramatic example of this occurred many years ago. A graduate student was running a personal growth group for students at a multicultural weekend retreat. The students who showed up for one group were White, with the exception of one young Latino man, who was there to spend more time with one of the young women in the group. Such groups seldom attracted non-White participants, for most Students of Color believe that they are a "White thing" as well as something that "Whites really need. As for us, we don't have any trouble relating to other people." The group was quite successful, and it did not take long before people were sharing deeply: talking about feelings of disconnection from parents, isolation, and loneliness. At a certain point, the young Latino man could contain himself no longer and blurted out, "I don't understand what you are all talking about. I am part of a big extended family; there is always someone around. I can't imagine feeling alone or isolated." Only from such experiences can one realize that the "universal malaise" of loneliness and isolation is, in fact, a cultural experience and artifact of the Northern European lifestyle.

5.1 *Dimensions of Culture according to Brown and Lundrum-Brown*

Psychobehavioral modality: The mode of activity most preferred within a culture. Do individuals actively engage their world (doing), more passively experience it as a process (being), or experience it with the intention of evolving (becoming)?

Axiology: The interpersonal values that a culture teaches. Do they compete or cooperate (competition versus cooperation)? Are emotions freely expressed or held back and controlled (emotional restraint versus emotional expressiveness)? Is verbal expression direct or indirect (direct verbal expression versus indirect verbal expression)? Do group members seek help from others or do they keep problems hidden so as not to shame their families (help seeking versus saving face)?

Ethos: The beliefs that are widely held within a cultural group and guide social interactions. Are people viewed as independent beings or as interdependent (independence versus interdependence)? Is one's first allegiance to oneself or to one's family (individual rights versus honor and protect family)? Are all individual group members equal, or is there an acknowledged hierarchy of status or power (egalitarianism versus authoritarianism)? Are harmony, respect, and deference toward others valued over controlling and dominating them (control and dominance versus harmony and deference)?

Epistemology: The preferred ways of gaining knowledge and learning about the world. Do people rely more on their intellectual abilities (cognitive processes), their emotions and intuition (affective processes, "vibes," intuition), or a combination (cognitive and affective)?

Logic: The kind of reasoning process that group members adopt. Are issues seen as being either one way or the other (either/or thinking)? Can multiple possibilities be considered at the same time (both/and thinking)? Or is thinking organized around inner consistency (circular)?

Ontology: How a culture views the nature of reality. Is what's real only what can be seen and touched (objective material)? Is there a level of reality that exists beyond the material senses (subjective spiritual)? Or are both levels of reality experienced (spiritual and material)?

Concept of Time: How time is experienced within a culture. Is it clock-determined and linear (clock-based)? Is it defined in relation to specific events (event-based)? Or is it experienced as repetitive (cyclical)?

Concept of Self: Do group members experience themselves as separate beings (individual self) or as part of a greater collective (extended self)?

Source: Brown and Lundrum-Brown, 1995.

COMPARING CULTURAL PARADIGMS IN AMERICA

M. Ho (1987) compared the cultural paradigm of White European Americans to the paradigms of the four cultures of People of Color. He used five dimensions: three similar to those identified by Brown and Landrum-Brown's (psychobehavioral modality or work and activity, concept of self or people relations, and concept of time or time orientation) and two of his own (nature and the environment and human nature). It is worth reviewing these in some detail to better appreciate the breadth of difference that can exist. It should be remembered, however, that these comparisons are generalizations and may not necessarily fit or apply to individual group members, especially those who have acculturated. In addition, each of the five racial groups described is in actuality made up of numerous subgroups whose cultural content may differ widely. In the United States, for example, Manson and Trimble (1982) identified 512 federally recognized Native "entities" and an additional 365 state-recognized Indian tribes, each with its own cultural uniqueness.

Nature and the Environment

Ho classified the four Cultures of Color—Asian Americans, Native Americans, African Americans, and Latino/a Americans—as living in "harmony with" nature and the environment, whereas European Americans prefer "mastery over" them. For the former, the relationship involves respecting and coexisting with nature. Human beings are part of a natural order and must live respectfully and nonintrusively with other aspects of nature. To destroy a fellow creature is to destroy a part of oneself. European American culture, on the other hand, views human beings as superior to the physical environment and entitled to manipulate it for their own benefit. The world is a resource to be used and plundered.

The Cultures of Color see the component parts of nature as alive and invested with spirit, to be related to respectfully and responsibly. Great value is placed on being attentive to what nature has to offer and teach. Out of such a perspective comes notions such as the Native American idea of Turtle Island, a mythology that views the nonhuman inhabitants of the continent as an interconnected system of animal spirits and archetypal characters. A "mastery" mentality results in environmental practices such as runaway logging, strip mining, and oil drilling as well as the impetus for institutions such as human slavery that exploit "inferior" human beings for material gain.

Time Orientation

There is great diversity among the five cultural groups in regard to how they perceive and experience time. European Americans are dominated by an orientation toward the future. Planning, producing, and controlling what will happen are all artifacts of a future time orientation. What was and what is are always a bit vague and are subordinated to what is anticipated. At the same time, European Americans view time as compartmentalized and incremental, and being on time and being efficient with time are positive values.

Asian and Latino/a cultures are described as past–present oriented. For both, history is a living entity. Ancestors and past events are felt to be alive and impacting present reality. The past flows imperceptibly into and defines the present. In turn, both Native Americans and African Americans are characterized as present-oriented. The focus is the here and now, with less attention to what led up to this moment or what will become of it.

As a group, and as distinct from European American culture, the Cultures of Color share a view of time as an infinite continuum and, as a result, find it difficult to relate to the White obsession with being on time. Interestingly, each of these groups has evolved a term to describe its "looser" sense of time: "Colored People's (CP) Time," "Indian time," "Asian time," and "Latin time." Invariably, time becomes an issue when non-Whites enter institutions in which European American cultural values predominate. Lateness is often mistakenly interpreted as indifference, a provocation, or a lack of basic work skills or interest.

People Relations

Ho distinguished European Americans as having an "individual" social focus compared to the "collateral" focus of the four Cultures of Color. *Individual behavior* refers to actions undertaken to actualize the self, while *collateral behavior* involves doing things to contribute to the survival and betterment of family and community. These differences, in turn, become a basis for attributing value to different, and opposing, styles of interaction. European Americans, for example, are taught and encouraged to compete, to seek individual success, and to feel pride in and make public their accomplishments. Native Americans and Latino/a Americans, in particular, place high value on cooperation and strive to suppress individual accomplishment, boasting, and self-aggrandizement.

Having pointed out this shared collateral focus, it is equally important to understand that the four Communities of Color differ significantly in their communication styles and the meaning of related symbols. Native Americans place high value on brevity in speech, while the ability to rap is treated like an art form by African Americans. It is considered impolite in certain Asian American subgroups to say no or to refuse to comply with a request from a superior. Among Latino/a Americans, differential behavior and the communication of proper respect depends on perceived authority, age, gender, and class. The same handshake can be given in one culture to communicate respect and deference and in another to show authority and power.

Work and Activity

On the dimension of work and activity (similar to Brown and Landrum-Brown's psychobehavioral modality), European Americans, Asian Americans, and African Americans are described as "doing" oriented, while Native Americans and Latino/a Americans are characterized as "being-in-becoming." Doing is an active mode. It involves initiating activity in pursuit of a goal. It tends to be associated with societies in which rewards and status are based on productivity and accomplishment. But even here, there are differences in motivation. European Americans' work and activity are premised on the idea of meritocracy—hard work and serious effort ultimately bring the person financial and social success. Asian Americans, on the other hand, pursue activity in terms of its ability to confer honor on the family and concurrently to avoid shaming the family or losing face. African Americans fall somewhere between these two extremes.

Being-in-becoming is more passive, process-oriented, and focused on the here and now. It involves allowing the world to present opportunities for activity and work rather than seeking them out or creating them. It is a mode of activity that can easily be misinterpreted as "lazy" or "lacking motivation." On a recent trip to the Sinai in Egypt one of the authors had a traveling companion who was a hardworking lawyer from New York City, clearly high on the doing dimension. After spending several hours visiting a Bedouin village, the lawyer could barely contain his shock at how the men just sat around all day. The guide, himself a Bedouin, suggested that they were not merely sitting, but were thinking and planning. "There is a lot to think about: where to find water, missing goats, perhaps a new wife, maybe a little smuggling." This didn't satisfy the lawyer. "I don't understand how they can get anything done without meetings. Give me six months and I'd have this whole desert covered with condos."

Activity and work, whether of the doing or becoming variety, must occur in the context of other cultural values. For example, in many cultures, work does not begin until there has been sufficient time to greet and properly inquire about the welfare of one's family. To do otherwise is considered rude and insensitive. In White European American business culture, such activity is seen as lazy, wasteful, and shirking one's responsibilities.

Human Nature

This dimension of culture deals with how groups view the essence of human nature. Are people inherently good, bad, or both? According to Ho, African Americans and European Americans see human nature as being both good and bad and as possessing both potentials. But for each, the meaning is quite different. In African American culture, where all behavior involves a collateral focus, or what Nobles (1972) calls "experiential communality," *good* and *bad* are defined in relation to the community. Something is laudable if it benefits the community and bad if it does not. Thus, human nature is seen as existing in the interaction between the person and the group. European American culture, on the other hand, sees good and bad as residing in the individual. Freud's view of human nature is an excellent example. The instinctive urges of the id are seen as a negative force that must be controlled. The ego and the superego play a positive role in containing baser drives. In addition, Freud hypothesized a life instinct that is balanced by a death instinct. Thus, the two sides of human nature, the good and bad, are seen in constant opposition and conflict within the individual.

Ho described Asian Americans, Native Americans, and Latino/a Americans as viewing human nature as good. The tendency to attribute positive motives to others has, however, at times proven less than helpful in interaction with members of the dominant culture. Early treaty negotiations between Native American tribes and the U.S. government are a case in point. Tribal representatives entered these negotiations under the assumption that they were dealing with honest and honorable men and that agreements would be honored. By the time sufficient experience forced them to reevaluate their original assumptions, their lands had been stolen. Similarly, in the workplace, when members of such groups exhibit helpfulness, generosity, and caring for fellow workers (behavior that follows from an assumption that others are basically good), they are frequently viewed as naive, gullible, and in need of "smartening up."

A CASE OF CROSS-CULTURAL MISCOMMUNICATION

Sue and Sue (1990) offered the following example of cross-cultural miscommunication in a school setting.

> Several years ago, a female school counselor sought the senior author's advice about a Hispanic family she had recently seen. She seemed quite concerned about the identified student, Elena Martinez, a 13-year-old student who was referred for alleged peddling of drugs on the school premises. The counselor had thought that the parents "did not care for their daughter," "were uncooperative," and "were attempting to avoid responsibility for dealing with Elena's delin-

quency." When pressed for how she arrived at these impressions, the counselor provided the following information. Elena Martinez is the second oldest of four siblings, ages 15, 12, 10, and 7. The father is an immigrant from Mexico and the mother a natural citizen. The family resides in a blue-collar neighborhood in San Jose, California. Elena had been reported as having minor problems in school prior to the "drug-selling incident." For example, she had "talked back to teachers," refused to do homework assignments, and had "fought" with other students. Her involvement with a group of Hispanic students (suspected of being responsible for disruptive school-yard pranks) had gotten her into trouble. Elena was well-known to the education staff at the school. Her teacher last year reported that she was unable to "get through" to Elena. Because of the seriousness of the drug accusation, the counselor felt that something had to be done, and that the parents needed to be informed immediately. The counselor reported calling the parents in order to set up an interview with them. When Mrs. Martinez answered the telephone, the counselor had explained how Elena had been caught on school grounds selling marijuana by a police officer. Rather than arrest her, the officer turned the student over to the vice-principal, who luckily was present at the time of the incident. After the explanation, the counselor had asked that the parents make arrangements for an appointment as soon as possible. The meeting would be aimed at informing the parents about Elena's difficulties in school and coming to some decision about what could be done. During the phone conversation, Mrs. Martinez seemed hesitant about choosing a time to come in and, when pressed by the counselor, excused herself from the telephone.

The counselor reported overhearing some whispering on the other end, and then the voice of Mr. Martinez. He immediately asked the counselor how his daughter was and expressed his consternation over the entire situation. At that point, the counselor stated that she understood his feelings, but it would be best to set up an appointment for tomorrow and talk about it then. Several times the counselor asked Mr. Martinez about a convenient time for the meeting, but each time he seemed to avoid the answer and to give excuses. He had to work the rest of the day and could not make the appointment. The counselor stressed strongly how important the meeting was for the daughter's welfare, and that the several hours of missed work [were] not important in light of the situation. The father stated that he would be able to make an evening session, but the counselor informed him that school policy prohibited evening meetings. When the counselor suggested that the mother could initially come alone, further hesitations seemed present. Finally, the father agreed to attend. The very next day, Mr. and Mrs. Martinez and a brother-in-law (Elena's godfather) showed up together in her office. The counselor reported being upset at the presence of the brother-in-law when it became obvious he planned to sit in on the session. At that point, she explained that a third party present would only make the session more complex and the outcome counterproductive. She wanted to see only the family.

The counselor reported that the session went poorly with minimal cooperation from the parents. She reported, "It was like pulling teeth," trying to get the Martinezes to say anything at all.

(From *Counseling the Culturally Different,* 2nd edition by S. W. Sue & D. Sue, pp. 118–119. Copyright © 1990 John Wiley & Sons, Inc. Reprinted with permission.)

This is a clear case of cultural misunderstanding. The counselor proceeded with her normal modus operandi, irrespective of the obvious cultural differences. She misread the parents' reactions and intentions and drew erroneous and insulting conclusions about them. She communicated these to the Martinezes, who immediately withdrew and became silent.

What are some of the assumptions the counselor made and cultural artifacts she missed? First, it is very possible that because of her ethnicity and her involvement with a group of other Latino/a students, Elena was being carefully watched as a potential troublemaker. Second, the counselor appeared unaware that, in a traditional Mexican family, the wife would not make a decision without first consulting her husband, which she did by "whispering on the other end." Similarly, it is the husband who represents and talks for the family in a formal situation. Third, the counselor assumed that Mr. Martinez was indifferent about his daughter because he seemed reluctant to miss work on her behalf. She had no idea what his work situation was or what the consequences of missing work might be for him and his family. But like most middle-class professionals, she assumed he could make himself available during the day. She then presumed to moralize about several hours of missed work being more important than his daughter. This was something he probably was not used to from a woman. But at the same time, she was unwilling to accommodate herself to the family's need for an evening session and hid behind bureaucratic rules to avoid doing so.

Finally, she thought too narrowly about what constitutes a family, was used to dealing with nuclear as opposed to extended families, and had no idea of the appropriateness of the brother-in-law's presence. Godfathers in Latino/a culture are responsible for the spiritual lives of their godchildren, and Elena was possibly in the midst of serious spiritual difficulties.

ARE EDUCATIONAL THEORIES CULTURE-BOUND?

In Chapter 3, *cultural racism* was defined as the belief that the cultural ways of one group are superior to those of another. It can exist within the mind of an individual, as in the case of Elena's counselor, who seemed largely unaware that she was imposing her cultural values on the Martinez family. Cultural racism can also assert itself through the workings of institutions, such as the schools and teacher education institutions in which most teachers work and learn, and through the theories and practices they hold and subscribe to as educators. It is the strong belief of many researchers that the assumptions and practices of mainstream education are based on Northern European cultural values (Sleeter, 2001). Because of this, serious questions exist about whether teachers educated by such theories can adequately serve culturally different students.

Anthropologists draw a distinction between emic and etic approaches to working cross-culturally. *Emic* refers to looking at a culture through concepts and theories that are indigenous to it. For example, making traditional stories available to Native American students is an emic approach to teaching.

Etic means viewing a culture through "glasses" that are external to it. This is the strategy that most educators have adopted. It has been assumed that this approach has relevance for all people, irrespective of their cultural backgrounds, but this may not be true. Some critics argue that, since the origins of the teaching profession are Northern European ideas, values, and sensibilities, it is not appropriate for individuals who hold different cultural values and assumptions (LeCompte, 1994). Educational models naively misjudge their own universality and are in reality "emic approaches—that are designed by and for middle-class European Americans" (Atkinson, Morten, & Sue, 1993, p. 54).

CONFLICTING VALUES IN EDUCATIONAL THEORY

Many of the assumptions and practices that are central to the teaching professions are in conflict with the cultural worldview or personal paradigms of non-White students. By way of example, we now focus on four such meta-values that are central to mainstream teaching approaches, yet are culture-bound—that is, at odds and in conflict with the cultural worldviews of most non-White students and their families. These meta-values include an emphasis on self-disclosure, the value of long-term goal-setting in educational planning, the importance of students' learning to adapt to the world in which they live, and a focus on developing the individual.

Self-Disclosure

A child spends a great deal of time in the classroom. In many ways, teachers and students develop close personal relationships, and this naturally leads to an expectation of personal sharing by the student and possibly by his or her family. Most teachers believe that such self-disclosure is an important part of the educational process and that, to the extent that they are in possession of personal information and data about the student, they will be in a position to better understand and adapt the learning environment to their needs.

The Cultures of Color do not, however, share this value, and their members do not feel comfortable talking about themselves or disclosing personal material to relative strangers. Asian Americans, for example, learn emotional restraint at an early age and are expected to exhibit modesty in the face of authority as well as subtlety in dealing with personal problems (Atkinson, Whitely, & Gin, 1990; Ho, 1994). To reveal intimate details to strangers is seen as bringing shame on the family and is experienced as losing face. Native

Americans and Latino/a Americans both feel threatened by the demand for such disclosure (Fleming, 1992; Vontress, 1981). For both, intimate sharing is done only with friends of long standing.

African Americans, in turn, tend to be suspicious of requests by Whites for intimate life details (Gordon, 1964; Sue & Sue, 1990). The African American community sees not hiding feelings from Whites until their trustworthiness can be assured as dangerous and potentially self-destructive. Educators obviously need to be aware of how culturally different individuals view and experience the teacher's desire for relevant personal information as well as to be careful about drawing conclusions about a student's reluctance to self-disclose. Such behavior is normative in many cultural groups and should not necessarily be interpreted as defensiveness or as reflecting resistance, shyness, or passivity.

In the classroom, culturally different students may hesitate to share details of their lives with volunteers and teachers who are not known to them as long as their motivations and commitment to caring are unknown. Self-disclosure may come much later in the relationship process, yet end up being fuller when the barriers to sharing are lifted naturally, according to individual cultural standards. But in general, sharing personal information is held suspect in nonmainstream cultures, and this is at odds with the Western European penchant for freely exchanging personal information, even with strangers.

Long-Term Goals

Most educational theories place importance on long-term planning and goal setting. Teaching is envisioned as an ongoing long-term process in which educator and student interact with the objective of the student's accumulating knowledge, skills, and certain values over time; even the intrapersonal lives of students are seen in developmental terms. Many People of Color, however, tend to be more action-oriented and short-term in their goal setting, and less logically oriented in their approaches to problem solving.

Individuals of Color, for example, may find directive approaches more helpful than nondirective approaches, and they often express confusion or frustration about abstract, long-term goal setting. The differences may result from differing time orientations, a belief that the individual's purpose is to serve the collective (rather than an all-consuming focus on the self), or the fact that "sitting around and talking" is a luxury most people can't afford or don't see as potentially helpful (Sue & Sue, 1990). In a school setting, for example, while teachers may be looking forward to end-of-year tests and covering the textbook, culturally different students may want to focus on immediate peer-oriented relationships and an educational process that seems more communally and culturally relevant. A good example of such a value difference is discussed in greater detail in Chapter 8, when we talk about the preference for a more authoritative discipline style by teachers that is found in some Communities of Color, particularly among African American students.

Changing the Individual or Changing the Environment

Educators differ somewhat about the role of schools in bringing about change in the lives of students and exactly where the change process should be located. Is it better to change students to fit their circumstances in the greater society, or to educate students to try to change the world around them? These are referred to technically as "autoplastic" and "alloplastic" solutions. Helping individuals cope with difficult life situations by accommodating or adapting to them (changing the person) is autoplastic; encouraging or teaching individuals to impose changes on the external environment so that it better fits their needs is alloplastic.

Cultures of Color differ widely on this issue. Asian American culture, for example, tends to stress passive acceptance of reality and transcendence of conflict by adjusting perceptions so that harmony can be achieved with the environment (D. R. Ho, 1994). African Americans, on the other hand, tend to point to a racist environment as the cause of many of their distresses and advocate changing it rather than themselves (Kunjufu, 1984). To this end, in the late 1960s African American psychologists in California called for and got a moratorium on testing minority children in the public schools (Bay Area Association of Black Psychologists, 1972). They argued that White teachers and administrators, who were not comfortable with students' non-white ways, were using culturally biased psychological assessment to funnel culturally different children into special education classes. Northern European culture, for its part, tends to encourage the confrontation of obstacles in the environment that restrict freedom (Holtzman, Diaz-Guerrero, & Swartz, 1975). But this is not necessarily the position taken by most White teachers.

Sue and Sue (1990) offer an interesting perspective on this question. They suggest that much student behavior can be understood as a result of their beliefs about locus of control and locus of responsibility. *Locus of control* refers to whether individuals feel that they are in control of their own fate (internal control) or are being controlled externally (external control) and have little impact on the outside world. *Locus of responsibility* refers to whether individuals believe that they are responsible for their own fate (internal responsibilities) or cannot be held responsible because more powerful forces are at work (external responsibility). Sue and Sue propose four different worldviews based on combining these two dimensions and argue that People of Color may exhibit any of the four.

Generally, it is our feeling that European American teachers believe in internal control and internal responsibility—that individuals are in control of their own fate, their actions affect outcomes, and success or failure in life is related to personal characteristics and abilities. This position, however, is at odds with the beliefs of certain Communities of Color. Many Latino/a Americans with strong religious beliefs, for example, tend to favor external control, that a higher power is in charge of their lives. Similarly, individuals who feel socially and economically powerless also tend to ascribe to a position of external control. The bottom line is that mismatches between a student's and a teacher's perceptions of how the world works are likely to reflect serious differences regarding educational goals and just what constitutes useful learning.

Conflict over the question of changing the child or changing the environment can lead to serious controversy within schools and educational communities. Parents who have chosen to assimilate or accommodate into mainstream American culture want schools to educate their children to become fully participating members of the school culture—to internalize its values and emulate its personnel. Yet many culturally different parents are critical of the role of schools in negating the cultures of their family. Although they want students to succeed in school and society, they believe that school culture must be adapted to support the cultural needs of the children, and thus they favor a more alloplastic or internal-control approach to education.

It is possible, however, for both to be in parallel—for a classroom's notion of achievement and the child's culture and values to be mutually supportive of each other. Students are clearly very sensitive to the existence of such discrepancies. Delpit (1995) provided an excellent example of such a dynamic: when Native Alaskan children know they are being watched, they act as if they do "not get it" when their Anglo teacher does or says something that is devaluing of their culture. When they believe they are not being observed, however, they will mock that same teacher. Also consider the Asian mother and European American teacher who experience a basic incongruency in their goals for a child. The teacher believes that the child should act on the environment and influence other members of the class, while the mother believes that such actions are culturally inappropriate. Their communication is hampered not only by their conflicting goals for the child, but also by the cultural reluctance of the mother to question the authority of the teacher and her desire to be in harmony with the school culture. The mother may not say much, but the conflict is still very real and will impact the student. It is our belief that a successful, culturally competent teacher shows respect for the culture of all children and seldom places children in a position where they feel the need to make a choice.

Focus on Developing the Individual

Educators have also tended to adopt Northern European cultural definitions of healthy and normal functioning. Self-reliance, autonomy, self-actualization, self-assertion, insight, and resistance to stress are seen as hallmarks of healthy adjustment and functioning (Saeki & Borow, 1985; Sue & Sue, 1990). These are the characteristics toward which individuals should be encouraged educationally. Such a focus on developing the strengths of individual character is not, however, shared or seen as of value in all cultures. Asian American cultures, for example, value interdependence, inner enlightenment, negation of self, transcendence of conflict, and passive acceptance of reality (D. R. Ho, 1994). This view is highly antithetical to that of mainstream Western thought. What Asian American cultures share with the other Cultures of Color, and what sets them apart from and in opposition to mainstream White culture, is the diminished importance of individual autonomy and self-assertion. A similar idea is expressed in the ways Native American culture views health and illness (Duran & Duran, 1995). Both mental and physical illnesses are thought to result from disharmony between the individual, the family and/or the tribe as well as between any of these and the ways of nature and the natural order. Healing can occur only when harmony is restored. Restoring harmony is the goal of traditional healing practices.

Another way to describe this important difference is the distinction made by Brown and Lundrum-Brown (1995) between the individual and the extended selves. The individual self is characteristic of Northern European culture. It exists autonomously, is fragmented from its social context, and has the goals of personal survival and betterment. The self develops very differently in cultures that limit narcissism and free expression. The term *extended self* is used to describe ego development in group members who conceive of themselves not as individuals, but as part of a broader collective. All behavior occurs with an awareness of its impact on the larger social group. Referring back to the axiology and ethos dimensions of culture suggested by Brown and Lundrum-Brown, the subvalues of competition, emotional restraint, direct verbal expression, and help seeking and the subbeliefs of independence, individual rights, egalitarianism, and control and dominance (all typical of the Northern European cultural paradigm) represent ideas that support the existence of an individual self. Similarly, their opposites (the subvalues of cooperation, emotional expressiveness, indirect verbal expression, and saving face and the subbeliefs of interdependence, honor and family protection, authoritarianism, and harmony and deference) are more typical of the worldview of Communities of Color and are related to the existence of an extended self. Independence, for example, allows for greater self-assertion; interdependence allows for greater intergroup harmony. In speaking of the extended self, we are reminded of a graduate Student of Color who, when introduced to a model of identity development that described the final stage of growth as "transcending specific group identities," reacted: "This can't be right. How can they see this as optimal growth. The person is no longer a part of the community."

It is important for teachers to be aware of the basic incongruity between their own notions of what is optimally healthy in human development and the kinds of educational goals that should be set for individual students, on the one hand, and the view of optimal functioning within the culture from which the student comes, on the other. Where differences exist, they must be respected, and great care must be taken to not project one's own values onto the educational process or to judge, even unintentionally, a student's behavior as inferior or deficient when it varies from the teacher's internal standards.

Such conflicts can exist at all levels of schooling—from graduate teacher education programs to the ways preschool programs are structured. The daunting task is to allow room not just for moments of cultural congruency as add-ons to the curriculum, but for a full-time expression of preferred definitions of successful education and optimal growth for individual students. The basic question turns out to be whether a teacher can allow for choice in everything from the desired lighting level to preferred learning styles to varying forms of peer interaction, or instead assumes without reflection that teaching methods and classroom structure must be congruent with her or his own unexamined cultural assumptions.

CONFLICTING STRATEGIES ABOUT MULTICULTURAL EDUCATION

In turning to the question of what educators can do about these areas of potential conflict, the easiest and most immediate answer is fairly simple: alter and adjust education to accommodate cultural differences. Recall from Chapter 2 that one of the central skills associated with cultural competence is being able to adapt mainstream practices to the needs of culturally different groups. For example, it does not seem unreasonable to expect teachers to alter their expectations, especially when first meeting a student, regarding self-disclosure. Teachers should also be able to adjust the type of interaction that occurs in the classroom and, when helpful, move into a less ambiguous and more directive problem-solving mode. Similarly, it should be possible to adapt the educator's view of where change should take place (changing the individual versus changing the environment) to align with the student's cultural tendencies and to rethink classroom goals and outcomes in light of the student's cultural beliefs.

Sue and Zane (1987) suggest two additional strategies for improving teacher credibility. The first is to ensure that students feel that their cultural backgrounds and life experiences are understood by the teacher. This involves both appreciating their worldviews in terms of the intricacies of their cultural backgrounds and being able to communicate that awareness to them. The second is to ensure that students get some immediate benefit or reinforcement from the teaching process. This may involve advocating for them, teaching them a skill or practice that might help them better navigate the system, or

even directly intervening in a situation on their behalf. Although such interventions may push the boundaries of what is considered appropriate among
mainstream teachers, it should be remembered that educational practices
were developed primarily for working with dominant-culture students. Limita-
tions may not make cultural sense when working with Students of Color.

Some critics, however, believe that merely making adjustments to a predominantly Northern European model of education is not sufficient. Their
belief is that approaching the problem of cross-cultural teaching in this manner is akin to "rearranging the deck chairs on the *Titanic.*" They argue that
merely making cosmetic changes in a process whose very nature is destructive to traditional people and their culture does not get to the heart of the
problem. Duran and Duran (1995), for example, believe that Northern European culture and its application through Western educational practices and
psychology have been instrumental in fragmenting Native American culture
and lifestyle. One need only remember the Indian Boarding Schools and
their expressed goal of eradicating Native culture. Duran and Duran contend
further that an inability to tolerate the existence of alternative ways of knowing and experiencing the world is inherent in Western thought.

> The critical factor in cross-cultural psychology is a fundamentally different way
> of being in the world. In no way does Western thinking address any system of
> cognition other than its own. Given that Judeo-Christian belief systems include
> notions of the Creator putting human beings in charge of all creations, it is easy
> to understand why this group of people assumes that it also possesses the ulti-
> mate way of describing psychological phenomena for all of humanity. In reality,
> the thought that what is right comes from one worldview produces a narcissistic
> worldview that desecrates and destroys much of what is known as culture and
> cosmological perspective. (p. 17)

Diamond's (1987) work offers an equally useful metaphor through which
to compare traditional cultures (which include the Cultures of Color in the
United States) with the culture of postmodern Northern Europe. Like Duran
and Duran, Diamond believed that something is inherently wrong with
civilized culture and that something essential has been lost. Only through a
careful analysis of the dimensions of traditional culture can one discern what
that is. Diamond summarized eight characteristics of "primitive" culture that
he believes have been lost in the "civilizing" process. These include good
psychological nurturance; many-sided, engaging relationships throughout life;
various forms of institutionalized deviance; celebration and fusion of the
sacred/natural and individual/society in ritual; direct engagement with nature
and natural processes; active participation in culture; equation of goodness,
beauty, and the natural environment; and socioeconomic support as a natural
inheritance. Diamond would suggest that not only has the content of primitive cultures been lost, but also their traditional methods of socialization and

teaching the young. In such cultures, education is a natural function of family structure, where the learning of content and process go hand in hand.

Like Duran and Duran and Diamond, Diller (1991) documented a destructive tendency in contemporary Western culture. Specifically, he looked at Jewish emancipation in nineteenth-century Europe and described the manner in which it radically altered traditional Jewish culture. The result was widespread fragmentation and the destruction of traditional Jewish ways, community, and identity.

> As chaos reigned supreme within the ghetto, it simultaneously intruded itself into the inner psyche of the assimilating Jew, rupturing previous bases for self-understanding and identity. The internal consequences were staggering. One major symptom was a fragmentation in the way people thought. Mind increasingly came to function independent of emotion and intuition, and the integrity of the Jewish self fell prey to self-consciousness and compartmentalization.
>
> With the Enlightenment, Jews became self-conscious about their own Jewishness and in time they grew alienated from it. In the ghetto, being a Jew was a given, a fact of life that required no further exploration. Jews uncritically followed customs and habits thousands of years old and participated in a lifestyle that defined all aspects of their existence. They questioned the fairness of God, the reasons for their sad plight and exile, but never the fact of who they were.
>
> A given becomes a matter of debate, an absolute becomes relative, only when there is an alternative available. Emancipation provided Jews with that alternative in the form of potential escape and assimilation, the possibility of no longer being Jews. In so doing, it forced them to inquire into the nature of their Jewishness, thereby objectifying it and setting them apart from it. By asking the questions: "Why am I a Jew and what does that mean?" by tasting of the tree of Knowledge as Adam had, post-emancipation Jews set into motion a process which would eventually and permanently alienate them from the past. (p. 32)

These concerns have led educators to seek alternative and more comprehensive solutions to replace approaches that merely adapt and adjust dominant-group classroom theories and practices for use with culturally different students. One alternative has been to call for the creation of individual ethnic-specific (emic) global educational theories, each developed by teachers and researchers from a given ethnic community, aimed at a unique and unbiased understanding of the educational needs of that community (Banks et al., 2001; Foster, 1994; Ladson-Billings, 1994). In arguing for such an approach, authors have contended that principles and theories developed to educate White students do not have sufficient power to engage and take into consideration the behavior that occurs in the African American classroom. C. Clark (1972), in a similar vein, suggested the need for "creating an alternative framework within which black behavior may be differently described, explained, and interpreted" (p. 1). Each of the evolving models would dictate a unique and culturally sensitive approach specific to educating members of that community.

A second approach was suggested by Duran and Duran (1995), who advocated a return to the use of traditional education practices from the student's own culture. Each Community of Color has over time developed its own conceptions of learning and education in the process of socializing children into the cultural ways of the group. Availing oneself of such approaches, first of all, helps guarantee that the knowledge being learned has not been compromised by dominant cultural ways. Second, it provides an avenue for strengthening ethnic identity and cultural ties. Finally, introducing such culturally congruent teaching methods is especially useful to students who remain steeped in traditional cultural ways and values, for whom dominant American culture has little relevance and to whom dominant culture feels unsafe.

A logical compromise, at least for the present, is to include traditional learning practices as part of a broad range of educational services within a community. Such a strategy above all provides a strong statement about the value of cultural diversity to the teaching profession.

Most culturally different students, however, have experienced some level of acculturation or, to put it differently, are bicultural in varying degrees. For these individuals, a full return to traditional cultural ways is probably neither possible nor desirable. More relevant to their situation is the use of models of teaching and helping that have been sensitively and extensively adapted to the cultural needs of their group by educators, either indigenous or culturally different, who are truly culturally competent. As the demand for cross-cultural education continues to grow and as increasingly complex and effective strategies for serving culturally diverse students are developed, it is just a matter of time before dominant forms of learning begin to lose their decidedly Northern European perspective and become increasingly infused and informed by the wisdom of a variety of other cultures.

REFLECTION QUESTIONS AND A TECHNIQUE FOR SOLVING PROBLEMS

Again using the steps from creative problem solving (Parnes, 1967), consider what you have learned in this chapter. As before, write down any conflict, controversy, question, or surprise that comes to mind about the material. After completing this step, "the mess," continue through the steps outlined at the end of Chapter 4. Return to that chapter as needed for more details and for the criteria list, which is not repeated here.

Next list three to five facts that have been established about the material covered.

Based on the facts and your original concern, complete the statement, "In what ways might we_____?" Generate several IWWMW statements, and choose your favorite.

Use brainstorming to answer your IWWMW statement. Include ideas you found in the chapter. Remember the brainstorming rules:

- No judgment.
- Generate many ideas.
- Piggyback for more ideas.
- Include wild ideas.

Apply criteria from the list in Chapter 4. Give your ideas points based on the criteria. Take an idea or two with the most points, and plan to implement your ideas.

SUMMARY

Culture is the ways in which distinct human groups have learned to respond to life's problems. A useful analogy for understanding culture is a paradigm. A paradigm is a set of shared assumptions and beliefs about how the world works that structures an individual's perception and ideas about reality. Our paradigms or worldviews tell us what is possible and impossible, what the rules are, and how things are done. Culture is the stuff that human paradigms are made of. It provides their content: identity, beliefs, values, and behavior. The culture into which a person is born defines the dimensions of that individual's personal paradigm. Different cultures generate different paradigms and experiences of reality.

Increasingly, social scientists have chosen to distinguish among human groups on the basis of culture rather than race. There are many problems with the concept of race. There seems to be as much variability in physical characteristics within traditional racial categories as between groups. The term *race* has become highly charged and politicized. The definition of race in U.S. census data has been quite variable, and the social reality of race in the United States does not conform to the existence of five distinct racial groups.

Brown and Lundrum-Brown (1995) defined eight dimensions along which cultures can vary. These include psychobehavioral modality (mode of activity more preferred); axiology (personal values); ethos (beliefs about social interaction); epistemology (preferred ways of gaining knowledge and learning about the world); logic (preferred style of reasoning); ontology (how the nature of reality is viewed); concept of time (how time is experienced); and concept of self (whether group members experience themselves as separate or as part of a collective). Each culture generates a unique profile along these various dimensions and, as a result, generates a unique experience of living and reality that is generally shared by members of the cultural group. The Cultures of Color in the United States share many dimensional similarities and, as a group, differ considerably from Northern European culture. Ho (1987) compared the five racial groups on the following dimensions: nature and the environment, time orientation, people relations, work and activity, and beliefs about human nature. An example of cross-cultural miscommunication between a school counselor and an Hispanic family was presented and analyzed.

Can educational theories and teacher-training programs be culture-bound—that is, exemplify the values and perspectives of a single cultural orientation, as opposed to espousing values and strategies for teaching that transcend specific cultural forms? Many educators believe this to be the case and argue that the educational framework adopted in most teacher-training programs derives exclusively from White Northern European cultural forms. By way of example, four values central to educational professionals are identified as being at odds with the cultures of Students of Color. These include an emphasis on self-disclosure, long-term goal setting, changing the individual versus changing the environment, and individuality and autonomy as optimal goals for student growth.

Finally, there is lively debate within the field of multicultural education about how to move from dominant-paradigm teaching strategies to those that are more responsive to the needs of Students of Color. Some theorists believe that it is possible to adjust and adapt existing dominant-group–oriented paradigms. Others feel that there is something inherently destructive to traditional peoples and cultures in the Northern European worldview and call for the creation of ethnic-specific education and teaching theories, each created for and developed by teachers and researchers from a given ethnic community. An alternative but related view is to use traditional cultural teaching and learning practices within the schools of a community. A good compromise seems to be a combination of the above, especially in light of the great variation in acculturation of most ethnic communities.

INTRODUCTION TO CHAPTERS 6, 7, 8, AND 9

We have so far focused on two key aspects of cultural competence—understanding racism in its various forms and understanding culture and cultural differences—and have seen how each shapes the way teachers interact with culturally different students. In Chapters 6, 7, 8, and 9, a slightly different question is explored: how do race and culture in America shape the psychological and educational experiences of students of color?

We begin in Chapter 6 with a consideration of how human development, parenting, and family structure and dynamics are affected by race and culture.

Chapter 7 looks at psychological variables that have relevance for the classroom. With what kinds of emotional issues do Students of Color struggle? What societal factors place Students of Color at special risk for mental and emotional problems? What types of internal problems are they likely to bring with them into the classroom? Chapter 8 looks at various forms of bias as they play out in the educational system and why culturally different students tend to underutilize and avoid mainstream teachers. Finally, Chapter 9 tackles several critical and practical issues in working cross-culturally, specifically bilingualism and maintaining respectful and caring classrooms through classroom management and a safe verbal environment.

CHILDREN, PARENTS, AND FAMILIES OF COLOR*

*How beautiful they are (yet) everywhere they turn
They are faced with abhorrence of everything that is black.*

—Margaret Burroughs
From "What Shall I Tell My Children Who Are Black?"

Parents of Color face a most difficult and frustrating task: preparing their children for entry into a society that often does not truly value them. Besides suffering from psychological wounds associated with racism, Children of Color may encounter problems navigating some of the developmental tasks of childhood because of the preponderance of negative messages from the White world. Of particular concern are potential difficulties in internalizing a positive self-concept and in developing an unconflicted racial identity. Given this situation, families and schools must serve as buffer zones between Children of Color and mainstream society, protecting and nurturing them.

The structures and dynamics of Families of Color vary widely due to ethnic and cultural differences and often bear little resemblance to mainstream White families. Of special interest to educators are the biracial children whose numbers are growing rapidly and who have unique challenges adjusting to their roles in bicultural families and the larger society. Often teachers, assuming they will work with children and families similar to themselves, tend not to be sensitive to these differences or prepared to teach cross-culturally.

This chapter begins with a discussion of issues related to child development that particularly impact Children of Color: cultural differences in temperament at birth, the development of racial awareness and its impact on self-concept, personal identity formation in Adolescents of Color, and differences in cognitive and learning styles. Next we turn to the question of parenting.

---

*Many of the issues presented in this chapter relate to White ethnics as well as to People of Color.

What unique tasks face Parents of Color vis-à-vis society and their children? How can Children of Color be prepared cognitively and emotionally for the racism they will inevitably encounter? Given the existence of racism, what child-rearing strategies and school practices are most likely to produce emotionally healthy and academically successful children? The final sections of the chapter focus on working with Families of Color and biracial children.

Four Scenarios

The following four scenarios, drawn from real-life situations, highlight the kinds of differences, demands, and dilemmas that characterize ethnic families. Most striking is the complexity of the dynamics that impact these children, parents, and families, to which they must respond and adapt. More often than not, forces in the broader environment impact them in negative ways, requiring creative intervention or accommodation for the child or family system to follow a healthy developmental course. Frequently, this involves drawing on the strengths and unique attributes of the family's cultural norms.

Scenario 1. K. B. Clark (1963), in early literature on the topic, described a Black child referred to therapy because of severe racial identity confusion. " 'I got a sun-tan at the beach this summer,' a seven-year-old Negro boy repeated over and over again to a psychologist. His mother, he said, was White and his father was White and therefore he was a 'White boy.' His brown skin was the result of a summer at the beach. He became almost plaintive in his pleading, begging the adult to believe him" (p. 37). Clark commented more broadly on this phenomenon: "General studies of a thousand Negro psychiatric patients in a mental hospital and detailed case histories of eight of them revealed that Negro patients frequently had delusions involving the denial of their skin color and ancestry. Some of these patients insisted that they were White in spite of clear evidence to the contrary" (p. 49).

Scenario 2. One of the authors was once awakened early in the morning to attend an emergency meeting of a Jewish religious school's board of directors. During the previous night, someone had broken into the school, made a mess, scrawled anti-Semitic graffiti on the walls, and destroyed religious articles and artwork. A night janitor had discovered the break-in, and board members were meeting to decide how best to handle the situation. In a very heated and emotional discussion, some directors argued that the school should remain closed until all signs of the vandalism were removed. They felt that seeing the damage would be too traumatic for the five- to twelve-year-old children because they were not old enough to understand what had happened. One parent summarized this position: "There will be plenty of time in their future for the children to learn about this kind of hatred." Others felt that it was "never too early."

Their suggestion was to show students the school now and give them ample opportunity to talk about what had happened. Still others favored exposing only the older children to the reality or letting individual parents choose.

Scenario 3. An interracial couple came into one author's practice to talk about marital problems. The Chinese American husband and Irish American wife disagreed bitterly about his mother's role in their lives. He said that it was normal in his culture for the mother of the family to give advice and guidance to the daughter-in-law and that, even though the advice might at times be a little "heavy-handed," it was done out of love and caring. He further believed that his wife should be more tolerant out of respect for his culture. She, in turn, responded that she had spent the last ten years trying to recover from an abusive home situation and refused to subject herself to further abuse from the mother-in-law, no matter how pure her intentions or how normal such behavior might be in Chinese culture. "I married you, not your family, and don't feel it is fair or very loving to ask me to continue to subject myself to your mother's intrusive and abusive ways." The husband just lowered his eyes, as if embarrassed by what his wife was saying.

Scenario 4. Lewis (2003) shares the following story from her long engagement with Students of Color in the schoolyard.

> One day in the yard I witnessed a conversation between Rodney, an African American fourth-grader, and two of his former teachers, Ms. Sullivan and Ms. Hill. Ms. Sullivan had been explaining to me her efforts to get her students to think about their futures and what they wanted to do with their lives. She stopped Rodney, a student in her class the previous year, and asked him what he wanted to do. He said he wanted to go to college but first he had to go to prison. When Ms. Sullivan looked horrified and asked him what he was talking about, he spelled it out for her: "All black men go to prison." He thought it would be more efficient to get his prison term out of the way before he went to college rather than having to do it afterward. He was impervious to both teachers' efforts to convince him that it was not true. (p. 54)

These are real-life scenarios about individuals caught in society's norms of culture, beauty, traditions, and expectations. We will explore how these values impinge on the development of families and children with different norms and challenges.

CHILD DEVELOPMENT

Temperament at Birth

The characteristics and development of children from different ethnic groups vary greatly from birth (Trawick-Smith, 1997). It is easy to discern dramatic differences, for instance, in temperament and activity levels of newborns and infants. Freedman (1979) offers the following examples. White babies of

Northern European background cry more easily and are harder to console than Chinese babies, who tend to adapt to any position in which they are placed. Navajo babies show even more calmness and adaptability than the Chinese babies. They accept being placed on a cradleboard, while White babies cry and struggle to get out of the strapped confinement. Japanese children, in turn, are far more irritable than either the Chinese or Navajo children. Australian aboriginal babies react strongly, like Whites, to being disturbed, but are more easily calmed.

Differences are also found in the ways mothers and infants interact (Seifer, Sameroff, Barrett, & Krafchuk, 1994). There is far less verbal interaction between a Navajo mother and baby than between a White mother and baby. The Navajo mother is rather silent and gets her baby's attention via eye contact. White mothers talk to their children constantly, and their children respond with great activity. These mothers are equally adept, however, at gaining their children's attention. According to Freedman (1979), the differences result from the continual interplay of genetic predispositions and patterns of cultural conditioning through early child–parent interaction. Thus, children's genetic temperamental tendencies are reinforced by cultural learning about the proper way to respond emotionally, and the result is children who increasingly take on the temperamental style of their culture (Garcia Coll, 1990; Scarr, 1993). These early temperamental differences continue to be evident and influential as the children enter school and begin to interact with teachers and peers.

Development of Racial Awareness

Children are aware of differences in skin color and facial and body features as early as age three or four, and by the time a child is seven, it is possible to begin to discern the rudiments of racial awareness (Aboud, 1988; Grant & Haynes, 1995). Majority-group children are generally slower to develop a consciousness of being White because race is not as central to their families' lives as it is to the lives of People of Color (York, 1991). Racial identity evolves in relation to the sequential acquisition of three learning processes. The first is racial classification ability (Aboud, 1988; Williams & Morland, 1976) and involves learning to accurately apply ethnic labels to members of different groups.

For example, in the classic doll studies designed by Clark and Clark (1947) to measure racial identity in African American children, the child is asked to "Show me the Black doll" or "Show me the White doll" when presented with dolls of varying skin tones. The child who can accurately perform such labeling on a regular basis is ready to move on to the next stage of forming a racial identification (Aboud & Doyle, 1993). Put simply, racial identification involves children's learning to apply the newly gained concept of race to themselves. According to Proshansky and Newton (1968), this process requires a kind of inner dialogue through which children learn that, because of their own skin color, they are members of a certain group (the child is black or yellow or brown) and, as such, visibly different from others. Thus, racial identification results from an interaction between children's comparisons of their own skin color with those of parents, siblings, and others and what they are told about who they are racially. The final stage, called racial evaluation by Proshansky and Newton, involves the creation of an internal evaluation of the child's own ethnicity. It involves how children come to feel about being black or yellow or brown. Racial evaluation develops as children internalize the various messages regarding their own ethnicity received from significant others and society in general. By age seven, most ethnic children are aware of the negative evaluation that society places on members of their group (Thornton, Chatters, Taylor, & Allen, 1990).

By the time children enter kindergarten, these processes are well underway. In general, children at this point of development rarely show racial preferences in their choice of play and learning partners. But one does periodically see children who have already been socialized within their families to avoid children of a certain skin color.

Racial Awareness and Self-Esteem

Early studies of racial awareness by Clark and Clark (1947), Kardiner and Ovesey (1951), and Goodman (1952) found that African American children had difficulty successfully completing the last two stages. These children would deny the fact that their skin was dark (as in Scenario 1), devalue people with dark skin and Black culture in general, or do both. In addition, these same African American children often exhibited negative self-concepts. The authors concluded that such outcomes were inevitable for Children of Color. Living in a White-dominated society, they could not help but internalize the negative attitudes and messages that bombarded them daily, and the resulting negative self-judgments inevitably translated into a diminished self-image.

As the ethnic pride movements of the 1960s gained momentum, however, the inevitability of such conclusions was vehemently challenged. Some referred to this early work as the "myth of self-hatred" (Trawick-Smith & Lisi, 1994). Earlier studies were criticized as being methodologically weak or as reflecting an earlier psychological reality that was no longer accurate. New studies showed no differences in the self-esteem of African American and White children (Powell, 1973; Rosenberg, 1979). In racially homogeneous settings, in fact, African American children scored higher than their White counterparts (Spenser & Markstrom-Adams, 1990). The more extensive their interaction with Whites and the White world, however, the lower their self-concept scores. The accuracy of these newer findings was challenged in turn, as too conveniently fitting the researchers' political agendas.

The Usefulness of a Dual Perspective

Critics of the earlier studies argued for the usefulness of a dual perspective in resolving this question. They believed that the messages sent by the child's immediate environment (made up of home, community, and significant others), rather than those sent by the broader society, can be internalized and, thus, become the basis for self-esteem. Earlier researchers had assumed that society's negative views and stereotypes were directly reflected onto the child and internalized into the sense of self. Norton (1983) argued for the usefulness of differentiating the child's immediate environment from that of society in general. For Whites, there is little difference between the two kinds of messages.

However, the situation is very different for People of Color; the two systems send very different and conflicting messages. Norton asserted that the more immediate interpersonal world of the child is most critical in the development of healthy self-esteem and that the family can act as a buffer between the child and the broader society and, thus, become the primary sculptor of feelings about self. Norton concluded by raising a number of questions that still need to be answered: "What happens in the interaction between Black parents and their children in those stable nurturing families from any educational or socioeconomic level who manage to rear children with a strong sense of self? How and with what patterns do these families defy the 'mark of oppression'? How can we determine the strengths and healthy coping mechanisms in the interaction between black parents and their children?" (Norton, 1983, p. 188).

Clarifying the Question

To bring further clarity, Williams and Morland (1976) carried out an extensive longitudinal study of racial identity formation in African American and White preschoolers, following them into their teenage years. Part of the value of the study was that it controlled for the various methodological criticisms that had been leveled at the earlier "doll" studies. What they found can be summarized as follows.

First, by the age of three, preschoolers were responding differently to black and white. Both Euro and Afro children (Williams and Morland's terms) tended to favor white over black. This trend continued for both groups throughout elementary school. By junior high school, however, the Afro children had done a complete turnaround in attitude and were generally favoring black over white. The authors suggest that the initial preference for white over black in all children probably derives from a biological tendency to prefer light over darkness, which generalizes to the differential favoring of white over black. They further suggest that this early preference creates a general context in which specific learning about race can occur. But this is all merely conjecture.

Second, racial identification was measured by asking children which of the variously colored dolls (light- or dark-skinned) looked like them or looked like a parent. Preschool Euro children chose the light-skinned figure 80 percent of the time and the dark-skinned figure 20 percent, whereas Afro preschoolers evenly distributed their choices between the dark- and light-skinned dolls fifty-fifty. By the third grade, however, the Afro children were also choosing the dark-skinned figures 80 percent of the time, paralleling the differential responses of the same-aged Euro children. By junior high school, both groups were almost 100 percent in their respective choices.

Third, racial evaluation was assessed by asking the young subjects to choose a figure (light- or dark-skinned) in response to a description that included a positive or negative adjective (for example, choose the good parent). Both Euro and Afro preschoolers overwhelmingly assigned the positive features to the light-skinned figures (pro-Euro response) at a rate of 90 percent and 80 percent, respectively. These same patterns repeated for both groups through late elementary school. In junior high school, however, the Afro students' responses changed dramatically to pro-Afro (that is, assigning positive adjectives to dark-skinned figures), ending with a rate equal to that of Euro junior high students.

Fourth, racial acceptance was measured by showing the subjects photos of dark- and light-skinned individuals and asking if they would like to play with this person. Euro preschoolers were significantly less accepting of Afro photos than Afro preschoolers were of Euro photos. In fact, Afro preschoolers accepted Euro pictures slightly more frequently than they did Afro photos. By elementary school and beyond, both Afro and Euro students grew increasingly less accepting of photos of the other group, with Afros always a bit more accepting than Euros.

By way of summary, Williams and Morland (1976) found that by third grade African American children were appropriately aware of their racial identity, accepted it, and preferred playmates from their own group. They did find African American preschoolers regularly making pro-Euro responses on all measures, which could be interpreted as indicating some early identity confusion (as suggested in the pre-1960s studies discussed earlier). The authors, however, attribute this to early response bias rather than to any underlying pathology, and their interpretation seems to be borne out by the fact that with further socialization and by the third grade all except one of the measures showed group-appropriate responses. Regarding racial evaluation, however, there do seem to be lingering pro-White attitudes among Black youth until junior high school, when there is a dramatic reversal to predominantly pro-Afro responses. From these data, it seems likely that African American children to some extent internalize the attitudes of society at large.

But it is not clear whether their pro-Euro preferences can be interpreted as indicative of negative feelings about themselves or their group. In any case, the effects are not lasting, and there does not seem to be any concurrent difficulty in racial identification. It is probably fair to say, however, that this is a critical period in the developmental life of Children of Color and may be potentially problematic for the development of self-esteem as long as pro-Euro attitudes linger. A more recent study by Spenser and Markstrom-Adams (1990) supports these conclusions.

Such studies clearly show that Children of Color regularly exhibit positive self-esteem and unconflicted racial identities. But this does not mean that racism poses any less risk for them. It simply implies that active measures must be taken to protect them, whether through Norton's (1983) notion of creating a buffer zone around the child or McAdoo's (1985) belief in creating ethnic pride to psychologically insulate the child from the experience of racism.

A word of caution: It should be obvious by now that issues of skin color and racial identity are very powerful forces within families. We think teachers should realize that balance is needed when such dynamics come into play. Teachers must beware of either overlooking or overreacting to issues. Consider the following two stories. One biracial child reported long after the fact that he was referred to by the "n-word" every single school day for many months. It became clear only in retrospect that this racial slur had become a nickname used by some of his classmates, who would call this epithet across the playground to get his attention. His parents did not know the details of this labeling and believed it was only occasional. One has to ask where teachers and administrators were during this long scenario. On the other end of the continuum, an African American mother became quite concerned when her biracial child said she hated "Suzy," the only other Black child in the classroom. After further investigation and discussions with the teacher, however, the mother discovered that it was a personality conflict (Suzy was not popular with any of the children) rather than a matter of race.

A final perspective on the impact of racism on self-esteem can be gleaned from interviews with People of Color who came to the United States as adults after growing up in countries where they were in the racial majority (Diller, 1997). Only after they arrived in this country did they have their first personal experiences with prejudice and racism. How did they respond? Their first reported reaction was shock and disbelief. However, once they had sufficient time to process what had happened and to label it as a "racial attack," they were able to put up sufficient ego defenses to protect themselves emotionally as well as physically. They quickly learned to identify such situations before or as they happened and to deal with them quickly and effectively. They uniformly believed that it was only because of their own strong sense of self and well-developed ego defenses that they were able to come out of these experiences relatively unharmed. When asked how they might have felt as children facing such experiences, they all indicated that they would have been clearly overwhelmed and likely scarred in some essential way.

Formation of Adolescent Identity

Another potential area of difficulty for Children of Color involves the formation of personal identity (that is, a stable and positive sense of who one is) in adolescents. In a study comparing lower-class urban African American and White adolescent boys, Hauser and Kasendorf (1983) found very different patterns of identity formation in the two groups. Building on the work of Erikson (1968), they looked at the manner in which adolescent boys integrated various images of themselves into a coherent sense of self. Erikson saw adolescence as a time of self-exploration during which the young person tries to find a comfortable synthesis of past experiences, sense of family, present questions and concerns, and hopes and plans for the future. Hauser and Kasendorf found that the African American adolescents formed a stable integration of self-image much earlier than did their White counterparts, who seemed to experience a lot more confusion, disequilibrium, and personal exploration. In fact, it took the White youth all four years of high school to reach the same level of identity stability achieved by the African American youth after one or two years.

At the same time, African American adolescents showed a striking sameness in how they saw themselves compared to Whites, who showed much greater variability and flexibility in content. According to Erikson's model of adolescent identity development, the Whites were experiencing "identity progression and moratorium" (slow but steady movement toward a coherent definition of self with extensive confusion and time out for exploration). The African American adolescents, on the other hand, were seen as exhibiting "identity foreclosure," stabilizing their identities very early with a premature closing off of possibilities in terms of content.

Hauser and Kasendorf found additional difficulties for the African American youth. Images of themselves as future parents were equally fixed and rigid, especially if the father had been absent from the home. In such cases, fathers were disparaged figures who foreshadowed what they themselves would be as fathers, and on this basis there was little hope for being any different. Thus, early foreclosure seemed a natural consequence.

Similarly, their image of the future was rigid and established early, connoting little hope for what was to be. Images of the past self showed great discontinuity, reflecting some discomfort and shame over the historical past (slavery and exploitation), instability in families (not knowing one parent's background), and even a kind of racial self-hatred (although there was no desire to be White). Finally, similar negative patterns were evident in relation to the kinds of fantasies they reported: lacking hope for their futures, especially in relation to what they could accomplish and become, the work available to them, and the role models they could emulate.

Although times have changed and many populations have significantly improved their financial and social situations, the study still clearly points to the difficulties that can exist for Children of Color growing up in a racist environment that dramatically limits what they can do and become. The data also show the great capacity for coping found in these African American males, for their everyday lives showed little evidence of the negativity and hopelessness that one might have predicted. Their self-images, in fact, differed little from those of their White counterparts. Finally, it should be acknowledged that cultural differences may be related to these findings. Erikson's model is clearly Northern European and reflects a view of adolescence (and what should be happening during this period) that may not be accurate or appropriate for a different cultural group. Some anthropologists have even suggested that the prolonged period of confusion and moratorium that typifies Western adolescence is a symptom of the loss of much-needed rites of passage, which in many other cultures create a clear sense of direction and identity for the young person.

Academic Performance and Learning Styles

A final aspect of child development that has special relevance for Children of Color has to do with the relationship between academic performance and cultural learning styles. Research regularly shows that Children of Color perform at a lower academic level than their White counterparts in the public school system. Obgu (1978) explained this phenomenon by looking at differences in ethnic cultures. He began by distinguishing between three types of ethnic minorities and their relative success in academic performance: autonomous, immigrant, and castelike. The first group, which includes relatively small populations such as Jews, Amish, and Mormons, tends to experience prejudice but not widespread oppression. They possess distinctive cultural traits related to academic success as well as cultural models of success and do not suffer from disproportionate degrees of school failure. The second group includes recent immigrants to the United States, such as Koreans and Chinese. They came here voluntarily to improve their life conditions and are ready to assimilate and/or accommodate. Although mainstream individuals may view them negatively, they do not hold similar views of themselves. Their living conditions in this country are a marked improvement over what they experienced in their countries of origin, and if they were to grow dissatisfied here, they can return to their home countries. In spite of cultural differences, their children perform well in school and on academic tests. The third group, what Obgu called "castelike minorities," includes African Americans, Latinos/as, and Native Americans and tends to experience disproportionate amounts of school failure. They are the objects of systematic racism and disadvantage both within and outside of the schools and, according to Ogbu, often view school success not as a path to advancement but rather as "acting White" or "Uncle Tom" behavior.

Closely related to poor school performance among these populations is the issue of cultural differences in learning styles. As children grow, they internalize and become progressively more comfortable and proficient with learning styles congruent with their own culture. There is much evidence to show that poor school performance among ethnic children is related to conflicts in learning style; that is, the U.S. school system as an institution is based on and rewards a mode of learning that is characteristic of Northern European culture (Anderson & Adams, 1992; Wolkind & Rutter, 1985). Those who do not adapt, or become comfortable interacting educationally in this mode, are clearly at a disadvantage and are, over time, likely to fail. When educational efforts have been made to adjust classroom interaction to the cultural needs of different individuals, the results have been dramatic increases in performance and school success (Wolkind & Rutter, 1985).

Cultural learning styles develop pragmatically. Native Americans, for example, developed their keen sense of visual observation out of necessity and in relation to their home environment. Their survival depended on "learning the signs of nature," and thus observation became a central mode of learning: "watching and listening, trial and error" (Fleming, 1992). Storytelling was the primary mode of teaching values and traditional attitudes, and it was often stylized through the use of symbols, anthropomorphizing, and metaphor, a particularly powerful way of teaching extremely complex concepts. Today, according to Fleming, "modern Indian children still demonstrate strengths in their ability to memorize visual patterns, visualize spatial concepts, and produce descriptions that are rich in visual detail and the use of graphic metaphor" (1992, pp. 161–162).

Contrast this with the very different learning paradigm emphasized in mainstream schools: auditory learning, conceptualization of the abstract out of context, and heavy emphasis on language skills. Similarly, African Americans (Hale-Benson, 1986), Hawaiians (Gallimore, Boggs, & Jordan, 1974), and Mexican Americans (Kagan & Madsen, 1972) exhibit learning styles that have a heavy relational component, in contrast to the Northern European style, which emphasizes individualism and competition. Mexican American children, for example, are less willing than White students to enter into rivalries or competition or to internalize a drive to perform well to meet the expectations of teachers. Neither do Hawaiian children feel any need to forsake their strong need to affiliate with peers for a more individualistic modality that reinforces goal-oriented behavior.

Although children from these cultures can learn to process information in the Northern European manner, it is counter to their preferred mode of interacting. Put simply, it feels foreign and unnatural, and rather than adapting many Students of Color choose to shut down and thereby exit the formal U.S. education system. The real task of education in a multicultural society is to broaden the dimensions of the classroom to make room for the learning styles of all students (Collett & Serrano, 1992; Pang, 2001). Similarly, teachers should be aware of optimal learning styles for students in order to maximize their potential during the learning process.

Overall, Children of Color learn better and show higher achievement levels when learning activities are culturally relevant and directly related to their larger lives and context. Learning to walk, talk, and internalize simple rituals and concepts occurs naturally in the family home and other familiar environments. Mainstream schools tend to introduce a basic disconnect between what is familiar in the child's life and the activities and content of the classroom. Its tendency is toward abstraction and out-of-context learning. Children of Color, indeed all children, learn best when their classrooms and activities mirror and build upon what is familiar to them, and where this occurs in as many ways and at as many different levels as possible. Such an approach to teaching and learning grows most authentically out of the lives and stories of the children and their natural relationships to each other, their families, and their neighborhoods.

Examples include authentic service learning projects that address real needs in the community (and focus the child on the collaborative good) and concurrently provide opportunity to develop skills and concepts that will ultimately form a foundation for achievement of mainstream teaching goals. An urban child's already strong sense of buildings, cars, and movement can be used as the basis for teaching the physical sciences. Most mainstream teachers tend to start with a canned curriculum and add-on connections, rather than start with the child, the environment, and the cultural learning style and then find creative ways to transform these learning foundations to meet schoolwide and statewide standards and goals.

PARENTING

All parents face the similar task of creating a safe environment in which the child can move without harm through the various developmental tasks and stages of growing up. For mainstream White parents, threats to the child's health or safety, when they do exist, are random and unpredictable. Children of Color, however, are systematically subjected to the harmful effects of racism. Parents of Color, having grown up under similar conditions, are aware of what awaits their children and know that there is only so much they can do to protect them. What can Parents of Color do? First, as suggested earlier in the chapter, they can create a buffer zone in which children are protected from the negative attitudes and stereotypes that abound in the broader society. Part of this process involves instilling a sense of ethnic pride. In such a safe environment, the child is more likely to develop a more positive sense of self. Second, parents can teach their children how to deal emotionally with the negative experiences of racism. Third, parents can prepare their children cognitively for what they will encounter in the world outside the buffer zone.

In each of these activities, schools and teachers must partner with parents. They must realize the importance of creating a safe and racism-free zone. They must realize the necessity of preparing children both emotionally and cognitively for racism and recognize the importance of doing this as part of a curriculum. Above all, they must appreciate the destructiveness of racial hatred to young psyches and realize that much harm may already have occurred. "It often will not be enough just to listen; one might have to work to create an environment in which a silenced voice feels the confidence or security to speak" (Burbules, 1993, p. 33). More often than not, such efforts produce results only slowly over time. Previously silenced students or parents may require multiple opportunities based on mutual respect and trust, before they feel safe enough to express what is on their minds and in their hearts.

Creating a Buffer Zone

The creation of a buffer zone in which a child can develop without harmful intrusions from the outside is the essence of good parenting. All young children must be protected and nurtured until they are able to venture forth with sufficient skills and abilities to protect themselves. Children of Color are often at risk, and it is especially critical for their parents to create within them a good psychological base grounded in a strong and positive sense of self. Research has repeatedly shown that a positive self-concept is correlated with effective social functioning, higher levels of cognitive development, and greater emotional health and stability (Curry & Johnson, 1990). The buffer zone against racism and negative racial messages can provide a place and time for optimal personal growth.

Children's concepts of self result directly from the messages they receive about themselves from the world. Psychological theories about the development of the self speak of mirroring and reflection and imply that children take in and make a part of themselves these reflected views of others (Wylie, 1961). If they are loved, they will love themselves; if they are demeaned or devalued, that is how they will come to feel about themselves and treat others. In this regard, K. B. Clark (1963) has written, "Children who are consistently rejected understandably begin to question and doubt whether they, their family, and their group really deserve no more respect from the larger society than they receive" (pp. 63–64). This is why the idea of a buffer zone is so critical to Parents of Color. By substituting the reflection of loving parents and significant others for that of an often hostile environment that may routinely negate the value of children because of their ethnicity, a more positive sense of self is guaranteed.

Norton (1983) describes the ingredients for parent–child interaction most likely to foster heightened self-esteem as follows: "Early consistent, loving, nurturing interaction is the ideal process of interaction leading to a good sense of self. The child who is loved, accepted and supported in appropriate reality-oriented functioning in relationship to others comes to love himself and to respect himself as someone worthy of love" (p. 185).

The idea of a buffer zone should not, however, be limited merely to parents and family. The institutions of the entire local community, especially its schools, can function to protect the children. The African adage that "it takes an entire village to raise a child" is relevant here. At an elementary school in Portland, for example, where one of the authors directs a preservice teacher immersion program, children are taught and cared for by all staff members. The school functions more as an entity than as a series of discrete classrooms. An intangible spirit of community and of being together both in and against the outside world wraps the children in a protective envelope. Often, the older Black women who are teaching assistants function as "other mothers," a common role that has its cultural roots in African societies (Delpit, 1995). In many African languages, the same word is used to mean "mother" and "aunt," and child-rearing is the responsibility of all adults in the whole village.

Parenting for Self-Esteem

Wright (1998) offered an interesting but controversial perspective on the relationship of parenting, race, and the nurturing of self-esteem. She believes that there are three crucial ways in which parents, especially African American parents, can support or negate their children's developing sense of self-worth. The first is disciplinary style. According to Wright, "many parents in the black community hold a strong belief in the value of corporal punishment." Whether it is done to follow the Biblical injunction to not "spare the rod," because it is "cultural" for African Americans to use physical pain in disciplining their children, because it toughens children to prepare them for life in a hostile world, because it "worked well for me," or because African American children "need more severe discipline than the children of other races" and it works with them, physical punishment may erode self-esteem. Wright further suggests that the lesson children learn from physical punishment is less about internal control and self-regulation and more about fear and hostility. Even more importantly, Wright states, when Black children are spanked for whatever reason, their caretakers may be sending "the same message that white society has traditionally sent to blacks" (p. 131). Gentler discipline, on the other hand, may foster greater emotional health by sending a very different message: that the child is worthy of such treatment and respect. It is important to point out that many Black parents take exception to Wright's position on corporal punishment.

A second factor in the promotion of self-esteem, according to Wright, is parental closeness or distance. When parents are present and emotionally involved in the daily lives of their children, there is greater likelihood of the development of positive self-worth. This at times has been a challenge for many in the African American community. Fathers may be absent, due to the cycle of poverty and racism; single mothers may be torn between earning a living and being with their children, and often lack the traditional African American extended support system; and today addictions are taking a toll on family life. All threaten the emotional health of the children who are touched by them. When a parent is unavailable for whatever reason, children tend to blame themselves for the absence, too often interpreting it as evidence of their own worthlessness.

A final factor in promoting a child's sense of self-worth is the parent's attitude about race and life. Wright describes working with children who seem "unusually vulnerable to perceived and actual racism." Some have personally experienced excessive amounts of discrimination and hatred. But many, according to Wright, "come from families that habitually blame their children's problems on race and bring the children up to believe that they are victims because they are Black" (p. 6). Prematurely sensitizing children to racism before they are developmentally ready may take an enormous toll on their future ability to cope. In this regard, Wright would argue for the usefulness of the buffer zone. Similarly, she was concerned about the basic attitude toward life that the child internalizes from the parent. She distinguished between what she calls attitudinal "impoverishment" and "enrichment." Parents may influence their children to see the glass as half empty or to see it as half full, and the perception may shape how the children feel about themselves and their futures. This factor, like the others, is controversial, and some might even see it as another example of "blaming the victim."

Preparing the Child Emotionally for Racism

Poussaint (1972) offered ways to help children deal emotionally with negative racial experiences. He first emphasized that children should not be allowed to feel alone in their struggle. They must not only feel the support of their parents, peers, and teachers, but also understand that they are part of a long history of African Americans, for example, who have similarly struggled against racism. Parents should model active intervention and mastery over the environment as well as help their children develop competence and the ability to achieve personal goals. If children can experience their parents as powerful, they gain a sense of vicarious power. Children should generally be allowed to try to deal with racial situations on their own, with parents prepared to intervene if necessary. It is the parent's job to be sure that the situation is resolved quickly and satisfactorily and, above all, that the child's self-esteem is protected.

Poussaint described a number of "compensatory mechanisms" that African American parents may adopt in the process of supporting and preparing their children for life. In doing so, these parents may be compensating for their own insecurities. More often than not, such efforts tend to be highly counterproductive. Some parents, for example, repeatedly tell their children that "Black is beautiful," hoping to reinforce positive identity and self. Children, however, may begin to wonder whether repeating the same phrases over and over really implies that maybe Black is not so beautiful after all. In a parallel dynamic in a school setting, rhetoric around "achievement regardless of race or previous academic performance" sets up the same sense that maybe the children can't achieve after all.

Other parents adopt a permissive stance, being overly generous and accommodating with their children, as if to assuage their own guilt or make up for the harshness that the children will eventually encounter. This strategy does not allow children to test themselves and their abilities in the real world and, in so doing, develop feelings of competence and self-worth. Still other parents are overly authoritarian and feel that the best they can do for their children is to toughen them up so that they will be familiar with functioning in a hostile environment. But this strategy may lead to abuse, which teaches children to be abusive in their own right. It also gives them a green light to act out in the world. A final compensatory mechanism involves encouraging a child to remain passive and to avoid aggressive behavior of any kind, as if such a strategy would somehow mollify racial hatred.

Poussaint also pointed out the importance of helping children learn to manage the righteous anger that they will feel as objects of racial hatred. Suppressing anger eventually leads to self-loathing and low self-esteem. Overgeneralized anger is counterproductive, leading nowhere and consuming a vast amount of undirected energy. A more balanced approach seems optimal: teaching children to assert themselves sufficiently, to display their anger appropriately, and to sublimate and channel much of it into constructive energy for actively dealing with the world. "Our job," Poussaint wrote, "is to help our children develop that delicate balance between appropriate control and appropriate display of anger and aggression, love and hate" (p. 110). He continued: "As parents we must try to raise men and women who are emotionally healthy in a society that is basically racist. If our history is a lesson, we will continue to survive. Many Black children will grow up to be strong, productive adults. But too many others will succumb under the pressures of a racist environment. Salvaging these youngsters is our responsibility as parents" (p. 111).

Preparing the Child Cognitively for Racism

Equally important to providing children with a strong emotional base is preparing them for what will be encountered in the broader world. This is the issue that members of the Jewish religious school board were arguing about in Scenario 2. Although many researchers have written about this process, the early work of Lewin (1948) offers suggestions on how to prepare children for the eventual experience of prejudice and discrimination.

First, never deny children's ethnicity or underestimate its possible impact on their lives. Some parents feel that it is best to put off such discussions as long as possible, thereby protecting children from the "horror of racism" until it can no longer be avoided. There are real problems with this approach. It models, first of all, a kind of denial of reality that not only confuses children, but also sets them on the course of not actively dealing with their ethnicity. Parents who choose to avoid discussions of race also tend to underestimate the level of children's knowledge and may be avoiding issues that have already become real and problematic for the children. (As cited earlier, some ethnic children are aware of racial differences as early as three years of age, and by seven all are aware of the negative judgments that society holds about their group.) Ethnic children might want and need to discuss their experiences but may feel that they must remain silent because of the family rule: "We do not talk about these things." By such tactics, parents unintentionally remove themselves as important resources for their children.

Lewin also pointed out, using the analogy of adoption, that "learning the truth" can be much more damaging and hurtful for an older child. In other words, the longer one lives with a picture of reality, the more devastating it can be to have that reality shattered. Although Lewin's work initially focused on assimilating Jews who could more easily hide their identities than can most People of Color, his points about avoiding the topic of ethnicity are still well taken. It is clearly best to allow children to bring up the subject and to deal with it in the context of their ongoing reality. Parents should answer questions in as simple a manner as possible and not overwhelm children with more knowledge than they need. More often than not, a small amount of information will suffice. Parents should answer questions in a manner that fits with the children's level of cognitive development. Similarly, children should not be overwhelmed emotionally with difficult information or stories. Preparing children for dealing with racism is not a single event; it is an ongoing developmental process. As they encounter racism in the real world, it should be discussed and processed; and as they mature, information and explanations should also grow in depth and comprehensiveness.

Second, it is important to help children develop a strong and positive ethnic identity based on values inherent in group membership so as to internally counteract the negative experiences of being an object of prejudice. Children should be able to say, "I am an African American, and I come from a rich cultural tradition of which I am very proud. Sure, I experience a lot of racism, but that is just the way it is, although at times I get very angry. But I would never trade it for being White or anything else, even if it meant life would be a lot easier." An ethnic identity based solely on negative experiences of racial hatred is a very fragile thing that disappears as soon as the adversity is gone. If children are made to feel bad because of how they are different, it is psychologically crucial that they have and can draw on positive feelings about who they are ethnically and individually. If they do not, they may in time come to hate their group membership, seeing it as the source of all their problems. Jewish parents, for example, are now beginning to realize that identities based exclusively on the experience of the Holocaust or a long history of oppression eventually drive their children from the fold.

Third, racism should always be presented as a social, not as an individual or personal, problem. For example: "Why did Tommy call me that bad name? I didn't do anything to him." "Of course, you didn't. Sometimes when people get angry or unhappy, they take it out on others who are different from them. There is something wrong with people when they do that." Children must not come to believe, consciously or unconsciously, that something they did brought on the racist behavior. Parents should not assume that a child has not personalized a negative racial experience. They must check it out. Young children, in their egocentric mode of experiencing the world, tend to take responsibility for most things that happen to them. Parents must actively make sure they do not do so. An ethnic child can be transformed from a happy and carefree young person to one who is negative and sullen by a single experience with racism. Much of the damage could be alleviated by working through the incident with the child. Parents must also be careful to not expect special behaviors from children because of who they are ethnically. Such expectations also communicate to children that they are in some way responsible for their own plight and that better behavior could have averted the incident. This is an enormous burden to place on a child.

Fourth, children should learn two lessons about ethnic group membership. The first is that group membership is based not only on obvious physical or cultural features but also on an interdependence of fate. In other words, members of an ethnic group share the experience of being treated similarly by the world, and this should serve to heighten awareness of being part of a single whole. It is easy for children to learn to vent their frustration on subgroups within their community, blaming them for the bad treatment that all group members experience. Such internalized racism can become a tyranny of its own and lead to destructive intergroup wrangling and bickering. We are thinking, for example, of caste systems based on lightness and darkness of skin color that exist in Communities of Color.

The second lesson is that it is acceptable to have multiple allegances and belong to different social groupings at the same time. If children are made to choose between alternatives, they grow resentful and eventually get even with parents, usually by rejecting group membership at some level. Some parents, for instance, are very critical of their children's attempts at being bicultural (of trying to become competent in the ways of dominant culture as well as their own). Fearing that their children may lose touch with traditional ways and values, they force them to choose, and the result is unhappiness for all concerned. The same result may come from forcing the child to acculturate into the mainstream culture, which may engender later yearning for identity.

Fifth, parents must realize that children's feelings about ethnicity, ethnic identity, and group belonging are not likely to be more positive or less conflicted than their own. Put in a slightly different manner, parents may pass on inner conflicts and issues about their own ethnicity to their children. In preparing children for a hostile world, parents must focus not only on their children, but also on themselves as role models.

FAMILIES OF COLOR

The key to understanding and working with Families of Color is an appreciation of their diversity, especially in relation to mainstream White families. Their form, first of all, varies from culture to culture. As Gushue and Sciarra (1995) suggest, each culture has "differing ways of understanding 'appropriate' family organization, values, communication and behavior" (p. 588). For example, Mexican American families tend to be hierarchical and male-dominated, religious, traditionally sex typed, and often bilingual, with deep extended family roots. But to push such generalizations too far is to enter into the realm of stereotyping.

McGoldrick (1982), who almost single-handedly crafted the recent interest in the importance of culture in working with families, argued that no two families are ever culturally the same. Each internalizes in its own way aspects of the cultural norms of the group. Some aspects become very important; others are disregarded. McGoldrick saw these cultural choices as "starting points" for understanding a given family. She enumerated a variety of other factors that impact "the way ethnic patterns surface in families." Included here are acculturation, class, education, ethnic identity, reason for migration to the United States, language status, geographic location, and stage in the family life cycle at the time of migration.

Cultural differences in family structure must not be interpreted as cultural "deficits." The so-called Moynihan Report (Moynihan, 1965) on the status of the Black family, also referred to as "the myth of the Black matriarchy," is an excellent case in point. The report, which had great impact on public welfare policy in the 1960s and 1970s, implied that the strong influence of the mother in African American families was an aberration caused by racism. It further implied that in more equitable times, African American family structure would return to a more patriarchal form. Critics argued that the existence of strong women in the African American family is instead a cultural artifact that reflects greater role equality and flexibility of men and women than is true in White families. They further pointed to strong women as an example of the creative and adaptive strategies and strengths that emerged out of the African American family to deal with a hostile social environment. The critical conceptual difference here is seeing this phenomenon as a creative adaptation of a traditional African American cultural form and as a strength rather than as a deficit.

BICULTURAL FAMILIES

There are two kinds of bicultural families: families in which the parents come from two different cultures, and families in which parents from the same culture have adopted a child from another culture. Bicultural families and children are definitely on the increase. Perkins (1994) estimated that there were around 1 million interracially married couples in the United States, an increase of 250 percent between 1967 and 1987. According to government statistics, approximately 1 million children, or 3 percent of the population born between 1970 and 1990, were of mixed race. This was probably a substantial underestimate because there was no formal category for counting such individuals in the 1990 U.S. census. The 2000 U.S. census, the first to inquire about multiracial backgrounds, found that 6.8 million people, or 2.4 percent of the population identified as multiracial. Smolowe (1993) estimated that the increase in birthrate of multiracial children was twenty-six times that of any other group. In spite of these increasing numbers, however, there are still a number of myths and distorted beliefs about bicultural children. (This is perhaps not surprising; in 1967 sixteen states still had laws against interracial marriages.) Kerwin and Ponterotto (1995) described three of the most prevalent myths: (1) bicultural children turn out to be tragic and marginal individuals; (2) each must choose an identity with only one group; and (3) they are very uncomfortable discussing their ethnic identity.

Each myth is far from the truth. Bicultural children are quite capable of developing healthy ethnic identities and finding a stable social place for themselves. Contrary to having to choose membership in one group over the other, healthy identity development involves integrating both cultural backgrounds into a single sense of self that is an amalgam of both and yet uniquely different from either. Bicultural children welcome the opportunity to discuss and explore who they are ethnically. Such myths are likely created and sustained by individuals who are uncomfortable with the idea of intercultural relationships and who project their own discomfort onto the children.

Bicultural Couples

Clinical work with bicultural spouses (as in Scenario 3) yields a very informative psychological profile. First, bicultural couples tend to approximate extremes in healthy functioning. They are either very high functioning and bring to the relationship advanced communication skills, good cultural understanding of each other, and a strong motivation toward openness and working through difficulties, or they enter the relationship with a culturally different partner for reasons of which they are largely unaware and bring to the relationship very poor interpersonal skills and little insight.

Jacobs (1977) carried out extensive interviews with African American and European American bicultural couples and their children. Because his sampling methods were skewed, his adult subjects were primarily high functioning. All reported personal attraction rather than race as their reason for involvement with their spouses. Jacobs found that several of the spouses acknowledged a drive toward asserting autonomy as a secondary motive. For the White spouses, this tended to be autonomy from rigid and overcontrolling families, while for the African American spouses it tended to represent "overcoming limits placed on them by racism." None of the fourteen spouses reported feeling any guilt over their relationships. Spouses also seemed well differentiated from each other and, because of this, were able to allow their children to separate and become their own selves. The parents did report that it seemed easier to give their children more autonomy because the children were not exactly like either of the parents.

Only two of the seven White spouses reported that both of their parents accepted their intention to marry. In contrast, all seven of the Black spouses reported that their families of origin were generally accepting of their choices. This parallels previous research findings that ethnic community members seem more accepting of bicultural relationships and marriages than do Whites. But there are some notable exceptions to this tendency, especially among Asian American subgroups.

White spouses reported an interesting sequence of reactions to parental rejection, which again attests to the basic maturity and emotional health of the partners in Jacobs's sample. After initial anger lasting anywhere from several months to a number of years, they were able to develop empathy and understanding for the rejecting parent and continued to attempt to reestablish contact and attachment. Spouses who exhibited unhealthy attachment patterns found it impossible to make such movement and efforts at reconciliation. They tended to be flooded with guilt over their marriages, were heavily preoccupied with race (the healthier couples were not so preoccupied), harbored serious prejudices of their own, and continued to act out the same conflict that had drawn them into the interracial relationship in the first place.

Second, bicultural couples reported frequent focus on issues of race and ethnicity. Intimate interaction with someone who is culturally different cannot help but elicit racial material from both partners. Such issues must be discussed honestly and worked through if the marriage is going to continue. What exists in effect is a microcosm of race relations, with numerous opportunities to explore cross-cultural problems. For example, Memmi (1966) suggested that racial prejudices and stereotypes often surface during arguments between bicultural couples. Because of the hurtful nature of such attacks, resolution must be pursued and found. Jacobs (1977) also found that his interracial couples were much freer to discuss topics of race and ethnicity than were either African American or White monocultural couples.

Third, bicultural couples tend to be rather isolated as a unit, often experiencing social rejection and preferring social contact with other bicultural couples who can more easily understand what they face. In reaction, they often evolve patterns of strong interdependence, which, on the negative side, seems to lead to an unwillingness to acknowledge problems or seek help. A positive consequence is that such couples may try harder to resolve conflict on their own. At the same time isolation and mutual dependence may make the airing of problems a particular threat.

Fourth, bicultural couples face an added challenge that monocultural couples do not. Not only must they deal with their own individual differences and conflicts, but they must also navigate through the often complex and difficult terrain of cultural differences. Thus, interfaith couples—for example, Jewish and Christian—must agree on shared practices and their children's religious education. Or bicultural couples may find that they have very different styles, values, priorities, or expectations that are cultural in origin. For instance, Northern Europeans become quiet and distant during interpersonal conflicts and tend to move away from their partners, while individuals from more traditional cultures tend to become more verbal and emotional and move toward their partners in an effort to resolve conflicts (Orbé, 2004). If problems are to be resolved by such bicultural couples, they must learn to accommodate differences in style.

Patterns of Bicultural Interactions as Evidenced in Bicultural Marital Discord

Bicultural children bring to the classroom reflections of conflicts and tensions not only within society, but also possibly from their own homes. Difficulties in bicultural marriages represent a microcosm of the kinds of conflicts bicultural children face in their lives. Falicov (1986), for example, believed that cross-cultural marriages demand from each partner a certain kind of cultural transition. The couple must "arrive at an adaptive and flexible view of cultural differences that makes it possible to maintain some individuated values, to negotiate conflictual areas, and even to develop a new cultural code that integrates parts of both cultural streams" (p. 431).

Falicov identified three common patterns of cultural tension. The first pattern is "conflicts in cultural code." This involves cultural differences in how marriages are conceived and structured. Particularly important are differences in rules related to the inclusion and exclusion of others (especially extended family members) and the relative power and authority of spouses. In the hope of mutually adapting to each other's style, partners often minimize or maximize cultural differences. In either case, they tend to have only limited knowledge of the other's culture and are generally unable to carry out what Falicov saw as a necessary developmental task for the marriage: that of negotiating a new cultural code that implies the melding of their different ways. She also pointed out that errors in this arena often stem from "ethnocentric or stereotyped views of the other." As a result of this limited knowledge, cultural differences may be "mistaken for negative personality traits" of the other.

The second type of problem deals with "cultural differences and permission to marry." Here, Falicov included problems related to parental disapproval of the relationship and cultural artifacts such as trends toward enmeshment, which make separating from the family of origin a difficult and conflictual task. She identified two patterns of adaptation in couples who had not received emotional permission to marry. In the first, partners

> maximize their differences and do not blend, integrate, or negotiate their values and life styles. They lead parallel lives, each holding on to their culture and/or family of origin. Often, the counterpoint of the marital distance is an excessive involvement of one or both parties with the family of origin. There may also be unresolved longings for the past ethnic or religious affiliations, even if these were of little importance previously. (p. 440)

These types of problems have implications for the children pulled between families and caught in the tension this produces. The second pattern involves minimizing and even denying the differences, including possibly joining a third and alternative culture or cutting ties with culture and family. Such couples often develop an attitude of "us against them" (meaning the world) or "we only have each other." Structurally, they tend to construct rigid boundaries with the outside (especially with families of origin) and unclear boundaries with each other. Such isolation may also be transferred to the children.

Falicov called the third problem area in cross-cultural marriages "cultural stereotyping and severe stress." In such problems, some impending stress (such as the death of a parent) initiates the maximizing of cultural differences as well as increased cultural stereotyping of each other. Falicov suggested that cultural material, which in the past was dealt with constructively, is being used as a defense against looking at other noncultural problems, and that the stress currently affecting the couple has worn down their ability to cope. Children in families reacting to stress in this manner may need extra help negotiating the stronger pull of conflicting cultures during this time. Teachers alerted to impending stress within bicultural families may need to be prepared to offer more than the usual care and empathy for such children. As we shall see in the next section, Falicov's three patterns of cultural tension within marriage exacerbate the kind of unique developmental tasks that bicultural child must navigate.

Bicultural Children

While monoethnic children may eventually face the realities of a hostile social environment, bicultural children must additionally come to grips with their parents' racial drama and the perpetually repeated question, "What are you?" Kich (1992) suggested that the interracial child represents not only the parents' racial differences but also a unique individual who must work through very personal identity issues. Kerwin and Ponterotto (1995) summarized the development of racial identity in biracial children. In many ways, the process parallels that of monoethnic children, but with the added task of simultaneously exploring two (or more) rather than a single ethnic heritage and then integrating them into a unique identity. Perhaps the most salient point to remember in teaching biracial and multiracial children is that psychologically they are not merely reflections of their two or more sides but rather unique integrations of them.

Biracial children, on average, develop awareness of race and racial differences even earlier than monoethnic children, usually by age three or four. This is because they are exposed to such differences from birth in the confines of their own family. It is also likely that their parents are more attuned to these differences because of their own interracial relationship. Upon entry into school, biracial children are immediately confronted with questions that serve as major stimuli for their internal processing of "What are you?" Concurrently, they begin to experiment with labels for themselves. Children may create descriptions based on perceptions of their skin color (such as *coffee and cream*) or adopt parental terms (such as *interracial*).

Generally, biracial children are more successful moving through the identity formation process when race is openly discussed at home and parents are available to help them sort out the various issues of self-definition. Rate of development also depends on the amount of integration in their classrooms and the availability in school of role models from their two cultural sides. During preadolescence, children begin to regularly use racial or cultural as opposed to physical descriptions of themselves. They become increasingly aware of group differences other than skin color (physical appearance, language, and so on) and of the fact that their parents belong to distinct ethnic groups. Exposure to "racial incidents" and first-time entry into either integrated or segregated school settings also accelerate learning.

Adolescence is particularly problematic for bicultural children. It is a time of marked intolerance for differences. There are likely to be strong pressures on bicultural adolescents to identify with one parent's ethnicity over the other: usually with the Parent of Color if one of the parents is White. Peers of Color push the adolescent to identify with them, and Whites increasingly perceive and treat the bicultural adolescent as a Person of Color. Jacobs (1977) believed that identification with one ethnic side and the simultaneous rejection of the other, and then identification with the other ethnic side, is a natural part of identity formation in bicultural youth. Perhaps only by internalizing one aspect of the self at a time and vacillating between the two over the duration of adolescence and young adulthood can both identities be integrated. Dating begins in adolescence, which accentuates race as a central life issue. It is not unusual for biracial youth to experience rejection because of their color or ethnicity, and such experiences are likely to have a great impact on their emerging sense of identity.

Biracial women have a particularly difficult task meshing their body images with the differences in physical appearance of their two parents. Young Black women often opt out of the mainstream society's "beauty contest." They find themselves so far from White America's standard of beauty that they sometimes don't even try and, as a result, may in fact pursue a healthier, more realistic self-image. Biracial women can also be torn between ideal mainstream images as portrayed in the media and identification with body image type of a Mother of Color. The heightened sexuality of adolescence also stimulates such questions as "If I become pregnant or make someone pregnant, what will the baby look like?" Interactions between bicultural children and their parents are at times complex and conflictual. As children mature and become more aware, they are increasingly confronted with and confused by being different. The experience has been described by some as akin to "going crazy" or having no way of making sense out of how the world is reacting to them. Bicultural parents often have a more difficult time understanding what their children are going through. At the root of this misunderstanding is a parent's tendency to see the child as a personal extension rather than as an amalgam of the couple. The parents' growing realization that the child is really not like either parent, but something beyond both, can provoke anxiety in both parents and child.

In family situations where one of the parents has detached from his or her group of origin, bicultural children tend to feel particularly protective of this parent. Similarly, they may feel particularly close to the Parent of Color when he or she is feeling bad or rejected because of racism. Divorce can be especially traumatic for biracial children because it represents a severing of the two sides of their identity. They may feel a real need to keep their warring parents together at any cost. It may become especially difficult for the child if the parents use race against each other. Nor is it uncommon for a child to take on the prejudices of the individual parents during divorce. In single-parent families, difficulties can arise when the lone parent, usually the mother, feels great hostility toward the father for abandoning the family and unconsciously turns her resentment toward the child, who is a very visible reminder of the union. Additionally, the parent's or the child's resentment may come out as subtle racism toward the race of the missing parent.

Adopted Children

Intercultural adoption is a second source of bicultural families. Some people in Communities of Color, especially African Americans and Native Americans, have taken very strong stances against adoption and foster care across racial lines. Their feeling is that White parents are not capable of providing ethnic children with adequate exposure and connection with their cultures of birth or of training the children in how to deal with the racism they will inevitably experience. Serious efforts have been made to sensitize and train adoptive parents in cultural competence as well as to encourage them to keep their children connected to the ethnic community of origin. There are, however, real questions about whether such efforts can overcome the enormous cultural gaps, let alone a racially hostile social environment. White adoptive parents seldom understand the enormity of difficulties that their children face as People of Color. In addition, they often unconsciously deny differences between themselves and their children.

This puts children in a difficult psychological position. They feel isolated in dealing with the very complex issues of race and ethnicity. Often, there is the aforementioned sense of "going crazy" caused by the enormous gulf between how they are treated in the world and at home. Finally, adopted Children of Color can feel confused when their adoptive parents simultaneously represent nurturance and emotional support on one side and oppression on the other. A process somewhat akin to the identity vacillation suggested by Jacobs (1977) may occur for these bicultural children as well. More information on biracial children and their experience in the classroom can be found in Chapter 7 in the section Isolated Students of Color.

REFLECTION QUESTIONS AND A TECHNIQUE FOR SOLVING PROBLEMS

This chapter covers some highly emotional and personal material. Creative problem solving (Parnes, 1967) is particularly useful here, as it helps us step back, look at the facts, and, as difficult as it may be, begin to take steps toward solutions. As before, write down any conflict, question, concern, or emotion you have about the material. After establishing "the mess," continue through the steps outlined at the end of Chapter 4.

List a few facts on parenting from the chapter.

Based on the facts and your original concern, complete the statement, "In what ways might we _____."

Brainstorm to answer your IWWMW statement.

Apply criteria and choose one idea that rates well on your criteria.

Plan to implement your idea.

SUMMARY

This chapter focuses on various cross-cultural issues related to child development, the nature of families, and parenting. From birth, characteristics and development of children vary greatly across ethnic groups. Differences in reactivity, temperament, and mother–child interaction are good examples. Children of Color are aware of racial differences as early as three or four, and by seven they exhibit a beginning racial awareness. Majority-group members are slower to develop an awareness of their Whiteness. Racial identity evolves through three learning processes: racial classification, racial identification, and racial evaluation. Racial awareness has also been related to self-esteem.

Early studies suggested that Children of Color exhibited negative self-concepts and tried to deny their ethnicity as a result of racism. This "myth of self-hatred" has been challenged by subsequent researchers. In a landmark study, Williams and Morland (1976) found that by third grade African American children were aware of their racial identity, accepted it, and preferred same-race playmates, as did their White counterparts. These researchers did find some evidence of pro-White preferences in attributing positive and negative evaluations of Blacks and Whites until junior high school, when they reversed themselves to pro-Black preferences. Studies of personal identity formation in adolescence show that African American youth formed stable integration of self-images much earlier than did White youth, although they also exhibited identity foreclosure, a sign of premature closing off of possibilities of who they could become. Children of Color show higher achievement scores when learning activities are culturally relevant to their life experiences and when learning strategies fit cultural learning styles.

Parents of Color face the difficult task of creating a safe environment for children who are systematically subjected to the harmful effects of racism. They can create buffer zones in their homes and communities where children are protected from the negative attitudes and stereotypes of broader society and at the same time learn ethnic pride. Substituting loving parents and community for a hostile environment that negates the value of children guarantees a more positive self-concept. Parents can teach their children how to deal emotionally with racism.

Poussaint (1972) warned against "compensatory mechanisms" that parents may adopt to prepare their children for racism. Wright (1998) warned against the use of corporal punishment, emotional distance, and blaming family problems exclusively on racism. Parents can prepare their children cognitively for what they will encounter in the world outside the buffer zone. The topic of race should not be avoided, but instead dealt with in an age-appropriate manner. A strong and positive ethnic identity should be fostered. Racism should be presented as a social, not personal, problem. Children should learn to accept and value multiple allegiances and not to scapegoat other subgroups within their culture. Parents with conflicted ethnic identities are likely to pass their own attitudes on to their children.

Families of Color tend to exhibit more diversity in their form and structure than do mainstream White families. McGoldrick (1982) listed the following factors as important in how ethnic patterns surface in families: acculturation, education, ethnic identity, reason for migration, language status, geographic location, and stage in the family life cycle. It is critical to avoid interpreting cultural differences in family structure as cultural deficits. The example of the "Black matriarchy" is presented, with an emphasis on differing family patterns as indicative of creative and adaptive development within the family rather than as pathology.

Bicultural couples and families represent a special subset of ethnic families. Contrary to widely held myths, bicultural children can develop healthy personal and ethnic identities, are able to integrate both cultural heritages, and welcome and benefit from the opportunity to explore who they are ethnically. Bicultural couples tend to exhibit either very positive or extremely dysfunctional relationship patterns. Jacobs (1977) found that African American–White couples eventually resolved problems with parents, reported frequent focus on issues of race and ethnicity and greater freedom in discussing the topic, tended to isolate themselves as a unit, and faced significant problems that resulted from cultural differences.

Falicov (1986) pointed to three typical problems in bicultural marital discord: conflicts in creating a shared cultural code, differences in gaining permission to marry and in separating from families of origin, and culturally stereotyping the partner during times of crisis and stress. Bicultural children face not only prejudice and racism, but also the task of integrating two different ethnic heritages and identities. Bicultural children are aware of race and racial differences earlier than monoethnic children. They tend to proceed most successfully through the identity formation process when race and ethnicity are openly discussed at home and parents help them sort out issues of self-definition. Adolescence is particularly problematic for bicultural children. There is often pressure to identify with one parent's ethnicity over the other. There is often the experience of rejection with the onset of dating. The adolescent also tends to vacillate between identifying with one parent's ethnicity and then the other's. This is a natural process in which both sides are integrated into a new and unique sense of self and identity. Communities of Color have opposed the adoption of ethnic children across ethnic lines. They feel that White parents are not capable of exposing or connecting them to their culture of origin or preparing them to deal with racism. Adopted Children of Color often find themselves isolated and on their own in dealing with issues of race and ethnicity.

Return to the four scenarios at the beginning of the chapter to see how your understanding of ethnic children, parents, and families has expanded and grown.

PSYCHOLOGICAL AND EDUCATIONAL ISSUES

You may not be able to change the world,
but at least you can embarrass the guilty.

—Jessica Miltford

Ely (2001) tells a story that graphically portrays the process whereby young people are alienated from schools and isolated from full participation in both school culture and American society at large.

> Mr. Cur . . . was the teacher who sent "Jamar" out of his room because he was being "insubordinate and defiant." He perceived Jamar as rebellious because Jamar was wearing his hair in a traditional African-American way. Mr. Cur interpreted this as a statement of "black power." He was immediately frightened by it . . . and lashed out at Jamar.
>
> Meanwhile . . . Jamar had done nothing but show up to class!
>
> Mr. Cur acted in accordance with his own limited viewpoint. Driven by both his fears and his lack of understanding about African-American students, he "saw" Jamar "wearing a cloak of defiance," when, actually, Jamar was "naked" of any such emotion.
>
> (Adapted from pp. 91–92 of *Quo No More* by Arline Ely. Copyright 2001 by Arline Ely. Reprinted by permission.)

Ely suggests that such "disconnects" are routinely experienced by African American, Hispanic, and lower-socioeconomic children because teachers lack basic sensitivity to the cultural styles of their students. Rather than reacting unconsciously to their own prejudices and stereotypes, they must learn to see and understand students' behavior from within the students' cultural perspectives.

Such encounters take their toll on the innocent victims. In a most extraordinary book entitled *Black Rage,* psychiatrists William Grier and Price Cobbs (1968) explored the enormous anger they saw lurking below the surface of the African American patients who sought their help. All had been living reasonably functional lives until emotional crises knocked them down, and each had difficulty recovering. Psychotherapy revealed very negative perceptions of self that were deeply intertwined with their experiences as African Americans in the United States. According to Grier and Cobbs, African Americans, because of having to live in, adapt to, and survive in a hostile and racist world, are at perpetual risk for developing serious physical and emotional disorders. Most, in fact, survive, and many even grow strong. But all pay an emotional price that may, with sufficient stress and personal difficulty, result in some type of psychological breakdown. According to the authors, African Americans stand at a precarious juncture, "delicately poised, not yet risen to the flash point, but rising rapidly nonetheless" (p. 213). Cose (1993), in *The Rage of a Privileged Class,* has more recently echoed these findings.

This chapter focuses on issues that plague People of Color, particularly in educational settings. It explores a number of factors, like the racism described by Grier and Cobbs and by Cose, that put individuals at risk for psychological and educational difficulties. We provide an overview of various factors that affect the psychological health and educational functioning of People of Color. We begin with a discussion of problems related to ethnic identification and group belonging. Then we consider acculturation and assimilation, which may produce identity crises for individuals and Groups of Color. Finally, we address the perspectives and unique experiences of isolated Students and Teachers of Color as well as ways to encourage dialogue across differences, especially in parent–teacher interactions. Throughout the chapter, particular attention is paid to models of racial-identity development that have proven particularly useful in making sense out of cross-cultural interactions.

Chapter 6 looked at some of the psychological issues related to child development, parenting, and family dynamics in Communities of Color. Chapter 8 explores various sources of bias in the education of Students of Color. Together, these chapters provide a clearer picture of the kinds of psychological and educational issues with which culturally different students struggle and which they ultimately bring into schools. They also represent barriers that lead to underachievement.

RACIAL IDENTITY AND GROUP BELONGING

The controversy over whether Children of Color regularly experience problems in group identification and low self-concept as a result of racism was discussed in some detail in Chapter 6. Our conclusion, based on several sources of evidence, was that they did not necessarily, but that without sufficient and appropriate family and community support, Children of Color were certainly at risk for such problems. We also suggested that researchers have been hesitant in estimating the deleterious effects of racism and society's negative views of ethnic-group members. In this section, we expand this picture of identity difficulties.

The Inner Dynamics of Ethnic Identity

The term *identity* refers to the stable inner sense of who a person is, which is formed by the successful integration of various experiences of the self into a coherent self-image. *Ethnic identity* refers to that part of personal identity that contributes to the person's self-image as an ethnic-group member. Thus, when one speaks of African American identity or Native American identity or Jewish identity, what is being referred to is the individual's subjective experience of ethnicity. What does the person feel, consciously and unconsciously, about being a member of his or her ethnic group? What meanings do individuals attach to their ethnicity? What does people's behavior reflect about the nature of their attachment to the group? Answers to these questions are subsumed under the notion of ethnic identity.

Ethnic-identity formation, like personal-identity formation, results from the integration of personal experiences each individual has as an African American or Native American or Jew as well as the messages that have been communicated and internalized about ethnicity by family members and significant others. In general, ethnic identity can be positive, negative, or ambivalent, and individuals can be positive identifiers, negative identifiers, and ambivalent identifiers (Klein, 1980). The latter two situations have also been referred to in the literature as "internalized racism" and "internalized oppression." As emphasized in Chapter 6, ethnic children raised in a hostile racist environment are likely to have unpleasant experiences associated with their ethnicity. As these negative experiences accumulate, it becomes increasingly difficult for the child, and later the adult, to integrate them into a coherent and positive sense of ethnic self.

Inner conflicts in ethnic identity, such as those just described, ultimately find expression in overt behavior. In the case of negative identification (where aspects of the ethnic self are actively rejected or disowned), the individual tends to deny, avoid, or escape group membership in whatever ways possible. In Communities of Color, this is often referred to as "passing." It may include trying to change one's appearance so as not to look so typically ethnic, changing one's name, moving to a nonethnic neighborhood, dating and marrying outside the group, and taking on majority-group habits, language, and affectations. Such behaviors are usually experienced as offensive within ethnic communities. Specific derogatory terms have, in fact, been created in each of the Communities of Color to describe such individuals: "Oreos" among African Americans, "coconuts" among Latinos/as, "apples" among Native Americans, and "bananas" among Asian Americans. All refer to individuals as being of Color on the outside but White on the inside. As part of this rejection of ethnicity, the individual also takes on majority attitudes and habits, including the dominant culture's prejudices and stereotypes.

In relation to ambivalent identification, where rejecting tendencies exist concurrently with positive feelings about group membership, there is either vacillation between love and hate (where individuals move back and forth, pulling away from feeling too identified if they get too close and moving back toward the group if they grow too distant) or the simultaneous expression of contradictory positive and negative attitudes and behaviors. One form of accommodation is to compartmentalize ethnic identity (retain certain aspects and reject others). For instance, a Latino/a might refuse to speak Spanish, identify as a Catholic, or marry within the group, but at the same time may have strong preferences for native foods, prefer to live in a barrio, and become involved in civil rights activities. It is perhaps most accurate to conceive of ethnic-identity formation as an ongoing and lifelong process. It involves a series of internal psychological adaptations (that may eventually translate into changes in behavior) to an ever-changing complex of unfolding ethnic experiences.

A good example of such dynamics is offered by Tatum (1997) in *Why Are All the Black Kids Sitting Together in the Cafeteria?* Tatum points out that race and racial-identity issues become particularly salient when Children of Color enter adolescence. Changes in school groupings, dating, and broader participation in the social environment increasingly highlight the existence of racism and the need to understand what it means to be Black. In adolescence there is a greater likelihood of encountering experiences that may cause an individual to examine his or her racial identity. Boy–girl events and interactions become less racially diverse, and White peers seem less likely to understand or be able to provide support for the emerging identities of Children of Color. As a result, adolescents gravitate to like-race peers and often adopt an "oppositional stance or identity," absorbing stereotyped images of being of Color and rejecting characteristics and behaviors that they see as White. "The anger and resentment that adolescents feel in response to their growing awareness of the systematic exclusion of Black people from full participation in U.S. society leads to the development of an oppositional social identity. This . . . both protects one's identity from the psychological assault of racism and keeps the dominant group at a distance" (p. 60).

Tatum sees this attachment to the peer group as a "positive coping strategy" in the face of stress. It is not without difficulties, however. Images of Blackness tend to be highly stereotyped, and academic success is often discounted as White. As we shall see next, this stage of racial identity development—which Cross (1995) calls the "encounter" and which entails turning toward one's own group and rejecting the majority and its values—is followed by the emergence of greater individualization and diversification of racial identity. Models of racial-identity development are helpful for exploring both student and teacher interactions across cultures.

Models of Racial-Identity Development

An important but somewhat different approach to understanding the evolution of racial or cultural consciousness is offered by various researchers (Atkinson et al., 1993; Cross, 1995; Hardiman & Jackson, 1992; Helms, 1990; Tatum, 1997) who began in the 1970s to develop what have come to be called models of racial-identity development. These models, which were first developed in relation to the experience of African Americans, assume that there are strong similarities in the ways all ethnic individuals respond to oppression and racism. It is believed that People of Color go through a series of predictable stages as they struggle to make sense out of their relationship to their own cultural group as well as to the oppression of mainstream culture. Cross (1995), whose work is exemplary, hypothesizes five such stages of development. It is assumed that each Person of Color can be located in one of the five stages, depending on the level of racial awareness and identity.

In Stage 1, called *preencounter,* individuals are not consciously aware of the impact of race and ethnicity on their life experiences. They tend to assimilate, seek acceptance by Whites, exhibit strong preferences for dominant cultural values, and even internalize negative stereotypes of their own group. By de-emphasizing race and distancing themselves from other group members, they are able to deny their vulnerability to racism and sustain the myth of meritocracy and the hope of achievement unencumbered by racial hatred.

In Stage 2, *encounter,* some event or experience shatters individuals' denial and sends them deep into confusion about their own ethnicity. For the first time they must consciously deal with the fact of being different and what this difference means. People of Color at this stage often speak of "waking up" to reality, realizing that ethnicity is an aspect of self that must be dealt with and becoming aware of the enormity of what must be confronted out in the world.

Stage 3, *immersion–emersion,* is characterized by two powerful feelings: first, a desire to immerse oneself in all things "ethnic"—to celebrate all symbols of Blackness, for example—and second, to simultaneously avoid all contact with Whites, the White world, and symbols of that world. The immediate result is an uncritical belief that everything Black is beautiful and everything White is abhorrent. During this more separatist period, people may seek out information about ethnic history and culture and surround themselves exclusively with "their own kind." The enormous anger that is generated during Stage 2 slowly dissipates as the person grows increasingly focused on self-exploration and attachment within the ethnic world, and less in need of lashing out at the White world.

Internalization, Stage 4 of the model, begins as individuals become increasingly secure and positive in their sense of racial identity and less rigid in their attachment to the group at the expense of personal autonomy. Pro-ethnic attitudes become "more open, expansive, and sophisticated" (Cross,

1995, p. 114). While they feel securely connected to their ethnic community, they also become more willing to relate to Whites and members of other ethnic groups who are able to acknowledge and accept their ethnicity.

Stage 5, *internalization–commitment*, represents a growing and maturing of the tendencies initiated in Stage 4. People at Stage 5 have found ways to translate their personal ethnic identities into active commitment to social justice and change. According to Tatum (1992b), the Stage 5 person is "anchored in a positive sense of racial identity" and can "proactively perceive and transcend race" (p. 12). Race has become an instrument for reaching out into the world, rather than an end in itself, as in Stage 3, or a social reality to be denied or avoided, as in Stage 1.

Racial-Identity Development and the Teaching Process

The value of these models for teachers is twofold. First, they educate and sensitize teachers to the importance of cultural identity in the lives of Children of Color. Second, they suggest that individuals at different stages of development may have very different needs and values and may feel differently about what is supportive in the learning situation.

Students of Color at Stage 1 may do very well in learning from White teachers. According to Sue and Sue (1999), Stage 1 individuals may react differently to White and same-race teachers.

Those at Stage 2 tend to be preoccupied with personal issues of race and identity, but at the same time are torn between fading Stage 1 beliefs and an emerging awareness of race consciousness. They may do particularly well with teachers who are knowledgeable about their own cultural group and with teaching methods that allow maximum choice and self-direction. A child may still be more comfortable with a White teacher, as long as the teacher is culturally aware.

According to Atkinson et al. (1993), students in Stage 3 are absorbed in reexploring and engaging in ethnic ways, and they see personal problems as exclusively the result of racism. In classrooms, Teachers of Color are by far preferred. Teachers, whether White or of Color, will inevitably be seen as a "symbol of the oppressive society" and thus challenged. The least helpful response is to become defensive and take attacks personally. "White guilt and defensiveness" will especially exacerbate student anger. Teachers must realize that they will be continually tested, and they often find that honest self-disclosure about race is necessary to establish credibility. Lastly, Sue and Sue (1999) suggest adopting strategies that are more "action oriented" and "aimed at external change" as well as group approaches when working with Stage 3 students. Students of Color functioning at this stage may be particularly ready for the social action level of curriculum reform, which we visit in depth in Chapter 8.

Students in Stage 4 are struggling to balance group and personal perspectives and may need help sorting out these issues. They may still tend to prefer teachers from their own group, but they can begin to conceive of learning from culturally sensitive outsiders. Sue and Sue (1999) point out that those in Stage 4 appear in many ways to be similar to those in Stage 1. They tend to experience conflict between identification with their group and the need to "exercise greater personal freedom." Approaches that emphasize self-exploration are particularly helpful in integrating group identity and personal concerns of the self.

Those who have reached Stage 5, according to Atkinson et al. (1993), have developed their skills at balancing personal needs and group obligations, have an openness to all cultures, and are able to deal well with racism when it is encountered. Their preference for a teacher is most likely to be dictated by the personal qualities and attitudes of the teacher rather than by group membership.

In Chapter 3, Helms's model of White identity development was introduced (Brown & Lundrum-Brown, 1995). The model, which parallels and evolved from the work just described, enumerates stages of racial consciousness development in Whites and the eventual abandonment of entitlement. Just as it is useful to be able to identify the stage of identity development of individual Students of Color, so too is it valuable to be able to assess White teachers *vis à vis* Helms's model in order to better prepare and match them with Communities of Color. According to Sue and Sue (1999), White teachers will be most effective in cross-cultural teaching when they have successfully worked through feelings about Whiteness and privilege. Such individuals, located in the highest stages of Helms's model, are able to experience their own ethnicity in a nondefensive and nonracist manner. Sue and Sue also warn against mismatches, especially when the White teacher is at Stage 1 of Helms's model.

A Practical Interpretation of Racial-Identity Models

In order to make the theories of racial-identity development, particularly those of Cross (1995) and Helms (1990), more immediately understandable by and useful for teachers and students, Moule (2003c) proposed a four stage model using colloquial terms that are easy to remember in everyday school situations.

She calls Stage 1, the preencounter stage, "I'm OK, you're OK." It includes the often-seen "color-blind" perspective. The second or encounter stage is called "Something is not OK." In the third stage, "I'm OK, I'm not so sure about you," Moule summarizes many of the dynamics described by the theorists, in their stages 3 and 4 including anger, denial, pseudo-independence, immersion, and emersion. Stage 4, "I'm OK, you're OK, we're OK," is equivalent to the autonomy or independent stage, in which people are ready to work for change in a more fully integrated manner. The superficiality of "I'm OK, you're OK" is replaced by a deeper, more compassionate and complex understanding of the issues and the fact that individuals are "all OK" as they continue to progress.

The following story illustrates how racial-identity stages may play out for Children of Color.

Judy was seven years old. Her family had quietly moved into an all-White, mostly Jewish neighborhood. Judy's parents had hoped that, despite an act of overt racism—one morning Judy's father had seen "N——— go back where you came from" scrawled on the outside of the house and, without telling anyone, washed it off—the school personnel would treat Judy like any other child. Perhaps pretending there was no difference would allow Judy to "fit in." Judy's parents hoped that an "I'm OK, you're OK" attitude—a preencounter stage—would be enough to ensure Judy's safety and success.

The preencounter strategy failed, for race and culture did matter. Judy experienced being different even as she worked to assimilate, and the resulting dissonance separated her even farther from her peers. During a Jewish holiday, only two students attended school, and Judy was the sole student in her class. She wondered, "Why isn't the teacher teaching me today? I am here!" Both in school and socially, she was often alone. Something was not OK.

Judy's encounter phase, "Something is not OK," slowly progressed to anger and the "I'm OK, I'm not sure about you" stage. One day, when Judy's mother came to pick her up from second grade, the teacher said that Judy waited at the door of the classroom and stomped on the toes of her classmates as they exited.

The next year Judy and her mother moved from their East Coast urban area to a West Coast suburb, from a two-parent to a one-parent family. Her new school was as culturally diverse as any Los Angeles could offer. Miss Thomas's room was a secure and healthy place for her own emotions and her classmates' toes. Judy was learning about her own culture and became, in ways, immersed.

Miss Thomas used strategies that seemed to validate every child in her room. Each day, she wrote a Spanish phrase in the corner of the blackboard. She read it to the class, then had the children repeat it. In less than a minute of classroom time, she thus acknowledged her Mexican American students and opened the door to another language for all her students. Miss Thomas's classroom was safe from disrespect toward her or among students. In this situation, as a result of a caring and skillful teacher, Judy entered into the autonomy stage, "I'm OK, you're OK, we're OK."

(Adapted from pp. 1, 2, 16 of *My Journey with Preservice Teachers: Reflecting on Teacher Characteristics that Bridge Multicultural Education Theory and Classroom Practice* by Jean Moule, 1998. Reprinted by permission.)

ASSIMILATION AND ACCULTURATION

Ethnic group members can differ widely in the extent of their assimilation and acculturation. Conceptually, *assimilation* means the coming together of two distinct cultures to create a new and unique third cultural form. Many people envisioned the United States becoming a "great melting pot"—a term borrowed from the name of a popular play written by the Jewish playwright

Israel Zangwill at the beginning of the Twentieth Century—in which different races and ethnicities would merge into a new American cultural form. In time it became known as the "myth" of the great melting pot because Americans never totally assimilated into a single culture.

Gordon (1964) distinguishes several forms of assimilation, including acculturation, structural assimilation, marital assimilation, and identificational assimilation. *Acculturation* involves taking on the cultural ways of another group, usually of the mainstream culture. *Structural assimilation* means gaining entry into the institutions of society. It is also called "integration" by Gordon. *Marital assimilation* implies large-scale intermarriage, and *identificational assimilation* involves developing a sense of belonging and peoplehood with the host society. It is probably most accurate to say that White ethnics—of Irish, Italian, Jewish, Armenian, and other backgrounds—have assimilated into American society on all of these dimensions, but only to the extent that they have been willing to give up their traditional ways and values.

People of Color, on the other hand, were never really considered part of the great melting pot and have remained structurally separate. They have, however, acculturated in varying degrees to the dominant Northern European culture. In America assimilation has always been a one-way process, that is perhaps, according to Healey (1995), better referred to as "Americanization" or "Anglo-conformity."

> This kind of assimilation was designed to maintain the predominance of the British-type institutional patterns created during the early years of American society. Under Anglo-conformity there is relatively little sharing of cultural traits, and immigrants and minority groups are expected to adapt to Anglo-American culture as fast as possible. Historically, Americanization has been a precondition for access to better jobs, higher education, and other opportunities. (Healey, 1995, p. 40)

Acculturation, the taking on of cultural patterns of another group, is important in two different ways. First, it is critical to be able to assess the amount of acculturation that has taken place within any individual or family and, simultaneously, to discover to what extent and in what specific areas traditional attitudes, values, and behavior still remain. Just knowing that a student is Latino/a says little about who the person is or how he or she lives. To know where the individual falls on a continuum from traditional identification to complete acculturation offers more information. It is important, however, to not confuse group membership with the degree of acculturation that has occurred. The cultural values of the student may or may not be the cultural values of the student's ethnic group.

Acculturation can also create serious emotional strain and difficulties for ethnic students. A special term, *acculturative stress,* has been coined to refer to such situations. Take, for example, a newly arrived Vietnamese family. The children have learned English relatively quickly in comparison to their parents. As a result, they may end up translating for and becoming the spokespeople for the family. This is not a traditional role for Vietnamese children, who are trained to be very deferential to elders. Nor is it natural within the tradition for children to wield so much power. As the children Americanize, they feel increasingly less bound by traditional ways. The result is enormous stress on the family unit, as is usually the case when traditional cultural ways are compromised or lost as a result of immigration and acculturation.

Views of Acculturation

Researchers have long argued over how best to conceptualize the process of acculturation. Is it unidimensional or multidimensional? That is, does acculturation exist on a single continuum ranging from identification with the indigenous culture at one end to identification with the dominant culture at the other? Or does it make more sense to conceive of an individual's attachment to the two groups as independent of each other, with the possibility of simultaneously retaining an allegiance to the traditional culture and the dominant American culture? The unidimensional view implies that a person who moves toward dominant cultural patterns must simultaneously give up traditional ways. This approach has generated the notion of the "marginal" person, an ethnic-group member who tries to acculturate into the majority but ends up in perpetual limbo, caught between the two cultures (Cose, 1993; Lewin, 1948; Stonequist, 1961). Such an individual has transformed too much to return to traditional ways but, at the same time, cannot gain any real acceptance in majority culture because of skin color.

Other writers see acculturation as bidimensional or multidimensional. Proponents of biculturalism believe that it is possible to live and function effectively in two or more cultures (Cross, 1987; Oetting & Beauvais, 1990; Valentine, 1971). Unlike the marginal person, who is suspended between cultures with little real connection to either, the bicultural individual feels connected to both and picks and chooses aspects of each to internalize. Thus, in this view, it is possible for an Asian American to remain deeply steeped in a traditional lifestyle, while at the same time interacting comfortably in the White world, perhaps in relation to school, some socializing, and recreational activity.

Problems arise when aspects of the two cultures are in clear conflict. For example, an immigrant Latina woman must work outside the home, yet tries to remain true to traditional sex roles. Even if she is able to integrate the two, it will be very difficult for her children, not having been fully enculturated in traditional ways, to do the same (Casas & Pytluk, 1995; Waldschmidt, 2002). Also, biculturalism is not seen as a virtue in all ethnic communities. Some view people who have become proficient in majority ways with contempt, as turncoats who have rejected their own kind.

A third perspective, typified by the work of Marin (1992), suggests that the impact of acculturation can best be assessed by discovering the kinds of material that have been gained or lost through acculturation. Marin distinguishes three levels of acculturation. The superficial level involves learning and forgetting facts that are part of a culture's history or tradition. The intermediate level has to do with gaining or losing more central aspects and behaviors of a person's social world (such as language preference and use; ethnicity of spouse, friends, and neighbors; names given to children; and choice of media). The significant level involves core values, beliefs, and norms that are essential to the very cultural paradigm or worldview of the person. For example, Marin (1992) points to Latino/a culture's values of "encouraging positive interpersonal relationships and discouraging negative, competitive and assertive interactions," "familialism," and "collectivism" (p. 239). When cultural values of this magnitude are lost or become less central, acculturation has reached a significant point, and one might wonder what remains of an individual's cultural attachment. For many Whites, traditional cultural ties progressively slipped away, generation by generation, in America, according to Marin's model. The immigrant generation tended to trade more superficial cultural material. Their children, in turn, exchanged more immediate cultural material as they increasingly acculturated, and so forth.

Acculturation and Community Breakdown

Another dynamic is the psychological consequence of the breakdown of the broader community as a result of assimilation. As acculturation proceeds and group members feel less attached to traditional ways, they often choose to leave the community (or ghetto) in the hope of avoiding some of the animosity routinely directed toward the group. At this point, the ability of the community to protect the individual is weakened, and the use of distancing to avoid racial hatred is likely to prove counterproductive. We address some aspects of the dynamics of isolation, whether self-chosen or imposed, later in the chapter.

Immigration and Acculturation

Acculturative stress is most pronounced during periods of transition, especially during and after significant migrations (to the United States) and the exposure and necessary adjustment to a new culture. Landau (1982) points to a number of factors that either ease the transition or make it more difficult: (1) the reasons for the migration and whether the original expectations and hopes were met, (2) the availability of community and extended family support systems, (3) the structure of the family and whether it was forced to assume a different form after migration (for example, an extended family becoming exclusively nuclear), (4) the degree to which the new culture is similar to the old (the greater the difference, the more substantial the stress), and (5) the family's general ability to be flexible and adaptive. According to Landau, when the stresses are severe, the support insufficient, and the family basically unhealthy, family members are likely to try to compensate in one of three ways, each leading to even more stresses and a compounding of existing problems. The family may isolate itself and remain separate from its new environment. It may become enmeshed and close its boundaries to the outside world, rigidify its traditional ways, and become overly dependent on its members. Or it may become disengaged, with individual members becoming isolated from each other as they reject previous family values and lifestyle. Especially problematic is a situation in which family members acculturate at very different rates.

Perhaps the most common and problematic consequence of acculturation is the breakdown of traditional cultural and family norms. Among Latino/a immigrants, for instance, this may take the form of challenges to traditional beliefs about male authority and supremacy, role expectations for men, and standards of conduct for females. Such changes may not be limited to newer immigrants. Carrillo (1982) suggests that these same changing patterns are evident within the Latino/a community as a whole: "Clearly, Hispanics appear to be moving away from such strict concepts of role and authority within the family, and with this movement approaching new normative behavior for males and females" (p. 260).

Ogbu (1992) addresses difference in levels of acculturation and assimilation based on whether immigration is voluntary or involuntary. Voluntary immigrants, according to Ogbu, "are people who have moved more or less voluntarily to the United States . . . for economic well-being, better overall opportunities, and/or greater political freedom. Their expectations continue to influence the way they perceive and respond to events, including schooling." Involuntary immigrants, on the other hand, "are people who were originally brought into the United States . . . against their will. For example, through slavery, conquest, colonization, or forced labor. . . . It is involuntary minorities that usually experience greater and more persistent difficulties with school learning" (p. 8).

Implications for School Achievement

Ogbu's (1992) research on immigrant populations, drawing on data from the United States and other countries, has done much to identify underlying factors in the poor achievement scores of Children of Color. These studies find that minority children do not fail in school merely because of cultural and language differences or succeed because they have internalized the culture and language of the dominant group. Ogbu gives specific examples from many places around the globe where students do much better after immigrating because they see themselves as "immigrants" in the new settings, rather than as the lower-status oppressed group they were in their homelands.

This body of literature is key to understanding the effect of attitude on achievement. Whether a family or an individual acculturates or assimilates is partially based on how its members view themselves in the culture.

> Voluntary minorities seem to bring to the United States a sense of who they are from their homeland and seem to retain this different but non-oppositional social identity at least during the first generation. Involuntary minorities, in contrast, develop a new sense of social or collective identity that is in opposition to the social identity of the dominant group after they have become subordinated. They do so in response to their treatment by White America in economic, political, social, psychological, cultural, and language domains. (Ogbu, 1992, p. 9)

Assimilation and Acculturation in the Classroom

How do these underlying factors play out in the classroom? What differences arise from assimilation, acculturation, or schooling in a majority minority culture in contrast to schooling as a minority Individual of Color? Several factors come into play in these cross-cultural educational challenges (Ogbu, 1992). Poor achievement scores seemed to be most prevalent where

- Children begin school with different cultural assumptions
- Certain concepts in the core curriculum are foreign to the home culture
- Students are non-English-speaking
- Children's learning styles differ from the predominant teaching style in the classroom

> Voluntary immigrants are likely to view learning English as a necessity and the playing of "the school game" as useful, because they see a pay off later. With this "accommodation without assimilation" attitude, they are able to cross cultural boundaries and do well in school. On the other hand, involuntary minorities view education as "learning the culture and language of White Americans, that is, the learning of the cultural and language frames of reference of their "enemy" or "oppressors." Thus, they may feel that such learning is "detrimental to their social identity, sense of security, and self-worth." (Ogbu, 1992, p. 10)

The acculturated Child of Color, as exemplified by a voluntary immigrant, may be strongly influenced by a collective orientation toward making good grades as well as peer pressure to do so. In some involuntary minority groups, however, there is less pressure to achieve. Less stigma is attached to being a poor student, and there are fewer community pressures toward academic achievement. The peer group may also work against academic striving, especially if academic success is seen as "acting White."

Drawing upon his research with Black students, Ogbu (1992) enumerates the following strategies used by students who have consciously overcome the pressures against achievement.

1. Emulation of White academic behavior or cultural passing (i.e., adopting "White" academic attitudes and behaviors or trying to behave like middle-class, White students). Some students say, "If it takes acting like White people to do well in school, I'll do that." Such students get good grades. The problem is, however, that they usually experience isolation from other Black students, resulting in high psychological costs.

2. Accommodation without assimilation. Students behave . . . according to school norms while at school, but at home . . . behave according to Black norms. . . . Black students who adopt this strategy do not pay the psychological costs that attend the White emulators.

3. Camouflage (i.e., disguising true academic attitudes and behaviors). Students use a variety of techniques: become a jester or class clown . . . claim to lack interest in school . . . study in secret, to obscure their academic efforts.

4. Involvement in church activities. Students find an alternative peer group.

5. Attending private school where there are fewer anti-academic norms.

6. Mentors. Students find adult support for achievement.

7. Protection. Students secure the help of bullies from peer pressure in return for helping bullies with their homework . . .

8. Remedial and intervention programs. Students seek out help in areas of academic need.

9. Encapsulation. Students become encapsulated in peer group logic and activities . . . don't want to do the White man's thing . . . don't do their school work. (p. 11)

While Ogbu's work gives us some understanding of the underlying reasons that many children do poorly in schools, researchers such as Cose (1997) narrow the focus and cite studies that implicate specific factors. One such factor, by way of example, is the impact of negative cultural and personal expectations on educational achievement. In this regard, Cose suggests that

> Black Americans' generations-long passage through a sea of noxious stereotypes ensured that some of those stereotypes would be absorbed, that many blacks would come to believe, as the society insisted, that black brains were somehow deficient. The result is something of a psychological Catch-22. The belief that one is not intellectually inclined can itself be enough to prevent one from becoming academically proficient, which can make it impossible . . . to offer proof that one is not mentally inferior. (p. 65)

Spencer, as reported in a personal communication to Cose (1997), found clear evidence that when Black students were told they were taking a "culture free" test, their performance paralleled that of White students. When they were told nothing about cultural considerations, they did worse. Blood-pressure read-ings of Black students were significantly lower when they were told a test was culture free. Cose attributes this to "not carrying the burden of negative racial expectations" (p. 42). This pattern is substantiated by recent research by Helms (2003) that identifies concerns about race as the variable in the Black–White test-score gap. Steele (1997) refers to this phenomenon as *stereotype threat*, reporting that the threat is even more acute among individuals already perform-ing at a high level in their respective fields.

Similar patterns of achievement have been found in relation to gender (Spencer, Steele, & Quinn, 1997; Steele, 1992). Specifically, Spencer et al. found that women performed at the same level as equally qualified men when the stereotype of male advantage in math was artificially removed. When women were told that particular tests showed no gender differences, none were found. When gender differences were emphasized as reasons for differences in test scores, such differences emerged in test scores. What incredible implications for teachers and educators!

STRESS

How exactly do broad social factors, such as racism, acculturation, poverty, and so forth, get translated into the everyday physical and emotional dis-tresses that disproportionately affect People of Color? According to Myers (1982), the mechanism is stress. Put most simply, lacking resources and being the perpetual object of discrimination make life more stressful and increase the risks of instability and difficulty in school. Myers suggested that "for many blacks, particularly those who are poor, the critical antecedents appear to be the higher basal stress level and the state of high stress vigilance at which nor-mative functioning often occurs" (p. 128). In other words, poor African Americans tend to be in a "stress-primed" state of existence.

Myers showed how certain internal and external factors either increase or decrease (mediate) the subjective experience of stress and, as a result, the risk of stress-related dysfunction. Externally, economic conditions set the stage for whether racial and social-class–related experiences will be sources of greater or lesser stress. Internally, individual temperament, problem-solving skills, sense of internal control, and self-esteem reduce the likelihood that an event or situation is experienced as stressful. With these factors as a baseline, Myers described two additional conditions that seem to mediate the individual's response when a stressful situation is actually presented: the actual episodic stressful event that occurs and the coping and adaptation of which the individual is capable. In rela-tion to the former, Myers contended that episodic crises are more frequent among poor African Americans, and that such crises are more likely to be dam-aging and disruptive because of their higher basal stress levels. "Thus, for exam-ple, the death of a relative, the loss of a job due to economic downturns is likely to be more psychologically and economically devastating to the person who is struggling to find enough money to eat, to pay the rent, and to support three or four children than it would to someone without those basic day to day concerns" (pp. 133–134). Myers identified substantial differences among group members in their ability to cope and in the type of coping strategies used. Street youth, for example, resort to "cappin, rappin, conning, and fighting" as coping mechanisms for survival in the streets. For others, the "ability to remain calm, cool, and collected in the face of a crisis" is primary. Still others may turn negatively to alcohol and drugs or positively to religion and increased personal and social interactions to gain some distance from general stress or crisis events.

Myers believed that stress-related risks are higher for African Americans as a group than for the general population. But he pointed out that there are very real ways to reduce the risk.

> To the extent that ethnic cultural identity can be developed and stably integrated into the personality structure, to the extent that skills and competencies necessary to meet the varied demands can be obtained, to the extent that flexible, contingent response strategies can be developed, and to the extent that support systems can be maintained and strengthened, then resistances can be developed that will enhance stress tolerance and reduce individual and collective risk. (Myers, 1982, p. 138)

Daly, Jennings, Beckett, and Leashore (1995) amplified on Myers's findings by describing specific coping mechanisms that can be introduced into families within organizations such as schools and at the community level.

PROVIDING PSYCHOLOGICAL SUPPORT IN THE CLASSROOM

Previous sections of this chapter have focused on areas of psychological concern that may relate to some Students of Color. These included problems of racial-identity development, conflicts around acculturation, and stress-related reactions. To the extent that such dynamics are true for a given student, personal issues, concerns, and stresses will be brought into the classroom by the child or by concerned parents.

Generally, such reactions interfere with student learning, may lead to behavioral problems, and must in some way be addressed. Two general strategies are suggested. The first is the creation of a classroom environment in which a sense of personal safety abounds and in which specific coping strategies can be taught as part of the curriculum. The second, seeking of counseling services, depends on the availability of resources. In an ideal situation, teachers can seek ongoing consultation from counseling professionals on how to work optimally with a student in the classroom and/or refer the student for external assessment or counseling.

Awareness that students may bring specific psychological problems with them is a first step in creating caring and supportive environments that can lead to successful learning situations for all children. Such a focus increases the desire of teachers to provide a safe place for students. By *safe* we mean an environment in which the feelings of each individual are considered from an attitude of caring and willingness to dialogue across differences (Moule, 1998). Burbules (1993) and Ellsworth (1990) believe that sensible and fair rules of participation are not enough to make a classroom feel *safe* to many students. According to Burbules, "It often will not be enough just to listen; one might have to work to create an environment in which a silenced voice feels the confidence or security to speak" (p. 33).

A number of other learning goals can be introduced into the classroom to help students who are at psychological risk. For some teachers of students for whom risk and vulnerability are everyday experiences, promoting resiliency through classroom activities has become an increasingly important meta-goal. Promoting resiliency involves strengthening personal characteristics that permit better coping in stressful situations.

Myers and King (1985), for example, identify the following factors as critical to resiliency: an ability to not overreact to stress, specific coping and problem-solving skills, a history of success in coping with race-related situations, a perception of being capable of manipulating the world and controlling one's destiny, and a healthy and well-integrated sense of self. To the extent any of these personal characteristics can be addressed, students will benefit by the development of better coping skills. Obviously, such factors do not work in isolation, but rather reinforce each other. Success in coping, for instance, leads to personal empowerment and feelings of competency, which in turn increase the probability of future successes in adapting and coping.

In looking at specific populations, Canino and Zayas (1997) found that Puerto Rican children defined as "invulnerable to risk" tended to exhibit more sociability, dominance, endurance, energy, demonstrativeness, reflectiveness, and impulse control than those who were more at risk. Their research also pointed to the importance of ethnic identification, family values, and adaptation to biculturality as hedges against vulnerability to stress.

Dupree, Spencer, and Bell (1997) suggested the following guidelines for instilling resiliency in African American youth.

> One of the goals of counseling with African American children and youth is to promote coping strategies under unique circumstances. Therefore one should avoid using methods that encourage clients to accept their negative environmental circumstances and adapt to such an environment. Methods providing information that promote the effective use of underutilized resources and resource that are unattainable within their community should be employed. Help seeking strategies and greater social mobility will enable them to survive in their environment. (p. 258)

Another meta-goal is greater comfort and success in dealing with culture conflict and biculturality, both frequent sources of stress for Children of Color.

Pinderhughes (1989) underlined the importance of helping children tolerate competing cultural values and practices by learning to reduce the conflict and confusion inherent to bicultural settings. At times, such conflicts find their way into the classroom. Pinderhughes offered an example of a teacher's conflict with parents over allowing the child to fight. "A mother explained when I was questioning her values about allowing him to fight. 'I'll take care of his behavior; you take care of his education. Where we live he has to be tough and be able to fight. I'm not going to stop that. You set your standards here and I'll see that he understands he has to abide by them'" (p. 182). Pinderhughes suggested teaching the child to negotiate this duality—inconsistencies between home and school are likely to be ongoing realities that the bicultural child must learn to negotiate. Rather than unintentionally creating a conflict, educators must regularly monitor their own value judgments and teaching goals so as not to "undermine the children's ability to tolerate the inconsistency between home and school. What the children needed was a sense that while the values at school were different, those of their parents were not being undermined. The teachers . . . must be able to function as a bridge, respecting the children's cultural values while simultaneously upholding the values of the school" (p. 182).

Similarly, Ogbu (1992) suggested offering Students of Color skill development in overcoming pressures against achievement. He saw real value in teaching students how to cope with the anti-achievement attitudes frequently found in their communities by increasing "students' adoption of the strategy of 'accommodation without assimilation' . . . or 'playing the classroom game.' The essence of this strategy is that students should recognize and accept the fact that they can participate in two cultural or language frames of reference for different purposes without losing their own cultural and language identity or undermining their loyalty to the minority community" (p. 12).

Obgu also emphasized the value of introducing such learning more broadly within the school curriculum, as part of counseling and related programs intended to teach students how to separate attitudes and behaviors that enhance school success from those that lead to acculturation or "acting White." Such interventions may help students avoid interpreting achievement as "acting White" and thereby as a threat to their identity and sense of security.

ISOLATED STUDENTS OF COLOR

Whether through individual choice, job relocation, accident of birth, or adoption, isolation of individuals from their ethnic and racial communities causes particular challenges. As stated earlier and as seen in the following story, they often lack the support of the broader community and have less protection as well as more exposure to conscious and unconscious biases and racism.

An acquaintance told the following story about a simple, though often experienced, aspect of her life as an isolated Person of Color. Anecdotes like this one abound in the literature on race (Cose, 1993; Jones, 2001; Taylor & Whittaker, 2003).

> I had an encounter Wednesday morning. I was running down the main street of our town just as it was getting light. A man approached me going the opposite direction. As he got closer, he moved far to the edge of the sidewalk. Yet, as usual, I gave him the benefit of the doubt. I spoke in a loud, cheery voice, "Good morning." Silence.
>
> At that point my husband pulled up to pick me up. As I got in the car, I told him about the encounter. He said, "Some people are just like that." "Yes," I said, "They are just more like that if you happen to be Black."

This simple event, which highlights not a blatant, identifiable act of racism, but a minor slight that may indeed simply be the result of a bad day by the silent fellow, gives us a glimpse into the very different world inhabited by People of Color who find themselves surrounded primarily by White folks. The story continued.

> I find myself not as friendly as I'd like to be. I find I do not look into cars as much as other people. I do not even want to face the rejection, even if it is one in one hundred. This is a daily fact of life for me. I find my general, easy-to-please self becoming less friendly, and recently, less willing to overlook the often obvious.
>
> My husband noted a similar reluctance my African American acquaintances have in coming to my house in a predominantly White rural setting. They want very clear directions. Their spouses call with much concern to check if "they made it OK."

Taking with us the understanding that such everyday slights and burdens occur along with more blatant racism, let's look at what happens to isolated Students of Color in the schools.

The pull between the culture of the Community of Color and mainstream White culture asserts itself more powerfully on isolated Individuals of Color than on children who reside in a majority minority community. The pressure to assimilate is also greater on isolated individuals without a community to which to attach. Various authors (Delpit, 1990; Tatum, 1992a; Taylor & Whittaker, 2003) have used case studies of isolated Students of Color to highlight their particular problems. Paley (1979), in her classic book *White Teacher*, described the occasional Black students who found their way into her classroom: "One the child of the live-in maid of a prominent family, two others when the school board attempted some minor integration" (p. 7). Encounters with these children caused Paley concern. One avoided looking at her and responded to her questions with only a "Yes'm." Another, Fred, joined an aggressive group of six White children. When the teachers came into Paley's room under various pretenses to, as Paley said, "check out the two black children," they all singled out Fred. "You've got your hands full with him. Shouldn't he be in a special class?" (p. 7).

Paley's story highlights a particular burden for the isolated Child of Color—higher visibility. This higher visibility may lead to increased pressure to assimilate or to an increased tendency to exhibit behavior problems (Ogbu, 1992; Tatum, 1997). Delpit used Paley's work as a good example: "At the first faculty meeting Paley raised the issue that even though all the children in Fred's small group behaved as he did, teachers singled out Fred because of his color. After vigorous discussion, the faculty reached a consensus: 'More than ever we must take care to ignore color. We must only look at behavior, and since a black child will be more prominent in a White classroom, we must bend over backward to see no color, hear no color, speak no color'" (Delpit, 1995, p. 177).

This "color-blind" attitude probably did more harm than good. It allowed the teachers to continue to pretend that race didn't matter in the curriculum, in classroom images, and so on. Yeo (1999, p. 4) pointed out that teachers in communities with only a few isolated Children of Color tend to experience their schools as monoracial. They seem unwilling to acknowledge the existence of current or increasing demographic diversity of their communities. Such reactions cannot help but make Children of Color feel invisible as well as highly visible, certainly a confusing state for young children.

Isolated Children of Color also come under more intense pressure from institutionalized racism. Anderson (1988) was specific about the effects of the system on the children within it.

> In America, as White children leave the home and move on through the educational system and then into the work world, the development of cognitive and learning styles follows a linear, self-reinforcing course. Never are they asked to be bicultural, bidialectic, or bicognitive. On the other hand, for children of Color, biculturality is not a free choice, but a prerequisite for successful participation and eventual success. Non-White children generally are expected to be bicultural, bidialectic, bicognitive; to measure their performance against a Euro-American yardstick; and to maintain the psychic energy to maintain this orientation. At the same time, they are being castigated whenever they attempt to express and validate their indigenous cultural and cognitive styles. Under such conditions cognitive conflict becomes the norm rather than the exception. (p. 5)

We see these dynamics acted out in the experiences of Chris and Nicole.

Chris

At home, the "mom unit" as Chris affectionately calls his mother, has brought the detailed eye of her training as an engineer to matters of child rearing and homemaking. She surrounds her biracial children with sights and sounds of their African heritage and promotes citywide events for families with children similar in color to her children. The family's frequent vacations are varied and reflect the family's high income. Chris is a typical isolated Child of Color within a community from which individuals from underrepresented groups are heavily recruited by private companies and the university. While his socioeconomic status, home life, and parental expectations will be advantageous in his education, only time will tell how Chris's experience as an isolated Student of Color will affect his life.

The public school Chris attends is one percent African American. An African American intern teacher observed several race-related problems, although the teachers he interviewed said that there were none. Perhaps the European American teachers hadn't noticed when one boy asked another to pick up a dropped ball. "What color do you think I am?" was the disdainful response. Or perhaps only the African American intern or a student whose color had been the oblique object of the reference would even have caught the racial slur in the offensive response.

What does Chris experience? Does the lens of his racial heritage reveal incidents that his European American teachers, perhaps quite innocently, miss? Is race ignored or, worse, is he asked to be a token who guides the teacher through rituals such as Martin Luther King, Jr., Day? Does he encounter the teacher who planned to avoid racial offenses by sidestepping any mention of racial differences? Does his presence embarrass a well-meaning teacher who pretends not to hear direct student questions about racial or cultural issues? Whatever his experience, he almost certainly is learning to see the world through a double lens. He is learning to view events and interactions through the eyes of the dominant culture he is a part of, and he also learning to view the world through the eyes of an African American, partially because others see him as different. With support from his parents, he is coming to see his multiple perspective as the positive benefit that it is. Without this support and understanding, he would be unlikely to reach his full potential as an individual and a citizen (Moule, 1998, p. 4–6).

Nicole

Next we meet Nicole, an isolated Student of Color in a school district that is 89 percent White, as seen by a student teacher.

> A girl in my class . . . is the only Person of Color in our entire class and . . . she has a challenge other students don't. [She] looks for books with Black protagonists and she reads those . . . not as many as [with] White protagonists. One of the things we talked about [was] rules for the class. [We] brainstormed . . . she threw out 'Don't call Black people Indians.' People at her table group laughed at the time. So I approached them and asked her to repeat it. We decided that 'Treat other people with respect' incorporates it. She is swimming up stream. A question I've had, what am I going to do as a teacher in school . . . potentially mostly White students with a few Students of Color? What am I going to do to prepare kids to live in [this state] and be a positive influence . . . with numbers becoming more diverse?

Nicole is a proud and capable artist and writer, and it is in these areas that she usually shines in the classroom—when she reads aloud or when she shows her artwork. Generally she is shy. She does not bring up racial issues in her writing, and I haven't seen her color the people she has drawn to indicate any skin color. Her mother is Black and her father is White, and she doesn't mention that in any discussions about her parents. Because of her own hesitancy to talk about race or racial issues, I have always talked generally about multicultural issues or topics, taking care not to spotlight her. I think it would make her extremely uncomfortable. . . . I believe that we haven't done any damage this year to Nicole or the other students by just talking in generalities.

In this same classroom the children were rehearsing an African dance for the school awards ceremony. The mentor teacher directed a question to Nicole, asking her if she knew the tribe or culture in Africa that the dance came from. Nicole did not answer. There was no apparent reason why Nicole would know the culture in Africa the dance came from, except for the teacher's assumption that her brown skin gave her this specialized knowledge. Shortly after the silently unanswered question, the mentor teacher suggested that they practice the song and dance. Nicole did not join in. In the busy life of the classroom, only an observer watching one particular child was aware of a very subtle, yet seemingly disturbing event for an isolated Child of Color.

(From *My Journey with Preservice Teachers: Reflecting on Teacher Characteristics That Bridge Multicultural Education Theory and Classroom Practice* by Jean Moule, 1998, pp. 148–149. Reprinted by permission.)

The White student teacher learned some very important lessons from being in the classroom with Nicole. First, he learned how little he knew about the lives and experiences of Children of Color, especially those who are isolated in predominantly White communities. Second, he learned the value of active observation, especially when it comes to matters of race. For instance, he recognized the student's hesitancy to discuss race. In time he came to see the importance of making time for the discussion of race relations in the classroom, and how such discussion works against the unstated taboo that exists in most school environments. Third, he learned the importance of self-reflection and the need to look at his own feelings and experiences in relation to what was happening to Nicole.

Finally, and perhaps most importantly, this student teacher allowed himself to remain open to the humanity of one small Child of Color. We see this particularly in relation to the teacher's question about African dances. bell hooks (1994) refers to what happened to Nicole as becoming a native informant, writing that "one lone person of color in the classroom . . . is objectified by others and forced to assume the role of 'native informant'" (p. 43). The student teacher learned that, instead of forcing Nicole to be a native informant, the teacher may have more appropriately asked, "Does anyone know which people in Africa created this dance?" If Nicole or anyone else knew the answer, he or she could then have volunteered it. When teachers take the time to observe individuals and apply simple strategies, the classroom becomes a more supportive learning environment for all children.

Isolated Teachers of Color

Levon, an African American preservice teacher, provides a somewhat different perspective on the struggles of isolated individuals (Moule, 1998). Levon's interaction with other members of his preservice teacher cohort showed him open to others' views, well-versed in several cultures, and acutely aware of the interactional problems that could arise during his journey toward licensure.

On the first day of the multicultural issues in education course, Levon wondered how honest and authentic the interaction would be and whether his own racial experiences and issues would "be lost in the quest for diversity among other religions, genders, groups. Hopefully, people will say what's on their minds . . . politically correct language allows Americans to hide their racist beliefs . . . we can never solve any racial problems because people are always denying that racism exists in today's society. . . . Sometimes people's reluctance to change makes me want to holler." He spoke of his potential value as a Black man entering the teaching profession. "Considering the social, economic, and political situation of black men in America, I can bring a perspective to education that could prove quite beneficial in classroom practices. . . . Studies have shown that . . . black males in particular . . . psychologically drop out as early as third grade. . . . The idea and reality of black men in the classroom can serve as a catalyst for students who are otherwise 'checking out' of school" (Moule, 1998, p. 113).

While Levon sees the value of his presence and role modeling for the Students of Color he will teach, he is acutely aware of the more difficult journey he travels to become a teacher.

> Being the only African American in the . . . Cohort is a particular experience. . . . Sometimes I wonder how I managed to slip through the barriers (institutionalized racism) that impede the progress of my people. Being the only "one" means that I'm carrying all 22 million [African Americans] on my back . . . . I find it very strange that my graduate program takes pride in their diversity achievements. They need to realize that having one person of color in the program doesn't equate to true cultural diversity. (Moule, 1998, p. 114)

Along with his reflections on his future value to students and his own struggles, Levon clearly sees his value in the education of his White classmates through their interaction with him. "Some of the students found it very difficult to compromise their Eurocentric values. . . . As future educators, if we cannot honor another cultural perspective then we must reevaluate our decision to become educators . . . . Once you comprehend another person's life experiences, then you can have a meaningful conversation with them" (Moule, 1998, p. 115).

Through his experiences, Levon developed a new appreciation for the power of multicultural education, and through his observations we are able to get a first-person sense of the experience of an isolated Person of Color struggling with the mistrust and the racial attitudes of Whites. Fortunately, the outcome was positive and motivating for Levon and his White classmates, all preservice teachers.

INTERACTING WITH PARENTS OF COLOR

Whether Parents of Color are unique in their situation as isolated individuals or part of a larger Community of Color, interactions with teachers not like themselves will be a fact of life in all but a few of this nation's school districts (Delpit, 1995; Garcia, 2001).

Fox (1993), in *Opening Closed Doors,* carefully examined obstacles to trust and open communication between African American parents and White teachers. For the parents, contact with the teachers highlighted their own issues of internalized oppression and "the need to prove." For teachers, prejudice—real or perceived—and their own use of personal power emerged as issues.

Issues that emerged as problems in interaction included differing views of institutional racism, differing levels of trust and mistrust, and conflict in communication styles. Fox showed how each group viewed the other in ways that made sense only from a single perspective, and how such ethnocentrism kept them from "open communication, constructive conflict, a genuine expression of feelings, learning to act with each other in meaningful ways, and reexamining a learned fear of difference" (p. iv). She emphasized, above all, the need to develop trust. She pointed to interaction styles as the main cause of miscommunication, relying on Kochman's (1981) belief that "Whites invariably interpret black anger and verbal aggressions as more provocative and threatening than do blacks . . . . The problems occur most when White people and African American people assume that the meaning they are assigning to these behaviors are the same, and therefore the motives ascribed are also justified." Consider the role this plays in increasing the gap between parents and teachers, particularly when this "interpretation of behaviors between White people and African Americans and the covert role that it plays in the communication process is a discussion that rarely takes place" (p. 158).

A Parent–Teacher Scenario

As an example of these differences in perspective, we end this chapter with a somewhat humorous hypothetical look at a parent–teacher interaction. In this scenario, we not only read what each individual says to the other, but get a glimpse into their thoughts as well. The dialogue was created by students in a multicultural issues course (Diaz-Ramos, Null, Pentland, & Roush, 1996). In it the parent of an isolated Student of Color talks with his teacher.

The scene: Mrs. Pentland, a third-grade teacher in a public elementary school, is about to have a conference with the parent of a Korean student, Jisoo. This dramatization invites the audience to be "flies on the wall" where they will be able to hear not only the spoken words, but also the thoughts of Mrs. Kim and Mrs. Pentland.

P'S MIND: *Okay, now I've done my homework, I know the general Korean etiquette and this will go very smoothly. Oh, please don't let me treat Mrs. Kim as a stereotype—remember that Jisoo is a unique boy. I'm so glad I memorized how to say hello. Hope I say this right!*

MRS. P: *Anyung Ha So Yo!*

K'S MIND: *Did she say "porcupine?"*

MRS. K: *(smiles and nods)*

MRS. P: *Well, it is certainly a pleasure to have Jisoo in class! Do you have any questions I can answer?*

MRS K: *(after a pause) Yes. How old are you?*

P'S MIND: *Why is she asking this?*

MRS. P: *Um . . . 45.*

K'S MIND: *Ah—she is older than me. She deserves even more respect than just for being Jisoo's teacher.*

(silence)

MRS. P: *Oh, I see you've brought Jisoo's performance report! As you can see from the marks, Jisoo is doing very well. His developmental abilities are quite adequate in most areas, reflecting his stage of growth. He's still a concrete thinker, so he needs manipulatives.*

K'S MIND: *I have no clue what she's talking about!*

MRS. K: *(smiles and nods)*

P'S MIND: *Oh rats—quick, Beth, drop the jargon!*

MRS. P: *What I mean is that Jisoo is doing very well for his age. He has excellent attention, strong cooperative abilities, and his academics are improving rapidly.*

K'S MIND: *Jisoo brings honor to our whole family. I must write a letter to the grandparents; they will be so proud.*

MRS. K: *(smiles and nods, but more genuinely)*

MRS. P: *I'd like to review some of Jisoo's work with you. I'm so impressed by the improvement of his writing. I do wish he'd put more detail into his stories—they're such fun to read, I'd like to see him expand on his ideas.*

MRS. K: *(no nod—apprehensive face)*

K'S MIND: *No, the honor of our family and community depends on Jisoo's performance. If he is not working hard now how can he be successful later?*

MRS. P: *Please, Mrs. Kim, don't worry. I shouldn't have mentioned it. The detail of his writing will come naturally as his English continues to improve. It's really not important now. It will come.*

K'S MIND: *What does this mean, "It will come"? It will not come unless he works hard. He must work harder. Maybe it's because we speak Korean at home. If we spoke more English he'd be more fluent by now. Maybe it's because my English is not so good. We must make sure Jisoo learns better English.*

(silence)

P'S MIND: *This isn't going well. And there's way too much silence. Let's switch topics. How about . . . (think, think). . . social, yes, he gets along well with other kids!*

MRS. P: *You know, Jisoo gets along so well with the other kids! In fact, just the other day they were playing a game of soccer when an older student took the ball, and Jisoo was very upset. At first he was yelling at the boy, but then he calmed down and gained control and spoke up for himself and his friend. He was the hero who got the ball back. The children all look at Jisoo as a leader.*

MRS. K: *(shocked face)*

K'S MIND: *AAAaaccckkk! What is he learning here? No more TV, no more Power Rangers! Jisoo knows not to let his emotions show. He should not have yelled. How could he let this happen? He needs to blend in—not stand out. He shouldn't be drawing attention to himself.*

MRS. K: *I apologize for Jisoo causing a disturbance.*

MRS. P: *No, Jisoo didn't cause a disturbance. He is a natural leader, his handling of the situation was a great model for others. . . .*

P'S MIND: *Don't forget to ask her to come into the class!*

MRS. P: *I just had a thought—I'd love for you to come in and help with the class. Could you give us a presentation on Korean cooking?*

K'S MIND: *What?? Talk to the whole class? My English is not good enough. Jisoo would be so embarrassed—he is even embarrassed when I talk just to his friends.*

MRS. K: *(hesitantly—no smile) Yes.*

P'S MIND: *Uh oh. She doesn't really want to do that—what else?*

MRS. P: *Or, better yet, how about helping with our spelling lessons?*

K'S MIND: *What?? English spelling? That's even worse than speaking. Doesn't she realize I'm still struggling with this crazy language?*

MRS. K: *(still hesitantly) Yes.*

P'S MIND: *Uh oh . . .—Try painting!*

MRS. P: *No, wait, I have a better idea. How about painting? Jisoo mentioned that you like to paint. Perhaps you'd like to help me with the class next week?*

K'S MIND: *Finally, that sounds like something I will enjoy.*

MRS. K: *(relieved) Yes!*

P'S MIND: *Whew!*

MRS. P: *That will be great! Thank you so much for coming in, Mrs. Kim. I really am enjoying Jisoo this year.*
BOTH MINDS TOGETHER: *I wish we'd had an interpreter!*

(From *Parent–Teacher Scenario* by S. Diaz-Ramos, K. Null, B. Pentland, and M. L. Roush, 1996. This scenario, completed as a class project, is used with permission.)

REFLECTION QUESTIONS AND CREATIVE PROBLEM SOLVING

This chapter lists some practical solutions to the problems we have been identifying. Using creative problem solving (Parnes, 1967), list specific solutions from this chapter. For instance, for "IWWMW relate to parents," tease some solutions from the dialogue you just read. Then read over some of the solutions listed by Ogbu and others. Ask yourself: What specifics might I address in the classrooms I have seen or will work in?

> Identify a "mess."
> List a few facts from the chapter.
> Complete the statement, "In what ways might we _____."
> Brainstorm to answer your IWWMW statement.
> Apply criteria (revisit the end of Chapter 4 for the criteria list).
> Plan to implement your idea.

SUMMARY

This chapter focuses on psychological and emotional issues that plague People of Color and have particular relevance for the classroom. In various ways, racism and its many attendant consequences put People of Color at risk for psychological and educational difficulties.

Ethnic identity refers to an individual's subjective experience of ethnicity and reflects the nature of the attachment to the ethnic group. Ethnic-identity formation results from the integration of various personal experiences as the member of an ethnic group. Ethnic identity can be defined as positive, negative, or ambivalent. Positive identification represents a generally successful integration of ethnic experience into a coherent and positive sense of ethnic self. In negative identification, aspects of the ethnic self are actively rejected or disowned, and individuals tend to deny, avoid, or escape group membership in a variety of ways. They can avoid contact with the community and community members, alter personal characteristics, and adopt majority ways, including negative attitudes and stereotypes about their own group. In ambivalent identification, rejecting tendencies exist concurrently with positive feelings about the group. There is typically a vacillation between loving and hating who one is: moving toward it if one grows too distant, away from it if one becomes too close. Tatum (1997) offers excellent examples in *Why Are All the Black Kids Sitting Together in the Cafeteria?*

A related approach is offered by researchers in the development of models of racial-identity development. These models assume that there are similarities in the manner in which all ethnic individuals respond to the experience of racism. They also assume that People of Color go through predictable stages as they struggle to make sense out of the relationship to their own cultural group as well as the oppression of mainstream culture. Cross (1995) offered a typical model composed of five stages: reencounter, encounter, immersion–emersion, internalization, and internalization–commitment. The value of these models for teachers is that they highlight the importance of cultural identity in understanding the life experience of Children of Color and show how individuals at different stages of racial-identity development exhibit different needs and values and may feel differently about what is supportive in the learning situation. An easy-to-recall version of the model was offered by Moule (2003c).

Ethnic-group members differ widely in the extent of their assimilation and acculturation into mainstream White society. It is especially important to be aware of acculturation in order to assess traditional attitudes, values, and behaviors of a student or family. Acculturation can also create emotional strain and difficulties for students and their families. Such reactions have been called acculturative stress. There is some disagreement about whether acculturation is unidimensional—that is, where acculturation implies the giving up of traditional ways—or multidimensional—where one can be simultaneously attached to both groups and integrate aspects of both into the self. Marin (1992) suggested that the impact of acculturation can best be measured by discovering the kinds of material gained or lost.

Acculturative stress is most pronounced during periods of immigration. Ogbu (1992) found that voluntary immigrant groups have more success adapting to American culture than do involuntary immigrants, who tend to exhibit greater difficulties identifying with majority culture and succeeding in its institutions, which includes school achievement. Also implicated are negative cultural and personal expectations. For example, stereotypes of minority individuals often include beliefs about poor school performance that become self-fulfilling prophecies.

People of Color are at particularly high risk for physical and mental health problems. According to Myers (1982), stress is the internal mechanism that mediates between social factors such as racism and poverty and health and mental health problems. Poor African Americans tend to live a stress-primed existence. Also relevant are coping ability, basal stress levels, self-esteem, internal sense of control, and support systems.

Students of Color often bring into the classroom psychological and emotional issues related to racial-identity development, conflicts around acculturation, and stress-related reactions. Such reactions interfere with student learning, may lead to behavioral problems, and must be addressed. Two strategies are suggested: creating within the classroom a safe environment in which specific coping strategies can be taught, and finding outside consultation and counseling services. Other learning goals for the classroom can include an attitude of caring and willingness to dialogue across differences, resiliency, greater comfort and success in dealing with culture conflict and biculturality, and overcoming pressures against school achievement.

Isolated Students and Children of Color tend to be more torn between minority and majority cultures than do those residing in majority minority communities. They also experience greater pressures to assimilate, face more stereotyping, are more visible, are prone to exhibit behavioral problems, and are more vulnerable to institutional racism. Several case studies of isolated Individuals of Color are presented.

Finally, suggestions about interacting with Parents of Color are presented, along with a hypothetical interaction between a White teacher and a Korean mother.

CHAPTER 8

BIAS IN THE CURRICULUM AND IN THE CLASSROOM

There is not one Indian in the whole of this country who does not cringe in anguish and frustration because of these textbooks. There is not one Indian child who has not come home in shame and tears.

—Ruper Costo

(Adapted from *Quo No More* by Arline Ely. Copyright 2001 by Arline Ely. Reprinted by permission.)

Consider the following two stories. A four-year-old African American child ran past one of the authors in a brightly muraled hall of an inner-city elementary school. "Should you be running like that?" asked the author in her usual teacher voice and style. He kept going, paying no attention to her question. Having taught this age group before, she was familiar with such disregard, which conjured up past visions of small crossed arms and stubborn attitudes. His seven-year-old brother appeared on the scene. "Stop running," he said, and the boy immediately did.

Ely (2001) calls the second story "The Felon and the Fidget."

The school was a tiny, little K–12 building to which a judge assigned the 19-year-old boy who had been convicted of armed robbery. The class was one that I had created to assist students who had never passed a math course before. He qualified. With respect to my class, the felon came and went as inconspicuously as possible.

Determined to help all of the students succeed for the first time, I buried myself in creating lessons which would interest the students. Each week, the class pretended to "be" a different type of worker and performed math from that worker's job. The math had application.

One day the activity required a bit of a longer explanation than usual. The "fidgets" commenced around the fifth minute. I addressed one boisterous "fidget" and asked him to "sit still" and to "settle down." Keeping with his past behavior, the "fidget" continued to disrupt the instruction.

Now, the felon had been sitting quietly, as he always did. He was becoming more and more annoyed. A single electric fright bolted through me as he turned toward the "fidget." You could see the same single electric bolt strike the "fidget" as he became conscious of the reversed orientation of the humongous classmate in front of him. The felon and the "fidget" made eye contact.

In a quiet, deliberate, slow, firm tone, the felon leaned toward him and said, "The lady said, 'Sit down, and settle down.'"

The "fidget" was a cartoon caricature with larger-than-life "bugged-out" eyes and "strobe-light" skin that flashed comic strip colors. The "fidget" sat upright—possibly for the first time in his academic career! He folded his hands and fixed his eyes on me. The rest of the class breathed for the first time since the felon had turned around. I exhaled, too, and continued with the lesson.

The felon never said another word, outside of answering my questions. The "fidget" remained in that position, hands folded, feet flat on the floor, for the remainder of the school year!

Both the "fidget" and the felon passed the course. (pp. 83–84)

(Adapted from: *Quo No More,* by Arline Ely. Copyright 2001 by Arline Ely. Reprinted by permission.)

What happened in these two situations? In a paper entitled "No More Mister Nice Guy," Higgins and Moule (2002) offer advice to preservice teachers about classroom management with African American elementary students. They describe a dynamic common to inner-city schools and the interaction between White teachers and African American students that they call the "pseudo-questioning strategy of discipline" or "command versus caring." In the first example, the four-year-old processed the author's question not as a command or expectation, but as a question, leaving him free to continue his behavior. In this case, his actions said, "Yes, I should be running." The author assumed that the student's locus of internal control would say, "No, I shouldn't be running," somehow understanding the subtlety of the question. The youngster's brother, a caregiver, was aware of the need for a direct command and used the authoritative voice for safe and appropriate school behavior to simply tell him to stop. Consider a classroom teacher's statement, "Is this a good time to read your book?" This is not really a question, but a statement to put the book away. Yet from the student's viewpoint, it does not have the qualities of caring and command and is easily misinterpreted as a question to be answered freely, rather than as a behavioral directive.

Moule (2003a) found that preservice teachers with prior instruction were able to master a more directive disciplinary style. According to one teacher, "It worked. I was having trouble keeping a young student on task. I remembered what you said and told her quite sternly to 'put away those other materials and get to work.' She did and seemed, if anything, more friendly towards me. It was as if she did see my strictness as caring."

The point is that conflicting cultural norms, such as "question versus telling with care," often underlie the overt tension that can be found in multicultural classrooms. The storytelling and classroom language of a Student of Color may seem oppositional to a teacher who has unquestioned assumptions, adding to the cultural divide. Deeper understanding of cultural differences is the key to developing competence in working cross-culturally. How do we develop this deeper understanding? How many cultural norms are so imbedded that we don't even see them? As in McIntosh's (1989) well-read work on White privilege, the norms are, indeed, "invisible."

The experience in the hall and Ely's felon and fidget are not atypical. In a variety of ways, educators have repeatedly introduced bias and culturally insensitive understanding and curriculum choices into their teaching. By not examining their assumptions about teaching and classroom management, they do not work effectively with culturally different students. Many ethnic children, particularly by middle school, have already chosen to avoid school culture and teachers' misguided expectations altogether. The result has been a systematic lowering of achievement and educational attainment for many Students of Color (Garcia, 2001; Haycock, 2001; Noordhoff & Kleinfeld, 1993; Tatum, 1997).

This chapter delves into the sources of bias in cross-cultural teaching. It begins by looking at ways attitudes can shape expectations. We see how these attitudes are inadvertently supported through bias in testing. It will become clear how certain teacher attitudes and expectations are the natural out-growth of who teachers are and what skills and preparations they bring to the cross-cultural classroom. Next, we discover that many efforts at curriculum reform have remained superficial and may in fact do more harm than good. Finally, we focus on how to more effectively reform curriculum vis à vis cul-ture and ethnicity. As an aid, we provide an in-depth example of literature bias as well as ways to critically examine reading material.

What does a culturally competent classroom look like? What are the images on the walls, the books on the shelf, the materials prepared for use? How much input has come from the students? Has racism or stereotyping played a role in how teachers relate to students? Have teachers simply added materials for cultural relevancy, or have they examined deep cultural roots and adjusted the curriculum accordingly? These questions are addressed in this chapter.

THE IMPACT OF SOCIAL AND RACIAL ATTITUDES

A vast body of research in social psychology shows how attitudes can uncon-sciously affect behavior. Rosenthal and Jacobson (1968), for example, looked at the relationship between teacher expectations and student performance. Teachers were told at the beginning of the school year that half the students in their class were high performers and the other half were low performers. In actuality, there were no differences between the students. By the end of the year, however, there were significant differences in how the two groups performed. Those who were expected to do well did so, and vice versa.

In another experiment, Rosenthal (1976) assigned rats to beginning psy-chology students. Some were told that their rats came from very bright strains; others were told that their rats were genetically low in intelligence. The rats were all from the same litter. By the end of the training period, each group of rats was performing as expected. In these two experiments, what the teachers and the psychology students believed and expected was translated into differential behavior, which in turn became what Rosenthal called a "self-fulfilling prophesy." In other words, what we believe (our attitudes about people) shapes the way we treat students.

Most teachers begin with their own cultural perspectives and their own unexamined classroom experiences. They fondly remember their years as students and often unconsciously reproduce those classrooms. Unfortunately, as Sleeter (2001) pointed out, such models are more often than not culturally White and middle class. Sleeter analyzed eighty empirically based research studies on preservice teacher preparation. Included were studies of the recruitment and selection of preservice teachers as well as the effects of coursework, field practicum, and program restructuring. While these studies clearly demonstrated the existence of ethnocentric attitudes and a general lack of cultural knowledge on the part of White preservice teachers and high-lighted a few promising practices, very few actually followed preservice teachers into the classroom or tried to determine optimal strategies for creating culturally competent teachers. The bottom line is that we still do not know how to populate the teaching profession with excellent, culturally responsive educators.

Classrooms based on unexamined experiences will inevitably miss the needs of many culturally diverse students. Several Web sites have been developed to help people examine their racial and cultural attitudes. Similar in intent to the self-assessment exercises at the end of Chapter 3, they offer a quick, hands-on opportunity to assess the attitudes and beliefs you will be bringing into the classroom. We suggest a site developed by psychologists from Yale University and the University of Washington for the Southern Poverty Law Center. Located at http://www.tolerance.org/hidden_bias/index.htm, it includes a number of implicit association tests, each taking only five minutes, that together provide a broad picture of an individual's racial and cultural biases. The following introduction appears on the Web site.

> What is an implicit association? Sometimes called "unconscious" or "automatic," an implicit association is a mental response that is so well learned as to operate without awareness, or without intention, or without control. . . . Equality is a birthright in the United States, protected by the Constitution. . . . Yet, not a day passes without reports of unequal treatment of individuals. This discrimination is based on negative stereotypes and prejudice that, according to social psychologists, linger in most of us. Even if we believe in our hearts that we see and treat people as equals, hidden biases may nevertheless influence our actions. A new suite of psychological tests measures unconscious bias. We invite you to take these tests online and reveal to yourself what may be hidden in your psyche.

We encourage you to take the full range of tests and read the various interpretations of your scores. Together, they should provide useful information about your own built-in biases.

CULTURAL ASPECTS OF CURRICULUM DELIVERY

Some aspects of the teaching process limit its relevance to Students of Color. Many of these relate to the fact that current pedagogies and practices are often defined in terms of dominant Northern European cultural values and norms and, therefore, limit the ability of teachers to adequately address and serve the needs of non-White populations. Chapter 4 included a description of four characteristics that infuse the teaching process as it is currently constituted and directly conflict with the worldview of Communities of Color. Here, we explore additional sources of this cultural mismatch as well as describe ways in which current pedagogy often portrays Students of Color in a negative light: highlighting their "weaknesses" and assuming a lack of ability. The incident of the supposedly out-of-control African American four-year-old is an excellent example. From the perspective of mainstream norms, his lack of response to a veiled request appeared to be willful disobedience.

Heath (1983), an educational anthropologist, provided an example of how parents socialize children into different cultures. In a Black working-class neighborhood, children were taught to tell rich, creative, embellished stories with many gestures; in a White working-class community, the emphasis was on stories that were as accurate as possible, with easy-to-discern "correct" answers. Each group was, in a sense, trapped by its own norms. Teachers tend to value students who tell stories the same way they do, and they negatively judge students whose styles are different as "not up to my standard" because of, for example, creativity over accuracy or succinctness over many gestures. Because the styles do not match, the teachers may begin to form conscious or unconscious opinions about the academic ability of the young storytellers (Anderson, 1988; Asante, 1991; Kochman, 1981).

Finders (1992) struggled with voices from her past that echoed a seldom-recognized standard. Yet she saw the need to untangle her taken-for-granted assumptions from her teaching. The deeply held beliefs did not need to change; they simply needed to be recognized for what they were: taken-for-granted assumptions about the world that may not apply to everyone. Recognizing the boxes that keep us in our own worlds, so that we can understand and sometimes transcend them, is the root of cultural competence. If a norm is never questioned—and many are not—then that standard is inadvertently applied, with great harm, to children with different cultural norms.

A *script* is a set of expectations about what will happen next in a well-understood situation. In many life situations, participants seem to be reading their roles. Scripts lay out what is supposed to happen and how others' actions are to be interpreted and responded to. Schank (1990) argued that seeking out additional cultural experiences and becoming familiar with various interaction styles enable people to "feel comfortable and capable of playing [any] role effectively" (p. 8). In a very practical workbook, *Preparing for Student Teaching in a Pluralistic Classroom*, Blair and Jones (1998), basing their approach on research by Michaels (1981), showed how teacher–student interaction styles can severely hamper the learning process for a child whose cultural discourse style differs greatly from that of the teacher.

Bias in Conceptualizing Ethnic Populations

Western science has a long history of portraying ethnic populations as biologically inferior. Beginning with the work of such luminaries as Charles Darwin, Sir Francis Galton, and G. Stanley Hall, one can trace what Sue and Sue (1990) called the "genetic deficiency model" of racial minorities into the present, carried on by research psychologists such as Jensen (1972). As biological theories of genetic inferiority lost intellectual credibility, they were quickly replaced within social science circles by notions of cultural inferiority or "deficit." While political correctness would not allow educators with negative racial attitudes to continue to embrace the idea of genetic inferiority, they could easily support theories "that a community subject to poverty and oppression is a disorganized community, and this disorganization expresses itself in various forms of psychological deficit ranging from intellectual performance . . . to personality functioning" (Jones & Korchin, 1982, p. 19). These new models took two forms: cultural deprivation and cultural disadvantage. In relation to the former, non-Whites were seen as deprived (lacking substantive culture). *Disadvantaged*, on the other hand, a supposed improvement over the term *deprived*, implies that, although ethnic-group members do possess culture, that culture had become deficient and distorted from the ravages of racism.

More recent and acceptable terms are *culturally different* and *culturally distinct*. But as Atkinson, Morten, and Sue (1993) pointed out, even these can "carry negative connotations when they are used to imply that a person's culture is at variance (out-of-step) with the dominant (accepted) culture" (p. 9).

Research on ethnic populations has also tended to find and focus on deficits and shortcomings. E. E. Jones and Korchin (1982) stated that this body of research has been widely criticized for faulty methodology: "Studies typically involved the comparison of ethnic and white groups on measures standardized on white, middle-class samples, administered by examiners of like background, intended to assess variables conceptualized on the basic U.S. population" (p. 19).

Two additional tendencies have been even more insidious. First, researchers have chosen to study and compare Whites and People of Color on characteristics that culturally favor dominant-group members. Thus, intelligence is assessed by measuring verbal reasoning; and schoolchildren are compared on their ability to compete or take personal initiative. In other words, research variables portray White subjects in a more favorable light and simultaneously create a negative impression of the abilities and resources of ethnic subjects.

Second, where differences have been found between Whites and People of Color, they tend to be interpreted as reflecting weaknesses in ethnic culture or character. Looking at such studies, various researchers have asked why alternative interpretations stressing the creative adaptiveness or strengths inherent in ethnic personality or culture might not just as easily have been sought. Hampden-Turner (1974), for example, wrote the following about the Moynihan Report, which attributed various African American social problems to deterioration of the Black family and has been soundly criticized both for blaming the victim and for pathologizing to the exclusion of other possible explanations: "If we regard the social oppression of blacks by whites as a total dynamic, why is the black end of this dynamic more pathological than the white end . . .? And how does one distinguish a 'pathology' from an 'heroic adaptation to overwhelming pressures'?" (p. 83). Inherent in Hampden-Turner's critique is a most important point; negative portrayals and stereotypes of People of Color serve to justify the status quo of oppression and unfair treatment and thus serve political as well as psychological purposes.

An interesting and provocative example was offered by Tong (1981) about the representation of Chinese Americans as the model minority—that is, "passive, ingratiating, reticent, non-complaining and self-denying" (p. 3). According to Tong, these characteristics were more a survival reaction to American racism than a true reflection of traditional Chinese traits. He suggested that traditional culture includes a "heroic tradition" that portrays the Chinese in a very different manner: "Coexistent with the Conventional Tradition was the 'heroic,' which exalted a time-honored Cantonese sense of self: the fierce, arrogant, independent individual beholden to no one and loyal only to those deemed worthy of undying respect, on that individual's terms" (Tong, 1981, p. 15). According to Tong, perpetuating the myth of the model minority has led to the confusion of psychopathology and culture.

> Timid and docile behavior *is* indicative of emotional disorder. If Chinese Americans seem to be that way by virtue of cultural "background," it is the case *only* to the extent that white racism, in combination with our heritage of Confusion [sic] repression, made it so. The early Chinamans [sic] *consistently* shaped themselves and justified their acts according to the fundamental vision of the

Heroic Tradition. Their stupendous feats of daring and courage, however, remain buried beneath a gargantuan mound of white movies, popular fiction, newspaper cartoons, dissertations, political tracts, religious meeting minutes, and now psychological studies that teach us to look upon ourselves as perpetual aliens living only for white acceptance. (p. 20)

The traits that allowed Asian students to conform to and assimilate into White culture, however superficially, have led to classroom success to the extent that college admissions for Asian students exceed their representation in the overall population. In this case, bias in conceptualizing People of Color seems to work in favor of a group, but at what cost?

BIAS IN ASSESSMENT

Data from the National Assessment of Educational Progress (NAEP) conducted by the National Center for Education Statistics (1997) show trends in achievement across racial groups. In reading skills, for example, the average score for White students in fourth grade for the year 2000 was 224, for Asian/Pacific Islanders 227, for Hispanic students 198, and for Black students 191. From 1992 to 2000, the scores of all groups were relatively the same, with the exception of an increase among Asian/Pacific Islanders. Such data, however, represent only a narrow understanding of achievement, since they highlight one subject at one grade level in one year. They tell us little about whether student scores fall into a proficiency level. According to Taylor and Whittaker (2003), proficiency levels for the reading test used by the NAEP show that all groups need improvement in reading. The weaknesses in our assessment methods are obvious.

Assessment across ethnic groups has suffered from additional problems. Racism and oppression may lead to groupwide deficits in performance on tests that have nothing to do with native ability. A test may measure different characteristics when administered to members of different cultural groups. Culturally unfair criteria, such as level of education or grade point average, may be used to validate tests expected to predict differences between Whites and People of Color. Differences in experience in taking tests may put non-White students at a disadvantage in testing situations. In short, it is difficult to ensure fairness in testing across cultures, and educators should exert real care in drawing conclusions based exclusively on test scores. They should, as a matter of validation, collect as much nontest collaborative data as possible, especially when the outcome of the assessment may have real-life consequences for the student.

In no other area of education has there been more concern about cultural bias than in testing. This is because People of Color have for many years watched their children being placed in remedial classrooms or tracked as having special needs on the basis of IQ tests. Serious life decisions are regularly made on the basis of these tests, and it is reasonable to expect them to be culture free—that is, scored based on what is being measured and not differentially affected by the cultural background of the test taker. In reality, there probably is no such thing as a culture free test, and it has been suggested, and supported by some research, that ethnic group members' abilities tend to be underestimated by intelligence tests (Snowden & Todman, 1982; Suzuki & Kugler, 1995).

Reynolds and Kaiser (1990) listed a number of factors that can contribute to cultural bias in testing. Test items and procedures may reflect dominant cultural values. A test may not have been standardized on populations of Color, only on middle-class Whites. Language differences and unfamiliarity or discomfort with students' culture can cause a tester to misjudge them or be unable to establish rapport in group and individual testing situations.

Hard numbers from rigorous testing, no matter how biased, are easier to obtain and compare than are more important measures of a sound education, such as critical thinking skills or problem solving ability, and they appear to be "reliable statistics," no matter how faulty their basis (Kohn, 2000). Standardized tests "fail to assess the skills and dispositions that matter most. Such tests are generally contrived exercises that measure how much students have managed to cram into short-term memory" (Kohn, 2000, p. 316). Studies of students at all levels have found significant correlations between scores on standardized tests and "relatively superficial thinking" (Kohn, 2000, p. 317). Kohn listed various reasons high-stakes testing should be reformed. His basic contention was that such tests foster a host of ills, including cheating, turning teachers against teachers, increasing overspecialization, creating defensiveness and competitiveness, driving good educators out of the profession, and narrowing the conversation about education (pp. 322–323).

Many states, such as Oregon, have attempted to add substantial portfolio reviews to student assessment. However, as much as educators might wish to use collaborative data, such measurements are the first to fall by the wayside when budgets are tight. Policymakers often cite cost savings as a reason to rely solely on unreliable tests (Haynes, 2003).

Much culturally questionable testing still takes place. Educators tend to be overattached to tests as a means of gaining student information. When they do try to account for cultural differences, instead of creating new instruments, they modify existing ones: adjusting scores, rewriting items, or translating them into a second language. In general, this creates new problems in the place of old ones.

The end result of culturally biased assessment is a gap in achievement not only as measured by test scores, but also in the placement and eventual educational attainment of students. According to Haycock (2001), based on U.S. Census Bureau (1998) data, for every hundred kindergartners, fifty-one Asian-Americans, twenty-eight Whites, sixteen African-Americans, and ten Latinos will earn bachelor's degrees.

WHO ARE THE TEACHERS?

According to Liston and Zeichner (1996), the majority of prospective teachers are White females, come from middle-class homes, and have had very little contact with other cultures or with Children of Color. Although attempts have been made to bring a more diverse population into elementary education, the vast majority of preservice teachers remain monocultural and middle to upper-middle class. In 1996, for example, student enrollment across ethnic groups in public elementary and secondary schools was 64 percent White, 17 percent Black, 14 percent Hispanic, 4 percent Asian/Pacific Islander, and 1 percent American Indian/Alaskan Native (National Center for Education Statistics, 1999). In contrast, the 1994 teaching force was 87 percent non-Hispanic White, 7 percent Black, 4 percent Hispanic, 1 percent Asian/Pacific Islander, and 1 percent American Indian/Alaskan Native (U.S. Department of Education, 1997).

Many Teachers of Color have been retiring, and expanded occupational options for People of Color has meant few replacements. Meanwhile, the continual increase in the percentage of Children of Color has caused an increasing cultural mismatch. Sleeter (2001) suggested recruiting preservice teachers who are more likely already culturally competent by virtue of membership in a Community of Color or who have "experiences, knowledge, and dispositions that will enable them to teach well in culturally diverse settings" (p. 96).

While much lip service is paid to recruiting more Students and Faculty of Color, the numbers have remained consistently low. Hodgkinson (2002) reported that, as overall college "student enrollments become increasingly racially diverse, the teaching force is actually becoming increasingly White due mainly to the striking decline in Black, Hispanic, and Asian enrollments in teacher education programs since 1990, with a proportionate increase in minority business majors" (p. 104). In addition, both cost and the Northern European cultural climate that predominates keep many non-White Students out of the university (or contribute to their dropout rate). It is not only difficult for Students of Color, especially those who are not highly acculturated, to navigate the complex application and entry procedures that teaching programs typically require, but it is also a challenge to feel comfortable, safe, and welcome in a monocultural environment that is not their own.

An equally critical factor is the number of Instructers of Color within teaching programs. These statistics also continue to remain quite low. Teachers at the university level are overwhelming White. Whether because of the lack of input from Students and Faculty of Color or cultural incompetence, teacher educators and preservice teachers continue to replicate themselves and remain prisoners of their own experiences (Liston & Zeichner, 1996, p. 68). This situation will not easily right itself, for "when predominately White teacher education classes focus on race in the curriculum, without the presence of racially diverse standpoints there is the danger that the dialogue will privilege White viewpoints and add little to an understanding of how concepts of race and racism are experienced from different racial standpoints" (Johnson, 2002, p. 163). Without a more balanced perspective, cultural learning cannot help but remain superficial, residing somewhere outside the heart of preservice teachers, accessed only when time permits and the presence of culturally diverse students compels.

What is it like being an Instructer or Researcher of Color? Moule (2003c) offers the following insights.

> I have come to anticipate my Multicultural Education class with both dread and pleasure, a knotty journey we all take each quarter. In conversations with a new graduate teaching assistant, I am reminded of the difficulty of this work and how much I have grown in order to withstand this regular onslaught. After our first day, Adrian, a Chicano comfortable in diverse environments, but not yet in his role as a minority teaching at the college level, asks me, "Do you find the students . . . resistant?" He has begun to understand the complexities of bringing others to an open understanding of cultural perspectives. I even share with him research by Barry and Lechner (1995) that shows that courses in multicultural education can actually reinforce bias. Most preservice teachers in the class struggle both with the subject matter and their reactions to having their first African American professor. Add to this my commitment to teach in a constructivist and student-centered manner, a far different atmosphere from the usual university courses, and one can begin to appreciate the kinds of barriers to growth and openness that can get erected.
>
> Or with my colleagues. As an isolated Researcher of Color, I am routinely interested in identifying the race of the researchers in the articles I review. I find that this information is very central to my eventual understanding and evaluation of the material. When I share this kind of information with colleagues, I am met with blank stares, as if I have crossed some invisible line. They just do not see it as relevant. This conflict highlights one aspect of institutional racism a Person of Color routinely faces: insistence on an exclusively Eurocentric perspective. I like what Kochman (1981) says about this. "White[s] . . . consider an idea authoritative when it has been published. . . . Blacks consider it essential for individuals to have personal positions on issues and assume full responsibility for arguing their validity" (pp. 24–25). Or Reinharz and Davidman (1992), who assert that claiming objectivity is itself the biased stance of privileged White males. In any case, I am determined to include my personal position and the context of my current life in my work, even when my faculty colleagues want only hard objective facts. (p. 157)

TEACHER CHARACTERISTICS THAT MAKE A DIFFERENCE

Preservice teachers and teacher educators bring to their teaching a complex of personal and group identities that can serve as obstacles or as stepping-stones to successful multicultural classroom practice. Are certain traits likely to predict success in teaching, or more specifically success in teaching a diverse K–12 student population? Haberman (1996), for example, extrapolated the following research-based list of teacher characteristics likely to enhance cross-cultural teaching.

- Teacher's belief that it is the teacher's responsibility to engage *all* students in meaningful learning activities.
- Caring orientation: The expectation of the need for rapport with children and youth.
- Fallibility: The expectation and orientation of teachers to their own errors, reflectivity.
- Persistence: The predisposition to pursue activities at which children or youth will succeed and to solve problems that intrude on learning.
- Organizational ability: The predisposition to engage in planning and gathering of materials.
- Physical and emotional stamina: The ability to persist in situations characterized by poor home lives and other crises facing children and youth.
- Response to authority: The predisposition to protect children or youth experiencing success in learning against bureaucratic constraints.
- Explanation of success: The predisposition to emphasize effort rather than ability.
- Teaching Style: The predisposition to engage in coaching rather than directive teaching. (p. 755)

In related research, Moule (1998) identified four key teacher characteristics likely to promote successful interaction of teachers and culturally diverse students: care, dialogue, passionate pursuit, and openness-to-learn. Two traits appear on both Moule's and Haberman's lists. Care may be defined as giving permanent value—considering each child as of value regardless of behavior. How a teacher develops and expresses care and concern for students may depend on personal value system, character, and personal philosophy. If, however, the teacher lacks care for each student as a unique and valuable human being, no step-by-step techniques will transform the classroom into a safe environment for students. Similarly, Moule's openness to learn parallels Haberman's fallibility or reflectivity. They involve developing skills for lifelong growth, being open to new perspectives and ideas, and encouraging the flexibility to progress in new and different directions. In multicultural education, these characteristics allow teachers to model greater openness to a broader range of learning strategies, skills, and perspectives.

CURRICULUM REFORM

Head knowledge without heart empathy will lead to superficial curriculum adjustments. Though we may individually and collectively turn from overt to covert discrimination, there is little lessening of racism's powerful influence and pain unless changes are rooted in attitude and perspective shifts rather than political correctness. Once we address underlying attitudes and assumptions, we can begin to address curriculum reform that will lead to good teaching for all children.

Moule (1998) offered the following story to illustrate this point.

> As an eighth grader, I had to attend a summer session to raise my low history grade. I was one of very few Students of Color in the class. We were studying pioneers and the western migration, which actually interested me. I was devastated, however, when my teacher, a European American female, accused me of plagiarism. I had written what I thought was a stirring and creative beginning to my term paper. But she would not believe me when I said I wrote it myself. What was her reason for not believing the work was my own? I did not connect it with the color of my skin at the time. However, it took unconsciously take its toll on me both personally and professionally. I never bothered finishing the term paper and received another low grade. I had a strong aversion against history for the next 30 years, avoiding it as much as possible during my education and even having some misgivings about marrying my husband because he was a historian. The teacher's racism had its impact on me for years. But finally, at the age of 38, I was forced to do a history unit on the small Oregon town where I was teaching. As my students and I explored, learned, and researched the rich history of the town, I realized our efforts at learning had become a delight for both me and them. They won an award and much community praise, and I had done much to heal an old wound and to reclaim an excitement about learning that had been nearly extinguished by the racist attitude of one teacher.

(Adapted from p. 18 of *My Journey with Preservice Teachers: Reflecting on Teacher Characteristics That Bridge Multicultural Education Theory and Classroom Practice*, 1998. Reprinted by permission.)

Banks and Banks (2001) identified four approaches or levels of curriculum reform, each representing more extensive transformation. Banks and Banks's model can help educators understand the range of possibility in multicultural education as well as critically assess their own efforts at change.

- The *contributions approach* involves merely adding discrete items of culture to the existing curriculum. Examples include a focus on heroes, holidays, food, and other discrete cultural facts without any basic conceptual change in the material.

- The *additive approach* involves adding content, concepts, themes, and perspectives to the curriculum without changing its basic structure.
- The *transformational approach* occurs when the structure of the curriculum is changed to enable students to view concepts, issues, events, and themes from the perspectives of diverse racial and cultural groups.
- The *social action approach* encourages students to make decisions on important social issues and take action to help solve them.

Most educators are content to work on the first two levels. While such efforts may appear to meet a multicultural mandate, they are not sufficient to ensure a culturally competent educational design of curriculum. Take, for example, the requirement in most educational plans for the teaching of state history. Most begin, even today, with the myth of an empty land waiting to be discovered, totally overlooking the existence and contribution of Native Peoples.

Culturally insensitive teachers typically begin with discrete historical units, such as those that focus on the Oregon trail or Lewis and Clark, and teach them from the perspective of "the invaders," as one Native American student put it. A teacher, waking up to the possibility that this perspective may be missing a totally different viewpoint, may decide to add a day of Native American culture or even raise controversial issues such as immigration and land ownership, but is still centering the curriculum on White history. A step in a more inclusive direction might entail asking who really discovered America, providing students with materials that explore the issues from various cultural viewpoints, and encouraging them to critically examine all materials.

A more comprehensive example was offered by Rethinking Schools (1991) in their curriculum guide "Rethinking Columbus: Teaching about the 500th Anniversary of Columbus' Arrival in America" (1991). The introduction states:

> The Columbus myth teaches children which voices to listen for as they go out into the world—and whose to ignore. Pick up a children's book on Columbus: See Chris; see Chris talk; see Chris grow up, have ideas, have feelings. In these volumes, the native peoples of the Caribbean, the "discovered," don't think or feel. And thus children begin a scholastic journey that encourages them to disregard the perspectives, the very humanity, of people of color. (p. 3)

"Rethinking Columbus" includes poems and articles by Native children and writers; issue pieces on Native rights, school mascots, and Columbus Day; historical documents; and extensive resources and references. By deconstructing Columbus and placing his historical contributions in a truly multicultural context, it is an excellent example of Banks's final two approaches to curriculum reform. Students are being sensitized to a Native American perspective on the issues and challenged to think about and take concrete action on social issues facing Native Peoples today.

Ford (1996) suggested that Banks and Banks's levels not only speak to curriculum reform, but also reflect the level of cultural competence of the teachers who adopt them. The contributions approach, for example, reflects a generally superficial understanding of racially and culturally diverse groups. The additive approach tends to be adopted by individuals who fail to understand how the predominant culture interacts with and is related to racially and culturally diverse groups. The transformational approach tends to reflect educators who are active in seeking training and experience with racially and culturally diverse groups. Teachers who adopt a social action approach have become empowered to make meaningful contributions to the resolution of social issues and problems.

A culturally competent teacher devises a curriculum that enables students to view concepts, issues, events, and themes from the perspectives of diverse racial and cultural groups and/or leads students to make meaningful contributions to the resolution of social issues and problems. Teachers who add "multicultural fluff" do not meet the standard of multicultural education at a transformative level and may well decrease the ability of diverse students to interact effectively with the material.

ASPECTS OF CURRICULUM TRANSFORMATION

We are only now beginning to discover some of the pedagogical techniques most likely to lead to successful curriculum transformation, that is, movement into Banks's final two levels of curriculum change. Talbot (2003), for instance, emphasized the importance of helping students enter the reality of an historical figure. By way of example, she traced the evolution of Sacagawea, the Native woman who guided the Lewis and Clark expedition, as she has been portrayed in history textbooks. Talbot reported a slow evolution away from treating Sacagawea as an actor in the White drama of exploring the West, toward an image of a living, breathing Hidatsa woman with whom students can identify and into whose cultural world they can enter. Sacajawea's story may be told through European American eyes with an emphasis on her contribution, as in Banks's contributions approach, or her story can be told from her own perspective. Taking the latter approach, it is possible to sense who she was and understand her relationships and her role in a community that was focused on the whole and in harmony with nature, rather than trying to control nature. Then her part in the journey takes on a personal perspective, and we learn more about the deep culture that surrounded her. Too often, teachers bring their students to only a limited knowing and superficial understanding of many things without letting them fully experience and know viscerally the heart of what they are learning.

Such an approach can be useful in highlighting an era as well as an historical figure. Moule (2002) provided the example of a teacher in training, Sarah, who wanted her kindergarten students to more fully and directly experience Rosa Parks's defining moment as she refused to give up her seat on the bus. Sarah had already begun to investigate the use of a school bus so that the children could feel what it was like to lose their freedom of movement, but decided that the students would probably think it was fun to sit in the back. Her solution not only connected the students to the lived experience of Rosa Parks, but also through the emotions and reality of the learning experience stimulated compassion and understanding for the civil rights era.

Sarah put "no kindergartners allowed" signs on the playground equipment. She roped off part of the playground, putting one ball in the enclosed space. The children endured this limitation on their recess for several days. She also gave them two parallel art sessions, one with choice and one without. By this time, the children had internalized the message of the unit so well that one spontaneously said to another, "She's taking away our freedom." As a culminating activity, the children removed the rope around their limited space on the playground and gleefully destroyed the "no kindergartners allowed" sign. Photos of the children during and after the playground incident provide further evidence of the effectiveness of the learning (Knapp, 2001).

Such teachers in training will become risk takers as classroom teachers and will assume that they have much to learn about any topic. They believe that shared lived experience is one of the few ways to change young lives. They not only engage their students in meaningful learning experiences but also illustrate the best in constructive teaching and set the stage for self-directed lifelong learning.

Students lucky enough to find themselves in such learning environments continue to learn and grow beyond the classroom. They are beginning to know that they can make a difference as citizens in a democratic society. Such early training may result in a later generation of teachers who are aware of and moving beyond the taken-for-granted cultural norms many current teachers struggle to even recognize.

However, such felt experiences, if not carried out with great sensitivity and caring, can become trivialized and hurtful. A preservice teacher team, for example, made elaborate preparations to expose their peers to a unit on the Jewish Holocaust. At one point, they herded most of the class into a small, dark section of the room draped with black curtains. On the surface, the simulation seemed to have the potential of giving the participants a taste of the horrors of darkness, confinement, and crowding. But the simulation turned to giggles, and one student turned away with tears in his eyes. His family's experience of such terror was trivialized by the activity. Another preservice teacher, hoping to generate a lived experience in relation to civil rights and the African American experience, assigned the students roles from the U.S. Civil War era. One group decided to "reenact" a slave beating. One student laughingly writhed in mock pain, and the physical horror was reduced to a game. Such experiences can be powerful learning tools, and they should be undertaken only after much thought and consultation.

CHILD-CENTEREDNESS OF THE CURRICULUM

Moule (2002) also emphasized the importance of beginning all curriculum development, especially that related to reform vis à vis transformation, with a thorough understanding of the students' perspective: their questions, current level of knowledge and understanding, and inner images. It is critical for teachers to be able to see the material from students' viewpoints, rather than from just their own. She suggested five factors to consider in moving toward Banks and Banks's level of transformational cultural learning:

- Focusing on context-rich material that relates directly to students' life experiences
- Allowing children to engage material on their own terms, since they are usually more open to multiple perspectives than is the teacher
- Centering the investigation in student ideas
- Looking at what is not known instead of what is known
- Developing students' interest in how others viewed the events and locations being studied

The essence of curriculum reform is that the students and their needs are central to the curriculum, not the material to be covered. It is not "Your child does not fit my curriculum" or "I teach your child through my curriculum." The child is the center, not the lesson or the curriculum.

Ely (2001) further amplified child-centeredness, especially with difficult-to-reach students, in the following scenario.

> When I was an Assistant Principal, there were the "regular skippers," whom I was always chasing. When I finally caught up with the students, I asked them what it would take to get them to come to school. Many had been skipping for so long, that they really had no idea.
>
> But, I noticed a strange pattern with a few of the "skippers." There was one who would skip Periods 1, 2, 4, 5, 6, 7, 8, 9. I asked . . . "So what about Period 3? Did that teacher forget to mark you absent?"
>
> "No," the Skipper replied. "That is Ms. Zachary's class. I don't miss her class."
>
> "You mean you skip Periods 1 and 2 and COME IN for Period 3?"
>
> "Yup. Every day."
>
> "You're kidding. WHY?"
>
> "Mrs. Ely, you've got to understand . . . Ms. Zachary would KILL me if I didn't show."

"Aw come on," I said incredulous. "ALL of your teachers would tell you that! So what makes that class special enough to get you out of bed?"

Through shrugs and "ticks" and wiggles, the Skipper finally said, "Well, ya see, Mrs. Ely, I'm IMPORTANT in that class. Ya see, we do these group things. We all contribute. Sometimes, it is just an opinion. But it is MY opinion. I'm the only one who can give it! I matter. It is my PERSPECTIVE."

"And you don't feel this in other classes?"

"You kiddin'? They all just talk at me. They don't care what I think. They don't even KNOW what I think. Who cares about goin' there?"

"So, you come into Ms. Zachary's class to give your opinion?"

"That's not all of it. We do these cooperative things, too. I mean, we all have to work together on projects. We all have our parts, ya know? If I don't show with my part, I let down the whole team. Can't do that. So, I come in. Besides. It is fun." (pp. 85–86)

(From *Quo No More* by Arline Ely. Copyright 2001 by Arline Ely. Reprinted by permission.)

According to Ely (2001), "it all relates to developing a personal connection with the students." Ms. Zachary was able to accomplish this with the most difficult students. The traditional "skippers" felt a responsibility to both their teacher and their classmates. They were invested in the learning process and belonged to a learning culture. Ely also distinguished the needs of today's students and compared them to the classrooms in which their teachers were educated.

Today's students . . . want to know why they need to learn certain facts, have an expectation that they will be respected for who they are, are products of the "information age," who need to seek answers both alone and with peers, (and) need to have an active role in their learning process . . . (They) need personal connections to both their learning and to their teachers. . . . But today's students are being taught by teachers who grew up in classrooms where they, as students, were listening while teachers talked, working in isolation, answering only when questioned, learning in classes of 40 students, (and) sitting in perfect rows, one "tombstone" behind the other.

(From *Quo No More* by Arline Ely, p. 86. Copyright 2001 by Arline Ely. Reprinted by permission.)

Finally, let's turn to Banks and Banks's fourth approach, that of stimulating social action. Teachers may choose to look beyond the obvious, to address real needs in a relevant and timely manner. They may teach students to look outside the narrow confines of the given for a larger view that includes more factors, more perspectives, and alternate solutions. Teachers may begin the transformation process by helping students look for items that need action. They may then lead students to see the issue from multiple perspectives. From there, ties to curriculum items in multiple subject areas may be made.

For example, one student became concerned about conflicts on the playground over the limited number of balls available during recess. Another noticed newly planted grass being trampled by students. In both cases, the problem became a classroom focus in order to enable students to see issues from alternative perspectives and then take action to solve problems. One student found an inexpensive source of playground balls and sold the balls to class-mates. The students approached the school maintenance staff, and a small fence was soon erected to protect the grass. Even math benchmarks, for example, can be addressed by action items such as fence building and ball purchases.

TEXTBOOK AND LITERATURE BIAS

In addition to curriculum reform, Banks and Banks's (2001) model can help teachers bring a discerning eye to textbooks and readers. Do they add a brown-skinned, White-at-the-core character, or do they transform the curriculum to enable students to view concepts, issues, events, and themes from the perspectives of diverse racial and cultural groups? At first glance, a book that simply has a Character of Color may appear to offer a model for Children of Color as well as a sense of diversity. However, as well-intentioned as the effort may be, a high degree of superficiality can be found in books that we unquestioningly give children (Monroe, 1997).

An example of this was carefully uncovered by Atleo et al. (1999) in their review of Rinaldi's *My Heart Is on the Ground.* This book was aggressively marketed to nine- to twelve-year-old girls by Scholastic in 1999 as an authentic fictionalized experience of a young girl in an Indian boarding school. Atleo et al. uncovered wide distortion from known facts as well as a disservice to specific individuals and to a culture. For example, Rinaldi used the names of dead children taken off of gravestones in stories that do not accurately mirror how these children probably did die. Where she saw honor to their memories, those who know the tragedy of the boarding school see a continuation of denial and glossing over of the actual pain of individuals. Likewise, Rinaldi's well-intentioned efforts to share the cultural perspectives of the Sioux tribe are superficial because she did not reflect authentic cultural roots. Educators who miss this level of understanding miseducate their students, often relying on stereotypes, as Rinaldi did in her book. According to Atleo et al., she trivialized the culture by resorting to a stereotypical nobility, yet including derogatory references to girls and women in ways that do not reflect the reality of how Native American females are actually thought of and treated.

Even harder to discern are inappropriate language choices. Atleo et al. critiqued Rinaldi's overemphasis on compound words ("Friend-to-go-between-us"), romantic-sounding metaphors ("his spring is poisoned with anger"), and the stilted speech pattern that they call "early jawbreaker" ("Teacher tells it that I know some English, that she is much proud of me, but wants be more proud"). Instead of bringing a young reader to a sense of shared humanity in a truly sad chapter of our nation's history, such assaults on a groups' language allow the reader to remain distant and to see the group as "other," perhaps less than. Such treatment allows People of Color to be seen as appropriately excluded and oppressed by the dominant culture. Such details in literature, unfortunately, do little to change this status.

Is a Textbook Multiculturally Relevant?

While the following textbook analysis is a starting point for making choices about what to include in a nonbiased curriculum, teachers must take a much deeper look to insure the lack of subtle language and perspective bias. One way to begin is to check the credentials of the writer. Has the author lived in the culture? Is she a member of the culture? Has he checked the material with members of the culture? While we cannot expect every writer to be an expert in the cultural roots of a group, we can expect a sense of humility and some indication that the author is a fellow learner. This sense of shared learning and wonder will help readers enter their zones of unknowing in a supported, open, questioning manner. Are we learning along with the author? Does the language continually reflect respect, or is it limiting? Become your own critical consumer of information and perspective before serving it to your students.

The following seven criteria, adapted from Butler (2001), provide a further check on multicultural sensitivity.

- Are the authors members of different cultures? Check pictures if available.
- Does the preface make reference to multiculturalism or diversity?
- Do the illustrations, photographs, and drawings show more than one cultural group?
- Do written examples, problems, and/or samples draw from more than one culture?
- Is any reference made to help include speakers of other languages currently learning English?
- Are historical references to other cultures accurate?
- Do multicultural references emphasize individuals rather than stereotypes?

Reflection Questions and Creative Problem Solving

This chapter has covered several areas. You may wish to follow the steps of creative problem solving (Parnes, 1967) for more than one original "mess" you identify. Remember, you may return to the end of Chapter 4 for details on each step.

Identify a beginning "mess" you would like to solve.
List a few facts from the chapter.
Complete the IWWMW statement.
Brainstorm solutions.
Apply criteria. Choose one idea that rates well on your criteria.
Make a plan. Go for it!

SUMMARY

This chapter delves into the sources of bias in cross-cultural teaching. By way of example it explores a frequent dynamic between White teachers and African American students called the "pseudo-questioning strategy of discipline." Uncomfortable with direct commands and unaware of their importance as a reflection of caring within African American culture, White teachers are frustrated by student reactions to their indirect methods of discipline. Such cultural disconnects are often found within multicultural classrooms when teachers lack cultural competence and knowledge.

A vast body of research shows how social and racial attitudes can unconsciously affect behavior. Rosenthal and Jacobson (1968), for instance, showed how teacher expectations shape student performance. Research has also shown that most teachers base their behavior and attitudes on their own years as students and unconsciously reproduce those classrooms. Their referent and the cultural perspective from which they teach are typically White, Northern European, and middle class. We direct you to Web sites that will help you identify personal attitude and belief systems.

Teaching style itself can lead to serious cultural disconnects. Heath (1983) gives the example of a teacher's discomfort and entrenched value assumptions about storytelling styles in Black and White working-class homes. The former is richly poetic and embellished, the latter fact-based with clear morals. Students who tell stories in a cultural form unfamiliar to the teacher are likely to be judged as academically inferior.

Similar bias is found in the ways that People of Color are conceptualized in the educational and psychological literature. Old theories of "genetic deficiency" have been replaced by theories of cultural inferiority and "deficit." Terms such as *culturally deprived, disadvantaged, different,* and *distinct* imply that their cultural style is at variance with the dominant and accepted culture. Research on ethnic populations also tends to focus on deficits and shortcomings of Populations of Color. Alternative and more positive interpretations of the same data are certainly possible, but do not serve to justify the status quo of racism and unfair treatment. There is also much evidence that achievement testing suffers from cultural bias that causes significant gaps between racial groups. Test items and procedures may reflect dominant cultural values and experience. A test may not have been properly standardized. Language differences may exist, or testers may be unfamiliar or uncomfortable with a student's culture.

The majority of prospective teachers are White, female, and middle class and have had little previous contact with Children of Color. The increase in Children of Color in the student population, coupled with the retirement of many Teachers of Color who are not being replaced, is lessening the likelihood of same-race teacher–student matches. Teachers of Color also continue to be significantly underrepresented on the faculties of teacher education programs. There are, however, certain teacher characteristics that seem to enhance cross-cultural teaching irrespective of race. Haberman (1996) suggested the following: a sense of responsibility for engaging students in meaningful learning activities, caring, being fallible, being persistent in helping students succeed educationally, and coaching rather than being directive.

Curriculum reform vis-à-vis making material more cross-culturally sensitive has generally tended to be superficial, rather than substantive. Banks and Banks (2001) identified four levels of curriculum reform: contributions approach, additive approach, transformational approach, and social action approach. Most educators are content to work at the first two levels. Research also suggests that the adoption of these levels is directly related to the cultural competence of teachers. Culturally competent teachers develop curricula that help students adopt the perspective of racially and culturally diverse groups, understand how dominant culture interacts with those who are culturally different, and become empowered to bring about social change. The following variables have been found to be useful in transforming curricula: helping the student enter the reality of those who are culturally different, taking risks and being personally interested in the learning that is taking place, and centering the learning process on the child. The chapter ends with suggestions on how to assess textbooks and literature for cultural bias.

CRITICAL ISSUES IN WORKING WITH CULTURALLY DIFFERENT STUDENTS

The world changes according to the way people see it, and if you can alter, even by a millimeter, the way people look at reality, then you can change the world.

—James Baldwin

(From *Quo No More* by Arline Ely. Copyright 2001 by Arline Ely. Reprinted by permission.)

The following happens far too often in today's classrooms.

The Counselor was visiting a pre-Kindergarten class in another district. She entered the classroom to find five tables of three or four children each, busily working with crayons and markers.

Four-year olds are so cute! She couldn't resist stopping to watch for a moment. What she saw . . . when she really watched . . . was upsetting to her.

There was one table whose behavior was different . . .

There was nothing outstanding about what was happening.

The teacher was not ignoring these children.

The other children weren't teasing or tormenting them in any way.

But . . . they were different.

Somewhere between the molecules of air . . . these children had "gotten the message" already. In a world where the other groups were "bluebirds" and "cardinals" and "robins;" they were the "crows."

The young students, at four years of age, had already experienced, "Animal Farm," mentality . . . where they were the animals not quite as equal as the rest.

Among these children, some were "Children of Color" and all were not as well dressed . . . not as clean . . . not as accepted as the others. These children could see the invisible wall that separated them from the others as clearly as the children from the old fable could see that the "Emperor wasn't wearing any clothes!"

The Counselor knew that the students at the "fifth table," had already begun their educational experience lacking the "connections," necessary for success in school. (Ely, 2001, pp. 138–139)

Can such destructive practices be broken? Or as Murtadha-Watts (1998) wondered, "What will happen if the increasing numbers of teachers have no idea about what they are doing culturally, who they are working with, and what the students' circumstances are? Will we continue this cycle? Does the cycle of culturally incompetent teachers continue?" (p. 620).

As the proportion and number of Children of Color in the nation's schools increase, the need for teachers who know how to function in multicultural classrooms and sensitively relate to culturally diverse students heightens dramatically. Yet we are only now beginning to learn how to prepare teachers to work with children with differences (Sleeter, 2001). The challenges are substantial. As various studies show (Bollin & Finkel, 1995; Breault, 1995; Harrington & Hathaway, 1995; MacDonald & Sperry, 1995; Stachowski & Mahan, 1998), teacher education in a pluralistic society is dependent on a complex set of factors. Teachers must be willing to change their racial attitudes and sense of privilege as well as master a body of cultural material. Educational systems must be willing to adapt their structure and style to a changing student population. There is sure to be resistance from a variety of sources, including parents and students themselves, and as we have tried to show, gaining cultural competence is a personally demanding and at times arduous enterprise. Gay (2000) indicated the need for "the moral courage and the will to stay the course in efforts to make the educational enterprise more multiculturally responsive, even in the face of the opposition that is surely to come from somewhere" (p. 210). We have learned the hard way that it is possible to inadvertently cause students to become less culturally competent. Barry and Lechner (1995), for example, demonstrated that teaching about different cultural groups may actually increase or affirm preservice teachers' stereotypes.

We have so far focused on a variety of conceptual issues related to working with culturally different students. Earlier chapters defined cultural competence, explored the meaning of racism, especially as it impacts students and teachers, and defined culture and worldview as well as the cultural limits of mainstream assumptions that have shaped most teachers' thinking. In addition, we looked at a number of factors unique to the experience of ethnically diverse students. These included child development and parenting, differences in family structure, biracial/bicultural families, potential areas of psychological difficulty (conflicts in identity development, assimilation and acculturation, negative stereotyping, stress), and sources of bias in cross-cultural teaching.

In this chapter we focus more directly on the process of working with culturally different students and also look at some important issues unique to educating Children of Color. What is the best way to prepare for cross-cultural work? How is it different from other teaching situations? How can a teacher begin to establish rapport and maximize success with diverse student populations? What should teachers know about bilingualism, classroom management, and dealing with stereotyping in the classroom? We look in depth at what we believe is a particularly promising strategy for preparing preservice teachers for cultural competence—cultural immersion experiences. This chapter ends with an introduction to Chapters 10 through 14, which provide culturally specific information useful in working with Latinos/as, Native Americans, African Americans, Asian Americans, and White ethnics.

OVERCOMING ANXIETY

The previous chapters highlighted the kinds of life experiences that impact culturally different students as well as teaching strategies that may require modification in order to work most effectively cross-culturally. No amount of preparation, however, can totally allay the anxiety typical of teachers who first contemplate working with culturally diverse students. Student teachers regularly ask, "But what do I do when I find myself standing in front of a room of children who are culturally different?" The usual answer is, "Just do the same thing you do with any group—begin to teach." The anxiety and hesitancy reflect a basic discomfort with cultural differences and the fact that most teachers have grown up in a racist society separated from those who are different from them. They are afraid because of their ignorance about students' cultures, because they don't want to make a cultural faux pas or miss something very obvious. They are, in addition, anxious and uncomfortable due to feelings of guilt over the existence of racism or feelings of embarrassment because of past indifference, the racist behavior of family and friends, or feelings of personal privilege or entitlement. It feels like very dangerous territory. After reading chapter after chapter about the complexity of issues in working with diversity and how easily cross-cultural communication can break down, the prospect of facing students from a different culture and providing them with a sound education must strike the readers as daunting.

At such moments of doubt, it is important to remember several things. First, as a teacher and a student of learning, one is already, or is in the process of becoming, a skilled educator. Becoming culturally competent does not mean starting from scratch or learning everything anew. Rather, it means further honing existing skills, broadening teaching concepts that are too narrow, and gaining new cultural knowledge about students. Culturally competent teachers are, in general, better educators because they must remain more conscious about the cultural appropriateness of tasks, methods, and perspectives that others may routinely overlook. In a certain sense, every student carries his or her own unique culture, and the teacher's task is to respectfully gain entry into that culture and offer learning that is sensitive to its rules and inner dynamics.

Second, students are, above all, human beings, and this is the ultimate basis for connection. They, too, are anxious about schooling, especially if they are culturally different. More than likely, they have had experiences that make them mistrust the kind of system in which the teacher works. The initial task, then, is to set them at ease in a manner that has meaning for them. Teaching and learning are, above all, human processes, that start with walking and talking. Teaching is bound to fail (with all students, not just culturally different ones) when awareness of common humanity and caring is lost. Unfortunately, in the process of teaching people about cultural differences, there is a tendency (that must always be guarded against) to objectify and stereotype students by seeing them only in terms of their differences. By attending to these too fully, the teacher can lose sight of the individuals in the classroom. Focusing too heavily on differences, and thereby overlooking basic human similarities, can turn cross-cultural work into a mechanical process. Cross-cultural interaction must be based on the shared humanity of student and teacher.

Kroeber (1948), an early anthropologist, pointed out that there were three kinds of human characteristics: those that the person shares with all other human beings, those shared with some other human beings, and those that are unique to each individual. It is in relation to the first that cross-cultural communication and teaching are possible. A sensitivity to the second and third allows for human differences and uniqueness once a basic connection has formed. Again, it is through the very human capacities of caring, having sympathy and empathy for others, and identifying with the basic joys and predicaments of being human that differences can best be bridged.

PREPARING FOR CROSS-CULTURAL WORK

A number of concrete preparations can create support or allay some of the natural anxiety that may be felt when contemplating or actually beginning cross-cultural teaching. The development of cultural competence is a lifelong pursuit. This book is only a first step. The more you learn about racism, culture, diversity, cultural competence, and cross-cultural teaching, as well as about individual groups and their cultures, the more comfortable and conversant you become. Since the late 1980s, there has been an explosion of good material in this area and a dramatic increase in the availability of excellent professional development opportunities. You should take advantage of these whenever possible.

Prepare for working with students from a particular ethnic group by doing personal research on that group's culture, history, and educational issues. This can include not only academic and professional reading and Internet searches, but also novels, biographies, social histories, travel accounts, movies, videos, theater, art exhibits, lectures, and so forth.

A most valuable supplement is actual immersion in the culture. This can range from attending celebrations, cultural events, and political rallies; eating regularly at ethnic restaurants; and patronizing community businesses to more sustained contact such as volunteering in the community, learning the language, and traveling to countries of origin. We talk more about immersion experiences below.

FINDING SUPPORT FOR CROSS-CULTURAL TEACHING

It is also useful to consult on a regular basis with a professional teacher who is indigenous to the community and/or the culture of the children in your class. As a beginner in cross-cultural teaching, it is particularly useful to discuss problems, especially early in their development, with someone who is knowledgeable about the workings of the students' culture. With more experience and comfort, one might need consultation only in more difficult or problematic areas.

A teacher might also consider establishing a study group or peer support group with other educators who are involved in cross-cultural teaching. Regular meetings can involve discussing shared readings, presenting problems, having guest experts, and the like. Such a group can provide opportunities to share resources and knowledge, receive observation support when helpful, and remain focused on the cultural dimensions of cross-cultural teaching.

A final suggestion is to join local ethnic teacher groups and networks. Often, teachers who work extensively with a specific population join together to share information and resources, advocate for the needs of students and their families, and keep knowledgeable on current research and trends in education for the population of interest. Active participation in such a group is an excellent way to learn more about a student population, connect with other teachers who might be valuable resources, and demonstrate interest and commitment to cross-cultural teaching as a career focus.

HOW IS CROSS-CULTURAL TEACHING DIFFERENT?

There is general agreement among educators and counselors that cross-cultural work is more demanding, challenging, and energy draining than work with same-culture students. According to Draguns (1981), whose writings apply equally well to education and counseling, cross-cultural work tends to be more "experiential, freewheeling, and bilateral" (p. 17). By "experiential," he meant that it is more likely to directly and emotionally impact the individual. Draguns likened it to culture shock; the person is immersed in a foreign culture in which familiar patterns of behavior are no longer useful and new means of acting and relating must be discovered. It has also been described as more labor-intensive and more likely to result in fatigue.

"Freewheeling" refers to the fact that the learning process must be continually adapted to the specific cultural needs of differing students. As suggested earlier, the only constant is the shared humanity. Standard approaches are overwhelmingly culture-bound and Northern European in nature, and even efforts to catalog cultural similarities among racially related ethnic groups must be tentative and ever mindful of enormous intragroup diversity. To this end, Draguns (1981) in reference to counseling suggested: "Be prepared to adapt your techniques (e.g., general activity level, mode of verbal intervention, content of remarks, tone of voice) to the cultural background of the client; communicate acceptance of and respect for the client in terms that make sense within his or her cultural frame of reference; and be open to the possibility of more direct intervention in the life of the client than the traditional ethos of the counseling profession would dictate or permit" (p. 16).

Finally, "bilateral" implies collaboration. By the very nature of cross-cultural work, the teacher is more dependent on the student for help in defining the teaching process. Though it is common practice, for example, for teachers to get input from students on their prior knowledge and lesson direction, in cross-cultural work it is even more imperative. Teachers need direct and continuing student input on what is culturally valued so that what is created is culturally appropriate and useful, and minimizes ethnocentric standards. Since teacher and student begin at very different cultural places, it is reasonable to expect some mutual movement in the direction of the other. Culturally competent educators adapt and adjust their efforts to the cultural milieu of the student. At the same time, by entering into the learning process, culturally different students cannot help but gain some knowledge and insight into the workings of mainstream culture.

What Does Successful Cross-Cultural Teaching Look Like?

Cose (1997) reviewed a number of strategies that had proven successful at the college level in facilitating learning among Students of Color. From published reports and personal communication, Cose found that professors at Xavier University were able to combine attitude change and focused remediation work with a small student body of predominately African American students in order to increase academic success. Over a period of many years, the university went from four or five minority graduates entering medical school to seventy-five. While Cose did identify problems in the program, its overall "success in fostering an atmosphere of achievement" was clear (p. 57). The difficulties resided primarily with the educational system at Xavier, not its racially different students.

From this and other research Cose extrapolated six principles of successful cross-cultural teaching.

- Find a group of young people motivated to learn or find a way to motivate them.
- Convince them you believe in them.
- Teach them good study skills, including the art of studying in groups.
- Challenge them with difficult and practical material.
- Give them adequate support.
- Demand that they perform.

Cose's first principle focuses on motivation. Without motivation that already exists or that has been stimulated by the teacher, significant learning will not occur. Implied is an expectation of student-centeredness (in other words, student needs, and not those of teacher's, are the beginning of the learning process) as well as an acknowledgment that students from different cultural groups may be motivated in different ways and that the teacher must be cognizant of such differences.

The second principle involves the communication of caring and empathy for students. Moule and Ingram (2002) defined empathy as the "ability to acknowledge the feelings behind another person's lived experience" (pp. 4–5). Cose (1997) acknowledged that this "second step may be the hardest, for convincing young people you believe in them is not an easy task . . . unless you really do" (p. 65). In this regard, teachers can expect to have their sense of caring and concern tested by many Students of Color.

The third principle highlights the necessity of developing good study skills upon which to build further learning, acknowledging that Students of Color often find themselves left behind because of differential treatment or stereotyping early in their education. The result has often been underperformance and underachievement. Cose's emphasis on group learning reflected an understanding of the role peer pressure can play in devaluing classroom performance as well as the value placed on cooperative learning in Cultures of Color.

Principle four speaks to the use of difficult and practical learning materials: difficult so that accomplishment will feel significant and challenge feelings of inadequacy in the learning realm, and practical so that the relevance and value of what is being learned is obvious to the student.

The fifth principle implies the necessity of close, continual contact and support in overcoming feelings of self-doubt and inadequacy. For many students, a history of learning failures saps motivation and subsequent attempts in the classroom. A culturally sensitive teacher is always monitoring student frustration, self-criticism, and self-fulfilling prophesies and is ready to intervene and short-circuit such reactions.

The last principle, the demand that students perform, highlights the importance of ongoing caring and support—that is, communicating that

"I care about you enough that I will not accept less than you are capable of."
It also implies the modeling of resilience and sustained effort in educational
success. As Cose implied, if a teacher demands that students perform and is
really sincere, "lo and behold, they do" (p. 65).

The need for a culture that empowers students and allows for learning in
open and open-minded ways is known to be crucial for all children, not just
those for whom the existing school culture comes naturally (Rimm, 1997).
Anderson (1988) described yet another program that had been successful in
training and retaining Students of Color at the college level. It succeeded by
"creating an aura of family in which cooperation is highly valued, bonding
between the students and faculty is encouraged, and a maintenance of positive ethnic identity is fostered" (p. 8). Cuban (1989) noted the importance of
a sense of community in learning settings, although he believed that "no formulas exist as yet to explain how to put together the right combination of
people, things, and ideas to create a particular setting that succeeds with
at-risk students" (p. 799). Meier (1995), in *The Power of Their Ideas: Lessons
for America from a Small School in Harlem,* described a New York City
elementary school that came close.

Having reviewed various strategies related to actual teaching in the
multicultural classroom, we turn to several issues of special importance in
working with Children of Color. These include bilingualism, classroom management across culturally different groups, and addressing stereotyping in the
classroom.

BILINGUALISM

Starting in 1664, when eighteen tongues, not counting Indian languages,
were spoken on Manhattan Island, this country has known the challenge of
what language to speak in our institutions, our public places, and our schools
(Crawford, 1999). Ever since, from Germans seeking German-speaking
schools in the 1700s and the systematic repression of Native languages in
favor of the "civilizing" influence of English, to the current controversy over
bilingual education, the connection between language and culture has been a
key issue in education.

Currently, the debate centers around the use and support of a second
language in schools, Spanish being the language most contested due to the
increasing population of Hispanic school-age children in the United States.
The conflict over Spanish is particularly keen in California, and a closer look
at the struggle in that state is informative.

During the 1800s conquered Spanish speakers in the Southwest faced
repression of their language and culture. Although California's 1849 constitution required the publication of all laws in both Spanish and English, the

practice was soon abandoned (Garcia, 2001). California's 1998 law brought the discussion to perhaps its most heated and passionate level. The law required all children to be placed in English-language classrooms and schools to educate English-language learners though "structured English immersion" (Garcia, 2001, p. 69). Although the law allowed a one-year transition period and instruction in the child's language with a yearly written waiver, many effective bilingual classrooms and programs have already been shut down.

The debate over the education of culturally and linguistically diverse students centers around the instructional use of the two languages of the bilingual student (Ovando, 1990).

> At one end of the debate are supporters of native-language instruction. . . . [who] recommend the utilization of the student's native language and mastery of that language prior to the introduction of an English curriculum. This approach suggests that competencies in the native language, particularly as related to academic learning, provide important cognitive and social foundations for second-language learning and academic learning in general—"you really only learn to read once" (Hudelson, 1987; Thomas, 1998). At the other end of this debate, introduction to the English curriculum is recommended at the onset of the students' schooling experience with minimal use of the native language (p. 350).

As one might expect, a middle ground seems to be most productive. Emerging research indicates that comprehensive two-way bilingual immersion programs seem to have the most promise for both students who speak the dominant-culture language (English) and speakers of another language, usually Spanish (Foster, 2002).

While the debate rages on, ultimate clarity cannot be reached without careful consideration of how academic underachievement is fostered by society's mistreatment of minorities in and out of school (Garcia, 2001). The following story highlights this point.

> My sister will never forget her first day of school. She was asked by the teacher, "What is your name, little girl?" My sister responded, "Ciprianita." The teacher tried to pronounce the name and then respectfully requested, "Can I call you Elsie? It is my favorite name." In that one instant, my sister's linguistic and cultural heritage was politely and unintentionally challenged. . . . The teacher's intent was positive. She meant no harm. It did not seem like a significant incident since scenes like these are common then (as they are today). But my sister, to this day still goes by the name Elsie and tells this story with tears in her eyes. (Garcia, 2001, p. 7)

Such acts do more than damage a child's sense of self, culture, language, and family. They also tell the student and family that they do not belong, do not fit into the school culture as they are. Demographics show quite clearly that minority school-age children will soon become the majority in the United States. Yet their high school completion rate lags significantly. How much sense do policies on second language use and acquisition make for these students?

According to Garcia (2001), Ruiz (1990) identified three possible policy development positions vis-á-vis language acquisition for children, each having very different implications for the multicultural classroom and how bilingual students are to be taught.

1. *Language-as-problem* sees non-English languages as a social problem to be identified, eradicated, alleviated, or otherwise resolved. In this orientation, the "beneficiaries" are mainstream native speakers. This "subtractive multiculturalism" is seen as a means to provide equality of opportunity.
2. *Language-as-right* is a reaction to the previous orientation. "It confronts the assimilation tendencies of dominant communities with arguments about the legal, moral, and natural right to . . . identity and language; it refutes the notion that minority communities are somehow made 'better' through the loss of their language and culture."
3. *Language-as-resource* views multiculturalism and bilingualism as valued resources that can enrich broader society. It has received less emphasis. It not only holds promise for reducing social conflict in ways the other two cannot, but it also serves as a guide by which language is preserved, managed, and developed. (Garcia, 2001, pp. 52–54)

Viewing language acquisition from the policy position of language-as-resource, the National Council of Teachers of English and the International Reading Association (1996) offered the following principles for teachers in regard to the teaching of reading and the development of language arts.

1. Students must develop an understanding of and respect for diversity in language use, patterns, and dialects across cultures, ethnic groups, geographic regions, and social roles.
2. Students whose first language is not English make use of their first language to develop competency in the English language arts and to develop understanding of content across the curriculum.
3. Celebrating our shared beliefs and traditions is not enough; we also need to honor that which is distinctive in the many groups that make up our nation. (p. 3)

Garcia (2001) offered the following conclusions:

Information derived from recent research indicates that Hispanic students can be served effectively (Lockwood & Secada, 1999; Romo, 1999; Tashakkori & Ochoa, 1999). These students can achieve academically at levels at or above the national norm. Instructional strategies that serve these students best acknowledge, respect, and build on the language and culture of the home. Teachers play the most critical role in the students' academic success, and students become important partners with teachers in the teaching and learning enterprise. Although much more research is required, we are not without a knowledge base that can make a difference. (p. 153)

CLASSROOM MANAGEMENT AND INTERACTIONAL STYLE

According to Delpit (1995), many Children of Color value social aspects of the environment more than mainstream children do and tend to be especially attuned to "feelings, acceptance, and emotional closeness." African American children from lower socioeconomic groups are more influenced by the need to affiliate than by the need to achieve. In Chapter 6 we explored the possibility that such a factor might play a role in suppressing school achievement. It may also have serious implications for classroom management.

Optimal culturally sensitive classroom environments and teaching styles for some Children of Color may need to emphasize collaboration and opportunities for interaction. The teacher of such students may find it useful, for example, to view social interactions and side conversations during class in a light that recognizes the cultural value and importance of sharing and emotional closeness between students.

Foster (1987) offered the following analysis of Black Student–teacher interaction. Due to different interactional styles, Black Students, for instance, may

> Grant teachers a wide latitude of emotions in which to make their expectations and dissatisfactions known. Assertive, aggressive and even angry behavior are all rated as acceptable means of communicating one's intentions as long as these emotions are perceived as genuine. If expressions of emotion are too subtle, however, students are likely to misread a teacher's intentions and become disoriented. Responses lacking a sufficient emotional quality are likely to be read as non-caring. Totally unacceptable, however, is non-responsiveness. Students expect a response, and failing to see one will generally interpret this behavior as non-concern. From students' perspective the non-responsive teacher demonstrates not only lack of control, but a non-caring attitude as well. (pp. 67–68)

Delpit (1995) further suggested that the implication of such perceptions is that, in the African American community, teachers demonstrate their caring for students by "controlling the class; exhibiting personal power; establishing meaningful interpersonal relationships; displaying emotion to garner student respect; demonstrating that all students can learn; establishing a standard of achievement and 'pushing' students to achieve the standard." Teachers hold student attention by "incorporating African-American interactional styles in their teaching." The community will view a teacher as "ineffectual, boring, or uncaring" if he or she does not exhibit these behaviors and firmly control the class (p. 142).

Consider the interactional styles of Asian students. Nieto (1996), for example, pointed out the disparity between traditional American classroom style and that expected by a recently arrived Vietnamese immigrant student. "Such a child might feel extremely off-balance and uncomfortable in a classroom environment in which teachers are informal and friendly, students are expected to ask questions and speak in front of the class, and group work is the order of the day" (p. 144). Compare such preferred interactions with that of the child's native land, where "teachers are revered and have a formal relationship with their students, and students are expected to learn individually and by listening and memorizing" (p. 144). Similarly, Marshall (2002) pointed out that Asian American students perceive greater emotional and social distance between themselves and their teachers. She suggested that "without repeated urging from teachers, some may be disinclined to initiate interactions with teachers that include asking questions or participating in class discussions." What to do? Marshall (2002) quoted Uba (1994), who suggested becoming attuned to "subtle body language" and noticing that students wishing to participate may sit straighter or make a bit more eye contact. Direct eye contact, viewed by most mainstream teachers as a sign of respect, is often avoided by Asian American students, who have been taught to avert their eyes in the presence of authority.

Latino/a students also bring their own unique cultural styles to the classroom. Falicov (1996), for instance, offered the following description of Mexican students' interactive style.

> Indirect, implicit, or covert communication is consonant with Mexicans' emphasis on family harmony, on "getting along" and not making others uncomfortable. Conversely, assertiveness, open differences in opinion, and demands for clarification are seen as rude or insensitive of others' feelings. The use of third-person ("One could be proud of . . ."), rather than first-person ("I am proud of . . .") pronouns is a common pattern of indirectness, and is viewed as a way of being selfless as opposed to self-serving. Thus, Mexican Americans sometimes are left guessing rather than asking about the other's intentions; they often make use of allusions, proverbs, and parables to convey their viewpoints, which may leave an impression of guardedness, vagueness, obscurity, or excessive embellishment, obsequiousness, and politeness. (p. 176)

Classroom interaction that calls for competition between individuals, emphasizes individual accomplishment, or promotes excessive directness or assertiveness may well make many Latino/a students uncomfortable and silent.

Regardless of cultural specifics, sound and safe classrooms depend on a few basic principles. In sound multicultural and empowering classrooms, teachers give permanent value to each student. *Permanent value* means considering each child to be of value regardless of behavior. It could be called *unconditional love.* How teachers develop and express this valuing of students may depend on their own value systems, characters, and personal philosophies. Dreikurs (1968) recognized the importance of permanent value: "The child's realization that he has permanent value and that his value is recognized by his teacher regardless of what he is doing at the moment or where he may fail opens the way for an unselfish desire [for the child] to do his best" (p. 66).

Avoiding the Stereotyping of Individual Group Members

Each of the chapters that follow focuses on working with a different ethnic community. As is described in greater detail at the end of this chapter, each is written in conjunction with an educator from that community. Multicultural educators are divided about the value of presenting culturally specific information in this manner. Although enumerating formulas or "recipes" for understanding and dealing with groups of people is a convenient way to summarize culturally specific information, it does present certain pitfalls.

To begin with, the division of America's nonWhite populations into four broad racial categories, although a common practice, is artificial and serves to mask enormous diversity. For example, Americans who have immigrated from Asian countries do not generally identify or call themselves Asian Americans. They may self-identify as Chinese Americans, Chinese, or of Chinese descent, or even according to more regional or tribal groupings. Some may find being called Asian American offensive. The term is, in fact, bureaucratic in origin, having been developed by the U.S. Census Bureau. It is used here, as elsewhere, for convenience, but it should not be assumed to imply sameness. In actuality, as Atkinson, Morten, and Sue (1993) pointed out, the term *Asian American* refers to "some twenty-nine distinct subgroups that differ in language, religion, and values" (p. 195). The important point is that the broad categories subsume many different ethnic groups, each with its own unique culture, and lumping them together on the basis of certain common geographic, physical, or cultural features merely encourages an underestimation of their diversity and uniqueness.

Thinking about People of Color through such categories also serves to encourage stereotyping. Such thinking tends to be most common among inexperienced teachers who find the prospect of cross-cultural work anxiety producing. Stereotyping reduces what might be experienced as unpredictability in the behavior of culturally different students. Thus, less experienced teachers often project cultural characteristics onto all individuals they identify as belonging to a specific group. It works this way: If I can be sure that all students will act similarly, I can more easily develop a general strategy of how to deal with them in class and, therefore, feel more in control. If I believe, for example, that all Native American students are reticent, I can prepare myself to be more active in seeking information, or if I know that all Asian Americans are taught to suppress emotions or to be hesitant to respond in class, I can be on the lookout for more subtle forms of emotionality or work to give them a safer place and manner for sharing in class. Similarly, teachers who wish to limit complexity can incorrectly assume that approaches that have been successful with a given student population are the only approaches to be adopted. In sum, then, taking the material that appears in the following chapters as gospel limits teacher creativity and adaptability and at the same time suppresses sensitivity to intragroup differences. Instead of assuming unanimity among students from the same group, a far better way to proceed is to treat all guesses about what is going on with a culturally different student as hypotheses to be verified or rejected.

A Four-Step Method of Addressing Stereotypical Statements

Teachers in multicultural settings will eventually be faced with stereotyping within their classrooms. Such an occurrence represents not only a very teachable moment, but also a rich opportunity for attitude change and increased dialogue about race and ethnicity. Knowing how to address the stereotypical statements of others, including students and colleagues, is an extremely valuable skill.

Fennimore (1994) offered a four-step method of addressing prejudiced statements. She indicated that teachers and educators must support the goal of accepting the dignity and equality of children, both within and outside the classroom. She quoted Nieto (1996) in further suggesting that educational institutions must continue to confront federal, state, local, and internal practices that reflect negative perceptions of racially, ethnically, or socioeconomically diverse children. These practices include labeling, deficit terminology, and tracking and ability groups, which tend to segregate both more- and less-advantaged students. She acknowledged that most training in prejudice reduction and multiculturalism seldom offers practical advice about meaningful application. Her four-step method was offered as an antidote to this trend.

According to Fennimore, teachers do not feel comfortable about confronting prejudiced statements for several reasons. They fear that they will become too angry or aggressive or that they will alienate the speaker and invite retaliation, or they feel hopeless about what one individual can accomplish. They also lack practice in confronting such statements. Letting such statements go unchallenged not only misses an opportunity to confront what is usually unintended racism, but silence also can be interpreted as agreement. Fennimore believed that her method allows educators to gently correct a prejudiced statement in a productive manner without creating a climate of rejection or negativity.

Fennimore indicated that personal responses to prejudiced statements should entail four characteristics.

1. Pull the prejudice out of the comment and restate it in a calm and objective way.
2. State personal beliefs in a clear and assertive manner.
3. Make a positive statement about the specific subjects of the prejudice.
4. Gently turn the subject to a new direction.

She offered the following two examples.

Example 1

Prejudiced Statement   Why would a talented and well-educated teacher like you choose to work in a neighborhood like that? Aren't most of your students African American (Asian American, Hispanic American, or any group experiencing discrimination)?

Response

- Many people seem to think that African American (Asian American, Hispanic American, Native American) children, particularly if they live in disadvantaged communities, are less capable. (Characteristic 1)
- I have always acted on my own belief that every child is filled with potential and deserves the finest possible education. (Characteristic 2)
- If you visited my classroom, you might be surprised to see how intelligent and successful my children really are. (Characteristic 3)
- In fact, you might even want to visit sometime. Do you still travel into the city frequently for your work? (Characteristic 4)

Example 2

Prejudiced Statement   I just cannot understand why a wonderful, healthy boy like you would confine yourself to dating that woman in a wheelchair.

Response

- I know that many who haven't had the chance to get to know people in wheelchairs think they are less capable or not as much fun to be with (Characteristic 1), but I have always thought that people's personal strengths and qualities are much more important to a relationship than possible disabilities. (Characteristic 2)
- My friend and I have enjoyed so many social experiences together, and she and her many successful disabled friends have certainly changed my former stereotyped ideas about people in wheelchairs. (Characteristic 3)
- Maybe the three of us could go to a movie sometime. Are you still fond of spy stories? (Characteristic 4)

Fennimore pointed out that training in such a method requires behavior application. Students need assistance in developing self-confidence and assertiveness in regard to such interventions as well as concrete opportunities to practice making assertive responses to prejudiced statements in risk-free classroom environments. They also benefit from observing role models responding to such situations.

IMMERSION EXPERIENCES

Immersion experiences involve placing teachers in culturally different school settings unfamiliar to them, so that they can learn firsthand about culturally different student populations. According to Sleeter (2001), some weaknesses of immersion-based learning are that the immersion experience is too short in duration and intensity, that it is too superficial and lacks sufficient depth, that it does not include living within the community in which the immersion school is located, and that authentic immersion settings may be located at a distance from the teacher education program, requiring time and money to travel and relocate for the period of the experience. If these factors can be addressed, as we shall see, such a learning strategy can have powerful effects in promoting cultural competence.

The material that follows, taken from Moule (2003a), is a description of an immersion program created for preservice teachers in a predominantly African American elementary school in Portland, Oregon.

The first task of an immersion experience, no matter how long or short, is to establish trust and the awareness that the student teacher is an integral part of the community, even if only for a day. In one program, for example, as the visitors arrive, they are asked to complete a form on their expectations for the day, including their thoughts as they entered the neighborhood and building. This moment of reflection allows them to express their fears and/or note their first impressions. The completed forms also identify those who may need special attention during the day. People who visit for a short time are given a complete tour of the school, during which they locate their assigned rooms and see the children and staff who happen to be in the halls, gym, cafeteria, or playground. These group tours give university visitors a sense of safety and an opportunity to ask questions of their familiar and trusted teacher educator. A "pep talk" explains their roles in the classroom as volunteers rather than as observers. Differences in teaching styles, classroom management techniques, and what they might be asked to do are anticipated. The existence of a long-standing and positive relationship between the teacher education program, the on-site teacher, and the immersion site's school staff is quite helpful, as is the on-site teachers' familiarity with the goals of the visiting preservice teachers and the school staff's familiarity with the university setting from which the preservice teachers come.

In immersion programs of longer duration, preservice teachers typically develop deep rapport with cooperating teachers and quickly discover that getting to know students on a personal level is most appealing educationally. New relationships and experiences quickly emerge. Student teachers are usually paired on-site, so that perceptions and experiences can be checked out with a peer. They are required to write about their experiences, which provides an opportunity to reflect on and consolidate learning. These reflective pieces give the participants time to self-reflect before sharing in a smaller or larger group. As Pang (1994) stated, "dialogue with their peers is crucial because it gives teachers the opportunity to clarify their beliefs and to better understand what they felt and saw" (p. 292).

At the beginning, most preservice teachers are guarded and uncomfortable, and they offer predictable and safe expectations for the forthcoming experience. One student, for example, hoped to "gain deeper insight into the African American culture and to be a better teacher for African American kids." By the end of the first week, however, they are more comfortable and begin to focus on the emotional lives of the children in their classroom, seeking them out on a human and personal level. One student teacher commented:

> One of the things I most want to gain from this experience is to start to form a bond with the students in the class. Now they know that I am a constant in the class and I feel with that stability some of the learners will begin to let their guard down. . . . On Friday one of the students wrote me a letter that said, "Thank you for believing in me." Maybe this child is my chance to form a bond and possibly make a difference. I was amazed at the compliment . . . the fact that the child noticed and was thankful for someone believing in him. (Moule, 2003a, pp. 1–2)

Now the preservice teachers begin to appreciate the important connection between emotional bonding and cultural expression. For example, as discussed earlier, discipline styles in predominantly African American schools are connected to increased emotional interactions, and that deep caring is evidenced in teacher–student and student–student relationships, even when the style seems particularly strict and authoritative.

Next they begin to recognize the difficulties in many of the children's home lives in poor neighborhoods, where poverty influences parents' ability to provide for children and their education. They come to understood that single mothers and parents with two jobs are less likely to be able to participate in their children's schooling. They begin to realize the need to adjust their lesson plans to match the learning styles of the children, and to incorporate more hands-on kinesthetic lessons and socially interactive components. The preservice teachers eventually become part of the instructional team, teaching a work sample to their assigned class. This working together appears largely responsible for a growing sense of belonging, community, and effectiveness.

An often-reported outcome of immersion experiences is that teachers feel less "scared" and "uncomfortable" in new multicultural settings. Most realize that their initial discomfort came not from previously imagined stereotypical fears, but from a lack of experience with discipline or the emotional interactional styles at the school. In difficult situations, student teachers received quick and contextual feedback on their actions that helped them gain confidence in their ability to work with culturally different populations. Significant learning also results from living in the community surrounding the school, although it took time for some participants to consciously relate the community to the classroom. "I have felt relatively comfortable and safe . . . a lot of similarities . . . inside the school. When I drive around the neighborhood I get a little nervous. . . . The area is like nothing I have ever experienced. It is definitely a unique experience outside the classroom" (Moule, 2003a, p. 3).

Moule's research showed that, after three weeks of the immersion experience, about half the students reported significant improvement in classroom management skills, and an equal number felt that their experience would transfer to working with other diverse populations. None showed increased bias. At worst, preservice teachers left with the same "kids are kids" attitude they came with, an attitude that may or may not cover unchanged assumptions and taken-for-granted cultural norms.

The following exchange underscores the conflict around classroom management that many of the preservice teachers felt.

> I have conflicting tendencies as a teacher. One is to be the Queen of the Classroom. To be in control of the structure. The other is to be the facilitator—to shepherd students along their educational journey, letting them construct meaning as they go. I can't be both. [My cooperating teacher] is Queen, and I'm not her. I couldn't teach like her even if it were my classroom. Kids can't be chief architects of their own learning when there is a Queen or King. (Moule, 2003a, p. 3)

Most teachers struggle with the question of control, or rather the lack of control. Yet it is often the ambiguity that makes things happen in the classroom. Too much control limits the educational spontaneity of students. Too little control, and the results are amorphous—which is why a "fail safe outer boundary," whether physical or psychological, is necessary. In the cross-cultural classroom, the ideal situation is freedom within limits, with both the freedom and the limits carefully constructed and mindful of cultural norms and needs.

A final question Moule asked her preservice teachers was "What have you learned about yourself that you did not realize before this experience?" Some participants saw themselves, for the first time, through the eyes of another culture. One wrote, "I realize I am perceived as being very reserved, quiet and serious." Many expressed delight at their new adaptability: "I realized how adaptable I am to situations . . . in terms of grade level, academically, culturally." One reported on learning "things not to do." Others simply said, "one of the best experiences I've ever had." The following comment summed up the experience for one student teacher.

> I have also learned that I really enjoyed working in a more diverse setting here at King. I have learned that change is good. Sometimes I am very opposed to change and I was very nervous, scared and not looking forward to this

experience. However, I have found that having this huge 180 degree turn in my life has been very positive, very mind altering and a very incredible learning experience. The main thing I have learned about myself from this experience is that I *really* can do whatever I put my mind to. I *can* learn from things I'm not looking forward to. (Moule, 2003a, pp. 3–4)

Once preservice teachers have had such an experience in a culturally different school—especially where staff is highly multicultural and integrated and the student population a minority majority—their previous learning about multicultural education begins to make real-life sense, and they begin to realize that practical details are easily dealt with and implemented. Without a deeper understanding of the lives of Children of Color and the cultural dimensions of their classroom, efforts at change will almost always be surface and have little real effectiveness.

REFLECTION QUESTIONS AND CREATIVE PROBLEM SOLVING

Apply CPS to this chapter (Parnes, 1967): a "mess"; facts; IWWMW; brainstorm; evaluate; plan.

SUMMARY

This chapter focuses on issues of the classroom and direct contact with culturally different students as well as on the preparation of teachers as they move toward cultural competence. People often express anxiety as they contemplate standing in front of a classroom of children who are culturally different from themselves. At such moments, it is important to remember that you are already moving toward being a skilled teacher. Cultural competence doesn't mean beginning from scratch, but rather broadening what you already know, gaining specific cultural knowledge and remaining vigilant as to the cultural appropriateness of various tasks, methods, and perspectives you might routinely take for granted. Teaching is, above all, a human interactive process. Students are also likely to be anxious, especially when the teacher is culturally different. Your first task is to set students at ease in a manner that has meaning for them. Retain an awareness of your common humanity and an attitude of caring, and the rest will follow naturally. Being aware and sensitive about cultural difference is very important, but no more important than being aware of similarities.

A number of suggestions are presented for preparing for and gaining support for cross-cultural teaching. Cross-cultural teaching tends to be more demanding, challenging, and energy-draining, but can also be more rewarding. According to Draguns (1981), it is also more experiential (more likely to emotionally impact the teacher), freewheeling (more demanding of ongoing awareness and an ability to continually adapt material and methods to the specific cultural needs of differing students), and bilateral (more collaborative). What does successful cross-cultural teaching look like? Cose (1997) pointed to the following. Teachers need to find ways to motivate students; convince students that they believe in them; teach them good study skills, including the art of studying in groups; challenge them with difficult and practical material; give them adequate support; and demand that they perform.

Several issues directly relevant to cross-cultural learners are next discussed. Today, the bilingualism debate centers on the instructional use of the two languages of bilingual students. At one end of the continuum are supporters of native-language instruction, which involves mastery of the student's native language before the introduction of English. At the other extreme is the position that English curriculum should be introduced immediately, with minimum use of the native language. Research demonstrates that a middle position is best, especially two-way bilingual immersion programs. Most authors, however, also emphasize the importance of the native language as a source of self-esteem and cultural pride.

In turning to the question of classroom interaction, most authors emphasize the necessity of considering cultural variables in understanding behavioral problems in the classroom. For example, African American students seem most comfortable with teaching styles that emphasize collaboration and opportunities for interaction as well greater latitude in emotions in teacher expression of expectations and dissatisfaction, including the expression of aggression and anger. Asian American students seem most comfortable with formal relationships with the teacher and with individual learning rather than group work. Latino/a students tend to communicate in more indirect, implicit, and covert ways. Often, classroom management problems result from a teacher's misreading the cultural style of Students of Color and interpreting behavior ethnocentrically.

Teachers in cross-cultural classrooms are often confronted with racist and stereotypical statements about students who are culturally different. They must address such statements as part of the learning process. Fennimore (1994) offered a four-stage model of how to do this most effectively: restate the prejudicial statement in a calm and objective way; state one's personal beliefs about the object of the statement in a clear and assertive way; make a positive statement about the specific subjects of the prejudice; and gently turn the subject in a new direction. Training in this method requires behavioral practice.

The final section of the chapter discusses the value of immersion experiences in developing the cultural competence of preservice teachers. Such experiences are optimal when they are of longer duration and greater intensity, involve actually living in the community in which the school resides, provide an opportunity to focus on the emotional lives of the students, and provide exposure to the daily realities of students' lives. Students tend to report that immersion programs allow them to get beyond their initial fears and stereotypes of Students of Color, gain comfort with and knowledge about student populations, and better understand classroom material presented earlier in their education.

INTRODUCTION TO CHAPTERS 10, 11, 12, 13, AND 14

What follows are five in-depth interviews, four focused on working with students from the four Communities of Color, and one focused on students from White ethnic backgrounds. Each is written in conjunction with a teacher from that community who is an educator with extensive experience working with students from his or her respective group. All were asked: What do you think is important, or even critical, for a culturally different teacher to know in relation to working with a student from your community? Their responses are presented according to a number of distinct topics that provide the structure for the interviews. Included are educator and ethnic autobiographical material, demographics and shared characteristics of their community, group names, history in a nutshell, family and community characteristics, cultural style, values, worldview, socioeconomic issues, subpopulations, optimal styles, and a short case study.

The text of each chapter was generated through an interview in which the teacher summarized his or her thinking about the general characteristics that community members share. This is not an easy task, since each racial category represents an array of diverse ethnic groups. Each interviewee tried to speak broadly enough to fairly represent the cultural and psychological characteristics shared by the majority of members of the ethnic group he or she is representing. At the same time, each tried to distinguish among subgroups where necessary. Since no single teacher can claim expert knowledge or experience working with all subgroups or divisions within any racial category, the interviewees were asked to discuss specifically and draw examples from subpopulations with which they are most familiar. Answers to the various questions in each interview have been left close to verbatim to retain their personal and cultural flavor.

WORKING WITH LATINO/A STUDENTS

An Interview with Aurora Cedillo

DEMOGRAPHICS

With the 2000 census, Latinos/as became the largest racial minority in the United States, numbering 35,305,818 or 12.5 percent of the U.S. population. These figures represent an increase of 58 percent over the last decade and are in actuality an underestimation, since they do not reflect the undocumented and illegal migrants who are continually entering the U.S. Garcia (1995) estimates illegal immigration at approximately 200,000 per year. Projections suggest that Latinos/as will make up one-third of the U.S. population by 2100. This dramatic growth is attributed to high birthrates and fertility rates, immigration patterns, and the average young age of the population. As a collective, Latinos/as are quite diverse, including individuals whose roots are in Mexico, Cuba, Puerto Rico, and South and Central America. Those of Mexican descent, now numbering 20 million, make up 64 percent of the Hispanic population. Puerto Ricans number 3.4 million and 10 percent, Cuban 1.2 million and 4 percent, and Central and South Americas 3.1 million and 9 percent.

For the purpose of the census, the government considers race and Hispanic origins as "two separate and distinct concepts." The term *Hispanic* is used to denote a Spanish-speaking background. A notable exception, however, are Latinos/as of Brazilian descent, whose native language is Portuguese. Racially, individuals of Mexican descent identify their roots as "Mestizo" (a mixture of Spanish and Indian backgrounds). Puerto Ricans consider themselves of Spanish descent, Cubans of Spanish and Black descent, and those from Latin America as varying mixtures of Spanish, Japanese, Italian, and Black. In the 2000 census, 48 percent of Hispanics identified themselves as White only and 42 percent as White and one other race.

Geographically, Latino/a populations are largely urban and are concentrated in the Southwest, Northeast, and the state of Florida. According to country of origin; Mexican Americans are a significant proportion of the population in Texas, California, Arizona, New Mexico, and Illinois; Puerto Ricans are often found in large urban areas in the Northeast and Cubans in the Miami area.

The vast majority of Latinos/as are Spanish-speaking and Catholic, and share in varying degrees a set of cultural characteristics described below. It is very important to distinguish between traditional Latino culture and alterations in traditional cultural patterns that result from life in the United States. Three factors—generational status, language use, and adaptation to acculturative forces—play a major role in creating diversity among individuals and families within Latino communities and in the emergence of new cultural forms. The interplay between tradition and acculturation is in fact a powerful dynamic. For example, conflict within families often arises when children adapt to acculturative forces and parents struggle to maintain traditional values and beliefs. In short, one must be careful to not underemphasize the differences within and across groups, for there are as many of these as there are similarities. Klor de Alva (1988), for example, points out that "Different Hispanic groups, generally concentrated in different regions of the country, have little knowledge of each other and are often as surprised as non-Hispanics to discover the cultural gulfs that separate them" (p. 107).

Compared to non-Hispanics (again, a census term rather than an identity of choice among most group members), Latinos/as tend to be younger—on average, below thirty, and nine years younger than the average White American; poorer—40 percent of Hispanic children live below the poverty line; less educated—approximately 30 percent leave high school before graduation (the highest rate of all minorities); and more consistently unemployed or relegated to unskilled and semiskilled jobs.

A unique set of factors, related to their entry and circumstances in the United States, puts Latinos/as at high risk for physical and psychological difficulties. Included are pressures around bilingualism, immigration and rapid acculturation, adjustment to U.S. society, intergenerational and cultural conflict, poverty, racism, and the loss of cultural identity. As we shall discover from our expert guest, Aurora Cedillo, central factors in understanding the educational situation of most Latino/a students are their individual experiences and the experiences of their family units in migrating to and residing in the United States.

FAMILY AND CULTURAL VALUES

As a collective, Latino/a subgroups share a language, Spanish; a religion, Catholicism; and in varying degrees aspects of traditional cultural values that define and structure group life. Carrasquillo (1991) lists the following shared values.

- Importance of the family, both nuclear and extended or *familialismo*
- Emphasis on interdependence and cooperation or *simpatico*

- Emphasis on the worth and dignity of the individual or *personalismo*
- A valuing of the spiritual side of life
- An acceptance of life as it exists

Garcia-Preto offers an excellent description of the nature of traditional Latino/a families.

> Perhaps the most significant value they share is the importance placed on family unity, welfare and honor. The emphasis is on the group rather than on the individual. There is a deep sense of family commitment, obligation, and responsibility. The family guarantees protection and caretaking for life as long as the person stays in the system. . . . The expectation is that when a person is having problems, others will help, especially those in stable positions. The family is usually an extended system that encompasses not only those related by blood and marriage, but also "compadres" (godparents) and "hijos de crianza" (adopted children, whose adoption is not necessarily legal). "Compadrazco" (godparenthood) is a system of ritual kinship with binding, mutual obligations for economic assistance, encouragement, and even personal correction. "Hijos de crianza" refers to the practice of transferring children from one nuclear family to another within the extended family in times of crisis. The others assume responsibility, as if children were their own, and do not view the practice as neglectful. (1996, p. 151)

Family roles and duties are highly structured and traditional, as are sex roles, which are referred to as *machismo* and *marianismo*. Males, the elderly, and parents are afforded special respect, while children are expected to be obedient and deferential, contribute to family finances, care for younger siblings, and act as parental surrogates. Males are expected to exhibit strength, virility, and dominance and to provide for the family, while females are expected to be nurturing, to submit themselves to males, and to self-sacrifice (Sue & Sue, 1999). Both boys and girls are socialized into these roles early. Boys are given far more freedom than girls, are encouraged to be aggressive and act manly, and are discouraged from playing with girls and engaging in female activities. Girls are trained early in household activities and are severely sheltered and restricted as they grow older.

The authoritative structure of the family also reflects a broader characteristic of Latino/a culture, what Marin and Marin (1991) describe as the valuing of conformity, obedience, deference to authority, and subservience to the autocratic attitudes of external organizations and institutions. Individuals from what Marin and Marin call "high power distant" cultures are most comfortable in hierarchical structures where there is an obvious power differential and expectations are clearly defined. Professionals and helpers who do not respect this power distance—by de-emphasizing their authority, trying to make the interaction more democratic, communicating indirectly, or using subtle forms of control such as sarcasm and causing an individual to lose face—tend to confuse and alienate, Latino/a students. Respect for authority can also have a darker side by forcing individuals from high power distant cultures to adapt to the status quo as well as restraining them from asserting their rights. Garcia-Preto (1996) offers the example of illegal migrants whose cultural hesitancy is exacerbated by the fear of being caught and sent back to more oppressive and dangerous circumstances.

Personalismo, an interpersonal attitude that acknowledges the basic worth and dignity of all individuals and attributes to them a sense of self-worth, serves as a powerful social lubricant in Latino/a culture. Unlike mainstream American culture, where respect is garnered through achievement, status, and wealth, in Latino/a culture the individual merits respect by the very fact of his or her humanity. *Simpatio,* or the placing of value on cooperation and interdependence, is a natural outgrowth of *personalismo.* Competing, undermining the efforts of another, asserting one's individuality, and trying to inflate one's ego are all viewed negatively within Latino/a culture. In cultures in which the needs of the individual are suppressed in order to better serve the interests of the group (the dimension of culture Brown and Lundrum-Brown, 1995, call "the individual versus the extended self" [see Chapter 3]), the individual ego must be contained. This is done through *simpatico,* which serves to promote cooperation, noncompetition, and the avoidance of conflict between individuals.

It should again be noted that this traditional picture of the Latino/a family can be radically altered as a function of education, generational status, and income. For example, rigid sex roles are often the first cultural element to change with acculturation. Similarly, some cultural dynamics tend to go against the value patterns just described. Traditional culture, for instance, shows a great degree of egalitarianism in decision making and childrearing. Latinos/as have a long history of asserting their rights in labor—for instance, the mine strikes and the work of Cesar Chavez—and education. And what better example is there of achievement motivation than the efforts of an individual or family to immigrate, leaving everything and everyone they know in search of a better life.

A final series of values in Latino/a culture relates to beliefs fostered by the Catholic church. These beliefs include

- A focus on spirituality and the life of the spirit
- A fatalistic acceptance of life as it exists
- A time orientation toward the present

Latino/a culture places as much emphasis on nonrational experience as it does on the material world. Belief in visions, omens, spirits, and spiritual healers is commonplace, and such phenomena are viewed from within the culture as normative rather than as pathological. Latino/as are also willing to forgo and even sacrifice material comfort in the pursuit of spiritual goals. To a large extent, this focus on spirituality derives from the unique blend of traditional religious practices and indigenous spiritual beliefs that together have created a practice that has served as a kind of resistance to colonization that has endured for over five hundred years.

At the same time, Yamamoto and Acosta (1982) suggest that the Latino/a church emphasizes that sacrifice in this world promotes salvation, that one must be charitable, and that wrongs against the person should be endured. Sue and

Sue (1999) assert that because of such beliefs "many Hispanics have difficulty behaving assertively. They feel that problems or events are meant to be and cannot be changed" (p. 290). This relates in turn to a time orientation to the present that is shared by most Latinos/as. Focus tends to be on the here-and-now, not on what has happened in the past or will happen in the future. Present-oriented cultures, according to Marin and Marin (1991), place special value on the nature and quality of interpersonal relationships as opposed to their history or functionality. Such an orientation is psychologically related to the kind of fatalism described above and is particularly common in peoples who suffer from economic deprivation and powerlessness and find themselves at the whim and mercy of those with more power. Our interviewee, Aurora Cedillo, gives a personal voice to many of these cultural patterns and values, offering valuable insights into Latino/a students and their behavior and needs in the classroom.

⟨━◆━⟩

Our Interviewee

Aurora Cedillo is a bilingual elementary resource teacher in the Salem-Keizer School District in Oregon. She has taught grades kindergarten to adult. She graduated from Oregon College of Education with an elementary teaching major and a Spanish minor. She has a master's degree and an administrator's certificate from the University of Oregon. She is currently enrolled in a doctoral program at Oregon State University, and teaches numerous inservice and teacher training workshops.

A Texas-born, Oregon-grown Chicana, Aurora migrated with her family from south Texas to the Willamette Valley in Oregon to harvest crops when she was 12 years. Out of 18 children born to her parents she is the first surviving female and the fourth of 10 surviving siblings. Of her personal life she writes: "I am a single mother and grandmother who loves to dance, sing, and tell cultural and family stories. I have written books about my family, my beliefs, and my experiences. In my work I share my culture and my perspectives on how ones' culture impacts educational experience as a learner and a teacher."

The Interview

Could you begin by talking about your own ethnic background and how it has impacted your work?

I'm caught between ethnicities. As I've grown older, I realize I have a multiple identity. I describe myself as Chicana, of Mexican American heritage and experience. But, as I look deeper, I realize that Mexican means mixed race. My mom is French. My dad is more indigenous, though his last name was

Cedillo, a very Spanish name. Therefore, I am French and Spanish and indigenous. My father's father, or my grandfather, lived with my mom at the beginning of her marriage, so she learned a lot from him about his indigenous culture. Many of his ideas, beliefs, and practices were taught to us. Therefore, I would describe my ethnic background as Mexican American, Chicana, and all of my responses in this interview derive from *my* lived experience.

The political and social terms, Mexican American and Chicana, I chose to describe myself have greatly impacted all areas of my personal, social, and educational development. I am a totality of my experiences. My cultural belief on destiny, which is a very strong belief in my culture, compels me to understand that my ethnicity impacted me even before I developed any consciousness of my ethnicity. Through this belief in destiny, I have understood and accepted my place and purpose in my life, my work, and family. Through destiny and the will of God, I have been allowed to learn from others and to share with others. In my work, I have had the opportunity to experience my ethnicity directly and indirectly. I have lived, read, and shared the Chicana experience in my work, communities, and the worlds of English and Spanish speakers as well as the bilingual speakers. I have read what is written about me, and others like me. I have experienced the fire that melts and molds us as a community. By that I mean the political, social, and economic oppression that limits and bars access to an appropriate education, health care, shelter, and dignity as people.

As a bilingual educator of diverse language, culture, and color, my work involves balancing the cultural, linguistic, and socioeconomic scale for students, staff, and parents. Opening means of communication, increasing awareness and acceptance between the groups is a continuous daily task. I confirm the efforts of the groups and value their input, but progress is slow in coming. Success comes one grain of sand at a time; teachers are overwhelmed with students that don't understand the language and culture of the school, parents that seem to not care about the education of their children, and administrators that can't support the teachers' efforts. Institutional, historical practices of silencing and promoting invisibility are alive and vital constantly in every element of the educational experience for Teachers, Students, and Parents of Color.

At times, the work seems to be worthless, and that is very discouraging. There is a lot of bilingual educator burnout. I've been doing this for thirty years, and nothing has changed. In fact, I think it is more difficult today. So I embrace the little successes, the small seeds of communication, and I am hopeful for a better future for all my Mexican American community.

Who are the Chicanas/Chicanos, Latinos/Latinas? What characteristics do they share as a group?

Everyone has their own definition of *Chicanismo*. To some it is positive and proud. To others it is negative and repulsive. My personal definition of who the Chicanos/Latinos or Hispanic are is based on personal lived experience and my readings on that topic. I used to think it meant being U.S.-born, first-generation Mexican American. Since then, I have learned that it is more than that. *Chicanismo* is a powerful inner force that energizes one to act and to self-identify as Chicano/a. It is based on a collection of similar lived experiences Mexicans, Mexican Indigenous have in common in Spanish-speaking communities throughout the United States. Experiences of oppression, invisibility, silencing, and complete rejection, yet succeeding against all odds, are the ingredients that create and define Chicanos.

Chicanos tend to be highly educated Mexican Americans or Latinos who have learned to survive in the mainstream while maintaining the barrio ways. They are advocates of the collective community. They are often excluded from top decision-making positions even if they have the required experience and education that would prepare them for that position.

A characteristic Latinos share is a belief in destiny. The belief is that we are not in complete control of everything that happens in our lives. "Si Dios Quiere" (God willing) is a typical yet simple statement of such belief. A higher being, God, has a purpose and a plan destined for each of us. "Uno pone y Dios Dispone" (one purposes and God disposes) states that one can plan, but if God is not willing it will not be. To Latinos destiny is being. No plan, no objective, no road map, no timeline. I never planned to be in this interview. I never planned to attend Oregon State University as a student participating in a doctoral program. I never planned to be a teacher, to travel nationally and internationally to share my teaching experience. Terms like *goal setting* and *objectives* and *plans* are words I learned in the mainstream world. I learned to use them; however, I can tell you that the plans I have made have very rarely been achieved. Our beliefs on destiny are based in our indigenous experience of European conquest, of genocide, of never having choice in our lives. I can't choose my place of employment; I can't choose where to live my life; I can't choose my doctor. I can't even tell you I will see you tomorrow, because even that depends on someone else.

Another fundamental belief that guides Latinos is the belief that we are born into a family and that the family becomes the most important element in life in this world and beyond. The family is the centerpiece, the glue that bonds one to nature. Family is plural and multifaceted. It is elastic and fluid-like. To Latinos, family is much more than the biological members one is born into. Family is broad and deep. It is inclusive of several generations, social relationships, and local community members. Family includes mother, father, sister, and brother. It includes sister cousins, political sisters, and growth sisters. Also included are aunts, uncles, grandparents, and great-grandparents. It includes children, grandchildren, and great-grandchildren.

Latino families are united to the fifth generation. The saying "hasta la quinta pinta" (tainted to the fifth) relates the exhibition of biological traits, genes, physical similarities, language, cultural practices, and psychological beliefs being present in the lives of members through five generations: great-grandmother to great-granddaughter.

Social families are initiated and implemented by the adults in the family as family members move away or to far-away places. Through processes of religious ceremonies, the families officially unite with dear and special friends as *compadres, comadres, haijados,* and *haijadas* (co-father, co-mother, son-like, and daughter-like). This newly acquired family fills in the void of missing my family and supports new parents in rearing the young.

The community family includes members of a rural community meeting in faraway places and uniting to assist one another in surviving in the new place. Individuals share housing, food, medicine, and money. They provide guidance in survival in the community, employment, and resources. Once able to sustain themselves, they leave and set up another place to assist the newcomers. Everyone from your birth farm, community, or state is a brother and sister. The term *paisano* relates to the brotherhood.

So, we are community centered in the family, defined by destiny, and our connections extend socially, religiously, and politically. We are one. This belief, if misunderstood, creates problems on the job and in relations in mainstream culture. Something as simple as a statement in an invitation to an event can be misunderstood. For example, the statement "no children please" to some Latinos may mean that he/she wasn't really welcomed because if one is invited, all are invited.

Another characteristic of Latino culture is collaboration and cooperation. "One" does not know "it" all. However, everyone knows something. So collectively, as a family or as a community, we Latinos are able to solve the immediate concerns. All members are responsible for something. Some are good at speaking and negotiating; others are good at thinking; others are good at math; others are more spiritually inclined; others are better caregivers. Everyone in the family is an expert in something. Depending on the task or individual funds of knowledge, different leaders arise. When we came to Oregon, my father did not speak, read, or write English. He could not read a map, a road sign, or was unable to ask for directions. My sixteen-year-old brother took the map, read it, and another brother asked directions. The rest of us participated by cleaning and feeding the crew in the cabin.

Could you talk about the various names that the group uses to describe or identify themselves and some of the names that have been used historically to identify the group by others?

Today, the most preferred term by political and social groups is *Hispanic.* Mostly used by non-Latinos describing those who speak Spanish: those coming from the Americas, Spain, Puerto Rico, Cuba, the Dominican Republic, the Caribbean islands, some from the Philippines, and anyone with Spanish surnames. Few Latinos use that term; some are offended by it. In asking about the term, I asked a peer, and he shared that *Hispanic* was a term that arose during the Reagan era. Former President Reagan was so overwhelmed with the influx and rapidly overpowering growth of Latinos in the United States that Latinos became "His Panic." I laughed and embraced that thought.

Other terms used are *Latino* or national terms such as *Mexican, Puerto Rican,* and *Guatemalan.* First-generation Latinos and a few others include *American* to their parents' nationality as in *Mexican American.* Others use terms that identify the tribe or group. *Chicano, Cholo, Pachuco, Tarazco, Huichol,* or *Cora* are such terms.

Terms used by outsiders to describe Mexicans born in the United State are *Pochos* (those lacking, or short of) Mexicans, *foreigners, los del otro lado* (those from the other side), *wetbacks, illegal aliens* and *migrant workers, braseros* and *pandilleros.* Mexicans call us *Mexican born in the United States, Pochos. Pocho* rhymes with *mocho* (without a limb) and means diluted, incomplete, or lacking Mexicanness. To Mexicans, Mexican Americans lack proper Spanish, disrespect the Mexican culture, and have not yet acquired the English language and United State culture. As for me, I detest the term *pocho.* There is no Pochaland in this world. The French have France. The Spaniards have Spain. The Mexicans have Mexico. Pochas, what do they have? Nothing! These terms are derogatory and are used to inflict shame. It is important to realize that each individual identifies oneself according to the term that is most meaningful to them.

Could you highlight for us key historical events in a nutshell? What historical experiences should educators be aware of in relationship to the Latino/a community and Latino/a students?

Historical events that include the histories of the students in the classroom are very important. Teachers must be inclusive of the countries represented in the classroom. For Latino students, a teacher must look to include members of communities represented in her class. For Mexican American, farmworkers, and migrants, a teacher must include Cesar Chavez. It is up to the teacher to discuss what he did and how it affects the present. It's amazing how quickly Heroes of Color fade away in the daily tasks of teaching. Once I asked third-grade students to tell me about Cesar Chavez. Eager and enthused students discussed a boxer also named Cesar Chavez. In less than ten years, Cezar Chavez had been lost to a new generation of teachers and students!

Teachers must celebrate the sixteenth of September, Mexico's day of independence, as well as many other Central American countries that celebrate their independence day in September. As teachers, we must know what event happened on the fifth of May and why we celebrate that day. For Mexican Americans and Chicanos Cinco de Mayo is especially important. The battle in Puebla, Mexico, on the fifth of May is a day to remember—that regardless of poverty, training, or language, positive change can happen if we fight a battle as a united people.

Teachers must be inclusive when discussing historical events. Many of our teachers were not exposed to the history of Latino countries and are not informed. I would suggest that teachers invite community members, parents, minority staff within the school to come and share with the students. Not only will the students feel included; the teacher will benefit greatly from this activity. Also important is the discussion of the contributions made by members of these communities in the development of this powerful nation.

Opportunity for inclusion is present everywhere in the curriculum and, guess what, you do not even have to speak Spanish. One of the great people I know, named David Bautista, said to me, "It is not about language." It is much more than that. It is about being inclusive, bringing the community into your class, asking for information, and being humble. It is about being passionate about your work as a teacher. Teaching the Constitution, the Pledge, and always learning. Learn to be resourceful. Learn from your students, parents, and other staff. Look for the great local community leaders. Invite them into the classes. Share your story, and invite others to share.

Could you speak more about family and community and how these shape what happens in schools with Latino students?

The popular saying that "it takes a village to grow a child" is also true in the Latino community. The only difference is that in the barrio we say, "It takes a migrant camp or a barrio to grow a child." Everyone in a community takes responsibility to assist in growing a child—parents, grandparents, co-parents, aunts, uncles, neighbors, church members, teachers, friends, and even older siblings. Authority to discipline a child if needed is given to the caregiver. My mother would say, " Spank her if she does not listen, and tell me, and I will spank her also." When you hear such words, you know you are responsible to all your elders regardless of who they are.

As a collective culture, Latinos tend to hand their child over to the teacher. They trust that the teachers and other school staff will do what is best for their child. In the subconscious mind, the teacher holds a sacred place. Next to God and mom, the teacher is respected and honored. Parents will not invade a teacher's space unless an obvious act of violence or disregard for the child are exposed.

Creating change and shaping the school culture is difficult when parents feel intrusive or rude if they question things at school. Parents will discuss issues superficially and may not confront the issues in a direct way. Added to this is the concern that parents do not speak and understand English at a level needed to address the needs. Many times, parents will bring a son or daughter to interpret for them. Schools are ill equipped to deal with this both linguistically and culturally. They judge these actions as irresponsible, for how can parents even consider including the child in these discussions.

After many unproductive meetings with school staff, Latino families learn that coming to school alone is very ineffective. They share their experience with others. Those with typical experience share what they know. They contact support within the community, and together in a group they call for change. Grandmothers, who are central to these activities, have been around; they experienced it with their children, and since they are elders they carry the discussion. These grandmothers bring their whole family to come and listen. (Many different ears can understand what one set will miss.) Once again, the culture that respects the experience of elders clashes with the culture that throws elders away to retirement homes.

With time and experience, parents realize that schools will only listen when lawyers and money talk. Through the grass-roots efforts, parents can create a situation where they will be heard. They bring attention to issues and make school accountable for all students' success. What works best is to include parents as partners—informing them of school processes and getting informed of the unique cultural, linguistic, and social and academic elements of the student and his family.

Are there any subpopulations in the Latino/a community you feel deserve additional attention in the classroom?

The two groups that I think deserve additional attention are the newly arrived to our communities from indigenous backgrounds and the locally born and grown Latino children. Our indigenous Indian populations intermixed racially with Latino/as as they come from Mexico, Central American, and Guatemala. We know very little about their background, how they learn, where their historical places are, or their lifestyles in their countries of origin. We are unfamiliar with their social practices and do not speak their language if it is not Spanish. Frankly, we are at a loss. Right now in our schools, we are looking for representatives from these indigenous communities who will come and share with us information on how we can reach their students and families. They tend to be even harder to reach than Chicano students, fall through the cracks, drop out, and underachieve at even higher levels.

A second group, particularly at high risk, are the first- and second-generation Latinos, both immigrant and U.S.-born. These students grow up in two worlds. They learn two languages at one time. They live between worlds and have not developed a strong foundation in either one. The minute they are born, they're listening to English as well as to the Spanish of their parents. So they must learn two languages. Educators in charge of instructing these students have little knowledge about bilingualism. In desperation, Spanish-language experts from Mexico and other Central Americans are hired to work with these students. These teachers know Spanish but do not know how to work with bilingual students. (Just because you speak two languages does not make you a teacher of bilingual students.)

Inappropriate or no assessment of these students' academic skills leads to inappropriate placement and instruction. Many of these students attend high-risk schools where the least experienced teachers tend to teach. Since they require a bilingual placement, they are taught by teachers who are just learning Spanish as their second language. They have not yet developed the depth or the breath of the language in order to provide students with rich embedded language required in academics.

Students from these two Latino subgroups tend to be the ones who drop out of school the most. They are also the fastest growing population in penal institutions. They also tend to be disconnected from the cultural practices and linguistic foundation that strengthen the first generation.

Could you talk a little more about the controversy among bilingual educators, their approaches and what needs to be done for bilingual students?

Controversy among bilingual educators centers on pressures from the mainstream society dictating that English is the only language to be taught. Research shows that if you teach children in the language they understand, they will be successful. But there are political pressures coming from the educational establishment that allow non-English students three years in special programs and then push them out. Research, however, says that it takes five to seven years for a child to develop the academic proficiency of an English speaker. But new educators want to keep their jobs and want to make sure they are doing what the system tells them to do. Older educators who have seen the research and know from firsthand experience are more likely to challenge the political pressures and push for teaching them in their native language. But basically, educators are caught between these forces, and what are you going to do?

Another great controversy is the misalignment in bilingual education. So-called programs are planted on hard soil. Allocated funding is misused; programs are left to the discretion of unqualified staff; and resources are either lacking or inappropriate.

Higher education institutions provide very little in bilingual education courses. Bilingual teachers have to figure it out on their own. Due to the lack of bilingual staff, multicultural education, language acquisition, and foreign language are some how supposed to prepare bilingual educators. Bilingual education is very political. It involves learning the rights and the Constitution. It involves moving students, parents, and staff to question the system. This is very scary, and very few teachers feel strong enough to battle.

All of these misalignments take a toll on teachers who are on the front lines. She is the one who sees the failure, the student dropout rate, who attends the parent conferences, and sees the angry letters from the mainstream community against bilingualism. And finally, she is blamed for the lack of support given to non-English speakers in such a crucial time in their development.

Does class or other socioeconomic issues play a role in considering aspects of this population?

Class plays a big role. Titles are important. Money is very important. Age is very important. Experience is very important. But class represents the dividing line that sorts one into social groups. If you have money, you tend to relate to others who have money. Especially among newcomers, few are not poor and all struggle to acquire money. And if one does acquire money, it becomes a big privilege, a big benefit, affords both greater protection and influence. If you are poor and have less money, you have little influence on the system.

How do different cultural styles, values, and worldviews affect education of Latino/Latina students?

The biggest thing I see in the classroom as far as different cultural styles is that the teacher tends to come from an "I" perspective and is in charge of teaching students who are from a culture with a "we" perspective. Not being aware of this cultural difference can result in confusion and arrogance on the part of the teacher that desires to control everything. The "I" perspective is an egocentric attitude that predominates in Anglo culture. I need to plan, I need to do, or I need to fix. For the mainstream culture, the idea is that you fail because one failed to plan. This "I" perspective creates misunderstanding toward people that have a "we" perspective. In order for "I" to do something, "we" needs to happen. In order for "I" to attend, "we" need to have a car, pay the insurance, get a license, learn to read English, and learn to drive. "I" is dependent on how many resources "we" can gather.

Also, the cultural elements of destiny and family are very important. The element of time heavily impacts the class. In situations where the relationship is more important than the event, measuring time can be problematic. For mainstream culture the clock runs the show. In Latino culture, the relationship runs the show. So it is more important to save the relationship than it is to save time. In Latino culture, the concept of time is different; *luego, despues, al rato, al ratito, ya* all have a different time value, If a teacher does not know that, it could cause disruptions in transitioning times.

Another issue is the concept of collective ownership. In Spanish the word *la, el* is used instead of *my* or *mine.* In English we say "my pencil," "my house," or "my car."

Communication style is another cultural element that needs to be considered when working with Latinos. Latinos tend to speak in colorful statements that surround the issue. This type of communication style is called "circular" and/or *peogeon* style of communication.

What are some of the common problems that Latino/a students might bring into the school setting?

I guess I would not call them problems. Unless if you would consider physical challenges. Not being able to see is a problem; not hearing is a problem; not having an anus is a problem. But not speaking English is not a problem. Not being aware of the mainstream culture is not a problem. Not knowing the school system is not a problem. The problem, as I see it, is that we, the educators, want students who look like us, act like us, think like us, and see like us. We as a people, even among a common group, have problems. We have problems with teenagers, elders, obese or thin people. Our biggest problem is "I." I need to see that I am not the center of the world. If I accept that idea, then I can move on to understand that not all people live like me. If one is late, it could be that they did not have a car. Or it could be that they had to wait on someone else and that someone else had something that they had to wait on. Or maybe they did not have a phone to call. It was raining so hard and walking to the nearest telephone would mean leaving the baby alone.

Another problem that I see could be that I accepted a job that required the use of Spanish, and my high school Spanish or my summer in Mexico did not prepare me to teach content and academics in Spanish. Another problem could be that, because I was taught to make eye contact and face people to show I am attentive and sincere, I have a difficult time when students hide their eyes from me.

In Spanish we say *el carro, la casa, el lapiz.* Even your personal parts don't belong to you. So it's *los manos*, the hands, wash the hands. Not wash *your* hands; wash the hands, wash the face, clean the ears. But in Anglo culture, it's I washed *my* hands, I washed *my* face. So this little boy or girl comes to school. He or she needs a pencil, so they pick one up off a desk. Not my pencil or her pencil, but the pencil. Another child yells out. "He stole my pencil. She took my pencil!" The Latino child says, "I did not take your pencil." "You have the pencil right there!" The teacher intercedes: "Is that her pencil? Give her back her pencil!" "But why?" Now he goes home and he takes a dinner plate. He had that plate yesterday, now his sister has it today. "That's my plate!" he says, and his mother disciplines him, feeling the need to remind him about sharing. "This is not your plate; it belongs to the family; it belongs to whoever gets it first."

Another issue is eye contact, and this is very important. In Latino culture, it is considered disrespectful to look directly at an elder when they are talking to you. However, in Anglo culture averting one's eyes is experienced as defiant, as showing guilt, as being rude.

There is also the high respect given to food in Latino culture. It is a community where everything is shared, especially food. Nothing is thrown away, and you share your food rather than throw it away. You don't play with it. At home one gets scolded or spanked for wasting or throwing away food. In the classroom, when food like rice or salt or macaroni or beans are used in learning activities, that is playing with it; the child is put in a difficult bind. He doesn't participate. He refuses to play with it. He may be graded down. But if the teacher is aware of these cultural things, they can use rocks or popsicle sticks, anything but food.

When teachers are unaware and cross cultural lines, they may inadvertently trample on their students and not even know it unless the child speaks up. And it is the rare classroom where Latino/a students feel free enough to speak up. There is the story of a classroom where the children obviously felt free enough to do so. The teacher gave out treats, little cakes, because it was someone's birthday. She said, "Please wait until the party person eats first, and then we will all eat." But the Spanish speakers didn't understand it, because it was said only in English. So the minute they got their cupcakes, they ate them. The teacher responded by saying, "You are eating like pigs!" One little boy responded, "Teacher, please don't call us pigs again." She began to answer "No, I said you ate like pigs," but then caught herself. "What should I have said?" The boy answered, "You could have said we ate a lot." The teacher subsequently learned that comparing a person to an animal is considered a deep insult in Latino/a culture. Again, these are not problems; they are challenges that must be discussed openly by students, parents, teachers, and other school staff.

Finally, a problem could be that, because I am used to seeing groups of cowboys in Wranglers hanging out in the streets, I do not feel scared. However, because I am not used to seeing a group of Latino men dressed in Khaki slacks, I feel funny and sacred. There are not problems, only challenges to overcome.

Could you discuss some of the factors important in assessing the learning style of Latino/Latina students and suggest what classroom factors could be manipulated to match these styles?

Learning styles are basically the different ways humankind learns. We learn by seeing. We learn by doing. We learn by acting out. We learn by observing others and modeling their behavior. We teach children by modeling the things we expect from them. It's a continual process in the classroom. You reach out to the kids, you model, you show, you do, you explain. You have other people explain. Look at José, he did it really well. Could you tell us how you did that, could you show us? I do much of my teaching in the context of small cooperative learning groups. You give them tasks to practice, problems to solve, explain your expectations step by step. Put things on the wall that reinforce the lessons, always giving them references to what they need to do. Reviews for when they are absent from the classroom. All of these little efforts or bricks of support provide scaffolding for learning and succeeding. Especially where language is an issue, a spoken lecture is not enough. You have to show them many times, to model behavior. In working in small groups, it is important to find a student leader who understands the lesson and is able to tell what he learned. I always tell my bilingual teachers, when you set up your cooperative groups, you want to find someone to lead who is fluent in English as well as someone fluent in Spanish. Also a balance of gender, girls and boys. In classes for bilingual children, everyone must be a teacher to each other. English speakers are going to learn Spanish; the Spanish speaker's going to learn English. The bilingual children are going to learn everyday. Also look to language ability when you're forming your groups. With different levels of ability, you're not the only teacher. You cannot teach such a classroom alone. You need your environment to help you. You need your students and their peers to help you. You need the materials to support you, and above all you need the cultural awareness of where those kids are coming from and their home experience. Finally, learn by doing. Create the experience for and with students. Learning involves all the senses. Use them. If you do all of these things and make all of these connections, kids will be more successful.

Are there teaching strategies that are more effective in working with Latino/Latina students?

I have spoken of many strategies through out the interview. Of all the ones I've spoken about, communicating is the most important. Be a learner and make sure to include the families; they are not there alone. "I did not get this A; we all got it." So if you leave the parents out of the learning loop, if you leave the aunts or the grandmothers, you are only using half of your resources. You need to bring the families into the learning environment. They know their students best. They know their children the most. They know if their children are morning people or afternoon people, their abilities and capabilities, their individual histories. We have a lot of kids who bring trauma with them to the classroom: abandonment, abuse, neglect, just being poor, not having the right foods, medical care, attention. We can't expect them to read and write when their teeth are falling out or they have an ear infection that has never been corrected or when they have been abandoned by their moms in their grandmother's house without any food because mom was trying to find her husband in the United States. Having access to a counselor is very important, someone who understands these traumas and can talk to children and families about them. Even U.S.-born Latino, English-speaking students often lack resources they need to succeed. Our schools witness families who have experienced death, drownings, and fires. We tend to be quicker to help them if they are English speaking. The school gets together, brings boxes of food and clothes, making sure that the family gets the support it needs. When Latino kids get hurt or their families have problems, there is a tendency to expect other agencies to take care of things. Somebody else will take care of it. We need the kind of system that will respond equally to all students who are hurting. And in a language and style they can understand. Who's going to counsel the immigrant child when he or she just lost their cousin in a fire? The English-speaking counselor cannot do it. And someone who can only translate is not equipped to understand the deeper concepts of counseling: what is going on in the children's minds and how to get them to discuss the issues that need attention. Such resources should be available in all of our schools.

Okay, last question. Could you present a short case that brings together the different issues and dynamics we've discussed about working with Latino/Latina students?

The story of my brother in special education comes to mind. Our ability to teach bilingual children with special problems that are deeper and more complex is minimal. There are usually fewer resources, less information, and it's an area sheltered by various laws and practices that often get in the way. In general, special education is designed only for the English language learner. My brother was a junior in high school when the system realized that here was this child due to graduate the following year who didn't know how to read . He had gone through the entire school system without any reading assessment, without anyone ever checking it out. What are they going to do with him? He's not in a special education class, so they can't give him an achievement award and send him on his way. He's not reading, so they can't give him a diploma. He's not perpetually absent, so they can't kick him out. So what they decide to do is test him. I am eighteen years old and serve as an interpreter between the school and my family. "Mom, they want to know if it's okay if they do these tests to find out why my brother hasn't read." Of course, like most Latino families, they want to do the best they can for their children, even though they don't quite understand it all. "Go ahead. We want to know what is wrong." So my brother is taken to a facility and given all of these psychological things, and he tried to explain them to us, but it was pretty confusing. And we never even knew the names of the tests. A couple of months later, they call us back and say, "The tests show that your son will never learn to read." We really couldn't understand what they were talking about other than the fact that he had been diagnosed as EMR, that is, mentally retarded, and would be put into an EMR classes. In those days, such classes were separate from the regular schools. At our school, they were housed in trailers behind the main building. So my brother goes the next day after the family has talked about it. But he is no longer with his group of friends. He's a junior, but is in this room with various-aged kids. They look different; they act different; some of them are sitting; some of them crying. It is your typical "mental class." My brother said that when he saw this, he slid to the floor, crawled out the door, and would never to go back to school again.

Working with Native American Students

An Interview with Jack Lawson

Demographics

The only word that adequately captures the horrors that befell the Native Peoples of this continent at the hands of the White majority is *genocide*. According to Churchill (1994), the population of Native Peoples of this hemisphere fell from estimates as high as 125 million to a quarter-million during the period of 1492–1892. This figure represents 90 percent of their population. The U.S. government expropriated (a fancy word meaning legal theft) 98 percent of Native lands. Today, debilitating alcoholism, high suicide rates, unresolved historic grief, economic hardships, and loss of cultural ways affect many Native Americans. Educationally, Native students exhibit some of the highest school dropout and underachievement rates in the country. In short, Native Americans represent a true American tragedy.

Today, American Indians and Alaska Natives (the U.S. census category) number 2,475,956 individuals or 0.9 percent of the population. By including people who identify themselves as multiracial with Native American as one of the components the number goes up to 1.6 million. Over the past four decades, the Native American population has been increasing. Between 1960 and 1990, for example, the numbers increased 255 percent, and between 1990 and 2000 they increased by 516,722, or another 26 percent. Adding multiracial individuals brings the increase to 2.2 million in the last ten years, or 110 percent. Pollard and O'Hare (1999) offer a number of reasons for this upward trend.

- Census counting has improved.
- Birthrates are high.
- Mortality rates have gone down.
- People who were passing as White, Black, or another race as well as those with partial ancestry have reclaimed their Native American heritage and identity.

As a collective, Native Americans represent almost 500 different tribes and 314 different reservations. Seventy-nine percent report tribal enrollment. Tribes with the largest populations are the Cherokee (281,069), Navajo (269,202), and Latin American Indian (104,940), followed by the Choctaw, Sioux, and Chippewa. The largest Alaskan Native tribe is the Eskimo (45,919). Geographically, Native American populations cluster in certain regions. Forty-nine percent live in the West, 31 percent in the South, 17 percent in the Midwest, and 9 percent in the Northeast. More than half of the total population reside in nine states: California, Oklahoma, Arizona, Texas, New Mexico, Washington, North Carolina, Michigan, and Alaska. California has the largest total population (627,562), followed by Oklahoma (391,949). Alaska has the largest proportion of Native residents at 19 percent, followed by Oklahoma (11 percent) and New Mexico (10 percent). About half of the Native population is located in urban centers and half on rural reservations. There is, however, extensive mobility between the two locations: city dwellers return to the reservation for ritual and family business, and reservation Indians travel to the cities for work, advanced education, and other reasons.

FAMILY AND CULTURAL VALUES

Sue and Sue (1999) identified five values that typify Native American cultures.

- Sharing and cooperation
- Noninterference
- A cyclical orientation to time
- The importance of extended families
- Harmony with nature

Sharing and Cooperation

Sutton and Broken Nose (1996) quoted an Oglala Lakota elder on the Native American attitude about sharing: "When I was little, I learned that what's yours is mine and what's mine is everybody's" (p. 40). Status and honor are earned not by accumulating wealth, but rather by sharing it and giving it away. Gifts are profusely given, especially during life-cycle events, to thank others and acknowledge their achievement. Material possessions are expected to be freely shared. Great importance is placed on hospitality and caring for the needs of strangers. Working for wages is purely instrumental. A Native Person, for example, may stop working once enough money has been earned to meet immediate needs. Related to sharing is cooperation. As in Latino/a culture, competition and egotism are anathema to Native ways. The family and tribe take precedence over the individual, and an individual is expected to set aside personal activities and striving in order to help others. Interpersonal harmony is always sought, and discord avoided.

Of course, the selfless attitude toward material wealth and possessions may prove counterproductive in the mainstream economy. Sutton and Broken Nose (1996) described the traditional owners of a restaurant on the Navaho reservation who had financial problems because they felt obliged to serve free food to relatives, and most people on the reservation were relatives.

Noninterference

It is considered inappropriate in Native American culture to intrude or interfere in the affairs of others. Boundaries and the natural order of things are to be respected. Similarly, stoicism and nonreactivity are highly valued. A premium is placed on listening. Sutton and Broken Nose (1996) suggested that "silence may connote respect, that the person is forming thoughts, or waiting for signs that it is the right time to speak" and that the "non-Indian may treat silence, embellished metaphors, and indirectness as signs of resistance, when actually they represent forms of communication" (p. 37).

Time Orientation

"Indian Time" is cyclical, rhythmic, and imprecise. People are orientated toward the present, the here and now, not to future events and deadlines. Activities take as long as they take and have a natural logic and rhythm of their own. "Lateness" and defining time by external clocks and circumstances are Western concepts, the product of a linear time frame. Long-term goal setting is viewed as egotism, and life events are experienced as processes that unfold in their own time and way. As Sutton and Broken Nose (1996) suggested, "the focus is placed on one's current place, knowing that the succeeding changes will inevitably come" (p. 39). This notion of time, which has a tendency to frustrate mainstream teachers who work on tight schedules, interfaces perfectly with the value of noninterference in the natural order of things.

Extended Families

Although the specifics of power distribution, roles, and kinship definitions vary from tribe to tribe, the vast majority of Native Peoples live under an extended family system that is conceptually different from the Western notion of family. Some tribes are matrilineal, which means that property and status are passed down through the women. When a Hopi man marries, for example, he moves in with his wife's family, and the wife's brothers, not the father, have primary responsibility for educating the sons.

Family ties define existence, and the definition of being a Navajo or a Sioux does not reside within the individual's personality, but rather in the intricacies of family and tribal responsibilities. When strangers meet, they identify themselves by who their relatives are, not by their occupations or place of residence. The individual feels a close and binding connection with a broad network of relatives (often including some who are not related by blood) that can extend as far as second cousins. The naming of relationships reflects the closeness between relatives. The term *grandparent,* for instance, applies not only to the parents of one's biological parents, but also to the biological grandparents' brothers and sisters. Similarly, *in-law* has no meaning within Native culture; after entry into the family system, no distinctions are made between natural and inducted individuals (Sutton and Broken Nose, 1996). Thus, the woman identified as mother-in-law in mainstream culture is called mother in Native culture. The responsibility for parenting is communal, shared throughout the extended family. Sue and Sue (1999) pointed out that it is not unusual for children to live in various households of the extended family while growing up.

Harmony with Nature

Native American cultures emphasize the interconnectedness and harmony of all living things and natural objects. This spiritual holism affirms the value and interdependence of all life forms. Nature is held in reverence, and Native Peoples believe that they are responsible for living in harmony and safeguarding the valuable resources human beings have been given. Sutton and Broken Nose (1996) quoted Chief Seattle: "My mother told me, every part of this earth is sacred to our people. Every pine needle. Every sandy shore. Every mist in the dark woods. Every meadow and humming insect. The Earth is our mother" (p. 40).

This message, which implies the need for noninterference in the natural order and stewardship over the environment, stands in stark opposition to the mainstream value of mastering, controlling, and taking what we want from the earth. Spiritual harmony with the natural order also underlies Native beliefs about health and illness. Physical and emotional illness reflects disharmony between the person or the collective and the natural world. Only by bringing the system back into harmony can healing be achieved.

Unlike other Peoples of Color, Native Americans have found it difficult to improve their socioeconomic standing in American society. While the other Communities of Color struggle to increase their representation in the middle class, in professional and white-collar jobs, and in higher education, Native representation in these groups is all but nonexistent. Why these great disparities?

First, other cultural groups share more aspects of White Northern European culture than do Native Americans. The radical differences between their ways and those of mainstream White culture set the stage for their ill treatment. Their notions of stewardship of the land, fair play, honor, and dignity made them easy victims of mainstream values of capitalism and the philosophy that "might makes right."

Second, so horrendous were the actions against Native Peoples that mainstream culture made certain that their voices would not be heard. To make sure their stories would be discounted, Native People were turned into stereotypes: savages of the frontier, drunken Indians, Pocahontas, mascots for sports teams, and emblems for automobiles. According to Kivel (1996), mechanisms of denial included underestimating the number of Native Americans who lived in North America, questioning the vitality and stability of their culture, picturing the genocide as a natural process with a life of its own, and attributing their demise to biological inferiority.

Third, for generations, the government systematically destroyed Native culture and alienated individuals from their traditions and customs. Our guest expert, Jack Lawson, describes this loss of identity and disconnection from tradition as the source of many contemporary Native woes. He also sees respect for tradition as a key element in integrating Native youth into the classroom.

———————◆———————

Our Interviewee

Jack Lawson is the Native American Coordinator for the State of Oregon Youth Authority. He is responsible for establishing relations with the nine federally recognized tribes in Oregon, developing and implementing culturally relevant educational and treatment services, and helping to oversee the Oregon Youth Authority's mission of implementing cultural competency and community development in all of its efforts. He has worked, primarily with Native People, for over twenty-two years as a teacher and counselor. Ethnically, he is a member of the Creek Nation.

The Interview

Could you first talk about your own ethnic background and how it has led to your work in the classroom and as a counselor to Native youth?

I am a Creek. My family is originally from Oklahoma. I was born in California and moved to Oklahoma when I was about six years old, and then moved back to California when I was ten years old, where we continued to live. While in Oklahoma, I remember attending ceremonies and

(Used with permission of Jack Lawson.)

gatherings. Feasts, singing, and dancing are part of my memories of that time. After returning to California, I lost contact with my relatives in Oklahoma. As a consequence of moving back to California, I was separated from my Native culture and traditions. I attended public schools all my life, and for the most part the information I received about Native Americans has been negative and based on stereotypes. Most western movies portrayed us as drunks, heathens, violent, and dirty, which supported the information I received in the schools. I knew I was a Native American, but I didn't have any way of accessing positive information about who I was racially and culturally. Growing up in a situation where I was not exposed to my own culture and traditions left me lost as to who I was and open to accepting what others said about Native People. One of the first signs of oppression is when you start believing other people's version of history about yourself. I seemed to have only numb feelings about my Native identity back then.

Several memories do remain with me about school, however. I remember receiving a box of crayons and being especially aware of the "flesh" colored crayon. It was not the color of my skin; flesh was supposed to be White. In retrospect the message was very clear. There was something wrong with me, not being White. I also remember the images of American history and its portrayal of my people. We were heathens and savages, and the settlers were always portrayed as good, innocent, god-fearing folk who were preyed upon by us savages. I remember in the seventh or eighth grade talking about scalping. The teacher talked about Native people scalping settlers. How an incision was made around the skull, and the hair was pulled back and it would make a popping sound. I later learned that the practice was in fact started by settlers who used to sell scalps and get bounties for scalps from the government. In short, the images I received about myself in school were all negative.

Both my mother and stepfather were alcohol dependent. After their separation, my stepfather died in a fire. My mother remarried when I was about sixteen and has quit drinking. During high school, I developed an alcohol addiction. I took to alcohol like birds to flight. In retrospect, I realized what I was struggling with was issues of internalized racism and, as a result of it, a variety of self-destructive behavior. I received my first message about recovery from a couple of Native Americans who were active in Alcoholics Anonymous while serving in a military jail. After a couple of false attempts at sobriety, I was able to catch onto the program. My first two years of recovery were made possible by strict attendance at AA meetings.

Several years later, I had the opportunity to attend my first sweat lodge ceremony. Experiencing it seemed to make all the difference in the world for me. It directed my recovery in a way that would not have been possible without access to my culture and identity as a Native person. It was exposure to the traditions of my people that allowed me for the first time to develop long-term relationships with others and good connections with my community. As a result of this experience, I began to understand the influence of culture and identity in the recovery process and the influence of people who can teach these cultural ways and traditions to us. My own recovery experience taught me what has to happen for other Native People. It has been a real blessing to be exposed to people knowledgeable in the ways of our culture and traditions, who could and did teach me about myself, about who I am, and where I came from.

Having those mentors in my life, with their understanding of Native ways and identity issues, has allowed me to access areas of my life that otherwise would have remained invisible to me. I would have been left with a substantial void inside. Learning how I, as well as my people, reacted to being oppressed by oppressing others and losing ourselves in destructive behavior and thinking has made it possible for me to bring that understanding to my work and to those I have taught, so that they too can transcend those barriers for themselves.

How would you define Native Americans or Native People as a group and what characteristics do they share?

Native People comprise over 350 different tribes and languages that are unique to this continent. We are both very different and very similar. There is not, for example, one monolithic religion that belongs to all Native People. We have many languages, cultures, and many religions. We understand these differences, as we always have. But today, we are focusing more on our commonalities, on those things that pull us together. Paramount among these are historical experiences. As a group, we have all been systematically subjected to colonization, to the effects of losing our language and our culture, and to governmental policies that have been destructive to our people and eventually led us to a variety of social and health problems. Sadly, our schools have been a tool in accomplishing this process. These problems have, in turn, divided us in relation to ourselves and into differences in levels of acculturation. There are people that range from very traditional to fully assimilated, and differ enormously in how they relate to their culture and identity.

Differences among Native Peoples are small in comparison to those things that set us apart from members of the dominant culture. I think we stand apart both because of a value system that is qualitatively different and a set of historic experiences that cannot really be understood by dominant culture. When I take a look at the behavior of Native People, the first thing that strikes me is that we keep to ourselves, are very insular and private, especially in comparison to members of the dominant culture.

Some of this is certainly dictated by culture. But for Native Peoples it is also a matter of self-protection. This is because of a shared sense of historical oppression and victimhood. The historical experiences of genocide and culturicide have left a deep mark upon our thinking and feelings, which is all the more tragic because our only "crime" was being on this land first. Everyone else that is in America today has come from somewhere else, but as Native People, this is the land from which we originated. We believe that we were created here. This is where our people have come from. It is an intricate part of who we are: how we define our communities and our mental health. When we view many of the problems that have arisen in our communities, we know they arise because of the loss of our land and our way of life that is so tied to the land. And of all the peoples in America today, we have been the least welcome.

The process of becoming an "American" for most citizens involved willingly giving up one's cultural heritage or identity in order to assimilate into the dominant culture and its values. This has been a very damaging process for Native People. We did not ask to be part of this process; it was forced upon us. Native People experienced enormous and long-standing traumas in their lives as a result of the assimilation process. And it is not an experience that many dominant-culture people can really identify with: having your religion outlawed, having your language outlawed, and living in a world that has devalued your very existence. And that brings about feelings of justified anger that are present in our Native communities. Anger is everywhere, and it plays itself out in different ways as our people respond to both historical and ongoing oppression. It comes out in the form of self-destructive behavior, alcoholism and drug addiction, suicide, homicide, and massive failure within the schools. We have become very different as a result of our historical experiences in "America," and these differences have to be paid attention to in the classroom. Our experience in all aspects of life including the educational system involves the forced imposition of the dominant culture's value system over our indigenous value system and has resulted in vast conflicts and misunderstandings as well as much resentment and mistrust that exist in our community.

Culturally, Native People tend to be nonintrusive and nondirective. They let people make up their own minds. If people come and seek advice, it will be given, but not offered. Life is experienced as an interconnected entity. Nature, the people, the community all intertwine and depend upon each other for meaning and existence. We also tend to be very spiritual in our orientation, and the underlying force of our spiritual beliefs comes from the geology of the area from which we come. That spirituality infuses the community and becomes its base. It is central to the identity of each person and gets expressed through various religious and cultural practices. The creation stories of each people, for example, are set in the geographic area from which they came. The Navajo and the Hopi believe that they came up through the center of the world, and that center is located in their sacred places. For the Modoc people of central Oregon, their creation story is built around the lava beds of northern California, and they believe that humanity enters the world through the creation center which is located there. All things come from our ties to the land, and all Native People are joined in their commonality with the Turtle Island, as we refer to the continent.

Could you describe some of the names that have been used historically to describe and identify Native Peoples and the general process of naming within the culture?

In regard to names, there are the names that we call ourselves, and then there are the names that other people have given us. Most familiar to dominant culture is the term *Indian.* It is actually a misnomer. It comes from the time that Europeans first landed on this continent. Christopher Columbus mistakenly believed he had landed on the coast of India, and hence we got tagged with the name Indian, which has over time taken on a pejorative meaning for us. In spite of the fact that the term has been prevalent in describing us, it carries no significance in our world. At some point, we as a people decided to take control of how we identify ourselves. The process began with the term *Native American,* which signifies that we come from this continent. But then, because we predate the naming of this continent and the Americas, we have begun to look at ourselves as the Indigenous People or First People of this land.

Outside of these more political distinctions, we also have names which we prefer to use and with which we more closely identify ourselves. There are tribal names and affiliations, such as Creeks, Choctaw, Crow, and so on. There are often clan names within the tribes, and then there are individual names: how we identify ourselves personally. Many of us have a Christian name that was given to us. But we also have personal names that are received through ceremony, a spiritual name that is often kept secret and used only for special occasions. It is important to realize that Native People vary greatly in which of the various terms they prefer, and to some extent, our choices say something about where we stand politically and culturally. Some of us still refer to ourselves as Native American, and others prefer Indigenous People. Sadly, there are still many who do not care or feel anything about who they are.

When first making contact with a Native student or family, it is perfectly appropriate to ask where they are from, what their tribal affiliation is, and how they prefer to identify themselves. I think we get into trouble when we don't do that and start making assumptions or just randomly use a term without being respectful enough to ask.

Asking about this information is probably a good way to begin contact. In mainstream America, people are identified primarily by what kind of work they do. We don't ask people what they do for a living. Instead, we ask each other, "Where are you from?" or "Who are your people?" This is because we come from a relationship-based culture, and our relationships are defined by our communities, our relatives, and our tribal affiliations. We socially locate ourselves by our human connections, not by our activities or jobs. Two last points. Spiritual names are sacred and private, and used only during ceremonies. It is considered inappropriate to inquire about these names unless they are spontaneously offered. In addition to Christian names, nicknames are very commonly used in Native communities. One might go an entire lifetime calling someone by a nickname and never know their given name.

We have already talked some about history. Could you give us a nutshell version of historical events of which a teacher should be aware?

Historically speaking, Native People have suffered greatly at the hands of governmental policies and the actions of various religious groups. The experience of colonization is not just historical, but is still happening in our communities today. Loss of our culture, loss of religion, loss of community, and loss of family cohesion are contemporary realities. And these patterns, which are the consequences of oppression, continue to play themselves out emotionally and psychologically in the lives of our people. They are major issues that concern us deeply because they involve nothing less than the loss of our identities and integrity.

The boarding school experience is a particularly destructive example. Until the mid-1980s, many Native children were taken from their natural families and communities and forced to reside in boarding schools, where they were isolated from Native culture and ways, and then immersed in the dominant culture and Christian values. In these institutions, children were punished for speaking their Native tongue or practicing traditional ways. The motto of the time was "Kill the Indian, but save the man," and its purpose was to eradicate all traces of Native culture and identity. Once accomplished, the child could be molded as desired, which meant shaping them into White Christians with mainstream values and attitudes. To make the task easier, the government outlawed our religion.

Perhaps most insidious about this practice was its effect on the Native family and its cohesion. When the children were taken out of their families, they were separated from their grandparents, parents, extended family, aunts, uncles, community, and so on. For generations, many Native American children were robbed of the nurturing of their families, deprived of the opportunity to learn parenting skills and other cultural lessons that would have enabled them to raise healthy families of their own. These children were forced to reside in institutions that were harsh and brutal. Some of our elders believe that our many social problems stem from the boarding school experience. Many of the children, as adults, remained isolated from families, no longer able to communicate because their language had been beaten out of them. They felt no comfort returning to their communities and were generally left alone to deal with the many internal issues that had been created as a result of growing up in the schools: low self-esteem, negative feelings about being Native, and a deep self-hatred. We can now see very clearly how generations of such experiences have impacted our communities and made them into what they are today. It is little wonder that many Native People today view schools and the educational system with such mistrust and suspicion.

We have begun to look at the consequences of the loss of our culture and realize that some Native People have come to internalize the stereotypes Whites hold about them. As a result, they have become those stereotypes: the subtle ones and the not so subtle ones, the "drunken Indian," the "lazy Indian." How can all those negative stereotypes not affect us? I am thinking of one of my uncles. He once told me that during high school, he very much wanted to go on to college. He went to see a school counselor and was strongly discouraged from going on. "Native People tend to be better with their hands," he was told and encouraged to pursue a trade. And so, with that advice, he didn't go to college, but went on to a trade school. He also went on to become alcoholic and drug dependent, and has since been in recovery. He attributes a lot of his problems to that stereotype and how believing in it changed his life. So for some of us, it is all too easy to live down to the stereotypes and to begin thinking about ourselves in self-deprecating terms—that we are not very smart or that we are only good with our hands and that we are destined to become alcoholic. These issues—residual effects of the boarding schools and stereotypes—are still being played out in our present-day experience. But fortunately, there has been a growing movement among many Native Peoples to regain our self-identity, to regain cultural pride, to regain our self-respect, and to learn about the traditions of our families, tribe, and people. As I shall suggest later, schools are welcoming places for Native American children and their families to the extent that they support and encourage these processes.

Are there any other things you would like to say about the nature of family, community, and culture among Native People that have relevance for teachers?

There is a lot that teachers need to know about our culture and what we have faced historically to better understand the worldview, expectations, and reactions of our students and their families. Family structure in Native communities is very different from the nuclear family that predominates in dominant culture. Among Native Peoples, extended families are more typical, where an aunt may also act in the role of the mother or the grandparents raise the children or an uncle is the primary teacher for a youth or cousins are treated as brothers and sisters. Traditionally, responsibility for child care is communal. Also included in the family structure are clans, which are determined by kinship, and bands, which are people living in the same locale.

There are and have been many obstacles for the Native American family. As mentioned previously, the boarding school experience left many people devastated. Many of our social problems stem from them. Having been forced into these institutions, children were separated from an environment where they would have been socialized and reared culturally by parents, grandparents, aunts, and uncles and placed in an often harsh environment which did not recognize Native American beliefs as having any value. Today, alcoholism is our number one health problem with 100 percent of all Native Americans affected, either directly or indirectly. In the age group of sixteen to twenty-one, we lead the nation per capita in suicides and higher than national rates of diabetes. Currently, our average life span is forty-five. School failure rates are also astronomical. These statistics attest to the problems faced in the Native American community and more privately by family members, and most of these are linked to the destruction of the cultural family.

Other disruptions for the family come from state children services agencies that routinely adopt our Native children out to non-Native homes. Often in conjunction with religious organizations or acting on stereotypical beliefs about Native American families, these agencies disregard the critical importance of Native culture for these children. There are many horror stories from the past of White people coming into Native American communities and removing children. Fortunately, this is a practice which has been stopped by implementation of the Indian Child Welfare Act of 1978, which reestablished tribal authority over the adoption of Native children. Even though our rights have been reinforced, we are constantly struggling with agencies who are working to undermine the law. By these few examples, it is obvious how there has been a basis for the development of mistrust of schools and also social service agencies, a feeling that continues today.

Oppression has had a significant effect on our family structure. Some Native People have decided not to teach their children about the culture, language, or traditions because they do not want their children to experience the same treatment of degradation and rejection from the outside world. Others have successfully made the transition into dominant society, taking on mainstream values and religious beliefs and living happily. There are also many who have managed to hang onto and practice cultural traditions and beliefs, learning from elders who have been able to share their wisdom with a younger generation. Some families mix traditional and dominant cultural ways. Clearly, we are a community in transition, adjusting to significant changes in social structure and identity, with much from the past to set right. But in spite of the historical and contemporary obstacles, our Native community is healing itself. We have weaknesses and strengths within the Native families. We have oppression and discrimination to overcome. We have social problems with addiction and abuse. But our people are making a comeback in pride and dignity by reclaiming indigenous family values.

Do class or other socioeconomic issues play any role in these various problems?

Definitely. Unemployment rates can be astronomical on a reservation, and the same is true for Native Peoples living in urban areas. The Relocation Act of the 1940s was one in a series of efforts by the government to encourage Native Peoples to leave the reservation, move to cities where jobs are more plentiful, and become part of the American mainstream. That was the ultimate goal. However, the reality was not quite as simple as that. Although some did relocate successfully, many found the experience traumatic. In the move from reservation to city, many traditional ties were lost. Kinship ties weakened with distance, and some people became disassociated from their relatives and community. Many ended up living marginal existences in the skid row areas of cities, and those who followed them from the reservations would tend to migrate toward these same enclaves. What the logic of the Relocation Act did not envision was the reality that most of these people, familiar with a very different kind of existence, did not have the dominant cultural tools to survive successfully, let alone prosper in such a foreign environment where they were met with substantial discrimination and rejection.

The move to the city was also instrumental in cutting off many from traditional cultural ties to their people. In addition, certain patterns of connection between the reservation and urban settings began to emerge. First, it was not uncommon for individuals to move back and forth between the two, and for many, this became a lifelong pattern. Second, animosities and various conflicts developed between people from these increasingly divergent lifestyles, with each looking down on the other. In general, some people in the urban centers may tend to view those on the reservation as backward, their ways antiquated, rustic. Those on the reservation in turn tend to see the urban dwellers as having lost their way, as suffering from the same malaise as the White man. Today, increasing numbers of Native People are returning to their traditions and culture in both locations and striving for unity.

There is an important cultural point here as well. In mainstream culture, success is measured in economic terms, and socioeconomic success implies a certain lifestyle that depends on having sufficient monetary resources, accumulating wealth, regular employment, living according to a certain style, and so forth. Our traditional cultural values are very different from this. Our wealth is located in the richness of our culture, tradition, ceremonies, and in the richness of our lifestyle. Difficulties arise when a person tries to live by a cultural value system that is not based on material economic gain within a broader culture that is so absolutely dedicated to it. These are not value systems that are easily integrated. Such clashes set the stage for Native Peoples losing our lands and having our language and culture outlawed in the first place. Today, we struggle with a similar conflict around remaining attached to our traditional way of life that cares little about accumulating economic wealth. It comes down to the question of divergent value systems. Those who are bicultural know what they would need to do to be successful, and that would be to eliminate their culture and perform accordingly, but that would go against their beliefs, which are based in indigenous culture and tradition. The integration of two such diverse value systems is difficult, to say the least. And it is in the schools where most Native children have their first major contact with majority culture.

You've spoken a lot about the difficult history that Native Peoples have faced in this country. What kinds of emotional issues are Native students likely to bring with them into the classroom? And what kinds of problem behavior are they likely to exhibit in the school setting?

One hundred percent of Native People are affected either directly or indirectly by alcoholism. I believe that all Native People, especially children, are at risk for developing alcoholism or some other form of dependency. There are physiological issues—social, economic, and emotional ones as well. They have been passed down from generation to generation, and together create a "lump sum" of a risk for us as Native People. Underlying this are a host of complex problems related to the loss of culture, identity, and disruption of the family unit, all symptomatic of a long history of genocide and oppression. There are also a lot of anger and anger-related issues, depression and hopelessness, health problems, and unusually high rates of suicide and homicide, especially among the young. There has also been a serious increase in the diagnosis of HIV in our community, mostly related to IV drug use. At one time, it was prevalent in our communities to accept alcoholism as a way of life. That is how we tended to cope with oppression and the discrimination in our lives. It became part of our continual grieving process. Although in many places this is still the norm, there are many of us who are beginning to take more control over our lives and rediscover who we are.

Teachers need to be sensitive to these realities. Children from more dysfunctional homes may be absent or late more often or be called upon for greater responsibilities at home. Often families will be called back to the reservation to attend funerals, for example, or experience economic crises. Lifestyles in alcoholic homes are chaotic, and children do not always have their needs met. To the extent that you, as a teacher, are able to form relationships with Native families, and they have shared personal information with you, the more able you will be to be supportive. Native communities also have natural helpers, leaders, and healers within them. To the extent that you can form relationships with these individuals, you may be useful as a resource for gaining help for your students and their families.

As far as problem behavior, there are several different sources. First, when students disconnect from the educational process, they get bored, isolated, and often act out. Second, much perceived problem behavior revolves around cultural misunderstanding and the existence of racism and prejudice in the schools. There are certain kinds of behavior which are particularly problematic for White teachers, which don't fit the dominant cultural view of how education should occur. A good example is students "hanging out with each other."

When White kids hang together, they call them cliques or clubs, but if minority kids are hanging together then it's gang involved and is perceived as more dangerous. There's fighting that happens, of course, but generally the fight is instigated by others, often by racial slurs or somebody making offensive remarks. When the Native youth react, they are often the ones that get punished because they are seldom willing to talk about it. And there are often few consequences for the student who instigated the fight in the first place. A lot of it goes back to expectations and stereotypes, especially when teachers have no relationship with the Native students. Much of the bonding, I believe, on the part of Native students is out of self-protection. They are often harassed and hang together as a matter of survival, emotional and physical. I could give you many more examples, but the bottom line is that culturally insensitive teachers too often interpret culturally different behavior as negative, and as symptomatic of resistance, lack of motivation, lack of respect, or low intelligence. This is certainly one of the reasons that one finds a disproportionately high rate of Native American students in special education classrooms.

Can you now talk about how an understanding of Native American cultural style and worldview can facilitate teacher interactions with Native students and their families?

Before getting too specific, I want to say several things about cultural perspective and worldview. It is, first of all, vital—and I can't emphasize this enough—that teachers be aware of their own cultural values, biases, and barriers, and understand clearly how they themselves have been influenced by their own culture and its prejudices. This is especially true in regard to stereotypes of Native Americans. I can't tell you how many Native young people I have spoken to, especially in the juvenile justice system, who remember teacher remarks and comments that belittle, stereotype, or insult Native peoples and their heritage. Such little insults, especially coming from teachers, accumulate and serve to alienate Native students: telling them they are different, unworthy, and do not belong. I firmly believe that such cultural disconnects (as well as curriculum that has no relevance for the lives of Native students) are a major source of the low grades and achievement scores, dropouts, suspensions and expulsions that are the frequent plight of Native American students in our schools. Poor school performance is a proven risk factor for future involvement in the juvenile justice system. And there is an overrepresentation of minority youth in the juvenile justice system.

Secondly, all behavior is derived from a cultural context as are our educational philosophies. If one is going to teach a student whose worldview is culturally different from that of the teacher, then it is likely that, if the student displays a behavior that is appropriate within his or her culture, but not within the dominant cultural view of the teacher, then that action is likely to be labeled as "inappropriate" or even "deviant." For example, in dominant culture, a firm handshake is seen as a sign of honesty, sincerity, and straightforwardness, whereas if one encounters a person of traditional Native beliefs, a firm handshake is avoided because in our culture it is sometimes seen as being intrusive, rude, overbearing, and impolite. However, someone assessing that behavior from a dominant cultural perspective might construe it as reflecting dishonesty, nonassertion, withdrawal, and evasiveness. The same cultural disconnect often occurs in relation to eye contact. When working with people from different cultures, it's always important to understand, judge, and validate their reactions, motives, and experience in terms of their own cultural perspective.

Perhaps the most important piece of information you can gain about Native students is where they and their families fall on a continuum from assimilated to traditional. People that are assimilated will often feel uncomfortable around their own people, not knowing the behaviors and what is expected of them. They appear to be Native and possess all the physical features of being Native, but internally they're different. They may feel uneasy because of their lack of knowledge of traditional ways and may feel unaccepted because of it. Assimilated individuals tend to act differently than those who live by traditional values and possess a traditional belief system. The assimilated person may appear more talkative and open, even though there might be distrust. They will be the ones who know the "rules of the system" and "how to play the game." In short, they will have learned what one needs to do within dominant culture to survive. Traditional Native People present themselves as more reserved and quiet. But rather than being indicative of withdrawal, it comes from a cultural value of respect, nonintrusiveness, and honor.

I'd also like to say something about the value of relationship. We are a relationship-based culture. We put our relationships before other things. In our culture, learning and instruction occur within the context of a personal relationship. If, for example, a teacher sends a letter or note home, a Native American parent will look at it, but if they have no connection with the person who sent it, chances are they will not respond. But if they know the teacher and have a relationship with her or him, and get a letter, a call, or one shows up at their door and says we'd like to have you join us in school, if I am known to that parent and have a history of previous contact with them, their family, and the community, they will feel more comfortable attending the meeting, visiting the classroom, or talking to me about their child. Remember, there is a long history of mistrust in the Native community. Gaining trust is often a slow process and requires the teacher to reach out and actively learn about and be seen within and by the community.

Teachers have to be willing to get out and be visible. Maybe if there's a powwow going on, to be at the powwow. Or engage one of the students at the school to organize a powwow, you know, for the school. I mean, those are some things that can help. What such activities do is allow students to bring in other aspects of the community into the classroom, in addition to just their parents. Remember, there's a whole extended family that's actively important in the student's life. There's the aunts and uncles too, grandparents, etc. Going to powwows, being visible, that makes a difference. Meet the natural helpers in the community. It may be an elder; it may be a couple of elders; maybe someone younger who's doing good work within the community. The bottom line is that you have to develop a relationship there. It doesn't have to be all that difficult. Just start talking to people, meeting with them, show a personal interest in your students and their lives. I believe that it is only in the context of such relationships between teacher and community that Native youth are afforded the greatest opportunity for success in the school system. Similarly, it is when students feel isolated, are not personally connected with their teachers or with a meaningful curriculum, that we lose them. If you can enter the community as a respectful visitor and friend and erase the distance between what is taught in your classroom and what is important in the life experience of Native children and students, you will be well on your way toward cultural competence in teaching Native American youth.

Finally, there is the matter of peer and community pressure. There is this basic ambivalence within the Native community about school success and success in the White world. There is an old Native American joke about crabs. There's two guys out on the beach crabbing. One guy can't keep his crabs in the bucket. They're up out of there all the time. He's just constantly chasing those crabs down. But he notices this other guy over there, and all the crabs are still in the bucket. They can't get out, they're not getting out. So as a consequence he's filling the bucket up. The other guy's just running his legs off, can't keep the crabs in. So finally, he gets frustrated and he goes over and asks the other guy, "What are you doing to keep those crabs in the bucket? I just get one in there and they are just out again." The other guy says, "Well it's easy. I just get the Indian crabs." He says, "Well, what do you mean, Indian crabs?" "Yeah, about the time one of 'em gets out of the bucket, the rest of 'em grab him and pull him back in."

I think such pressures have two sources. First, being successful in White schools often means leaving the community, turning one's back on cultural traditions and ways, and "becoming White." There is a real fear of losing the person from the family and the community. Family members are proud of their child's success, but fear their eventual loss and react by doing things to pull them back and keep them from leaving and rejecting the culture. There are also individuals who devalue school success, not out of a motive for cultural survival, but because of their own inability to succeed in school they need to rationalize their failures by pressuring others to also fail. Teachers need to realize that such ambivalence does exist in the Native community, understand its source, and thereby be able to more competently deal with it.

What additional suggestions can you give regarding developing rapport with Native American students?

It's not about learning all the ins and outs. We are dealing with a very diverse population. It's impossible for me to say: "Well, this is the one thing you will need to say, or this is the one thing that you do in order to develop rapport." I would be merely creating a new stereotype. We are all going to make mistakes, and mistakes are a common thing in working with diverse cultures. But if one really comes from a place of acceptance and respect as a teacher and educator, then that is going to translate into developing rapport with students and their families. As I said before, relationship is a crucial ingredient in working with the Native American community. As teachers, we have a certain goal in mind: trying to develop an environment where our students can learn to their best ability. I would add in the case of Native American students that that environment should also be a place in which they can heal and reconnect with their Native culture. But there is more than one road we can travel to get to the same place.

In order to develop rapport with Native students, one has to learn to not be afraid of their anger. You can be sure that there is going to be mistrust and anger that may very well be directed toward you personally as a White teacher. But if you can tolerate it, not be frightened by it, and just allow it to be expressed as honest communication, you will be on the road to making a connection. There is the possibility the student will see you as part of the White establishment and, as such, unlikely to be of any real help. Remember: historically, Native Peoples have had their feelings discounted, been patronized and demeaned and chronically abused by the system. You may be witnessing justified anger running rampant. In short, you may be stereotyped and lumped into this category of the enemy. The only way to get beyond this is to acknowledge your Whiteness and the feelings they are likely to project onto you as well as your general understanding of what they have experienced as a people. But be clear, the walls are not going to come down overnight, but only with time and patience. In addition, becoming aware of the effects oppression has on a people will aid in understanding the self-destructive behavior that one often finds among Native youth.

Are there any learning styles that typify Native American students and, if so, ways to manipulate the classroom environment to match these learning styles.

I am aware of the research on learning styles, but feel that such an approach is premature and secondary to some of the other issues I have been raising about teaching Native American students. Besides, we are a very diverse people with a variety of learning styles depending upon the kind of geography we evolved in, our lifestyle such as hunting or gathering societies, migratory or stationary, peaceful or war, and what specifically happened to us in our interactions with White America. As far as classroom strategy, I would suggest using a wide selection and sampling of learning approaches, thereby engaging as wide a range of learning strategies as possible. What I am suggesting is trying to find an effective model for teaching Native students that addresses many learning styles and does it in a way that validates Indian lifestyle and experience.

But learning strategies will not matter if there is not a sufficient relationship between teacher and student upon which to build. And part of that relationship has to do with bringing the Native community and culture into the classroom, thereby validating who the students are. Schools that exist on reservations which are responsible for their own curriculum and bringing the community into the classroom tend to have dramatically more success than public schools in engaging and fostering success with Native American students. To the extent that classroom education leads to students feeling pride about who they are personally and culturally, and receiving validating information about themselves, they will become engaged in the learning process.

Having said all of this, I do believe I can make several suggestions about working with storytelling. Storytelling is not only a great way to engage people in learning about themselves and the world around them, but also a very effective means of developing community and transmitting culture. This is a traditional method of teaching among my people. There are many different types of learning stories which teach cultural values and right behavior. Listening to stories is actually a very active process whereby students engage the story through their personal understanding and interpretation of it. I believe all human beings are drawn toward myth and mythology. In dominant American culture, however, myths and mythology are held suspect and viewed as inferior to fact and science. Ironically, all we have done is choose a certain type of story and called it science and placed it above the myths and stories of other cultures.

For instance, all societies have creation stories which tell about how this world came into being. Hopi people believe that they came from the center of the earth through a hole located in a sacred site on Hopi land. Another creation story suggests that there were these atoms and particles which collided in space and created this big boom which in turn created gravitational forces which created the planets and eventually amoebas and finally us. From our perspective there are many, not just one right creation story. If we can ever get to a point where teachers can validate a student's own cultural experiences such as the creation stories I've been talking about, I think we'll see more successes in our schools.

I think two other aspects that all Native cultures share and which particularly lend themselves to classroom learning are our shared history in the United States and our relationship to the earth. Introducing such material supports cultural differences and engages and validates our students. To talk about Native history as if it were of value to everyone and being able to identify what it is that Native culture has contributed to dominant culture, that give students a sense of pride, a sense of connection that "this is mine and comes from my people," versus not hearing anything about yourself and what you have given to the world.

Finally, could you give us an example that brings together the issues and dynamics about which you've been talking?

Sure. Actually, let me tell you about my daughter who has been with us throughout this interview. We're getting ready to send her to school. We've been working with her on the culture, and being tied to her culture. And you know, she's been in a sweat lodge, she smudges, she does the cere-monies, she goes to the powwows. But you know, when she gets to the educational system, I really see my role as working with the educators to make them aware that, keep it on the table that she is Native, and if there are stereotypes, stereotypical information that comes up in the classroom about Native people, I'm gonna be there to challenge it. I am going to be an advocate for her to get accurate information about who she is racially and culturally. Of course there are many people in our communities that may not feel comfortable playing such a role. That's why it is so important to train teachers to be doing this themselves. But as for us, we're going to make sure she gets accurate information about who she is and that the teachers are being attentive to those kinds of things and not propagating stereotypical information.

We've decided not to enroll her in public school right off the bat. We're going to find a good private school for now. We've found one we like. They are doing some pretty good things. They're not going to stay in the classroom all the time. They take kids out on field trips and debrief their experiences. And they actively explore alternatives to the way things are usually done. But perhaps most important is their attitude. When I talked to them about cultural issues, and the cultural needs of my daughter, they got excited and questioned me further. They wanted more information. That kind of reaction says it all to me. They were sincerely interested. I'm well familiar with the opposite. "Yeah, that sounds good . . . We'll have to schedule you in some time to talk about that stuff."

WORKING WITH AFRICAN AMERICAN STUDENTS

An Interview with William Cross

DEMOGRAPHICS

The term *African American* subsumes a diverse array of peoples, including African Americans born in this country, people from Africa, and people from the West Indies and Central and South America. The 2000 census numbers African Americans in the United States at 34,658,190 or 12.3 percent of the population. Since the time of slavery, African Americans made up this county's largest minority, but the 2000 census showed that Latinos/as have become the largest minority. Projections show African Americans increasing to 13 percent of the population by 2010 and then leveling off into midcentury. They are the most widely dispersed ethnic group both geographically and economically. In 1997, for example, 55 percent lived in the South, 36 percent in the Northeast and Midwest, and 9 percent in the West.

While most African Americans are descendants of families who have been in the United States since slavery, immigration has slowly been increasing over the last two decades, leading to increasing levels of linguistic and cultural diversity. Immigrants from former British Caribbean colonies have brought a mixture of African and British customs, and those from former Spanish, French, and Dutch colonies have done the same. In 1980 only 3 percent of African Americans were foreign-born. By 1998 the figure had risen to 5 percent, with most of the increase a result of immigration from the Caribbean. Increasing immigration from sub-Saharan Africa is projected. Previous immigration from Africa has primarily come from Nigeria, Ethiopia, Ghana, Kenya, and Morocco (Pollard & O'Hare, 1999). Such diversity leads Hines and Boyd-Franklin (1982) to warn teachers against assuming the existence of a "typical" African American family.

FAMILY AND CULTURAL VALUES

Black (1996) pointed to four factors that have shaped the African American experience and culture.

- "The African Legacy, rich in culture, custom, and achievement;
- "The history of slavery, a deliberate attempt to destroy the core and soul of the people, while keeping their bodies in enforced servitude;
- "Racism and discrimination, ongoing efforts to continue the psychological and economic subjugation started during slavery; and
- "The victim system, a process by which individuals and communities are denied access to the instruments of development and advancement, and then blamed for low levels of accomplishment and achievement, while their successes are treated as anomalies." (p. 59)

Black slaves brought a rich amalgam of cultures from West Africa; according to Hilliard (1995), rather than eradicating African culture and consciousness, slavery actually preserved it. Aspects of an African worldview still infuse African American life: a deep religiosity and spirituality, cooperation and interdependence, and a oneness with nature. According to Marshall (2002), enslavement added emphases on resistance, freedom, self-determination, and education. African culture also contributed a tradition of strong family structure in which extended families and close-knit kinship systems were the basis of larger tribal groupings.

According to researchers who have worked to understand how the classroom can better accommodate the needs and cultural realities of African American families, three strategies are critical.

- Understanding the cultural context of the family
- Viewing differences in family dynamics as adaptive mechanisms and strengths
- Developing practices that take into account the needs, cultural dynamics, and style of African American culture

Further, these researchers favor classroom strategies that educate students in the context of existing African American family structure and communities and oppose helping students adapt to a White world and its culture. Hill (1972) identifies three factors as positive strengths to be built upon in the classroom: kinship bonds, role flexibility within the family, and religion. Each offers insight into the workings of African American culture, values that infuse the culture, and arenas where teachers can find additional support and encouragement for their work in the classroom.

Kinship Bonds

Most African American families are part of complex kinship networks of blood relatives and unrelated individuals. Stack (1975) found typical patterns of "co-residence, kinship-based exchange networks linking multiple domestic units, elastic household boundaries, and a lifelong bond to three generation households" (p. 124). White (1972) pointed to a series of "uncles, aunts, big mamas, boyfriends, older brothers and sisters, deacons, preachers, and others who operate in and out of the Black home" (p. 45). Such extended patterns must be acknowledged as legitimate by teachers and called upon as useful resources as a bridge between school and family as well as when it is necessary to involve family in educational issues that arise for individual students. Key family members must be identified and included in educational decision making, even if their inclusion goes beyond the teacher's personal definition of who makes up the family. It is critical that all members of the family, as defined by the family, be invited to participate in the process of educating their student. One is reminded of Elena's godfather in the case study of the Martinez family in Chapter 5.

When first meeting African American students and families, teachers, especially White teachers, should exercise caution in seeking personal information about the family and its members. African American families, with good reason, are often suspicious of "prying" professionals. Authors, such as Hines and Boyd-Franklin (1982) and Boyd (1982), suggest delaying the seeking of personal data until adequate trust of the school situation has been developed and when information can be sought in a natural as opposed to a forced manner. Extended kinship bonds suggest that teachers consider working with subgroups of the extended family when it is necessary to involve family members in discussion about a student's classroom behavior and only those who would have direct input on a particular issue. Of course, this assumes a certain level of knowledge about a given family's members and structure. It may also be necessary to schedule home visits in order to include key figures who cannot or will not come to the school. Again, entering a home, like seeking information, should be done with sensitivity in light of past abuses of the welfare system against poor families.

Role Flexibility

Role flexibility within the African American family, like extended kinship bonds, is highly adaptive for coping with the stresses of oppression and socioeconomic ills. It is most evident in the greater role diversity found among African American men and women as well as in the existence of unique familial roles. African American males have been traditionally seen by social scientists as peripheral to family functioning (Moynihan, 1965). Hill (1972), among others, has challenged this notion. He argues that the father's frequent absence from the home does not reflect a lack of parenting skill or interest, but rather the time and energy required to provide basic necessities for the family. The father's precarious economic position coupled with the need for African American females to work outside the home often lead to extensive role reversals and flexibility in childrearing and household responsibilities. These circumstances have led White (1972) to suggest that African American children may not learn as rigid distinctions between male and female roles as their White counterparts.

Hines and Boyd-Franklin (1982) and Boyd (1982) caution against routinely excluding the father, as has frequently been done by those who subscribe to the myth of the peripheral male. Instead, they suggest doing as much as possible to include him, even if for only a cursory introduction. Teachers are encouraged, if possible, to regularly inform the father of what is happening educationally for his student if he is unable to participate more fully. The authors also caution teachers against assuming the absence of a male role model when the father has abandoned the family. Given the variety of extended family figures in the extended family and community, someone else may emerge to fill this role.

While the African American male has been viewed as peripheral, the African American female, often forced to assume responsibilities well beyond those typically taken on by White women, has frequently been mislabeled as overly dominant. African American couples are, in fact, often more egalitarian than their White counterparts. Scanzoni (1971), for example, found that, more often than Whites, Black males and females grow up with the expectation that both will work. Minuchin, Montalvo, Guerney, Rosman, and Schumer (1967) offer interesting insights into the dynamics between African American males and females. Discord tends to be dealt with indirectly, not through direct confrontation. Solutions to long-term disharmony are typically informal, and long periods of separation may occur without the thought of divorce.

African American couples tend to remain together for life, often for the sake of the children, and typically seek therapy for child-focused issues rather than for marital dissatisfaction. In spite of ill-treatment by a husband, an African American woman tends to resist the dissolution of a relationship. Hines and Boyd-Franklin (Boyd, 1982) suggest that this may result from three factors.

- Greater empathy for the husband's frustration in a racist society
- An awareness of the extent to which Black females outnumber Black males
- A strong religious orientation that teaches tolerance for suffering

Economic demands and oppressive forces have, in addition, created unique roles in the African American family. Included are the *parental child*—an older child who has parental responsibilities when there are many younger children to attend to or when both parents are absent from the home for considerable amounts of time—and the extended generational system of parenting, in which the parent role is shared and distributed across several generations within the home. Such adaptive strategies, while clearly a potential positive force, can become sources of additional problems. This occurs when their intended function becomes distorted, overutilized, or rigid. According to Pinderhughes (1989), "if the mother's role is overemphasized . . . it can become the pathway for all interactions within the family. This requires children to relate primarily to her moods and wishes rather than to their own needs. The result is emotional fusion of the children with the mother" (p. 113). Parental children can be forced to take on responsibilities well beyond their abilities and at the expense of necessary peer group interactions (Minuchin, 1974). Shared parenting in the multigenerational family can become highly chaotic or a source of open conflict and dispute. If teachers are aware of such patterns and their impact upon a student, they may better understand why a student may be chronically late, absent or always tired, or with whom to speak when they need to contact a family member about their student.

Religion

Religion is extremely important in the African American community and provides a valuable source of social connection as well as self-esteem and succor in times of stress. Religious leaders often become "family members" as part of the extended family structure, and are often sought out by religious families for personal help and support as an alternative to White mental health or social service agencies. Such religious networks are frequently overlooked by teachers as a resource and source of support and information about the community in which a student's family lives. Educators may find it useful to seek necessary information from religious leaders, to call on church networks for help when a student's family is in crisis, or to ask a minister to intervene with a particular student or family problem. On the other hand, religiosity itself may become a source of conflict in the African American family. For example, Larsen (1976) reported the situation of a highly religious family dealing with the rejection of religion and traditional values by a rebellious preadolescent. An understanding of the impact of a family's religious practice on the personal development of a student (for example, strict adherence to harsh physical punishment and discipline of children based on religious maxims such as "spare the rod and spoil the child") may help explain her or his classroom behavior or difficulties.

The trauma of slavery and the long history of racism have shaped and defined the African American experience in the United States. It is impossible to understand the African American psyche without keeping these two events clearly in mind. Kivel (1996) stated the facts of slavery succinctly: "From 1619 until slavery ended officially in 1865, 10–15 million Africans were brought here, and another 30–35 million died in transport" (p. 121). The magnitude is staggering. The effect of slavery was intensified by the systematic destruction of African culture and identity by slavers and slave masters, the tearing apart of families, and the creation of myths of inferiority and subhuman status to justify what was being done. The entire nation benefited economically and socially from this cruel institution.

Racism replaced slavery as a vehicle for the continued exploitation of African Americans as well as a justification for continuing to deny them the equality guaranteed by the U.S. Constitution. As a people, they survived, grew strong, and fashioned a new culture in America, but they continue to pay an awesome price for the color of their skin. Hacker (1992) argued that the United States is functionally "two nations," Black and White, and that there is an enormous disparity in the access of these two groups to the resources and benefits of this rich nation. The long list of statistical inequities—from average salaries to unemployment, from incarceration to education levels, from teenage pregnancies to poverty—is staggering. For example, poverty rates among African Americans are almost three times those of Whites. Life expectancy is six years shorter. Infant mortality rates are twice those of Whites, Asians, and Latinos/as. African American households have the lowest annual median income at $25,100, while African American men experience the highest rate of unemployment among ethnic minorities (Hacker, 1992).

African Americans have been the "point men" in the struggle against inequality and social injustice in this country. Through the civil rights and other social movements, they have been the voice of conscience in America, not allowing the nation to forget grave injustices that are still very much alive. As Kivel (1996) suggested, they have been the "center of racial attention," and all other oppressed groups have learned from and modeled their fights on those of African Americans. It is little wonder, as our guest points out, that the complexities around relationships and identity in America impact African American students.

⫘⬥⫘

Our Interviewee

William E. Cross, Jr., Ph.D., is Professor and Coordinator of the Social-Personality Doctoral Program in Psychology at City University of New York. He has taught on the faculties of Cornell University, Pennsylvania State University, and University of Massachusetts–Amherst. Dr. Cross is also a con-

(Used with permission of William E. Cross, Jr.)

sultant to government, education, and industry on business and educational implications of America's changing demographics. One of the leading experts on the study of African American identity, his text, *Shades of Black: Diversity in African-American Identity* (Temple University Press, 1991), is considered a classic. His model of African American identity development has significantly shaped the study of ethnic identity in the fields of psychology and African American studies and has influenced scholars theorizing and doing research on Jewish identity, Asian American identity, White ethnic-group identity, Latina and Latino identity, and gay and lesbian identity.

The Interview

Can you begin by talking about your own ethnic background and how it has impacted you and your work?

Because the color variation in my own family was so dramatic, when I was pretty young, I thought that being born blonde or White was random. And so my earliest memories are not about race, but that it was somehow disturbing that your mom would produce a brown child one day and a white child the next. As a young boy I had mostly very rich, positive memories of youth. And there was the vaguest notion of race; it wasn't negative, it was more a sense of culture. Because I was raised on the South Side of Chicago, I was growing up in the golden age of African American Renaissance. I was born in 1940 so this was after World War II. The unemployment rate for men and women was very, very high. There were sections in the Black community which could be financially stable, but they were very modest. We had baseball teams, and Robinson was in his prime. So my primal memory, meaning when I was a young child, was being happy.

There would be these moments, however, when there were certain markers in the community; and I didn't know why we weren't supposed to walk beyond that bridge, or across the river. As my images of Whites evolved, this was somewhat compartmentalized because where we were was a heavily integrated community. It was not uncommon for us to have White neighbors. But there was this notion of Whites, particularly White males, who were angry. And because I was so steeped in the family, the neighbors, and the good people that were around us I didn't quite understand what they were angry about. And so I hadn't internalized their stereotypes of us. Then we moved to Evanston, Illinois. I guess that's where I began to be more conscious of race, in terms of its constructions, in terms of it being a label that somehow was problematic to other people.

My mom, who was very fair, raised us to understand that she would use the label Negro, but then she would very quickly say, "You can be whoever you want to be." My father had more of a race consciousness. But because of his alcoholism, we just didn't pay as much attention to Dad. So, in my adolescence, my mom had a greater influence on me. I probably went through adolescence knowing I was Negro, but having pretty close to a racelessness notion of race. Racelessness in the sense that I was a Negro, but, so what? The school system that I attended did not teach us at all about Negro/Black history. My father would bring me books. However, his status in the family didn't make him someone that we would listen to. I think if we had more conversations when he was sober and he made history more, I don't want to say more fun, but more engaging, it might be different. But that just didn't happen. And Mom didn't push it.

I was very much a Negro by the time I reached late adolescence. Issues across race were there. We would date White girls. I had Black and White girlfriends in high school, but I think by the time I was in high school I probably had a distorted aesthetic in that I began to deify White beauty. Yet, all the way through college I had mixed relationships. Sometimes they'd be Black, sometimes they'd be White. And I was even engaged once to a Black woman for a short time, even though before her and after her I dated the same White woman.

In college I was heavily affected by the Pi Lambda Phi experience. Now, anyone who knows fraternities knows that Pi Lambda Phi is a traditionally Jewish house. At the university in Denver a radical Jewish man reorganized the chapter and he made the point to integrate it. And so, I became the first president of what was essentially an integrated fraternity. That had a deep effect on me. It didn't cause me to become a "race-man" or "come back into a culture" man, but it meant that I could be more openly a Negro, and this person could be more openly Jewish, and this person could be Catholic. So it was a very multicultural kind of thing. So much so that in the early 1960s—I came out of high school in '59, went to Denver between '59 and '63—when the civil rights movement began picking up, I was almost unprepared for it.

When I went to grad studies in clinical psychology at Roosevelt University in Chicago in the early to mid-1960s, there was a nascent move toward nationalism, and toward a more caustic discourse across the racial barriers. I remember having a miserable year my first year at Roosevelt University. A lot of it was tied around the fact that I had come out of this Denver experience where we had built real bridges across, or what we thought were bridges across, race and culture. And that scaffolding had no value, for the most part, at Roosevelt. I think I began to be, also, not ashamed, but wondering why I was so hesitant to just commit myself to what other Black people were saying and doing and wanting.

Then with Martin Luther King, I got swept up in the notion of nonviolence. I certainly was not a ruffian and didn't know what value one saw in that, so there was a whole bunch of reasons I would be attracted to his philosophy. But when King was assassinated, that released a lot of my pent up feelings, views, and so on. In my own history, my turnaround in having a Black focus would be in the sixties. The death of Martin Luther King caused me to very consciously and deliberately reconstruct what I thought was my old identity—to unload myself of the sense of shame, guilt, and anxiety about being the wrong kind of Black person, and to understand to whom am I anchoring myself. Whose identity am I trying to impress? So, I just totally immersed myself in what I perceived to be Black culture, tried to go through those emotional and psychological hoops that would make me an authentic Black person. And, shyly but steadily began to, I should say hesitantly began to keep notes.

Over time this was reinforced by others, and the next thing you know, 1971, I was encouraged to publish my notes as the Black emersion experience. One other thing happened to me that was awesome is that Joe Hall, who was in counseling psychology, was mentoring me at a very key point. I was wanting to go to the clinical side, he says, "No, no, no. Go into traditional academic psychology. Become more theory oriented, because almost all clinicians use other people's theories." And, he in part was right, because our people need original thinkers who are actually developing theory.

Now, as to the original question, "How do I see myself ethnically?" When I was first raised I don't think I had a notion of race and culture. When race and culture began to evolve, it was very positive; I can still draw on that. Then in my early adolescence, it became a stigma, and that was bad. I experienced a lot of shame, because I bought into the stereotypes of the larger society. Being fair skinned, I was sometimes able to melt into larger White society, and there'd be other times when I'd felt this sense of tension with other Black people. Because I was so fair, my features were so sharp, that even when I declared myself to be Negro, what have you, there was still in the eyes of some of the folks that I saw a sense of questioning. When I went through the Black sixties, I had an afro as long as I could get it. And wore dashikis and so on—a mirror of conformity. Like any young man, I wanted to be accepted, and loved, and have women who'd love me. I was taking Blackness to another level. Being a doctoral student, I was able to fuse this sense of ethnicity and race with long-term studies.

Coming out of Princeton, I then went into Black studies and over the next twenty years that was a search toward solidifying my frame. I very early on went from just viewing the issue as race to viewing it also as culture. And I almost had to do that because, since I racially didn't look like the very people I was identifying with, I had an existential understanding of Blackness. And then once I got rid of enough shame and anxiety and guilt and rage, I became aware that actually this existential component was true for all people, whatever their ideals. So I came to understand that essentially, identity is a choice, a choice that's often fostered by the ecological niche into which you are immersed. My boyhood flirtation with Black nationalism in a very narrow sense was real, but it was limited. And early on I became aware that I was an African American. An Afro American if you will. And that, it was very difficult, but there were these other roots, Native American roots, White roots, because that was all there in my family. By the way, I should tell you that I received tremendous support within my family for my own identity change; they were going through changes too. But, their love was so sustaining and unequivocal that even though I'd come home talking, you know, crazy ideas, they'd listen. But most importantly, my mother, who as you recall I said earlier in the interview was almost the key person for our racial ideas, and she'd work on a racelessness notion, she actually would reengage with the children that'd been home and she became radicalized herself in the sixties. My dad was angry because he tried to show us the power of race and culture early on, so the irony is that in becoming Black I became even closer to my mother because she changed. And my father remained estranged, but close to my sisters.

I stayed with the Africana Center at Cornell for twenty-plus years; I loved it. It's the cornerstone of my being, but I shifted from a psychologist to a cultural psychologist: that's what happened to me at Africana. At Africana, I became someone who was friendly to those students who pushed the limits of a nationalist frame. Who kind of pushed us over into viewing the issue as bicultural, biracial, binational. And of course, in some instances, even flirting with multicultural, but that would come a little bit later. Starting with the "bi-" component. We are not just Africans, we are not just Americans, we are some sort of hybrid. And where hybridity is not viewed as a negative, but just simply means it's the fusion. And when Reagan took office in the eighties and his policies began to sink through, and I don't say this in any negative way toward my colleagues at the Africana Center, there was a rightful reemergence of this nationalist frame. And I became aware I was a little bit estranged, because I wanted people who were bicultural to come, I wanted people from Japan to come, to the Africana Center. I wanted the few White students who came in to succeed. And, I think I was misperceived. Some people thought I spent a little too much time with these "other groups." I could see that there were actually some of our professors who were explicitly hostile to anyone who was not Black. So I thought I was friendly to our African American students, but also made the point to be the bridge to these other groups. Because my vision at Africana was that we wanted to have students graduate from our program and teach in China, Japan, Russia. Well that meant you had to welcome someone from China, Japan, Russia. And the group as a whole, from my point of view, was not always there.

So when I moved from Africana to Penn State, that was symbolic, in terms of my own ethnicity, of shifting from a nationalist-focused identity to a multicultural-focused one. So today I see myself as very much African

American, but with a decided Black cultural and multicultural frame. My multicultural frame is limited by the fact that I don't know other languages, and I think you really do have to know other languages to pull off the multicultural frame. But I do consider myself more than a friend to movements of certain aspects of Jewish identity. I separate that out from Zionist identity—I understand Zionism but that's not where my connection is—but to Palestinian identity, to women's identity, feminist identity, more recently gay and lesbian identity. I feel a connectivity to these other groups, which are sometimes marginalized for various reasons. I have in some cases intellectually become engaged in their concerns, and I have actually influenced the way some scholars write about them. Nonetheless, most of my writings have to do with Black people because I believe that in the short time I have on the earth, you know, I'm sixty-three, I want to do more. There's so much there you can't exhaust it, so before I spill over into a dedicated multicultural frame, I write about Blackness in a way that's *friendly*, friendly to the multicultural frame.

Who are the African Americans, and what characteristics do they share as a group?

My writing since 1971 has been trying to point out to people that while in a political sense we can be called a *group*, we are really *groups*. We welcome the psychology of what I'll call human ecology: that is to say, we try to figure out what kind of ecological niche or niches members of groups are being raised in. And the material conditions, the spiritual conditions, and political conditions under which Black people are raised vary. Yes, we have concentrations in what we call our communities—outsiders sometimes call them ghettos—but we say ghetto in a friendly way, and there's commonality whether you're here, Cleveland, so on. But we are disbursed and as a result when you find someone raised in Oregon or at a distance from a large population, or in my case where my late adolescence was in Evanston—just down the road from Chicago—there was just a different kind of frame of reference.

We are a community that is very diverse in its orientations. Now, having said that, the stigma that we have to wrestle with is real. And so, even when we achieve different class dispersion, there's a greater probability that we are a problem to other people, and as a result of being a problem to other people who have power, they do things to us that do affect our lives. And so, we are hyperconcentrated in a certain spatial sense. So we are, we choose to live sometimes with ourselves, but oftentimes it is more than choice, we are forced to. And, as a result, we, as a group, are more likely to experience certain kinds of plethoras of oppression that resonate on poverty.

But even when we have managed to escape poverty, the reach of certain types of racism, and there's not just one, there's many variations that can reach us. So even as a bourgeoisie, middle-class academic I have a history that I can tell of my moments of encountering racism. Moments which are going to be different across people, from the shoeshine guy, to the laborer, to the maid and whatever. But I have not escaped that racism, although my material well-being can allow me to create some zones of comfort, some buffers. I don't equate my life with someone who has been forced to make a choice that might make them end up in prison and so on. And I certainly don't feel better, but I'm not kidding myself that my life has been the same. Now that said, my own work has suggested that if there are a thousand ways in which African Americans come to view themselves, if there's great variation in our identity structures, some of the problems that we are almost all forced to encounter have such a repeated theme from Chicago to New York to Cleveland that I tend to focus in on these identity frames of reference to the exclusion of the others.

One cluster of identity types has to do with those people who for various reasons don't make race very important to their lives. And there could be some very positive reasons for that, or some very negative. Let's just give some examples. I could be Black, but I could be so into my religion or my Pentecostal church that I see myself as being a child of God and therefore I don't place that much weight on race because I have this positive other interest. In that situation I might be married to a Black woman, I might be going to an all-Black church, but I don't see race as a framing issue, I see it as my relationship with God. That would be a person who, from my point of view, is what I call preencountered because they have an identity, and it's a positive identity, but it's not anchored in race and culture. Or whatever race and cultural dimensions are there are understated, underplayed, getting secondary emphasis. So that'd be one way you can do it. So I call that low-salience.

Then there are other people who tend to have absorbed stereotypes about the group that cause them to feel some degree of estrangement from the group. They may even live in the community, but because they view the group as being about the stereotypes that are often racist, they don't often see the beauty or the strength of the community. So therefore they live in it, but they don't feel—they're kind of almost ambivalent about it.

Then, of course, the third category that I've studied a lot is those persons that have absorbed the stereotypes, who painfully not only see the group as negative, but they see themselves as negative and there's self-hate. Let me show you from my point of view, all three of those people end up being in the same category because if tomorrow something were to happen, and there was a call to race, there was a call to culture, the first person wouldn't come forward because they don't think it's important. The second person, the miseducated person, wouldn't come forward because they're not so sure that Black people do anything together. And then the third person would not come forward because he or she is hating the group. So therefore, all those persons end up not acting in the group's behalf. Some, again, have positive reasons, but others for real negative reasons.

And then on the other extreme, if you will, there are a range of people who do make race and culture part of their identity. But one of the things I've done in my work is show that people who have a Black identity are not the same. Some are Afrocentrically focused, that is to say they've raised a paramount frame in their identity. Some are biculturally focused, they feel very comfortable being American and they feel very comfortable being Black, they have a real fusion. And then there are people who are emerging more recently. I guess they've been around forever, but they have more of a strong voice, they are Black and they are multiculturally focused. So if you will, on either extreme, we have these clusters of identities. And then in the middle is something I call states of in-between-ness. There are people who you can find in the community who, they don't fit either of the two extremes, but they seem more volatile, they seem to be more agitated. Agitation not necessarily in a negative way. They literally are in between. And sometimes they live their whole lives that way. And I call that emersion–immersion. So, from my point of view, for all the diversity of identity you find in the Black community, nonetheless, these identities are paramount. You find them in barbershops and beauty salons, in conversations you and I might have. They're the driving points of identities, though leaving off the table some important ones, such as the spiritualist.

I find more recently in my work, I'm trying to look at how spirituality influences. But I think spirituality is like gender. Gender has never been that much of a part of my discourse. And people have said, "that's because you're male and you're leaving off women." That's the way people have said it, and I've had to walk up and look at that. And, I have been fortunate with the people I work with in that we have pinpointed those dimensions of Black identity that tend not to change that much across gender. So, we talk to Black women about stereotypes, and they resonate to that. And we talk to Black males about stereotypes and they resonate to that. And we talk to Black men and women about having moments when you have doubted your identity. I mean, we have been able to hit key themes that are quite gender neutral. Now, that said, if you go deeper into the stereotypes, we say, okay, you both have agreed that you have been influenced and you know about stereotypes. Are there gender dimensions to that? Yes there are. So it's almost as though there's a second and third level of the discourse on identity that you can hit. And we stumbled upon those dimensions of race and cultural identity that are transcendent across gender. That doesn't make gender irrelevant. So Black men, when they have to wrestle with the White aesthetic, they have to wrestle with the way a blonde male or a certain kind of physiology for maleness has been presented to them and they have to work against that. And God knows we know about the stereotyping of Black men. And yet, we ask Black women about that encounter, they're going to give you a gendered view. There's a very key component of gender that's there, but when you look at our work, and you look at our scales, and you look at our identity types, we find them as much in women as we do in men.

Could you talk about the various names that African Americans use to describe and identify themselves, and some of the names that have been used historically to describe and identify the group?

Now, this used to be rather easy to do when the focus was only on African Americans. We started out, of course, with our tribal or African names. Then we had the slavery experience. We now know that who we're named after often still maintained itself during slavery. There are certain names that you can hear that have very much a Southern bent to them. In my coming up I used to wonder who was Rufus. Rufus was always someone from Mississippi. I'm a William, but there were many Willies. And before the sixties, we used to, not that we were unique to this, but we would have fun making up names. In fact I just met a woman whose name was Decita. And I asked her whether it was a name from the islands. And she said, "No, that was a name made up by my mom and dad based on certain letters from certain names." In the sixties and seventies, African Americans became much more friendly to African names. And now you also have a large number of African American people that were born and flew across that are now Makaza Kuminika. I don't know what percentage that would be.

But now you also have, because of immigration from the Caribbean and elsewhere, an amazing mixture in New York City, for example, of people from Panama, from Haiti, from the Dominican Republic, and so on. And now there's a cross-influence. People will hear about a Dominican name they like and they'll name their child that. So, the reality now is that you can have people with very African-sounding names, or names that would suggest ethnicity, yet when you interview them they may be as preencountered as anyone else. So names often don't tell as much about people as we might think; however, if the person was born African American, and they have taken on an African name, that probably means this is someone who has a close relationship between their naming and how they think on some issues.

As a nation within a nation, we have gone through long periods of deracination. We stopped seeing ourselves as an African people, that's why the word *Negro* became so popular. In the sixties we began to rebel against Negro, but notice how in the sixties we didn't begin to take on African names right away. We said *Black.* It was still a struggle for us, as a people, to embrace our being African. And then, with the late movement of the sixties, there became a very self-conscious, new form of nationalism and we now notice Afrocentricity.

And then I guess it'd be in the late eighties, maybe as late as the nineties, we have this famous speech by Jessie Jackson in which he said we should stop calling ourselves simply Black, just as there are Italian Americans, just as there are Irish Americans, we are African Americans. And so today, you find that people that don't want to be called Negro—that term has almost become anachronistic. They're comfortable with Black. People from the islands, while they're in the United States, are wary of how they're going to be classified; in our research we have found they will compromise and say "I'm Black American," and they'll feel much better if you also give them the right to say, I'm Jamaican, Panamanian, so on. So we have a much larger spread of categories that we'll use in surveys and in general studies; people feel comfortable with the terms *White, Black, Native American,* and so on. You still find people using those categories and being OK if they were forced to make a choice.

Can you highlight for us key historical events, in a nutshell, what historical experience should educators be aware of in relationship to the African American community and African American students?

That's a pretty tough one and the answer may surprise you in part. Let me start out with, that especially going from 1900 to 2000, the long-term effect of racism has been to shunt or slow down the rate in which African Americans could become part of the mainstream. And we have many, many African Americans who remain poor. When you ask me a question from that angle, then the key markers for our push toward modernity, our push toward dispersal into the society would be, of course, the movement from the Deep South to the North or the urban centers. We went from a very rural-based people, farming, to a more urban proletarian one.

World War I was a tremendous eye-opener for us because tens of thousands of our men and women went abroad and saw how race, in a manner of speaking, was socially constructed. That system of segregation in the United States was a system created by people, and it did not have to be accepted. And then, those coming back from the war, agitated and produced some of the first great, great social movements, one being artistic: the Harlem Renaissance, and the other the Marcus Garvey movement.

Both these movements would end up having bridges to things that were happening in the sixties. There you have your great explosion of African American culture, literature, music, poetry, with regard to the Renaissance. Not to say there wasn't a Black tradition, but you have the codification of the Black aesthetic in the 1910s and 1920s. That's when a corpus of work so voluminous presented itself, and you have a basis for, if you will, African American studies, in music, in art, in labor, and so on. We made great progress in that level, and while we had some people who criticized our movement, we were stunted with regard to our breakthrough and the union movement. And so, in the 1920s through the 1940s, we were locked into lower-wage jobs and so on. The next great tragedy for us would be the Depression. The Depression began to weaken us; we were pushed so hard down on the ground in the urban scene and in the rural scene, that some of the vitality of the culture that could keep us hopeful, positive, almost resistant to certain nefarious activities began to weaken. Though not to the point that it became as much of a problem as it is now.

Then with World War II, we had another interruption of the grinding, grinding, grinding poverty. And we began to see the emergence of protest again. And from about 1945 to the 1960s, this is my interpretation, would be the golden age of African American working-class life. We had the dispersal of tens of thousands of Whites out of the factories into White-collar jobs because of the G.I. Bill and so on. And even though some of us went to college, nonetheless, the jobs we could take were often in these factories. And for a while, people would go from Mississippi to Chicago or Detroit, to the Ford plant, and if you study our ghettos, our communities, between the 1940s and the 1960s, they weren't nirvana, but they were very vibrant, healthy places. There was lots of money circulating,

Now, with this high employment in the working-class sector, we have vibrant but segregated colleges; we began to produce people who developmentally were now college trained, exposed to higher education along with this very healthy working-class strata. Our parents were often in this working-class strata, we were kind of nudging up. And with the end of World War II, the defeat of Nazis and so on, we began to slowly but surely have an agitation around our condition.

Then, finally in the 1950s, with Rosa Parks and so on, it was just inevitable that we would begin to push toward a greater sense of freedom. But keep in mind that you have to ask the question, "Where do those Black college kids come from and how do they come in such large numbers?" Well, they came from those working-class parents, and that's why I mentioned that. Then, we have just a series of things that happen between '55 and '65: you have the great Supreme Court decision. Not great in terms of its content, it can be critiqued, but it was the trigger that increased our expectations. That's why these Supreme Court decisions are important. The decision itself caused us as a people to rapidly expand what we should expect of ourselves and of the nation.

At first we tried to express this new expectation in a most amazing way, and that would be through a nonviolent movement, more in the tradition of

Gandhi. The civil rights movement—the movement of the common Black person for which King was the spokesperson—can't be studied enough. It has to be understood. It's an amazing, amazing groundswell. Then of course, that spun off into what we call the Black consciousness movement. I'm a product of the Black consciousness movement, but my actual frame of reference is when we as a people began to shift from "Let us in, let us just be Americans," because there's a very integrationist/assimilationist theme, to the civil rights movement—to not only are you going to let us in, we're going to force ourselves in, but you're going to have to change. That was the kind of dimension that happened with the Blackness phase.

Now, noticing at the same time that you have this explosive emergence of will and push for insertion in the sixties and seventies, the American economy was going through a radical shift such that many of the good-paying blue-collar jobs were being pushed out of the cities, offshore, what have you. And people have to understand this, it took a long time for that to happen, but it began to have a more immediate effect in the inner cities than it did in the suburban areas. So that, as early as 1955 people are able to trace how there was a sucking out of some of the good jobs that we as Black people were then able to have with the moving on of Whites. So, you have this irony that between 1960 and 1980 you have this explosive emergence of middle-class Black people. Now wealthy and so on, and a very hopeful sign of the society, and at the same time you have a large number of our people who were literally going backwards. I have no doubt in my mind that if the economy had maintained itself for at least another ten or twenty years, the proportion of Black people that would be poor today would be very very manageable. It's almost at times unmanageable.

But with the dropoff of the economic bridging into middle-class life, you have this irony that in some cases the material conditions, and maybe even the spiritual conditions, of some Black people in some hyperconcentrated poor arenas—and this causes some of my friends to get a little antsy—I'm not so sure if it isn't the same as, or worse than, slavery in the sense that the level of hope is so low. It causes us to entertain solutions that you're hard-pressed to find Black people entertaining these solutions, such as the underground economy, in such large numbers in earlier periods of history.

That creates problems in its own right. People on the right and a few liberals even will start blaming Blacks themselves, but we did not create our unemployment. And the unemployment is sustained, and that has to do more with the larger society.

And then, more recently we have the attempt to roll back the progress that was made by African Americans and the tensions that have been created in higher education. Here's an interesting thing, and my comment on this question was this: People tried to racialize affirmative action. But affirmative action is a recurring thing in American history. There's a bridge right near us called the Triboro Bridge, in New York. The Triboro Bridge was a project designed in the context of affirmative action to give preference to White male ethnic workers who were unemployed in the city of New York and figure out what could we do with them. But rather than to have makeshift work, let's create some projects that would add value to society as a whole, but also would employ them, keep them from becoming communists, keep them from rioting, keep them from making much mischief, political and otherwise. A project that would end up with a product that would serve the needs of the society for years to come. In a sense, we had to do such things earlier in times of poverty when most of the people were poor or working class, that would help them be transformed from working class to middle class.

The G.I. Bill in World War II is another example of transforming of a large group, tens of thousands, hundreds of thousands of White people who were poor, working class, and so on. Then repositioning them so they could, in a sense, become the new middle class. Now, these new middle-class Whites now have been around for two or three, sometime four, generations. And there's a tendency that, not always, but often, that once you make the middle class, it is easier for you to replicate your status, as long as the schools cooperate and so on. So, the middle class among us, who still are dominated by Whites, and especially the powerful middle class and the wealthy, want the society to be friendly to their replicative needs. Since I'm an adult and I'm middle class I want the society to sustain my own status, but in regard to my children I want you to help me to help them replicate my status.

Now, what does that have to do with issues of race and culture? Well, if I am poor, I need institutions that are going to help me transform my status. I need projects like the Triboro Bridge; I need projects like the G.I. Bill. Those kinds of activities will help to identify those persons amongst the poor who really could do well in college, but might need a little bit of assistance—extra programs to study, extra help, and so on. So not only do you need to be admitted, but you need to have programs within the university that assist. There's two ways. Even in admissions you can't set the standards that are so biased toward the middle class that you would overlook my value. In fact what are called standards are really not standards. It's simply a way of trying to give preference to those persons that are middle class. Because now, those people, the middle class, are so large in number that again, they want institutions that will be friendly to them. They cannot be serviced by private institutions, there's just too many of them. So now they've turned their attentions to public institutions, such as the University of Michigan, and so on. And you see what people are saying? Well, "I should be allowed to come in based on my test scores." Well, those test scores are inherently class-biased, and they're inherently geared toward replication.

If you go into the actual charters of public higher education institutions, it says right there in the charter, it says right there in the mission statement, "We are to make education accessible. We are to make education affordable." That is because when they were started, they were servicing the transformation of people who were not yet middle class. And now my long-winded discussion: You now are facing this battle between groups, because many of the people who are crying out for transformative operations on the society are People of Color. Some because they were immigrants, but with regard to African Americans it is this long-term negative result of their being stunted in their transformation to the mainstream. So they need flexible admissions so the institutions can identify quality within their ranks that are not identifiable by some of the markers of admissions that are useful for people that are already middle class. And yet when you see people like the fascist groups out of Maryland that call themselves "The Center for Equal Opportunity" or whatever, what they're really trying to do is try to blunt the number of People of Color who make it to these institutions and keep them as White as they can.

It's ironic that people say we want to have a race-neutral standard. Well the standards that they get actually increase the probability of having an all-White class. They claim it has nothing to do with race because they're using standards, but that's just bullshit. Anyone who knows the history of test measurements knows that what they're asking for is a narrow range of definitions of excellence that increase the probability that Whites and middle class will get in.

Affirmative action is about the business of saying, "No, you are missing, you are missing quality." And there are other ways than test scores and there's much merit in people who are poor and who have to work thirty hours a week while in school and so on. And that if the state is to have a bias it should not be toward those who are already middle class, but should be toward those people that need education that's accessible and affordable. It is just the opposite. But you have this tension between replicative status and transformed status.

The discussion of historical elements has led naturally to comments about the African American family and community. Can you talk more about family and community and how these shape what happens in schools with African American students?

Now we get into some of the great, great distortions in African American life, the Moynihan Report (1965) and so on. From 1900 to the edges of 1960, the employment rate of Black males was usually high, and the ability of women to also work was usually high, so that the existence of the two-parent household in the Black community is normative. Even when Moynihan wrote this report, 74 percent of Black families or so were two-parent households. Children were being raised in two-parent households. Recall I said that we had this transformation in the economy that takes place in the sixties, and it goes full-force in 1973 with the oil embargo. That's when we had the rapid closing down of factories and so on, and people began to lose their jobs. So that between the early 1970s and 1980s, we began to see what appeared to be a radical change in the structure of Black families. That's kind of ass-backwards. You can't have a family if you don't have a job.

The overall ecology of working-class life was radically affected by the pulling out of decent-paying jobs. Black people didn't stop relating to each other; they still fell in love. The irony of Black employment is that now sometimes the relationships took on more, not more importance, but took on a distorted importance from what would happen if I was working eight hours a day, coming home to be with my wife, my children going to school, et cetera. Hope just got pulled out of that. And so, men would have relationships, and women as well, where they couldn't look forward to marriage because there was no rational reason to get married. You and I have lived through thirty years, maybe longer than that, of people still relating, still in their mind's eye wanting to be like anyone else, but not being able to afford it. That and the hyperconcentration of such people in what we know as ghettos now produces people who are estranged from larger society. They love, then leave each other earlier and earlier, we now even see kids having kids.

The society puts almost all the pressure on the community itself, and says it's the community's issue; but, as you know for years and years, we continue to lose tens of thousands of good-paying blue-collar jobs in cities like New York. It's still going on and 9/11 has exacerbated it.

How does this affect our educational institutions? Well, when I was growing up, and we had the predominance of people employed, then when we went to school together we were in segregated schools. When the really low-income kids would come along, and there were always kids who came from situations where the parents were unemployed, they were a minority. And we set the tone for conformity and they would kind of conform to us. And they could almost discover their hope with us. They could almost discover their sense of future with us. That their life did not have to be defined by the avid poverty which they were experiencing.

But we had a shift in the sixties. Now at schools the majority of kids who were in school were coming from hyperisolated, segregated, poor situations; in some case the percentage of single-parent moms is very, very high; and they're bringing that ethos of day-to-day survival with them, they're sometimes brushing up against kids who come from less risky environments, but their numbers are so big that sometimes they begin to influence the culture of the schools. So it's almost been the reverse of earlier situations. Now add to that this interesting scenario: the Black kids who are doing OK, who want very much to communicate to their brethren who are not doing so well that "I identify with you. I am with you." And as a result we have some middle-class kids who because they want to be viewed as part of a group will some-times be perplexed as to how they should view school, whether or not "am I being White" in having strong performance. And we're kind of a little bit in the middle of that. I know history, we go through these cycles. And the Black communities can allow for coming out of a cycle.

Being real, being down and so on is driven by the underclass. But now the underclass has had a chance to play out its own agenda, and in some cases it is no less decadent than other agendas that class has critiqued. We have our hip-hop artists who on the one hand have messages that are sear-ing, searing not wonderful. We can't say they're wonderful, but they're awe-some because they're so truthful and they're so raw. But we're now going through a period where people are almost celebrating pimps. Celebrating the hos, I mean, I don't see how that's any less decadent than Germany where in the 1930s they got so hung up on sexuality and freedom that they weren't talking about political institutions, they weren't talking about rear-ranging society. So, we see now that some of the messages from hip-hop are very raw and very real and we need to listen, but their political consequences are not good and in some cases they're as reactionary as you can find.

I think we're spinning out of that. I'm not utopian, but I think what's going to happen is the coming together of progressive Blacks and Whites, and really, progressively oriented folks from hip-hop culture. I don't know what that's going to look like, but it's going to be different from what we are now.

But to get to your question, the schools are often beside themselves, because on one hand, they were designed for purposes of replication. The teachers were usually trained in middle-class teaching institutions. They work best when the kids come to school with attitudes like their own.

What the kids need are teachers and principals who are very competent in transformative experiences, you know, that help kids face up to, relate to their realities, but then say "you don't have to be satisfied with that, and I can be your ally in taking you to another place." The schools want to teach about the value of American society. The kids need raw discussions on "you are a part of stigmatized groups in the United States. Here's how people have organized to get the things that they need." And that would be called radical. I mean that many people would be highly distressed if that were in the schools. But that's exactly what you need. How do you organize welfare mothers? How do you organize people who are unemployed? That's what you need for people who are trying to transform. What does it look like to have a school that actually teaches how poor people are manipulated? Not for the purposes of making them angry, and therefore wanting to go out and perform anarchy, but for the purposes of organizing.

People should understand, in the fifties and sixties, when we got angry—and we went through an angry period—we were funneled,

tunneled, steered toward creating African American studies. New Black
unions. New Black art. I mean we took our energy and collectivized it. And
we set the stage for individuals having a better life but we did it through
our collective action. That often was done outside of the schools.

So when people ask me what can be done in the schools there's two
things. You can either change the schools in that way, and I have a very low
expectation that they'll change, or you try to figure out political-economic
forces that can cause the society to better distribute its resources. A better
distribution will result in a higher level of employment by people that are
poor, with jobs that are decent and that can sustain a family, and that can
sustain a community. And again, I'm not pie in the sky, we have a sanitation system that's stretched to the max, if we were to build on a national
basis for the next twenty years—it'd take us twenty years, probably more,
to get the kind of sanitation system we would need—that would employ
engineers, that would employ common laborers, and so on. If we had affirmative action we'd have our fair share of such jobs. If we were to transform our bridges—we would build new ones or first start out with making
sure the ones we've got are all they can be—again we'd employ architects,
engineers, we'd also employ common laborers.

If we were to build—if not all the schools—many of the schools that
we need in Washington, Chicago, Cleveland, and so on, make them up to
date and so on, here we go again, that would employ engineers, architects,
and so on. So, it doesn't mean we become a communist society, it means
that we borrow from American history, because all these things are like the
Triboro Bridge again.

You know, we could identify projects that add value to all of us, but it
goes against the grain in a sense. The market wants to maximize as much
money as they can into those market areas that they control. The government has an obligation to balance that somewhat. But with regard to our
infrastructure, with regard to our investment in our youth, that's not something that maybe the market people want to do, that's something that we
do. I'm going to make this number up: We'll make sure that 15 percent of
our tax dollars, 20 percent of our tax dollars are done in these activities,
and ironically end up pulling large, large numbers of common people.
They don't have to have a master's, they don't have to have a B.A., they
may not even have to have a high school degree, but they have to be pretty
clean in their habits and so on.

America thinks it's a great country; I think if we get that, we could be
an awesome country. We know from studies that that would work faster
than trying to change the schools. Families that have a reasonable level of
good employment that allows them to remain married—some may
divorce, others remain married or marry again—and where they're able to
feed their children, where they're able to go to church or live out their

spiritual lives, they send to school children who don't want to do battle with the school but want to learn from the school.

And it means the teachers themselves would not have to radically change; they could remain somewhat middle-class biased. Because the kids are becoming more malleable in terms of where they want to go, it'd just be easier. Things would be super better if in fact you get the teachers to be trained differently, if the schools were reorganized, in addition to the solid employment of the parents.

One thing is sure, as long as the parents of the children are devalued by the society, in the sense that you're almost treated as redundant workers, as leftovers, then there should be no surprise in us that the children of such redundant workers will reject that future and they will make what we call mischief. Because as they try on their own to manipulate those aspects of their environment that they can—that's what gangs are—they will produce short-run successes, but in the long run they will likely end up in jail, in prison, and when their spirits are broken, sometimes it leads to addiction and they commit—as we're seeing, but we don't want to see—suicide.

Right now, I don't have much hope in the short run. I think that people we have in office such as Bush are operating from the bell-curve agenda. I believe that they have a weird sense that the society is open, that the reason why people are on the bottom is because of their genes, that because they're on the bottom because of their genes, that nothing has to be done to assist them. And not taking action really makes a difference. That means they prolong White power. As you increase the probability of maintaining the status quo, you protect White power. They're willing to share the stage a little bit with some tokens, some Asian Americans, even some Blacks. Their image of the United States is not of a multicultural society, but of a society that's multicultural in demographics only, but which is still fundamentally a White man's country. And, I'm sixty three, I don't have any expectations that there'll be any breakthrough before I die. I don't wish that on us, I just don't think change will happen that fast. I think that right now we have a president who, it's reasonable to suggest, was not elected. We have a president who distorted information on why we should send men and women off to die. We have a power system that just collapsed because of something called deregulation. In each of these instances—the question of the election, the false notions about the war, and the deregulation—there's no reason to believe that the society is going to respond.

The reason why we're at war is an impeachable offense, and yet there's no movement to do that. It's ironic that we had Bill Clinton, who because of his sexual liaisons can be raked over the coals for two years, but history will show that we have a president now who committed impeachable offenses who will not be impeached, may even be reelected. This shows you how it has little to do with justice, and has more to do with might and your ability to control voters and so on. That's why I just don't have much hope.

My hope personally is working with young people. My own work is designed more recently to counter some of the vicious stereotypes about Black history and about Black people, so that maybe someday later someone can say, "At least somebody was writing on these things in a way that was more truthful." But right now, I don't even know if the truth matters.

As a country we could, not so much solve the problems with poverty that we have, but we could make the poverty more manageable. We can't have a zero-poverty society in a capitalist world, but we've gone through such a change, we're so imbalanced, that we're living with levels of poverty that need not be. So, I'm not utopian, I'm not a romantic; I pay a lot of attention to American history. What the society has done in the past when it steered some of its resources toward the working class has been nothing short of amazing. It is ironic that powerful Whites today who have their roots in the G.I. Bill, have their roots in forming unions and so on, could end up being so antipoor and antiBlack in their stances when the solutions that could cause them to have a better society would, in some cases, replicate some of the things that happened to their own groups in the past. That makes for great frustration for us to see the potential of the society and to see it being wasted. It's a very painful thing to see. Okay, your next question.

Are there any subpopulations in the African American community that deserve additional attention?

Yes. What's been emerging in the last ten years is that you have the Black race if you will, but there're always ethnic strands. It varies from one city to another, but in New York it really is exploding. The Dominicans, Black Cubans, Panamanians. And now in Harlem, 123rd in Harlem is like an African street—African street in a traditional sense of the term, as it is in African American. We're doing research in City University of New York and about three times we've gone out to collect data on African Americans, and three times we've ended up with a sample that is much larger for Caribbeans and African Caribbeans than African Americans. So, these subcategories would be crucial.

The multiracial category is increasing. The last time I went about research in California, 17 percent of Black males are marrying out of race. And not just White women. So, there is an explosion of biracial, multiracial children who may identify themselves as mostly Black, but they have these other connections. We are now getting more and more Black people who are successful economically. And I don't know what the spread is, but a number of them are drifting toward a conservative, right-wing orientation. So they're becoming more of a voice. Their percentage is small, but because we're living in an era of the right, they're often better funded, and their voices often louder. There's been a diminution, in some ways, of the voices of Black progressives. But you asked for new voices.

I think that you wouldn't necessarily call this a population, but gender remains a discourse within that community, some for positive reasons, some for negative. The horrific stereotyping and stigmatization of Black males is something hard to find in Western history. But we should also look at the stigmatization that is also occurring with Black women. And the issue of sexual lifestyle is real problematic in our community. We have delayed the aggressive reaching out to our homosexual brothers and sisters that are relying on us on some of the AIDS issues, although that's not the first thing one wants to think about.

Consider the incarceration of Black men, and the production of a group that defines themselves as not being gay, but who enjoy relationships within same-sex relationships, and do so with unsafe sex. It has now sprung over into heterosexual relationships, and now there's a population of Black women, often poor, relating to heterosexual men, but who've been in prison, who've had relationships. So there's a sort of category, you can't call 'em gay, you can't call them homosexual, but by their sexual activity, it's causing issues.

We have a large sector, more so than ever, of kids who are being raised in very, very poor environments, usually just with moms. Often they're hyperconcentrated in tenement houses.

Let's not overlook, however, that we have the largest Black middle-class subpopulation that we've had in our history. And if they go through the chain that we've seen Whites go through, we will produce our bohemian group, our rebels, our people who see life differently, we'll get our entrepreneurs. There's also a certain bit of unpredictability with the very, very poor and the very, very comfortable, and it makes for wonderful history. We'll see that unfold in the years to come.

You've addressed my next question on how class or socioeconomic issues play a role in determining aspects of the African American population. Let's continue. How do different cultural styles, values, and worldviews affect the education of African Americans?

Two things are going on. The kids sometimes do come with different styles, often couched in different language behaviors. But probably the biggest problem in the schools is not so much what the kids bring to the classroom, that's often varied, as much as the way our teachers have been trained and what they feel comfortable with. We had a time in the 1900s, 1920s that people coming in were Italian, Irish, and there were Eastern European Jews from Poland or elsewhere. Over two or three generations the schools did a pretty good job of helping them eventually achieve middle-class status.

What's kind of scary today is that the only hope that's being held out to these diverse kids, many of whom are poor, is the education system. And so you have a falling tyranny. I'll be a bit dramatic on this one. No other group, by that I mean, say, White ethnic group, no other ethnic group has achieved social mobility from lower-class status to the middle-class status through education alone. You can find many pockets of exceptions, but even when you find those exceptions you find the problem.

People are saying, well, there's the model minority, the Asian Americans. When you study the extent to which people from India, people from China, from Japan have made it very quickly—Asian Americans who have done well in our school system—you discover they didn't come in at a low point. Their parents had no money per se, but they often were middle class in the first place. So you've got middle-class ethnic groups coming here, learning the language, taking off. That's not the same as bringing in people who are boat people. For example, when we track Vietnamese boat people who are very, very poor, they have not gone up into the system. So, it's a myth that education alone can make all the difference.

And this is the part that is scary with our poor kids today, because society is trying to make education the singular platform by which social ability can be achieved. All other history shows us that it is a combination of employment of the parents in conjunction with the education of the children. If you don't have steady employment of the parents, then you don't move large masses of those kids, their progeny, if you will, into a better place. They become distracted, they get into issues of survival, and this phenomenon showed itself in the Depression when White ethnic groups became distracted, they were driven to street life and we had a duel economy with prohibition.

So, no other group has achieved social ability in one generation through education alone. That's what education is being asked to do, and that is scary stuff. Because when the kids don't achieve, then people turn around and say, "Ah ha! We invest in you, we have educational classes for you, and yet you don't achieve, therefore it must be you." They're not looking at the fact that while the children were in school, the parents were often divorced or couldn't even get married or living in tenement houses and didn't have good jobs. There has to be decent-paying jobs for the parents and that will lead to a sense of hope. Now do I again mean some sort of nirvana? No, but there has to be a critical mass of the parents, the adults, employed in decent jobs, not every single one. The Black community has been able to tolerate high employment of 15–20 percent, but the jobs had to be good-paying jobs. If not it leads to some mischief making by the kids.

What are some of the common problems that African Americans might bring into the school setting?

Instead of describing problems let's call them challenges. They often bring in a different alignment system. How they codify life is different. And they work better with teachers who outright know the code, who can fight back for them and understand that they have to transform the kid. We should place a greater value on outside activity, as opposed to staying in a class-room. They often are more engaged if there's a way in which the curriculum can move back and forth from the classroom situation to things that happen in the street. I don't mean to bring in crime from the street, that would be ridiculous. You almost need a core of teachers and administrators who rather than view the community as enemy, view the community as an anthropological wellspring. The challenge is how do I show the students that if I'm walking down the street, there's a building and a connection, there's a building and another connection, and cognitively recognizing the connections and the differences. How to bring in that kind of everyday sense of survival and connection. Keep the kids absorbed and bring into the classroom something that's fascinating and interesting. That's no small challenge. But if you have a school system that's busy talking about giving people tests, tracking them, and then talking about how you know that the kid can't make it, then the kid himself feels that sense of being trapped, feels that sense that you don't have much confidence in me, they fight back. They come to war. Especially by preadolescence and adolescence.

Could you now discuss some of the factors that you see as important in assessing the learning styles of African American students and share what environmental factors could be manipulated to match that style?

I'm impressed with the work of A. Wade Bodkin of Howard University and others. They have gone into the classroom and done anthropological studies, seeing how the classroom is in terms of its activities, teacher behavior, decorations. The child comes in and sees this culture as something fully integrated into the classroom. Is the culture something new and strange or does it have enough symbols that they have from their home, which is a permanent place, to the classroom, which is a permanent place? These researchers place a lot of emphasis not only on the teacher, per se, but the behavior, the language style, the competencies, and the actual physical structure of the school itself. This merging of the educational institutions and the home has value.

Is the disconnect a problem of a child or is it a problem of the teacher? Perhaps you're saying to yourself, we're going to bring in people to make a connection. It's somehow easier to understand it when they're from Hungary or Vietnam or so on. There's something about the ability of Americans to greet foreigners, strangers, in a way that it's understood that they're strangers. I'm using *stranger* now in a pejorative sense. But if the stranger is Chicano, if the stranger is Native American, or if the stranger is Black American, somehow people go brain-dead. Yet some of the solutions that we use for bringing in a stranger who's foreign, we'd want to see them do it also with African Americans.

It's hard for people to do this because they have to face up to their racism. People have to understand that the spatial isolation of African Americans into various residencies is not an accident. Nor is it an issue of choice. And you have to own up to that.

And you have to ask the question of given I didn't necessarily cause that, but I'm part of the solution, and I want to be part of the solution. Then what things do I have to do structurally, pedagogically, and so on to make this, not only a friendly environment—because that's a liberal solution, how to make it friendly—but more so than the issue of friendly, how do I make a child stronger? Because the issue is to push the kids, to create a sense of future, that's just as tough as it is for anyone else, and that requires people being very relaxed in taking a top to bottom look at themselves. And maybe it may mean, in a state like Oregon, going back to your schools of education and saying, "You're out to lunch." You know, you have to walk up to that and don't feel negative about it. You know, if you really, really do want to reach everyone then tracking is not the solution; simply cataloguing people is not the solution. As we know from history, the stories of poor, White Irish kids who were done to, they were catalogued as not making it, and they have made it. We have the same scenario, how do we not make the same mistake? How do we assume from the beginning that every kid can learn? And yet take on the challenge of creating an environment where that can take place?

Considering cultural differences and learning style what suggestions might you have concerning establishing rapport with African American students and families?

Yeah, if we did make connections earlier, that would help. But again I can't overstress what I said earlier. Schools can do an awful lot, and they could do more. But if the larger economic arena is not treating the parents with respect, the kids are going to come in with sand in their eye and they're going to be distracted.

There should be a lot more participatory surveys and discussions. Ask parents, "What do you need from us?" I know I'm friendly but we live in a world where there's racial/cultural barriers. What has to happen so that you as a parent can really feel as though you can walk in the door and feel friendly about it? How do we work together to go from low expectations for your child, you know, let's just get that on the table, to really high expectations? What kind of demands do we make of each other for that?

There should be a lot of time spent with parents and people of the community asking those kind of pointed questions, then translating those responses into programs that are doable, programs that teachers themselves can get excited about and that the various principals of the schools can be proud of. That's not an easy thing to do. You still basically use a middle-class model and that presupposes that kids kind of look alike, sound alike, talk alike, and act alike.

Could you present a short case that brings together the different issues and dynamics we discussed about working with African American students?

Well, this may surprise you, but I see these issues even at the college level. I took on a new job recently. When I came in there were a couple of African American kids who were falling through the cracks. This was generally a positive environment but somehow they just weren't being pushed enough. I don't know that I'd done much different than to suggest to them that they really can make it, but it's not going to be easy, and that I have confidence in them, so let's go for it. And now I've got two of them on the cusp of getting their degrees. When I think back in my days at Cornell, we used to admit students that were being rejected by other higher level schools in the area of Black studies. You could see where they weren't high testers, but they were solid students. We felt like they were like us.

We created, not a grueling, but a really rigorous two-year program with a master's degree. The thesis really tested their ability to not only think, but to write as well as think. And when we got through with them, we not only grew as professors, but more importantly they were going off to Yale, they were going off to U-Penn.

It's hard to say to people, but it's a combination of first and foremost believing in people when they walk in the door, and then understanding that it's work, and that one has to constantly monitor whether or not you're really allowing for systems, creating systems that allow the students to share their world value and world competencies.

I'll give you one more example. We have a program where you're supposed to take a test after the first year of graduate studies. It's called the first doctoral examination. Well, we found out that when you give a test that's middle-class skewed, that the kids that are going to do the best on it will be middle class. Yet the kids who are equally as smart and equally as bright, the very mechanism of the test will likely overlook them. So we changed it to a take-home test. Made it more transparent, not necessarily easier. We find that the well-trained middle-class student still excels in this vehicle, but now we're able to see better the emergent competencies or the actual competencies of our working-class kids, White and Black. Sometimes we still have to work harder or work differently with the working-class kids. They come in with some rough edges in writing. Their ability to translate their thinking into writing often is more of a mystery to them. But as you see from the smile on my face, we keep the attitude that we have faith in the kids.

And we're going to examine our systems to see how they're working, to see how they might have a middle-class bias to them. There's nothing wrong with being middle class, its just that if you allow some middle-class biases to come in, you skip over talent that would display itself differently. Now ironically you could say we end up at the same place. Each writes a dissertation. This is a written document, usually there's intense, thick, qualitative material, or there's actual quantitative material, or both. So in a manner of speaking we take all the students and they arrive, in a manner of speaking, at the same place. But we don't assume they have to start in the same place.

And I think that's the challenge to educators. We want all the kids to come out competent, probably not the same, but within a range of competencies. Using words differently, seeing the world differently. But as a result of having those competencies they have choices. If the society would allow us to really transform these kids the way we talked about earlier, on a minimalist level you would hope that they would be provided with such choices that with their own developing consciousness, they can take advantage of such choices. Yet we have poor decisions such as one reported recently in the state of New York, where in an attempt to equalize funding, a judge stood and suggested that all we need provide for the average high school child what is tantamount to an eighth-grade education—and we know already that an eighth-grade education is a limitation of choice, not a creation of choice. Such decisions suggest that we have a system that will replicate poverty rather than transform.

But I don't want to end on a negative note—though I told you earlier that I'm not too optimistic that in my lifetime I'll see people change. Our society is right now wrong-headed with regard to its attitudes toward the poor. It probably is overlooking a critical mass of people who could help to further revitalize our economy, our arts, all aspects of our society. To pull out those qualities in our children is hard work; it has to go beyond the middle-class curriculum that tends to dominate the schools right now. It does mean we'll lose some teachers that may retire early. But in the long run, just as the incorporation of the Eastern European Jews did nothing but infuse and revitalize parts of our community, just as the poor Irish were transformed into the middle-class, I see the same thing happening with African Americans and African children, Native American children. It's hard because there are many people that don't have faith in them. And it looks to me like they've done such a good job of communicating that lack of faith that sometimes the kids themselves now are turning off to school. We're losing them very early. I hope maybe this kind of book that you're writing and the attitudes you and your coauthor have will make a difference in how we train teachers. And maybe as importantly, how we socialize and educate not just teachers, but administrator, principals, counselors, and so on.

WORKING WITH ASIAN AMERICAN STUDENTS

An Interview with Valerie Ooka Pang

DEMOGRAPHICS

Asian Americans were the fastest growing racial group in this country from 1980 to 2000, their population nearly tripling (179 percent) during that period. The 2000 census (which now divides the larger group into two sub-groups) reported an Asian population of 10.2 million or 3.6 percent of the general population and a Native Hawaiian and other Pacific Islander popula-tion of 400,000 or 0.1 percent. Projections are for a population increase from 5 percent of the U.S. total in 2010 to 9 percent by 2050.

Like Latinos/as, Asians represent diverse ethnic groups with very differ-ent languages and cultures, and in some cases a long history of intergroup conflict and hostilities. Included are forty-three ethnic groups, twenty-eight in the Asian category and fifteen in the Pacific Islander category. Included in the former are individuals who identify themselves as Asian Indian, Chinese, Filipino, Korean, Japanese, and Vietnamese; and in the latter individuals from Hawaii, Guam, and Samoa.

With passage of the Immigration Act of 1965 and large-scale immigration from Southeast Asia and other parts of the Asian continent, the relative sizes of Asian American subgroups changed dramatically. According to the 1970 census, Japanese were the most populous, followed by Chinese and Filipinos. By 1980, however, Japanese were in third place, Chinese first, and Filipinos second. Today, Chinese are the largest Asian subgroup with 2.3 million, fol-lowed by Filipinos at 1.9 million, Asian Indians at 1.7 million, Vietnamese at 1.1 million, Koreans also at 1.1 million, and Japanese at 0.8 million. Native Hawaiians and Pacific Islanders make up only 5 percent of the total Asian population.

Most Asian Americans come from recent immigrant families. During the 1990s immigrants were responsible for two-thirds of the growth of the overall Asian population. In 1998, for instance, 59 percent were foreign-born, with

74 percent of them arriving after 1980. Many Chinese Americans and Japanese Americans, however, have been here for three or more generations. Originally a source of cheap labor in the economic development of the western United States, the Chinese and Japanese experienced extensive suffering and racial discrimination.

> Legislation enacted in 1790 excluded Asians and other non-Whites gaining citizenship by limiting citizenship to "free White residents." Because most Asians were foreign-born and not citizens, they could be legally kept from owning land or businesses, attending schools with Whites, or living in White neighborhoods. Asian immigrants were not eligible for U.S. citizenship until 1952. The 1879 California constitution barred the hiring of Chinese workers, and the federal Chinese Exclusion Act of 1882 halted the entry of most Chinese until 1943. The 1907 Gentlemen's Agreement and a 1917 law restricted immigration from Japan and a "barred zone" known as the Asian-Pacific Triangle. During World War II Americans of Japanese ancestry were interned in camps by Executive Order signed by Franklin D. Roosevelt. (Pollard and O'Hare, 1999, pp. 6–7)

Recent Asian and Pacific Islander immigration has followed two different streams. The first stream came from countries such as China and Korea that already had large populations in the United States. The majority of these immigrants were college educated and entered under special employment provisions. The second stream came from the Southeast Asian nations of Vietnam, Laos, and Cambodia after the Vietnam War to escape persecution. Most were poor and uneducated.

Forty-nine percent of Asian Americans and Pacific Islanders are concentrated in the western United States, with the largest urban populations located in Los Angeles and New York City. Sixty percent of the Chinese reside in California and New York; two-thirds of the Filipinos and Japanese live in California and Hawaii. Koreans and Asian Indians tend to be more dispersed, with the largest concentrations in California, New York, Illinois, New Jersey, and Texas. Southeast Asians, on the other hand, can be found in unexpected locations due to government resettlement policies. In 1990, for example, 40 percent of the Hmong resided in Minnesota and Wisconsin (Pollard and O'Hare, 1999).

Unlike African Americans, Latinos/as, and Native Americans, Asian Americans have been economically and educationally successful, even in comparison with the White population. In 1998 the average median household income was $46,637 for Asians, compared to $42,439 for White households and $25,351 for African Americans. Although they make up only 13 percent of the non-White population, Asian Americans account for 30 percent of all minority businesses. They also score high on business ownership rates (businesses per thousand population), with Koreans and Asian Indians surpassing Whites. Asians and Whites graduate from high school at the same rate, approximately 90 percent, but Asians are more likely than Whites to complete two or more years of college. In 1990, 13 percent of Asians and Pacific

Islanders earned graduate and professional degrees, in comparison to 9 percent of Whites; their rate was three to four times the rate of other minorities.

Because of such statistics and a cultural tendency to act deferential and not compete openly with White Americans, Asian Americans have been described as a model minority and a success story. Sue and Sue (1999), however, see this image as a myth based on incomplete data. In their view, the myth validates the erroneous belief that any ethnic group can succeed if its members work hard enough, stimulates intergroup conflict, and shortchanges Asian communities from needed resources. According to Sue and Sue (1999), a number of facts need to be understood. High median income doesn't take into consideration the number of wage earners, the level of poverty among certain Asian subgroups, and the discrepancy between education and income for Asian workers. Education in the Asian community is bimodal—that is, there are both highly educated and uneducated subpopulations. In large urban areas Asians live in ghettos with high unemployment, poverty, and widespread social problems. Underutilization of services does not necessarily mean a lack of problems, but may in fact have alternative explanations such as face saving, shame, or the family's cultural tendency to keep personal information hidden from the outside world. In short, the belief in Asian success does not mean that Asian Americans experience less racism or discrimination than other groups or that there are not serious problems within crowded urban enclaves. At a psychological level, model-minority status refers to the lack of threat Whites experience in relation to Asian Americans. Such an attitude has eroded somewhat, however, with increased economic competition from Japan and other Pacific Rim countries and the growth in the number of Asian American students competing successfully for college and university slots.

FAMILY AND CULTURAL VALUES

Lee (1996) offered the following description of traditional Asian families.

> in traditional Asian families, the family unit—rather than the individual—is highly valued. The individual is seen as the product of all the generations of his or her family. The concept is reinforced by rituals and customs such as ancestor worship, family celebrations, funeral rites, and genealogy records. Because of this continuum, individuals' personal action reflects not only on themselves but also on their extended family and ancestors. . . . Obligations and shame are mechanisms that traditionally help reinforce societal expectations and proper behavior. An individual is expected to function in his or her clearly defined roles and positions in the family hierarchy, based on age, gender, and social class. There is an emphasis on harmonious interpersonal relationships, interdependence, and mutual obligations or loyalty for achieving a state of psychological homeostasis or peaceful coexistence with family or other fellow beings. (pp. 230–230).

Family and gender roles and expectations are highly structured. Fathers are the breadwinners, protectors, and ultimate authorities. Mothers oversee the home, bear and care for children, and are under the authority of their father, husband, in-laws, and at time even sons. Male children are highly prized, and the strongest bond within the family is between mother and son. Children are expected to be respectful and obedient, and are usually raised by an extended family system. Older daughters are expected to be caretakers of younger siblings.

Traditional Asian values differ dramatically from those of White middle-class Americans. With immigration, there is the strong possibility of cultural conflict within the family. Lee (1996) described five Asian American family types that differ in levels of cultural conflict.

- "Traditional" families are largely untouched by assimilation and acculturation, retain cultural ways, limit their contact with the White world, and tend to live in ethnic enclaves.
- "Culture conflict" families are typified by traditional parents and acculturated, Americanized children who experience intergenerational conflict over appropriate behavior and values, exhibit major role confusion, and lack agreed upon family structures.
- "Bicultural" families tend to include acculturated parents, born either in the United States or in Asia but exposed to Western ways. They are professional, middle-class, bilingual, and bicultural. Family structures tend to blend family styles, but with regular contact with traditional family members.
- "Americanized" families have taken on the ways of majority culture; their ties to traditional Asian culture are fading, and they have little interest in ethnic identity.
- "Interracial" families are formed through intermarriage with a non-Asian partner; family styles from the two cultures can be successfully integrated, or there can be significant value and style conflict.

Sue and Sue (1999) similarly identified five value conflicts that may arise between Asian American students and Western-trained teachers.

- Asian students and families value a collective and group focus that emphasizes interdependence, while Western teachers focus on individualism and independent action.
- Asians tend to be most comfortable with hierarchical relationships, in comparison with the Western emphasis on equality in relationships.
- Asian cultures see restraint of emotion as a sign of maturity, while Western culture is more likely to see emotional expressiveness as healthy.
- Traditional Asian students and families expect teachers to provide solutions, while the Western educational perspective encourages finding one's own solutions through introspection.

- Mental illness and emotional problems are seen as shameful and indicative of family failure within the Asian context, while Western counseling views mental illness and physical illness similarly.

Our Interviewee

Valerie Ooka Pang is a professor in the School of Teacher Education at San Diego State University. She was a first- and second-grade teacher in rural and urban schools. Dr. Pang was senior editor of *Struggling to Be Heard: The Unmet Needs of Asian Pacific American Children,* which is the only multidisciplinary text on Asian Pacific American children. Her latest book is *Multicultural Education: A Caring-Centered, Reflective Approach.* She developed a philosophical framework called caring-centered multicultural education. Her philosophy is based on the work of scholars such as Nel Noddings, John Dewey, Vygotsky, Luis Moll, Vanessa Siddle Walker, Geneva Gay, and Michael Cole.

Dr. Pang is a sought-after consultant for *Sesame Street,* Fox Children's Network, Family Communications (producer of the fondly remembered *Mr. Roger's Neighborhood*). She has published in a variety of journals, including *Harvard Educational Review, The Kappan, Educational Forum, Theory and Research in Social Education, Social Education, Equity* and *Excellence,* and *Multicultural Education.* She received the Outstanding Teaching Award in the Liberal Studies Program at San Diego State University.

The Interview

Could you begin by talking about your own ethnic background and how it has impacted your work?

I am a third generation Japanese American. I was born in Seattle, Washington, and grew up in eastern Washington in the town of Ellensburg. The farmers there grew corn, potatoes, Kentucky bluegrass, hay, that kind of thing. I lived in town, but I would visit my friends out in the country, and we would ride horses. I rode horses as a child, but I never rode the subway until I was thirty-nine. Many folks do not see me in this way, I mean living in a rural town. I could milk a cow. I fed the steers. I've been to the roundup, where they brand them. I have a whole different kind of background than most Asian Americans, who tend to live in urban settings.

My interest in multicultural education began many years ago when I was a twenty-year-old and I started teaching at the only neighborhood Black elementary school in a large urban district. It was March and I had just received

(Used with permission of Valeria Ooka Pang.)

my bachelor's degree in education from a small private university. I felt I was ready to tackle the problems of the world. My first teaching assignment was in a school of three hundred children; 93 percent of the students were Black, 3 percent were Asian and Native American, and 4 percent of the youngsters were White. All my students were either on reduced or free lunch.

Of the fourteen teachers at the school, only three had more than six years of teaching experience. Most of us were new or had been teaching for less than three years. There was an underlying atmosphere of frustration and hopelessness in the school, especially in the upper grades.

Most of the staff didn't think that I, a relatively quiet, young, and short Asian American woman (barely five feet tall), would make it at this tough neighborhood school. The week after I took the job, the principal mentioned to me, "We had a knifing in the parking lot last year, so be sure to lock your car." I was definitely a greenhorn who would learn much from the school and parents in the neighborhood in the next year and a half.

As a beginning first-grade teacher, I was unaware that young children are sensitive to ethnic differences. The first days of the school year were spent in special orientation sessions: small groups of first graders came with their parents to become familiar with their new surroundings before attending school for an entire day. During one such session, I noticed a child and his mother huddled in discussion outside the classroom door. Finally, this mother came inside to speak with me. She said, "My son, Rodney, doesn't want to come in." My tension level beginning to rise, I wondered how I would coax this anxious body into the room. Politely, I asked her, "Is he scared?" "No," she said matter of factly. "Rodney says he doesn't want to come in because he can't speak Chinese!" At first I didn't understand what she meant; I don't speak Chinese either. Then I realized that peering into the room and seeing me, a Japanese American, the youngster assumed I was Chinese. I went over and spoke to Rodney, persuading him to join the other children. This misunderstanding, though easy to correct, demonstrates that Rodney, barely six years old, had already formed certain beliefs: first, that those with Asian physical features must be Chinese and not American, that if I were Chinese, I would not speak English.

I wish I had been a more effective teacher. I didn't know where to begin. What did I need to learn? What changes did I need to make to be a better teacher? This is how my interest in multicultural education began.

Who are the Asian Americans? What characteristics do they share as a group?

You did a pretty good job answering the question in the introduction to this chapter. Rather than talk about similarities, I would like to also emphasize our differences. Asian Americans are one of the most diverse groups that you will find in the world. There are more within-group differences than are between groups. They include people who come from the islands like the Hawaiians, and that is why we refer to the broad group as Asian and Pacific Islanders. Chamorros, they are from Guam. There's the people from the Marshall Islands, Micronesia. Then of course the Asians who first came to the continental United States. The first group were Filipinos, who jumped ship from Spanish galleons in 1765. I think that's the right date. They just celebrated 225 years in this country. You'll find the documentation in Fred Cordova's book: *Filipinos, Forgotten Asians,* I think that is the title. And then Chinese immigrants who came in the mid-1800s. I always think of Bing, after whom the Bing cherry is named. He was here in the 1850s and 1860s, working on the Llewing farm in Milwaukee, Oregon. Seth Llewing , the brother of the original orchardist, Henderson Llewing, named the cherry after Bing, his Chinese foreman. So there are a lot of other groups, the Japanese, they also came to the United States, but most immigration from other countries stopped in 1924 with the Asian Exclusion Act and didn't really start up again until 1965 with the new immigration act. That's when you get an influx of immigrants from Asia: more Filipinos, Koreans, and Southeast Asians. So I would say it is also diversity that is a main theme within the Asian and Pacific Island American group, each with its own unique culture.

Could you talk about the various names Asian Americans use to describe or identify themselves and some of the names that have been used historically to identify the group by others?

As you know Asians have been called Orientals, I think that term probably came from Westerners who went to China, Japan, and Korea when those countries were just opening up. At that time it was referred to as the Orient. But, as I tell my students, I am not a rug, so that's why I'm not an Oriental. I am an Asian because that denotes where my ancestors are from in a world context. And in the sixties, Yuji Ichioka from UCLA created the term *Asian American* because it was a description that we felt more signified who we are and is devoid of the negative connotation of terms such as Oriental and Yellow Peril. Many Asians in America prefer to be referred to by their country of origin.

Derogatory names are just part of the larger problem of racial discrimination and stereotyping and how children internalize them into their identities. Consider the words of Suzanne Akemi Negoro, a Japanese American female.

> In my junior high history class, I remember sitting in the rigid single desk, resting my feet on the bookrack of the desk in front of me. I always used to sink low in my seat, and on one particular day I was sinking even lower than normal as our teacher announced that it was Pearl Harbor Day. Usually anything that is given its own day is something that's good; there's Valentine's Day, Martin Luther King, Jr., Day, President's Day, Labor Day, and Independence Day. But Pearl

Harbor Day is one of the few dark-designated days, left in the same camp with D-Day. This day not only marks the day that Japan bombed the United States; it also marks that day that my family and other Japanese Americans officially became suspected traitors. Sitting in my junior high history class, this day also marked me. I can still picture the student in the row next to me leaning toward me and whispering, "So why'd you bomb us anyway?" Four generations and forty years, and not much had changed.

The biggest problem I had in dealing with this student's comment was my own inability to reconcile my cultural identity, both Japanese and American. I remember words from my childhood: being praised, "You speak so well; Your English is so good"; being questioned, "What are you anyway?" "No, what are you *really*?" and being criticized, "You don't speak Japanese? Why not?" "How sad that you've lost your language; How sad that you've lost your culture." I remember being about three feet tall with the voice of a mouse, trying to talk as loud as possible so that people could hear how well I spoke, that is, without an accent. I remember my years of adolescent female fun that always ended up matching me with the other Asian boy in the class. And I remember always wanting to be matched with every other boy but him. I wanted to prove to people that I was American, and to me that meant proving that I was White.

I was not, however, simply just trying to prove that I was White. I was simultaneously trying to prove that I was still "Japanese enough." As a child, the most difficult part was figuring what was enough (Pang, 2001, pp. 127–128).

Could you highlight for us key historical events in a nutshell? What historical experiences should educators be aware of in relationship to the Asian American community and Asian American students?

In 1882 the Chinese Exclusion Act, or Gary Act, was passed by Congress. It was the first U.S. immigration law that denied entry to a specific group of people on the basis of race. Then, in 1924, further legislation excluded most Asian groups from immigrating to the United States. It was primarily aimed, however, at the Japanese. Filipinos were allowed to come into the United States until 1934, when virtually all Asian immigration ceased. They were need as workers in the Navy yards, but were never given citizenship. Immigration did not resume again until 1965, and today 65 percent of the Asian community are immigrants.

And then, of course, one of the major defining events of our history was the bombing of Pearl Harbor, December 7, 1941. Unfortunately, many teachers and others have used this event as analogous to September 11, as akin to the bombing of Pearl. It's not, it's very different. First of all, the war on terrorism and September 11 in New York, the event was aimed at civilians. In Hawaii, the Japanese naval fleet bombed only the military installations there. My father was a teenager living in Hawaii at the time Hawaii was only a territory. Unfortunately, as we saw in Suzanne's story earlier, Pearl Harbor has become a very sensitive issue for all Asian Americans. When it's brought up in class, Asian American children feel singled out, as if they were directly responsible. Obviously, they weren't even born. How could they have anything to do with it? Yet, many feel guilty, sensing that other students are looking at them, wondering why they would commit so heinous a crime. Even though they wouldn't be born for many years, students like Suzanne were still linked with the event, seen as responsible. People still seem to need to make the connection. So there's that.

Then on February 19, 1942, Executive Order 9066 put 120,000 Japanese Americans into ten concentration camps across the western United States. My mother, her parents, and her brothers were sent to Minidoka, Idaho. Even though my mother was born in Seattle, she was still sent away. I don't think she posed much of a threat as a twelve-year-old.

And finally, another important event that I think teachers should be very aware of is the 1974 Supreme Court decision in *Lau* v. *Nichols,* a defining moment in the legal history of U.S. education. The Chinese American community had struggled for many years with the San Francisco school board in order to receive educational services for their children. As part of their moral commitment to education and students, members of the Chinese American community filed a class action suit asking the district to hire bilingual teachers. The teachers would teach students academic content in their primary languages so the students could progress academically while they concurrently developed English-language skills. Though it took over four years of litigation, the Supreme Count ruled in favor of the parents with this groundbreaking decision.

How did this momentous educational struggle begin? Kinney Lau and twelve other Cantonese-speaking students along with their parents filed a class action suit on behalf of 1,800 children against Alan Nichols, who was the president of the San Francisco School Board. For many years Chinese American parents had been concerned because they did not feel their children were receiving adequate instruction due to their English-language needs.

During the court hearing, the San Francisco Unified School District admitted that many children needed special instruction, but the district argued that it was not legally obligated to provide for those needs. In *Lau* v. *Nichols,* the Supreme Court unanimously took the position that in order for children to participate equally in school, their education must be "meaningful" and "comprehensible"; as a result, their civil rights had been violated. To address this problem, bicultural and bilingual programs were needed. The ruling became the backbone for bilingual education programs throughout the nation and supported the right of thousands of children who spoke languages other than English to equal access to education. So, a little Chinese American child in the first grade became an important hero in our country.

Since the discussion of historical elements has led naturally to aspects of the Asian American family and community, could you talk more about family and community and how these shape what happens in schools with Asian American students?

I think even though you don't want to overgeneralize, for Asian Pacific American children, family is probably the most important value. Family relationships are the core of how the child develops, how the child sees the world, how the child interprets the world, and how the child behaves in relation to the world. The family. Of course, there are many differences within families and across families. We are very aware of generational differences. Like I am third generation in this country, but my children are now fourth generation. There are also fifth generation Asians as well as first and second. Each generation has its own values and concerns, relationships to each other, and position in the family. Depending upon the ethnic community one comes from, even though family form varies somewhat. Like Hawaiian and Samoan families focus more on extended family. There are some more-assimilated Asian groups, maybe the Japanese, where the family form is the nuclear family. So even though family as a theme is important, how we interpret its meaning might be slightly different. Though from an outsider looking in, one may not be really able to understand that. Within the Asian family I think there is still a little bit more respect for elders and education than in other communities. But even this varies across groups. There are Asian groups who have come here, like the Hmong, still a preliterate people, for whom education in a formal sense is not something they are as oriented toward. But, I know they are educated in the customs and the ways of their families. Children learn culture from their families. Families are holders and transmitters of culture. Let me share a story about a friend of mine.

> When Gerry was ten years old, he went to his grandmother's eightieth birthday party in Hawaii. The family had the party at a Chinese restaurant. Everyone was smiling and talking. Gerry sat at a round table with nine other people. He sat next to his Auntie Sara. This was a big birthday celebration, and so the family wanted to honor their grandmother with a nine-course dinner.
>
> Many years ago, Gerry's grandmother traveled to Hawaii from Canton, China, by ship when she was only fifteen years old. She was betrothed to his grandfather, who at that time was about twenty-five years old. The couple eventually had eight children. His grandfather died when Gerry was four years old and left his grandmother as matriarch of the family.
>
> In honor of the grandmother, the family had golden peach pins for everyone. Peaches symbolize long life, and so every family member was given not only pins but vases with peaches painted on the front panel.
>
> As each course was brought out to the table and served, Gerry became more full. He wanted to rest his stomach, so he stuck his chopsticks into his bowl of rice. The chopsticks stuck straight up. His Auntie Sara placed her hand on his shoulder and whispered, "Gerry, don't do that because it means death."

Gerry quickly took the chopsticks from his bowl of rice and placed them on his white dinner plate; his face was slightly red because he was embarrassed. He knew children were not supposed to do anything to bring disgrace to their family. Just like in school, children were supposed to act properly.

One of the nine courses was a noodle dish. Noodles are served at birthday parties in many Chinese and Chinese American families because they are long and therefore represent long life. When the large blue platter of noodles was pushed before Gerry on the table's lazy susan, he took the large spoon and began to put noodles on his plate. However, some noodles were falling off the serving place so he cut them with the spoon. His Auntie Sara frowned and leaned down toward Gerry, gently whispering in his ear. This time she said, "Gerry, don't cut your noodles or you will be cutting the life of your grandmother short." The young man quickly scooped the noodles on to his plate and pushed the lazy susan toward the next diner.

In the course of the meal, each person was also given a small packet of dried coconut and fruit that had a sugar coating. The sweetness of the dessert represented more sweetness in life for his grandmother. . . . Gerry, like most children, learned values and beliefs besides other cultural elements like traditions and customs through social interactions with family members (Pang, 2001, pp. 7–8).

Are there any subpopulations in the Asian American community you feel deserve additional attention?

Each is unique in its own right, but Filipino Americans are a good example. They are one of the largest groups of Asian Pacific Americans, and people know little about them. Although there are hundreds of languages in the Philippines, Tagalog is one of the main ones. It should be taught in the schools, but it's not. In California, Filipinos are the largest single Asian group. And yet, people and teachers and other service providers have very little knowledge of their experiences. And it's hard for Filipino kids, often, because their parents are immigrants. They're first generation and trying to make it, and the children are like a bridge between old ways and new ways. I know some girls are not allowed to go out at night, or go out past ten o'clock even if they're older. I had a student, a senior in college, who couldn't go out past midnight. She had to have her parents' permission. She couldn't stay overnight at anybody else's house. So it depends on the family, it depends on how traditional. Some Asian families are very traditional and others are not as traditional. I also think Filipino Americans are often invisible within the Asian Pacific American community.

Do class or other social economic issues play a role in considering aspects of this population?

Class is an important component to society. Classism is prejudice or discrimination based on one's financial or economic status. Oftentimes classism and racism are intimately connected. For example, when a Latino or Pacific Islander faces continual societal prejudice, they may find it difficult to find employment or housing. In this way their opportunities to find economic success are limited, and they find themselves scrambling to survive economically. Then as they attempt to find additional opportunities, others may discriminate against them not only because of their racial membership, but also because they are from lower-income communities.

One of the problems with the model-minority myth, where all Asians are seen as economically and educationally successful, it's based on the successes of very small groups of people. Chinese and Japanese are the most culturally assimilated of all the Asian groups, and rates for marriages to non-Asians among Japanese American women approaches something like 65 percent. But then there are other Asian groups who marry within their ethnic groups exclusively. Class is the same thing. You will find more higher-income Japanese Americans than some groups among Cambodians and Hmongs who did not come here with the same level of education as the Japanese immigrants. And they haven't been established as long here. So there's a huge range of class differences within the Asian American community.

How do these various differences you have been talking about affect the education of Asian Americans?

For those Asian families who believe strongly in education and formal education and brought that to the United States, their values are more apt to mesh with mainstream America. They tend to achieve in the schools. Members of Asian groups with less formal education have a harder time. But, it's not necessarily the case that Asian Americans always are assimilated. It's just that in some cases their values may be in line with a more mainstream view of the world. They can still remain very traditional, but their traditional culture involves beliefs and values that allow a child to function naturally within the school environment.

What are some of the common problems that Asians face or bring into the school setting?

Well, some of the problems that they see, that the children see, is prejudice. If you look at the literature and you talk to children themselves, they will tell you that the level of prejudice that they feel that they experience in public schools is absolutely phenomenal. People will be calling them Cambodian, which is kind of like using the "n-word" in the way it is used on the playground. And they're often discriminated against because of physical differences. I mean, other kids have been taught racism at home, and unfortunately Asian American children have to deal with this. Teachers deal with them differently also. Because of the model-minority myth, teachers may expect Asian kids to do well in topics or subject areas like math and sciences. And sometimes they do do well, but what happens to the Asian child who doesn't do well in math, like me? Then something must be wrong with you. This is a stereotype we also internalize which creates a problem for those students who do not fit the mold.

Another area of concern is for Asian children whose family does not encourage them to articulate verbally what they think, who are taught to be deferential and quiet. When students who have been raised with this value go to school and are asked by teachers to join in the Socratic method and other discussions, they may find it difficult to participate due to shyness or a lack of practice in verbal communication style. It is the teacher's job to mentor and help them overcome these barriers and to do it in an emotionally sensitive way. Maybe they develop activities for the child such as a short speech of a couple minutes by way of practice. Or if the child is scared of making a mistake. Let's say they're bilingual and unsure of their language skills in English. The teacher can record a short talk of theirs on videotape, show it to them, and also provide them the opportunity to rerecord if they feel they're going to make a mistake. With such an opportunity their anxiety won't be as high. I think Asian Pacific American children have anxiety, communication anxiety.

The literature also shows that often the written work of Asian children is not as developed as it could be. I don't think enough teachers encourage Asians to be novelists, to be poets, to be actors, to be musicians, any of the fine arts or creative arts kind of careers. They are rather pushed primarily into technical areas of computer science, physics, mathematics. There are, for example, lots of children from the Black community who are great dancers. Is that because, innately, those children have genes to dance well? No, they've been practicing that ever since they were born. Similarly, Asians have been pushed into more technical fields and have had more practice at it. They have been developing those skills. I'm sure that if we had the kids dancing too, they would be great dancers. It's just a matter of, first, cultural priorities and, second, the expectations that are placed around certain types of behavior.

I want to say a bit more about the invisibility of certain Asian and Pacific American students and the need for school districts to look at disaggregate statistics. You don't hear about the dropout rates of Samoans, though in San Diego it's something like 50 percent. They have one of the highest dropout rates of any ethnic group in San Diego. But if you look at the scores of all Asian kids put together, such realities become masked over. It is critical to understand the enormous diversity that exists within the Asian American community, the needs of certain groups, and the tendency to overlook such deficits because so many of us want to believe in the myth of the model minority. Another area I want to allude to is mental health. There's a lot of alcoholism in Asian communities that people don't know about. There are also problems with self-image among our students. I did my dissertation on physical self-image in Asian American children. I looked at body image in Japanese American and Caucasian kids. Asian American kids in general may not like the way they look. They don't think they're tall enough. They don't like the shape of their eyes. The girls don't have big enough breasts. But this information gets lost with a broad analysis. If you use a general measure of self-concept where you can't separate out body image, you might not see a significant difference between White kids and Asians. Feeling good about academics or one's family may cover over the lower body image scores. Also, because of the diversity that exists across Asian American groups, it is important to not lump all Asian group members together in the analysis.

This leads to the next question. Could you discuss some of the factors you see as important in assessing the learning style of Asian American students and what environmental factors could be manipulated to match these styles?

There is some research that Clara Park did on Asian American learning style. She felt that Asian students liked demonstrations, but that teachers tended to use the blackboard a lot. Whenever the teacher spoke and tried to explain a concept she would write a definition, create a graphic or a map or a model. Whatever she did, it was visual. So, in order to learn with this teacher the kids need to be able to relate to visual representation. I think Asian American kids would benefit from hands-on methods that, unfortunately, are used least in our schools. Schools generally depend on paper and pencil type activities even though most kids remember more information and can process more comprehensively with a hands-on demonstration or modeling.

Say we do an experiment, and then the child is given the hands-on opportunity to repeat it. What happens? My preservice students do a lot of work out in the field with kids. One of the activities they've used is making bubbles to teach the concept of surface tension. They ask the children what shapes makes the best bubbles and why is the bubble round? Talking about this is one thing, but what they did was actually go into a kitchen and try out different things as bubble makers. They tried a strainer, etc. I can't remember all the things they used. One student brought a tennis racket whose holes are square and the teacher asked, "What do you think?" One child said, "I still think it's going to be round."

But why? He wasn't sure. So he tried the tennis racket and it was, Ah ha! They are round, And so that led to more discussion. Then the issue of surface tension was introduced. When you press on the bubble, it pops because the balance of the surface tension is weak. But students don't learn as much unless they can interact directly with the materials. You can tell them all you want about surface tension, but if you don't have them actually making the bubbles and blowing them all over the playground, they don't really quite understand it. Ninety-eight percent of children, especially Asian children, like hands-on activities.

I would also like to say something about teaching students, and also teachers perhaps, about what culture is. How do we give them an appreciation for its depth, complexity, and interconnectedness. Ramon Valle provides a multidimensional model to explain culture. Culture is defined by Valle as having three layers: language, symbols, and artifacts; customs, practices, and interactional patterns; and shared values, norms, beliefs, and expectations. These three levels can also be described as means of communication, means of interaction, and values driving people, groups. Culture is made up of many elements and together they make an integrated whole. Separating culture into distinct elements, as we often do in the classroom, tends to fragment it.

There are many aspects of culture that may be invisible. In caring-centered multicultural education, teachers know that culture is an important aspect of children's lives. They try to "unpack" the layers of culture and identify what children respond to and understand in human relationships. Remember Gerry's experience at his grandmother's birthday party. Gerry was learning the meanings behind many symbols in his family culture. He gained a better understanding of what behaviors were expected of him and why. His Auntie Sara helped him to "unpack" what was going on and what was expected of him in the cultural context of his family. She explained what to do and the reasons why.

Teachers must also learn to make these connections themselves and help their students to do so. My daughter learned these lessons through origami, Japanese paper folding. Origami represents not only the tangible product of a culture, but also interactional patterns and underlying values. To provide students with a more complete understanding of culture, teachers must share with them not only the how-to sequence of folding, but explain how it is an art form that reinforces the importance of observational skills, working with others, and patience, and it represents simple beauty. Using a single piece of paper, a person can create a myriad of objects and artistic expressions. There are various levels of cultural significance.

Considering cultural differences and learning styles, what suggestions might you have regarding establishing rapport with Asian American students and families?

Since family is a core value, relationship building is important. Even though there are many people who feel that the Asian respect for teachers has become almost stereotypical, I still believe it is true. For most children in the Asian Pacific American family, as in many other communities, the teacher is still seen as a respected and revered person. Even though a child may not necessarily always act in that way, they still know that the teacher is a person to be treated deferentially and always kept at a distance. So, I think it's absolutely critical that teachers develop relationships, trusting relationships where they actually talk to the kids, find out about their dreams, their disappointments, and their needs. Such open dialogue is quite important because the kids are dying to get to know the teacher more closely. Because they're seen as so quiet or as the model minority, the teacher may overlook them and not spend the time that they really should have in developing a personal connection. Every child needs that relationship, and I think it's even more so with Asians because of their family background and because they're seen so often as invisible. They're the good kids. We don't have to spend so much time because they do not seem as needy or disruptive or demanding of attention.

You also have Asians students I would not consider the most upstanding citizens, but that is more rare. They may be getting straight A's in school but are gang members in the evenings. So all this is extremely complex, and merely giving a teacher a book on Asian American values is not going to do it. Because not only are Asian groups different, but each family is different, and then there are individual student differences. And the context of where the child lives and all the groups that they're interacting with impact who they are and how they define themselves and how they act. There are Asian kids who know how to use the stereotype too. There's research that shows that Asian students know teachers think of them as model minority, so they'll pretend that they're behaving when they're really not. Someone else is likely to be the one that gets in trouble. Maybe the Black child, maybe the Latino child, a different child more likely to be seen stereotypically as acting out. But if you are a smart child you know, and you use all of your abilities and cultural knowledge to get by in school.

I want to re-emphasize relationship building, because a teacher can really have so much more power in motivating and mentoring when the kid trusts you. But teachers don't realize this. Because society does not reward them, teachers often feel unimportant in the general scheme of things. But children are still coming to school everyday. That says a whole lot. They're still sitting in that classroom even if it's so unbelievably boring sometimes. There is always hope; kids are always hoping for something more. Kids are also going there because of their friends. But there they are, waiting to get engaged, to get empowered. You as a teachers can send them out with knowledge and life skills, so they can live and make life better when you're not there anymore. You're trying to give them the skills and the attitude and the philosophy so that they can work with anybody in all types of situations, so they can create a more compassionate, just, and happy place for all of us. We often forget about that happiness, that joy. Life is supposed to be like that! Not a burden. Not always suffering.

Could you present an example or two that bring together the different issues and dynamic we've discussed about working with Asian American students?

Okay. There are several things I would suggest that teachers think about. First, is the enormity of the gulf that can exist across cultures and the possibility that we may fail because of that gulf. Second, is what a teacher can accomplish multiculturally and pass on to their students who can in turn change worlds.

One book that I would suggest they read is *The Spirit Catches You and You Fall Down*. It's about a Hmong child living in Fresno, California, who had epilepsy. She was about three years old when they first took her to the hospital. The Hmong parents did not speak English, and the doctors didn't speak Hmong. The story is about the struggles that they had in trying to understand each other in order to help the child. Unfortunately, even though the pediatricians worked so hard with the family, the parents did not understand why they had to give the medicine at a certain time every day, and eventually the child died. Western medicine did not make any sense to the parents, and, though they never doubted the sincerity and caring of the doctors, they were most comfortable seeking help from a shaman, a traditional healer who would come and pray over the child. Though the story is a sad one, it is critical that teachers really understand that culture defines, limits, and impacts the life of all children. We can do our best to understand and teach them, but in the end they are cultural beings and must remain so. That reality must be accepted in an essential way by all multicultural teachers.

I want to go to another one. I had a student that I had in class and her name is Lisa. She came here from Cambodia with her mother. They came as refugees by themselves, and the mother cleaned homes, was a janitor. She did whatever she could to get Lisa the financial resources she needed. They lived a very poor existence. Lisa eventually became a teacher and now helps kids like herself. She had teachers along the way that really believed in her, and that is why she is a teacher today. She is one of only five teachers in San Diego city schools, a system employing over five thousand teachers, that speaks Cambodian. She has become one of those cultural mediators that can help teachers understand what the child is going through culturally, a bridge between old culture and new. One of the joys of multicultural education is the impact we can have on our students who then go out and impact their respective worlds, sometimes in wondrous ways.

WORKING WITH WHITE ETHNIC STUDENTS

An Interview with Rachel Israel

DEMOGRAPHICS AND CULTURAL SIMILARITIES

Who are the White ethnics? Put simply, they are national groups of Eastern and Southern European descent who share a common experience of immigration to the United States. They include Italians, Poles, Greeks, Armenians, Jews, and various ethnic groups making up the former Russian Republic (Czech, Lithuanian, Russian, Slovak, Ukranian). Because of historical similarities, the Irish are also included in this category. All had long histories of oppression and racial hatred in their native lands, were met with suspicion and rejection as newly arrived immigrants, and for a generation or two were exploited as cheap labor.

The United States has experienced two major waves of immigration from Europe. The first, which occurred in the early nineteenth century, was made up of Northern and Western Europeans: Germans, English, Scandinavians, French. According to Healey (1995), these groups shared common characteristics with the dominant U.S. culture. They were Protestants, came from developing and industrialized countries, shared certain cultural values—such as the Protestant ethic of "hard work, success, and individualism" and a belief in democratic governance—and had attained levels of education and "occupational skill" that allowed them to compete in a modernized nation. The second wave of Europeans, coming between the 1880s and 1920s, immigrated from Southern and Eastern Europe. These White ethnics were mainly Catholic and Jewish, and they came from rural, village-based cultures where family took precedence over individualism. As Healey (1995) suggested, they "came from backgrounds less consistent with the industrializing, capitalistic, individualistic Anglo-American culture" and as a result "faced more barriers and greater rejection than the Protestant immigrants from Northern and Western Europe" (p. 458).

In the U.S. censuses White ethnics are counted racially as "non-Hispanic Whites." Respondents are allowed to self-identify as to "ancestry" (defined as national origin), but may choose not to. Because of inexact interviewing methods coupled with high levels of acculturation into "White" America, current White ethnic populations can only be estimated, not reported in exact numbers. The U.S. Bureau of Census (2000), for example, reports the following estimates: Czech, 1,248,159; Greek, 1,179,064; Irish, 33,067,131; Italian, 15,942,683; Lithuanian, 714,097; Polish, 9,053,606; Russian, 2,980,776; Slovak, 821,325; Ukranian, 862,762. The census does not report demographics for American Jews. They are considered a religious group, rather than an ethnic group, and are included in the census by national ancestry. Other sources, for example Singer and Seldin (1994), have estimated the number of Jews in America at 5.5 million.

Today, there are strong pockets of intact traditional culture within each of the White ethnic communities, although many descendants have taken the path of complete and irreversible assimilation. Because of the darker physical features and appearance of many, White ethnics were often viewed as nonWhite by Western Europeans and thus rejected both religiously and racially. In the United States, however, their skin color and physical features "paled" in comparison to the nonWhites who were already here. As their economic and social circumstances improved, they increasingly identified themselves as "White" in order to distinguish themselves from the People of Color with whom they competed for jobs and other economic resources. This dynamic is described by Ignatiev (1995) in his book *How the Irish Became White* and Brodkin (1998) in her book *How Jews Became White Folks.* Their identification with "Whiteness" allowed White ethnic-group members to more easily assimilate. As they did, they took on the racial attitudes and prejudices of the dominant culture to which they aspired. Thus, White ethnics exist in a kind of psychological "demilitarized zone." Being White in America, they share the privilege of Whiteness. But as ethnic-group members from cultures that have experienced long histories of oppression, they carry within them many internal dynamics similar to those of People of Color. Teachers working with students from these groups often face classroom situations and behavior that reflect these two very different psychological realities: that of the oppressor and that of the oppressed.

As students, White ethnics, especially those whose families have been in the United States for several generations, generally feel comfortable with the European American educational system. Some have assimilated so fully into majority culture, in fact, that they are culturally indistinguishable from other White students. Most, however, still retain some cultural connection to the past, and in considering the education of these students, teachers should be aware of four important points.

- First, although White ethnics may be seen and treated as White by society at large, they do not necessarily perceive or identify themselves as members of the majority. More typically, there is the sense that "I am not White; I am Irish (or Italian or Jewish)." Nor may they identify culturally with the dominant Northern European worldview. Thus, it is important to determine what a student's connection is to traditional ethnic culture and what traditional beliefs, values, and behaviors still remain intact. If White ethnic students do retain significant elements of traditional culture, teachers must become familiar with the content of that culture.

- Second, getting a sense of the student's cultural background should not be based exclusively on external characteristics. Like People of Color, White ethnics differ widely in terms of assimilation and acculturation. As suggested earlier, some have so fully assimilated and intermarried that there is little if any cultural material remaining beyond surface artifacts like family names and food preferences. Others are still very traditional, although they may have taken on some of the outward trappings of majority culture. Only by getting to know individual students and their families can one make an accurate assessment. In this regard, it is important to realize that external markers of culture disappear more quickly than internal ones. Thus, cultural artifacts such as values and worldview, psychological temperament, and family dynamics are more resistant to change and disappear more slowly.
- Third, the cultural identity of White ethnics may be conflicted in much the same manner as described for People of Color. This is true even for those who at first glance may appear to be highly assimilated. On a similar note, it is important to realize that, even if an individual has been spared the direct experience of racial hatred and discrimination, its emotional consequences can be passed on from previous generations through family dynamics.
- Fourth, the fact that White ethnics can so easily assimilate into American culture, thus seemingly escaping their collective past, creates a somewhat different identity picture. In comparison to People of Color, who are reminded constantly of their ethnicity, White ethnics can bury their conflicts much deeper and further out of awareness. But again, as in the case of People of Color, the rejection of such an important part of identity as ethnicity cannot help but cause deep inner conflicts that eventually affect behavior. Thus, it is not uncommon to find identity rejection and self-hatred among White ethnics.

In the pages that follows, we interview Rachel Israel about her work with Jewish students and their families as an in-depth example of working with White ethnic students. The interview is structured according to the same question-and-answer format used in Chapters 10 through 13. Unfortunately, space does not allow for an extensive treatment of each of the White ethnic groups in the United States. It is hoped that this interview will give the reader a good sense of the kind of educational issues faced by White ethnics in general.

Our Interviewee

Rachel Israel graduated from Bard College in 1999 and recently received a master's in education from Mills College, Oakland, California. She has taught in several Jewish day schools in the San Francisco Bay area and has served as a programming director and teacher for East Bay Midrasha, a Jewish studies program for Jewish high school students. She is currently studying in Israel.

The Interview

Could you begin by talking about your own ethnic background and how it has impacted your work as a teacher?

I was acutely aware while growing up that I was Jewish and therefore different in some way. I often felt responsible for being a spokesperson for my religion, which I more often than not identified as a culture and shared history, first in my suburban Pittsburgh community and then at a mostly White New England boarding school.

My family was active in the Jewish community but not observant. We went to a reform temple frequently but we didn't participate in other religious rituals at home. Yet there was constant identification and reinforcement of Jewish values in my family. My father's family felt comfortable as American Jews and were more assimilated, part of an earlier generation's migration, all born and bred in Pittsburgh, Pennsylvania's wealthy, take-care-of-our-own, Jewish community. They were very social people, whose experience at their reform temple was largely about who they spoke to and where they went. They didn't talk about the past, they didn't talk about ritual, practice and they didn't talk about G-d. My mother's family seemed like immigrants compared to them. Although both her parents were born in North America, my grandfather on the Lower East Side of Manhattan and my grandmother on a farm outside of Winnipeg, they were both the first children in their families born in the New World. They shared a desire for education, a striving for something better, and an interest in distancing themselves from anything that seemed "other." Yet they maintained a longing for family and spoke of tradition often. Both of them lamented education denied to them for financial reasons.

My father became an attorney and my mother a teacher/housewife. The only Jews that I knew growing up were from families like this: second to fourth generation, middle to upper-middle class, often spoiled. My parents were also both interested in history, encouraged my own interest in learning about the shtetl, the pogroms, and the Holocaust. I was told that if I married a non-Jew they would be very displeased, that I should never put up a Christmas tree in my home, that eating pork wasn't okay but shellfish was fine. From my father there was this fear of being "too religious" and an intense need to know history—not personal history but the history of the Jewish people. From my mother it was a personal history that involved never forgetting where we came from. I read quite a bit and what I came out with was: "You must never forget what your ancestors went through to ensure that you could be here, in America, getting education, with access to anything. You must never forget that persecution is in our blood and that, although we are home in America, nothing is guaranteed. The Holocaust must never happen again. The state of Israel must be supported even if you never go there." These things are important.

I developed an intense love for history and English and the telling of stories. I eventually, at boarding school, developed confidence in an intense love of learning. I learned that the best way to learn is to teach and that education is of utmost importance, whether for status, knowledge, or achievement. I knew that in some capacity I would be an educator.

My senior year in college I wrote about Jewish American women and through that process started to more actively explore my own connection to Jewish tradition. I eventually went to Israel for a year and when I came back to the states I started working in Jewish education. I think that there are a few reasons that I was drawn to Jewish education. First off, I wanted to be in a Jewish environment because it felt comfortable and also because there was so much about Judaism that I wanted to learn. Second, I felt that I could offer some balance and perspective to Jewish children; I felt as if I could do the most good in an environment that I was familiar with and excited about being a part of.

Who are the Jews and what characteristics do they share as a group?

First of all, Judaism is a monotheistic religion based around values articulated in the Five Books of Moses. As a group, Jews generally share an emphasis on literacy, the importance of asking questions and analysis, and the value of study and scholarship. There is also a shared family structure and dynamic and a strong belief in bringing change to the world and making things better. The emphasis is on this life that we're living now, not an unknown life after death.

Judaism has evolved through two thousand years of dispersion, persecution, and modernization to encompass a culture, ethnicities, and social identification. Some people would refer to Jews as a nation of people and many Jews feel a connection to that. Even so, within Judaism there are many different cultural, religious, and ethnic identifications, most of which are represented within American Jewry.

There are Jews dispersed throughout the world, with the largest concentrations in Israel and North America. The two main "ethnic groups" within Judaism are Sephardim and Ashkenazim. Sephardim are Jews who two thousand years ago went to Spain and North Africa and developed customs there in accordance with the cultures of which they were a part. Sephardim can also be found in Arab countries in the Middle East from the land of Israel. These Jews are called Mizrachim, meaning Eastern. Ashkenazim are Jews from Europe, the largest percentage from Eastern Europe. They too assimilated styles and customs of the lands in which they lived—German Jews, Hungarian Jews, Litvacks (Jews from Lithuania), Polish Jews, and so forth. One can even find Jewish communities in Ethiopia, India, and China. All share a connection, even if it's only a perception of their own otherness, formed over thousands of years of anti-Semitism. I've visited places and seen people with seemingly nothing in common culturally bond completely over the fact that they were both Jews.

Some Jews hardly identify as Jews at all, or only as "cultural" Jews, meaning that they define themselves primarily on the basis of external artifacts of Jewishness—food, language (for example, Yiddish), jokes, neighborhoods of origin, etc.—not on the basis of religion. It sometimes seems to me, teaching Jewish teenagers, that every Jewish student I meet has an individual conception of what it mean to be Jewish and that personal identification is loosely related to something having to do with text, culture, or history. Community is a very important element of Jewish life and many Jews seek out a community in which they feel comfortable. Religious identification ranges from ultra-religious to completely secular with a variety of group distinctions in between. There are Jews who believe that Israel should exist, Jews who believe that it shouldn't exist, and Jews who don't care either way.

In my own life I've gone through several different identifications and all have helped me to better understand my students and their process of understanding and accepting who they are as Jews and what it means to be a Jew in today's world. Most students I have taught identify themselves religiously as reform, conservative, or secular. Some would even say that they don't think of themselves as Jewish even though their parents are.

Could you talk about the various names that Jews use to describe and identify themselves and some of the names that have been used historically to describe and identify the group by others?

In the United States, and Canada to a lesser extent, Jews have separated themselves into religious subgroups. There are Chassidic Jews who, with the exception of the Lubavitcher sect, are fairly isolated in their own communities, ultra-religious Jews who don't identify as Chassidic, and Modern Orthodox Jews who strictly observe Jewish law but do so within the context of the modern world. There are Jews who identify as part of the Conservative movement, which has evolved primarily in America and represents a middle-range position in adjusting Jewish law to fit more modern sensibilities. The other movements or traditions had their beginnings in Europe and the Middle East. Finally, there are Reform, Reconstructionist, and Renewal Jews, who have done away with most traditional Jewish practices in favor of more humanistic values and practices. When two Jews meet, it is not uncommon for them to inquire as to the religious affiliation of the other. I am often asked this question and see Jewish students ask it of each other when they first meet. For many people religious affiliation within the Jewish world is an important source of identification. As for me, I was raised Reform and now consider myself a Baal Teshuva. *Baal Teshuva* means literally to return to oneself, and in recent years many Jews have chosen to become more traditionally observant in their views and practices. Historically, there have been many tensions between the various religious movements, and I would welcome a world where Jews can accept each other no matter how they identify.

In Europe, Israel, Australia, South America, and South Africa most Jews identify as secular, traditional, or religious. As I mentioned earlier, Jews can be either Sephardic or Ashkenazic, and may also identify according to their family's country of origin. For example, my family are Russian Jews. There are also Jews who identify themselves according to significant experiences they have had as Jews—such as Holocaust survivors or refugees from Iraq, Iran, Syria, Egypt, or Morocco. Jews living in Israel most typically call themselves Israeli, not Jews. And for many Israelis the term *Jew* even has a negative connotation. Every year I give my students the following list of terms—Israeli, Jewish, American, other—and ask them to rate their connection to each. *Jewish* and *American* usually get the highest responses. Half will identify themselves most strongly as American and the half as Jewish. For most of them, these are two separate identities which they cannot yet merge. They can see themselves as Americans who are also Jewish, but not as American Jews. That will hopefully come later.

There are also images and perceptions of Jews that one sometimes hears, not all of them complimentary. I've heard the Jewish people referred to as intellectual, political, communist, socialist, moneymaking, greedy, social, talkative, materialistic, weak, and successful. The history of anti-Semitism has given us a long list of derogatory labels as well as these stereotypes. I'll spare you the specifics. Jews have also been identified with a variety of social movements over the last century: socialists and labor organizers in the twenties and thirties, communists in the fifties, civil rights and antiwar activists in the sixties and seventies. There are also stereotypes of Jews as highly materialistic and successful and ruthless businesspeople and as power brokers and members of cabals that control American politics. Although there is usually some kernel of historic truth in all stereotypes, they tend to miss the fact that Jews like all groups are very diverse and just do not fit neatly into narrow categories.

Can you highlight for us key historical events in a nutshell? What historic experiences should educators be aware of in relation to the Jewish community and Jewish students?

The Diaspora, the dispersion of Jews from the land of Israel throughout the Middle East, Europe, and beyond, has defined Jews for the last two thousand years. When the Romans took over Jerusalem and the land of Israel in the year 70, the central Temple of the Jewish people was destroyed. After a series of rebellions the bulk of the Jewish community migrated into Babylonia and then into the lands currently known as Yemen, Iraq, Iran, and Syria as well as up into Russia and over into what is now Eastern Europe. A second wave of dispersions dislocated the Jews of Spain and Portugal during the Spanish Inquisition of the fifteenth century and led to their migration into North Africa and the Middle East. The experience of Diaspora marked by widespread anti-Semitism and genocide weighs heavily in much Jewish literature and forms a framework for religious practice that centers on the longing for a rebuilt Temple and the return to Jerusalem.

The events that most directly affected American Jewry, of course, are those that occurred after the colonization of the United States. Sephardic Jews came to America early on, possibly with Columbus and certainly in the early settlement days of New Amsterdam. Many were uprooted by the Spanish expulsions and found their way directly to the Americas. They tended to practice the Jewish religion privately, actively assimilating into the American culture, but still retaining some outward Jewish customs. German Jews began coming to America in the early nineteenth century and in larger numbers in the 1840s and 50s. They were highly assimilated and mostly businesspeople. In 1880s the largest Jewish population in the world was located in Poland and Russia. During this period, a series of edicts restricting the movement and rights of Jews were issued by local governments, which also encouraged the scapegoating of Jews and resulted in bloody pogroms throughout Russia and Eastern Europe.

Between 1880 and 1920 over 2 million Jews came to North America. They didn't come with any intention of going back to Europe. They came to stay. America was the Promised Land, the land of opportunity, and these new arrivals were ambitious and ready to sacrifice themselves so their next generation could taste success and be truly American. Most second- and third-generation Jews of my age remember at least some family members speaking Yiddish. My own memories are vague, but I know that my mother's whole family spoke Yiddish together. I still find notes in Yiddish in my grandmother's handwriting in books in our house. They were a generation anxious to assimilate and become fully American, so they would speak Yiddish only in the home or in writing notes, but outside the home their language was English.

The next major event affecting the North American Jewish community was World War II and the Holocaust. During the early years of the war the United States was fairly isolationist, and boatloads of Jews trying to escape Europe were even denied entrance. There was widespread anti-Semitism and some pro-Nazi sentiments in this country, and many American Jews, because of old fears, were in denial about what was happening in Europe. It was just too unfathomable and shattered their newly formed illusions of security. After liberation of the concentration camps, more Jews, especially those with family in the United States, were allowed entrance. Refugees who had escaped and survivor families cast a heavy shadow across the American Jewish community. Many survivors did not want to speak about their experiences, and many who survived the war on this side of the Atlantic were too ridden with guilt to ask.

The creation of the modern state of Israel in 1948 also had a huge impact on American Jewry. For two thousand years, consciously and unconsciously, Jews lamented the destruction of their homeland and associated their persecution as a people with their lack of nationhood. Most Jews came to America because it was the most accessible avenue of escape from persecution. Israel now represented a second "escape valve," as well as an opportunity to be involved in building a Jewish nation and to regain a sense of self-respect and safety. This new state revived for many images from the Torah and ancient history of Jews as pioneers, farmers, fighters, citizens living under their own laws. Many American Jews immigrated to Israel, and in time many Israelis came to America and settled here. And for many there has been a regular pattern of moving back and forth between the two countries. The United States has also seen an increase in immigration of Jews from Arab countries, often by way of some residency in Israel. For example, large numbers of Persian Jews left Iran in the sixties and seventies, and these refugees eventually found their way here to form their own ethnic communities. The most recent immigrants to the United States have been Jews from the former Soviet Union. Coming with little knowledge of Judaism, the flood of Russian refugees began in the seventies and increased significantly with the fall of communism.

Jews now make up about 2.5 percent of the population of the United States but have had a larger impact politically, socially, economically, and culturally. Many Yiddish words and phrases have become part of the American vernacular, and knowledge of Jewish culture and rituals have made their way into popular culture. As a group, Jews have been highly successful in business, media, politics, academics, and the arts. In general Jewish immigrants have risen to middle- and upper-middle-class status by the second generation. Their successful integration into the very fabric of this country is largely due to a strong cultural emphasis on education and an equally strong desire to assimilate. The rush to assimilate has also had a negative impact. The Jewish community is marked by widespread inter-marriage and disconnection from Jewish tradition. As I stated earlier, many Jews born into the culture no longer consider themselves Jewish, and there are even those who do not realize that they have a Jewish heritage at all.

Could you next talk about the Jewish family and community, and how these shape what happens in schools with Jewish students?

It is critical, first of all, to realize that American Jews have their own unique cultural values and worldview. Four central values define and infuse Jewish culture. These include: the centrality of the family, chosen-ness and suffering as a shared value, intellectual achievement and financial success, and the verbal expression of feelings. Jewish social existence is organized around these values, and the Jewish psyche is socialized to support and internalize them.

Jewish tradition is highly family-centered. Unmarried men and women and childless couples are seen as incomplete; intermarriage and divorce are looked down upon and viewed as violations of family togetherness. Sex and family roles are fairly rigid and remain so throughout life both within the primary and extended family. High expectations are placed on children as well as adults, and socialization is accomplished through the threat of withdrawal of love and the engendering of guilt. The basic building block of Jewish life is, thus, the family as opposed to the individual, and there are strong pressures for family members to place the well-being of the family and the community before personal needs. Strong boundaries around the family protect Jewish ethnicity.

Movement away from ethnicity is experienced and reacted to as rejec-tion of the family. Within the family itself, relations are very close, often with unclear boundaries. Children are afforded higher status than in most other groups. They are expected to give their parents pleasure by way of their accomplishments and to remain within the family complex through-out life. Traditionally, the sexes tend to be segregated, yet there exist within the Jewish family very strong ties and conflicts between fathers and daughters and mothers and sons. Owing to these complex interactions, Jewish men are often described as distant and dependent, and Jewish women as intrusive and controlling.

Jews tend to view suffering as a basic part of life. Jewish history has so often been characterized by persecution and oppression that the expectation of suffering, attitudes of cynicism and pessimism, and even paranoia have become a central aspect of the family's ethos. Suffering also serves as a shared basis for group belonging. In other words, it is seen as an intrinsic part of Jewish history. Suffering is seen as something that is visited upon the Jew from outside as opposed to being a punishment for one's sins. Dwelling on suffering and life's negatives often has the consequence of eclipsing the experience of happiness and pleasure, and it is not uncommon for Jews to find it difficult to enjoy life without concurrently accomplishing something. Similarly, the focus on suffering is probably related to a high incidence of hypochondriasis among Jews. Such patterns are especially evident in families of Holocaust survivors in which parental suffering overwhelms and incapacitates children and where feelings of loss are too strong to talk about.

Jews also place high value on intellectual achievement and financial success. Historically, religious learning and scholarship were the primary sources of prestige and status in the Jewish world. A man learned and all other aspects of family endeavor served to support that learning. As Jews assimilated into the Gentile world, non-Jewish standards of success including money, professional status, and secular educational accomplishment grew increasingly important. The support of intellectual achievement within the family made success in these new secular activities easily transferable. With assimilation, a growing conflict emerged between family and success. Especially for men, becoming successful meant less time available in the home for family activities and interaction. As an oppressed minority, Jews also tended to push harder to succeed and prove themselves equal to or better than majority-group members.

Within the family itself, there is enormous pressure on children and spouses to achieve. In exchange for their special status and treatment, children are expected to perform, often at unrealistically high levels. The perfectionistic demands of the family can easily create a sense of failure irrespective of one's actual accomplishments. Such demands and their attendant sense of failure can also lead to competition among family members and the devaluing of each other to bolster self-esteem. This cycle of unrealistic demands, failure, and mutual criticism leaves family members wounded emotionally and permanently poised against attack. Also related to success is the high value placed on helping others and taking care of one's own. Traditionally, success is viewed as carrying with it an obligation of charity and generosity. Doing good deeds and giving to those in need are considered highly meritorious.

Finally, verbal expression is highly prized in the Jewish world. The ability to articulate thoughts and feelings and a passion for ideas are encouraged and rewarded within the family. All members including children are expected to express themselves verbally, and it is not unusual for the intensity of interaction to escalate as passions rise. Jewish couples tend to deal with conflict openly and directly. They increasingly seek verbal resolution and understanding as arguments and disagreements intensify. Of course, external circumstances can do much to alter such family value patterns. For example, in the well-known silence of Holocaust survivors and their offspring, verbal expressiveness has been limited by the trauma of their experience.

Children are the center of Jewish families, and great importance is put on their success. This leads to quite a bit of pressure in the classroom and on educators to help them "produce." It's not uncommon to see third graders worrying obsessively about grades and their future prospects. Most Jewish children participate in a wide variety of extracurricular activities. Often they are pushed to do so by parents and in time by their peers, who are also experiencing similar pressures to succeed and excel. The goal is to become a well-rounded, accomplished individual. But to do so in a pool with others who are also being pushed and striving to succeed is no small task. One can never really relax. There is a lot of competition and an extreme sense of failure when a student is not ultimately successful. In this whole process children often feel quite accountable to their parents and at times come to resent it and may act out accordingly. Also related to this pressure to succeed is a sense of entitlement and again guilt when this entitlement is not realized. Children expect to be successful and have nice things. Many feel entitled to successful futures; some even expect it without the hard work that usually accompanies it. Demands to succeed are reinforced through guilt and the expectation that life involves suffering, both characteristics, as I suggest above, of the Jewish family. Teachers need to be aware of these cultural dynamics and provide a learning environment that provides some balance to the stress that Jewish students are already experiencing. They also need to be aware that parents may expect them to collude in setting up especially high demands and expectations for Jewish students.

Are there subpopulations in the Jewish community you feel deserve special educational attention?

Children and grandchildren of Holocaust survivors deserve special mention. There can be an extreme amount of uncommunicated fear, pain, and paranoia in these families that takes its emotional toll on students. I had, for example, a very sensitive fifth grader in one of my classes who felt responsible for everything that happened in the classroom. She was often quietly frustrated by misunderstandings that happened between students and tended to internalize and take personal responsibility for every incidence of injustice that we studied or talked about. Her grandparents were

Holocaust survivors and her mother suffered from massive feelings of guilt. There is often much grief in these families that gets passed down to the next generation.

Another interesting subgroup of which teachers should be aware is secular Israelis living in the United States. They generally identify themselves as Israeli rather than Jews and tend to remain in ethnic conclaves within the wider Jewish community. Israel, as a culture, has experienced a continual state of war since its inception in 1948, and recent years have witnessed a dramatic increase in acts of terrorism against the general population. Israel is a small country, and everyone knows someone who has been either hurt or killed in war or by terrorist attacks. I lived in Israel for only one year, but personally know three people who have been killed in the last two years. Many Israelis now living in the United States have fully assimilated to our culture and plan on residing here permanently. Yet they miss family, the life and culture of Israel and feel responsible for the plight of their home country. Many feel guilty living here, physically safe and earning a good living. Some back home even consider them traitors. If you ask an Israeli if he or she plans to stay in the United States, they will rarely answer with an unequivocal yes, but suggest instead that their time here is only temporary.

Children of intermarriage also stand on the fringe of the Jewish community, especially those who are biracial. I had a student whose mother was White and Jewish and whose father was African American. Since Jewishness is traditionally traced through the mother, he is considered Jewish by religious law. It was obvious, however, through his comments that most people assumed he was either adopted or not Jewish at all. Not surprisingly, he was very defensive of his ethnic identity and only with time and much learning about Jewish law and culture did he began to feel more comfortable and confident in who he was. Similarly, children of Jewish fathers and non-Jewish mothers who have not converted may consider themselves to be Jews while others do not and treat them as outsiders. This whole subject of who is a Jew can be a very sensitive and painful issue.

Do class or other socioeconomic issues play a role in the Jewish community?

The most obvious way that class plays a role is for students whose families don't have money. There is a general assumption among both Jews and non-Jews alike that Jewish people are at least middle class and more often upper-middle class or upper class. Jewish students whose families are struggling financially often experience great shame and embarrassment. There is, on the flip side, a tradition of feeling some guilt for being financially successful. Religious law requires Jews to donate money or time to charity. For some such behavior come from a tradition of giving; for others from a sense of guilt and unfair entitlement; for still others from a feeling of thankfulness for what has been given them and a desire to better the circumstances of others. Many Jewish students get involved in social action projects and many Jewish schools include such projects as part of their curriculum. As students learn about the financial injustices that exist in the world, they often become sensitive about their parents' affluence. As a child I remember trying to disassociate myself from the wealthy, suburban, materialistic culture in which I grew up. I didn't want to be associated with money and materialism and actively played down my family's financial comfort and security. Class issues are very difficult to discuss openly. Students at either end of the spectrum can feel very uncomfortable about issues of social class. The need to earn sufficient money and be successful in financial terms can place additional pressure on students and their feelings of overresponsibility.

What are some of the common problems that Jewish students bring into the school setting?

I've mentioned emotional pressure several times already. It informs a lot of the problems that Jewish students bring into the classroom. Many students are under pressure from their parents and community to succeed. Unfortunately it isn't pressure to succeed generally in whatever interests the student, but rather to succeed academically. To achieve high marks and special distinctions, getting into the right college and then go on to graduate school. There is also pressure to have a full and busy schedule including many extracurricular activities—activities that look good on one's transcript and make one competitive for entry into the best schools. Along with these pressure there is also often a sense of perfectionism that subtly communicates to students that they never quite do enough or as well as they could. The result of such emotional demands are students who are often tense, unable to relax, driven by ever-increasing inner standards, who have internalized their parents' often overzealous expectations.

It isn't unusual for parents to attend all school functions, to worry about their child's academic success, to enlist the teacher as an ally in motivating the student, and even to hold the teacher responsible if academic expectations are not met. Jewish parents in turn tend to pay less attention to their child's discipline or to reinforcing in them other forms of achievement or personal development. As a result, Jewish children are sometimes described as disrespectful, lacking in self-control, and argumentative. Part of this results from parents who focus on "being friends" with their children as opposed to assuming more traditional parental roles and who tend at the same time to set fewer boundaries. These differing parental roles combined with the pressures and expectations for success create a unique set of demands on Jewish children.

I once had a third grader who became hysterical when he did not receive an A. From talking with him it became obvious that he was already worrying about getting into college. There was also a fifth-grade student who was having a very hard time reading. I later discovered that his parents, both Ph.D.'s, were doing his homework for him, unknowingly robbing him of the essential practice he need to develop good reading skills. In talking with them it became clear to me that they honestly believed that they were just helping him.

I also at times experience in some of my students a sense of entitlement, a feeling that they deserve special treatment and consideration, which often translates into a lack of awareness that they need to work hard to accomplish specific learning goals. Such students are often given everything they desire without any responsibility for earning it, and come to assume that they are especially gifted or entitled. They expect good grades and success in extracurricular activities just because of who they are. Eventually this "house of cards" comes tumbling down. Parents, like the ones who did their child's homework or those who overestimate their child's abilities without allowing them to work hard and develop the necessary skills, place their children in a precarious position which will in turn become just another source of pressure on the child.

Finally, I see a lot of guilt and anxiety in some of my students. This is especially true of those who are more recent immigrants or from families tied to political hot spots. Children of Israeli parents may be affected by what's going on in Israel. There are Jews from Iraqi families, and there are also those who have been particularly hard hit by anti-Semitism. These are situations of which a teacher should be aware.

Could you now discuss what you see as optimal learning styles among Jewish students and how these can be built upon in the classroom?

Many students come from verbal homes where they learn to articulate at an early age. Energized debate within the family is not unusual. There is in fact a tradition of debate in Judaism and this can easily transform into being argumentative. Students may initially seem overly assertive in their manner of asking and answering questions as compared to students who come from more passive homes. All students learn by becoming engaged in what they are learning. For Jewish students such engagement comes especially through interaction, discussion, and even argument. When I have set up debates in a Jewish classroom almost everyone participates. In public school settings debates become the occasion for many students to become quiet—slinking into the corner, withdrawing, or just shutting down. Many Jewish students can easily carry on adult conversations and at home are challenged to discuss current events, explain their reasoning in a given matter, or asked to present the same argument from different perspectives. In the classroom such students benefit from an environment that allows then to discuss issues, challenges their ideas, and encourages them to come up with new thoughts. They want to be respected, treated as if they were adults, and challenged verbally. Still, no matter how conversationally adept they may be, they still need boundaries. It is easy to mistake their verbal skills for emotional maturity, and that is not necessarily the case. I would suggest teachers discuss the defining of classroom boundaries with students, letting them have some input, but once established keep the lines very clear. In general I would say that Jewish students are especially engaged by intellectual challenges, lively verbal interaction, and competitive classroom tasks.

A final point. Jewish students tend to come from homes where parents and siblings read quite a bit. Reading is an important activity for them because it fosters independent and exploratory learning skills. I have found that Jewish students are comfortable with out of school reading assignments. They also quickly become self-starters and are able to work on projects independently. But teachers must be a bit wary of this apparent independence because it does require ongoing support and encouragement. Jewish students may appear highly self-sufficient and not in need of help or support, but this is not always the case, and it is important to always check in with them, especially when involved in solitary or independent classroom activities.

What suggestions can you make for developing rapport with Jewish students and their families?

First, be aware that Jewish parents often focus on long-term goals when it comes to their child's education. In kindergarten, for example, some parents may already be planning for college and graduate school. Although such concerns have reduced a bit among parents after several generations of success in America, the desire to help their children "do better than they did" is still deeply ingrained in Jewish families. Some parents may be concerned not only about the current marking period, but also about a variety of other issues that may affect their child's future educational success. Obviously, such concerns can place quite a bit of pressure on the student. Some parents even believe that if they can do a good enough job communicating their concerns to the teacher, the teacher will naturally set their child's needs as a priority. Again, a bit of the entitlement that I mentioned earlier.

It is very important to remember to strike a balance between showing your concern about the issues that parents may raise with you and establishing your position as ultimate decision maker in the classroom. At times parents may seem rather aggressive about their child's needs and their belief that they know best about how education should proceed with their child. Never forget that in spite of their intelligence or professional standing, you are still the educator who knows their child in the classroom. Of course, their knowledge of the child at home and outside the classroom is valuable, but you are the expert here at school. It is best to foster a relationship of working together. Never let yourself be bullied or intimidated, and try as best you can to calm the overprotective fears that are likely to surface with such parents. I find that a balance of understanding, self-confidence, knowing where to draw the line, and keeping control works well with Jewish parents.

Finally, could you provide us with a short example of how the different issues you've raised about working with Jewish students and their families come together in the classroom?

Of course. I would like to go back to an earlier example, the fifth-grade boy whose parents were doing his homework for him. I was serving as a teaching assistant in the class, and watched with amazement the intrusiveness of these parents, their lack of any reasonable boundaries, and how the teacher did such a skillful job in dealing with them. My own observations of the student was that he was often nervous, unclear about what he should be doing, and definitely falling behind in several skill areas, but especially reading. His parents would often call the teacher at school, even during class, to speak with him about concerns about their child's education. They would want to know specifics about certain assignments he brought home, and would regularly question the teacher's choices of curriculum material and teaching approach. One parent was a teacher and the other a child psychologist, and together felt that their credentials gave them the right to judge and assess the teacher's performance, and suggest alternative methods and materials. From the quality of the homework being turned in, it was clear that the parents were actually doing some of the work for him. It also was clear to us that the child was suffering from the enormous pressure that the parents were unconsciously putting on him and also embarrassed by their frequent calls and visits to the school. It was also obvious that the parents were not aware of the impact they were having on either the student or the teacher. Nor did they realize the relationship between their intrusiveness into their son's learning and his suppressed performance and skill development.

After checking out his plan with the principal, the teacher invited the parents in for a conference. In a very understanding yet firm manner, the teacher made it very clear to the parents that when it came to the classroom he was in charge and aware of what was in the student's best interest educationally, that his choices of assignments were well-thought out, and that it would better serve everyone if the student was allowed to do more of the work on his own. I was very impressed with how the teacher could communicate an awareness and acceptance of their concerns and at the same time clearly define the boundaries of their relationship and also reflect back to them what he perceived as their role in negatively affecting their son's performance in reading. We did not know if the parents would keep their child in school, but evidently some of the message got through, because there was a lot less communication from the parents, the homework he was turning in was clearly his, and after a month or so, we began to see progress in his performance. We were also aware of the fact that he seemed less stressed and happier in the classroom.

References

Aboud, F. (1988). *Children and prejudice.* Oxford: Blackwell.

Aboud, F., & Doyle, A. B. (1993). The early development of ethnic identity and attitudes. In M. E. Bernal & G. P. Knight (Eds.), *Ethnic identity* (pp. 46–59). Albany, NY: State University of New York Press.

Adorno, T. W., Frankel-Brunswik, E., Levinson, D. J., & Sanford, R. N. (1950). *The authoritarian personality.* New York: Harper & Row.

Allport, G. W. (1954). *The nature of prejudice.* New York: Doubleday.

Anderson, J. A. (1988). Cognitive styles and multicultural populations. *Journal of Teacher Education, 39* (1), 2–9.

Anderson, J. A., & Adams, M. (1992). Acknowledging the learning styles of diverse student populations: Implications for instructional design. In L. L. B. Borders & N. V. N. Chism (Eds.), *Teaching for diversity* (pp. 5–18). San Francisco: Jossey-Bass.

Asante, M. K. (1991). The Afrocentric idea in education. *Journal of Negro Education, 60* (2), 170–180.

Atkinson, D. R., Morten, G., & Sue, D. W. (1993). *Counseling American minorities: A cross-cultural perspective* (4th ed.). Dubuque, IA: William C. Brown.

Atkinson, D. R., Whitely, S., & Gin, R. H. (1990). Asian-American acculturation and preferences for help providers. *Journal of College Student Development, 31,* 155–161.

Atleo, M., Caldwell, N., Landis, B., Mendoza, J., Miranda, D., Reese, D., Rose, L., Slapin, B., & Smith, C. (September, 1999). *My heart is on the ground* and the Indian boarding school experience. *Multicultural Review,* 41–46.

Banks, J. (1998). Approaches to multicultural curriculum reform. *Multicultural Leader, 1* (2), 1–3.

Banks, J. A., & Banks, C. A. (2001). *Multicultural education: Issues and perspectives* (4th ed.). Boston: Allyn & Bacon.

Banks, J. A., & Banks, C. A. M. (1995). *Handbook on multicultural education.* New York: Macmillan.

Banks, J. A., Cookson, P., Gay, G., Hawley, W. D., Irvine, J. J., Nieto, S., Schofield, J. W., & Stephan. (2001). *Diversity within unity: Essential principles for teaching and learning in a multicultural society.* Seattle: Center for Multicultural Education, University of Washington. (206-543-3386 or Centerme@u.Washington.edu)

Barry, N. H., & Lechner, J. V. (1995). Preservice teachers' attitudes about and awareness of multicultural teaching and learning. *Teaching and Teacher Education, 11* (2), 149–161.

Bay Area Association of Black Psychologists. (1972). Position statement on use of IQ and ability tests. In R. L. Jones (Ed.), *Black psychology* (pp. 92–94). New York: Harper & Row.

Bennett, M. B. (1993). Towards ethnorelativism: A developmental model of intercultural sensitivity. In R. M. Paige (Ed.), *Education for the intercultural experience* (pp. 1–51). Yarmouth, ME: Intercultural Press.

Black, L. (1996). Families of African origin: An overview. In M. McGoldrick, J. Giordan, & J. K. Pearce (Eds.), *Ethnicity and family therapy* (pp. 57–65). New York: Guilford Press.

Blair, T. R., & Jones, D. L. (1998). *Preparing for student teaching in a pluralistic classroom.* Boston: Allyn & Bacon.

Bollin, G. G., & Finkel, J. (1995). White racial identity as a barrier to understanding diversity: A study of preservice teachers. *Equity and Excellence in Education, 28* (1), 25–30.

Boyd, N. (1977). *Perceptions of Black families in therapy.* Unpublished doctoral dissertation, Teacher's College, Columbia University, New York.

Boyd, N. (1982). Family therapy with Black families. In E. E. Jones & S. J. Korchin (Eds.), *Minority mental health* (pp. 227–249). New York: Praeger.

Braginsky, B., & Braginsky, D. (1974). *Methods of madness: A critique.* New York: Holt, Rinehart & Winston.

Breault, R. A. (1995). Preparing preservice teachers for culturally diverse classrooms. *Educational Forum, 59* (3), 265–275.

Brodkin, K. (1998). *How Jews became White folks and what that says about race in America.* New Brunswick, NJ: Rutgers University Press.

Brown, M. T., & Lundrum-Brown, J. (1995). Counselor supervision: Cross-cultural perspectives. In J. P. Ponterotto, J. M. Casas, L. A. Suzuki, & C. M. Alexander (Eds.), *Handbook of multicultural counseling* (pp. 263–287). Thousand Oaks, CA: Sage.

Burbules, N. C. (1993). *Dialogue in teaching: Theory and practice.* New York: Teachers College Press.

Burroughs, M. (1968). *What shall I tell my children who are Black?* Chicago: M.A.A.H. Press.

Butler, K. (2001). Evaluating textbooks for bias. Unpublished manuscript. Oregon State University, Corvallis.

Canino, C., & Zayas, L. H. (1997). Puerto Rican children. In G. Johnson-Powell, J. Yamamoto, & W. Arroyo (Eds.), *Transcultural child development: Psychological assessment and treatment.* New York: Wiley.

Carrasquillo, A. (1991). *Hispanic children and youth in the United States : A resource guide.* New York: Garland.

Carrillo, C. (1982). Changing norms of Hispanic families: Implications for treatment. In E. E. Jones & S. J. Korchin (Eds.), *Minority mental health* (pp. 250–266). New York: Praeger.

Casas, J. M., & Pytluk, S. D. (1995). Hispanic identity development: Implications for research and practice. In J. P. Ponterotto, J. M. Casas, L. A. Suzuki, &

C. M. Alexander (Eds.), *Handbook of multicultural counseling* (pp. 155–180). Thousand Oaks, CA: Sage.

Churchill, W. (1994). *Indians are us? Culture and genocide in Native North America.* Monroe, MA: Common Courage.

Clark, C. (1972). Black studies or the study of Black people. In C. Clark (Ed.), *Black psychology* (pp. 3–17). New York: Harper & Row.

Clark, K., & Clark, M. (1947). Racial identification and preference in Negro children. In T. H. Newcomb & E. L. Hartley (Eds.), *Readings in social psychology* (pp. 169–178). New York: Holt.

Clark, K. B. (1963). *Prejudice and your child.* Boston: Beacon Press.

Collett, J., & Serrano, B. (1992). Stirring it up: The inclusive classroom. In L. L. B. Borders & N. V. N. Chism (Eds.), *Teaching for diversity* (pp. 35–48). San Francisco: Jossey-Bass.

Collins, P. H. (1990). *Black feminist thought: Knowledge, consciousness, and the politics of empowerment.* Boston: Unwin Hyman.

Cose, E. (1993). *The rage of a privileged class.* New York: HarperCollins.

Cose, E. (1997). *Color-blind: Seeing beyond race in a race-obsessed world.* New York: HarperCollins.

Crawford, J. (1999). *Bilingual education: History, politics, theory, and practice* (4th ed.). Los Angeles: Bilingual Educational Services.

Cross, T. L. (1987). *The Black power imperative : Racial inequality and the politics of nonviolence.* New York: Faulkner.

Cross, T. L. (Summer, 1988). Services to minority populations: What does it mean to be a culturally competent professional, *Focal Point.* Portland, OR: Research and Training Center, Portland State University.

Cross, T. L., Bazron, B. J., Dennis, K. W., & Isaacs, M. R. (1989). *Toward a culturally competent system of care.* Washington, DC: Georgetown University Development Center.

Cross, W. (1991). *Shades of Black: Diversity in African-American identity.* Philadelphia: Temple University Press.

Cross, W. E. (1971). The Negro-to-Black conversion experience: Toward a psychology of Black liberation. *Black World, 20* (9), 13–27.

Cross, W. E. (1995). The psychology of Nigrescence: Revising the Cross model. In J. G. Ponterotto, J. M. Casas, L. A. Suzuki, & C. M. Alexander (Eds.), *Handbook of multicultural counseling* (pp. 93–123). Thousand Oaks, CA: Sage.

Cuban, L. (1989). The "at-risk" label and the problem of urban school reform. *Phi Delta Kappan 70*(10), 780–784, 799–801.

Curry, N. E., & Johnson, C. N. (1990). *Beyond self-esteem: Developing a genuine sense of human value.* Paper presented at the National Association for the Education of Young Children, Washington, DC.

Daly, A., Jennings, J., Beckett, J. O., & Leashore, B. R. (1995). Effective coping strategies of African Americans. *Social Work, 40,* 240–248.

Delpit, L. (1990). Seeing color: A review of *White Teacher. Hungry Mind Review,* 15, 4–5.

Delpit, L. (1995). *Other people's children: Cultural conflict in the classroom.* New York: The New Press.

Devore, W., & Schlesinger, E. G. (1981). *Ethnic sensitive social work practice.* St. Louis, MO: Mosby.

Diamond, S. (1987). *In search of the primitive: A critique of civilization.* New Brunswick, NJ: Transaction.

Diaz-Ramos, S., Null, K., Pentland, B., & Roush, M. L. (1996). *Parent-teacher scenario.* Unpublished manuscript, Oregon State University, Corvallis.

Diller, J. V. (1991). *Freud's Jewish identity: A case study in the impact of ethnicity.* Cranbury, NJ: Fairleigh Dickinson University Press.

Diller, J. V. (1997). *Informal interviews about self-esteem and racism with People of Color raised outside of the United States.* Paper presented at the Conference on Race and Ethnicity in Higher Education, Orlando, FL.

Dollard, J. (1938). Hostility and fear in social life. *Social Forces, 17,* 15–26.

Draguns, J. G. (1981). Dilemmas and choices in cross-cultural counseling: The universal versus the culturally distinct. In P. B. Pedersen, J. G. Draguns, W. L. Lonner, & J. E. Trimble (Eds.), *Counseling across cultures* (pp. 3–22). Honolulu: University of Hawaii Press.

Dreikurs, R. (1968). *Psychology in the classroom* (2nd ed.). New York: Harper & Row.

Dresser, N. (1996). *Multicultural manners: New rules of etiquette for a changing society.* New York: Wiley.

Dupree, D. B., Spencer, M. B., & Bell, S. (1997). African American children. In G. Johnson-Powell, J. Yamamoto, & W. Arroyo (Eds.), *Transcultural child development: Psychological assessment and treatment.* New York: Wiley.

Duran, E., & Duran, B. (1995). *Native American postcolonial psychology.* Albany, NY: State University of New York Press.

Ellsworth, E. (1990). Why doesn't this feel empowering? Working through the repressive myths of critical pedagogy. *Harvard Education Review, 59* (3), 297–324.

Ely, A. (2000). *Quo no more.* Unpublished manuscript.

Erikson, E. (1968). *Identity, youth and crisis.* New York: Norton.

Falicov, C. J. (1986). Cross-cultural marriages. In N. Jacobson & A. Gurman (Eds.), *Clinical handbook of marital therapy* (pp. 429–450). New York: Guilford Press.

Falicov, C. J. (1996). Mexican families. In M. McGoldrick, J. Giordano, & J. K. Pearce (Eds.), *Ethnicity and family therapy* (pp. 169–182). New York: Guilford Press.

Fennimore, B. S. (1994). Addressing prejudiced statements: A four-step method that works! *Childhood Education, 70* (4), 202–204.

Finders, M. (1992). Looking at lives through ethnography. *Educational Leadership, 50* (1), 60–65.

Fleming, C. M. (1992). American Indians and Alaska Natives: Changing societies past and present. In M. A. Orlandi (Ed.), *Cultural competence for evaluators: A guide for alcohol and other drug abuse prevention practitioners working with ethnic/racial communities* (pp. 147–171). Rockville, MD: U.S. Department of Health and Human Services.

Ford, D. (1996, November). *Adaptation of Banks' curriculum model.* Paper presented at the National Association of Gifted Children, Indianapolis, IN.

Foster, G. P. (2002, September/October). Building a better tomorrow. *NABE News, 26,* 12–14.

Foster, M. (1987). *"It's cooking now": An ethnographic study of teaching style of a successful Black teacher in a White community college.* Unpublished doctoral dissertation. Harvard University, Cambridge, MA.

Foster, M. (1994). Effective Black teachers: A literature review. In E. R. Hollins, J. E. King, & W. C. Hayman (Eds.), *Teaching diverse populations: Formulating a knowledge base* (pp. 225–241). Albany, NY: State University of New York Press.

Fox, K. C. (1993). *Opening closed doors: Perceptions of African American parents and White teachers.* Unpublished master of arts thesis. Cambridge, MA: Lesley College Graduate School.

Freedman, D. G. (1979, January). Ethnic differences in babies. *Human Nature,* 36–43.

Gallimore, R., Boggs, J., & Jordan, C. (1974). *Culture, behaviorism and education: A study of Hawaiian-Americans.* Beverly Hills, CA: Sage.

Garcia, E. E. (1995). Educating Mexican American students: Past treatment and recent developments in theory, research, policy, and practice. In J. A. Banks & C. A. M. Banks (Eds.), *Handbook of research on multicultural education* (pp. 372–387). New York: Macmillan.

Garcia, E. E. (2001). *Hispanic education in the United States.* Lanham, MD: Rowman & Littlefield.

Garcia Coll, C. T. (1990). Development outcome of minority infants: A process oriented look into our beginnings. *Child Development, 61,* 270–289.

Garcia-Preto, N. (1996). Latino families: An overview. In M. McGoldrick, J. Giordan, & J. K. Pearce (Eds.), *Ethnicity and family therapy* (pp. 141–154). New York: Guilford Press.

Gay, G. (2000). *Culturally responsive teaching : Theory, research, and practice.* New York: Teachers College Press.

Gibson, M. A. (1976). Approaches to multicultural education in the United States: Some concepts and assumptions. *Anthropology and Education, 7,* 7–18.

Goodman, M. E. (1952). *Race awareness in young children.* London: Collier.

Gordon, M. (1964). *Assimilation in American life.* New York: Oxford University Press.

Grant, D., & Haynes, D. (1995). A developmental framework for cultural competence training with children. *Social Work in Education, 17,* 171–182.

Green, J. W. (1981). *Cultural awareness in the human services.* Englewood Cliffs, NJ: Prentice Hall.

Grieco, E. M., & Cassidy, R. C. (2001). *Overview of race and Hispanic origin, 2000.* Washington, DC: U.S. Department of Commerce, Economics and Statistics Administration, U.S. Census Bureau.

Grier, W., & Cobbs, P. (1968). *Black rage.* New York: Basic.

Gushue, G. V., & Sciarra, D. T. (1995). Culture and families: A multicultural approach. In J. P. Ponterotto, J. M. Casas, L. A. Suzuki, & C. M. Alexander (Eds.), *Handbook of multicultural counseling* (pp. 586–606). Thousand Oaks, CA: Sage.

Haberman, M. (1996). Selecting and preparing culturally competent teachers for urban schools. In J. Sikula, T. J. Buttery, & E. Guyon (Eds.), *Handbook of research on teacher education* (2nd ed., pp. 247–760). New York: Macmillan.

Hacker, A. (1992). *Two nations: Black and White, separate, hostile, unequal.* New York: Ballantine.

Hale-Benson, J. (1986). *Black children: Their roots, culture and learning style.* Baltimore, MD: Johns Hopkins University Press.

Hampden-Turner, C. (1974). *From poverty to dignity: A strategy for poor Americans.* Garden City, NY: Anchor Press.

Hardiman, R., & Jackson, B. W. (1992). Racial identity development: Understanding racial dynamics in college classrooms and on campus. In M. Adams (Ed.), *Promoting diversity in college classrooms: Innovative responses for the curriculum, faculty and institutions* (pp. 21–37). San Francisco: Jossey-Bass.

Hardy, K. V., & Laszloffy, T. A. (1995). The cultural genogram: Key to training culturally competent family therapists. *Journal of Marital and Family Therapy, 21* (3), 227–237.

Harrington, H. L., & Hathaway, R. S. (1995). Illuminating beliefs about diversity. *Journal of Teacher Education, 46* (4), 275–284.

Hauser, S. T., & Kasendorf, E. (1983). *Black and White identity formation.* Halabar, FL: Kreiger.

Haycock, K. (2001). Closing the achievement gap. *Educational Leadership, 58* (6), 6–11.

Haynes, D. (2003, February 8). CIM and CAM on the block again. *Statesman Journal,* p. 1.

Healey, J. F. (1995). *Race, ethnicity, gender, and class: The sociology of group conflict and change.* Thousand Oaks, CA: Pine Forge Press.

Heath, S. B. (1983). *Ways with words.* Cambridge: Cambridge University Press.

Helms, J. E. (1985). Cultural identity in the treatment process. In P. Pedersen (Ed.), *Handbook of cross-cultural counseling and therapy.* (pp. 239–247) Westport, CT: Greenwood.

Helms, J. E. (1990). An overview of Black racial identity theory. In J. E. Helms (Ed.), *Black and White racial identity: Theory, research and practice* (pp. 9–32). Westport, CT: Greenwood Press.

Helms, J. E. (1995). An update of Helms' White and People of Color racial identity models. In J. P. Ponterotto, J. M. Casas, L. A. Suzuki, & C. M. Alexander (Eds.), *Handbook of multicultural counseling* (pp. 181–198). Thousand Oaks, CA: Sage.

Helms, J. E. (2003, February 21). *How to use Black racial identity theory to solve the Black–White test-score gap.* Paper presented at the Winter Roundtable, Teachers College, Columbia University, New York.

Higgins, K., & Moule, J. (2002, April). *"No more Mr. Nice Guy": Preservice teachers' conflict with classroom management in an African American elementary school.* Paper presented at the American Educational Research Association, New Orleans, LA.

Hill, R. (1972). *The strengths of Black families.* New York: National Urban League.

Hilliard, A. G. (1995). *The maroon within us.* Baltimore: Black Classic Press.

Hines, P. M., & Boyd-Franklin, N. (1982). Black families. In M. McGoldrick, J. K. Pearce, & J. Giordano (Eds.), *Ethnicity and family therapy* (pp. 84–107). New York: Guilford Press.

Ho, D. R. (1994). Asian American perspectives. In J. U. Gordon (Ed.), *Managing multiculturalism in substance abuse services* (pp. 72–98). Thousand Oaks, CA: Sage.

Ho, M. (1987). *Family therapy with ethnic minorities.* Newbury Park, CA: Sage.

Hodgkinson, H. (2002). Demographics and teacher education. *Journal of Teacher Education, 53* (2), 102–105.

Holtzman, W. H., Diaz-Guerrero, R., & Swartz, J. D. (1975). *Personality: Development in two cultures.* Austin: University of Texas Press.

hooks, b. (1994). *Teaching to transgress: Education as the practice of freedom.* New York: Routledge.

Hoopes, D. S. (1972). *Reader in intercultural communication* (Vol. 1 & 2). Pittsburgh, PA: Regional Council for International Education.

Hudelson, S. (1987). The role of native language in literacy in the education of language minority children. *Language Arts 64,* (8) 827–841.

Ignatiev, N. (1995). *How the Irish became White.* New York: Routledge.

Implicit association test. Retrieved from the World Wide Web: Retrieved March 17, 2004 from, *http://ww.tolerance.org/hidden_bias/*

Jacobs, J. H. (1977). *Black/White interracial families: Marital process and identity development in young children.* Unpublished doctoral dissertation, The Wright Institute, Berkeley, CA.

Jensen, A. R. (1972). *Genetics and education.* New York: Harper & Row.

Johnson, L. (2002). "My eyes have been opened": White teachers and racial awareness. *Journal of Teacher Education, 53* (2), 153–167.

Jones, D. L. (2001). *Retaining African Americans in higher education.* Sterling, VA: Stylus.

Jones, E. E., & Korchin, S. J. (1982). Minority mental health: Perspectives. In E. E. Jones & S. J. Korchin (Eds.), *Minority mental health* (pp. 3–36). New York: Praeger.

Jones, J. M. (1972). *Prejudice and racism.* Reading, MA: Addison-Wesley.

Kagan, S., & Madsen, M. (1972). Experimental analysis of cooperation and competition of Anglo-American and Mexican-American children. *Developmental Psychology, 6,* 49–59.

Kardiner, A., & Ovesey, L. (1951). *The mark of oppression.* Cleveland, OH: World Press.

Kendall, F. E. (1997, June). *Understanding White privilege.* Paper presented at the National Conference on Race and Ethnicity in Higher Education, Orlando, FL.

Kerwin, C., & Ponterotto, J. G. (1995). Biracial identity development: Theory and research. In J. P. Ponterotto, J. M. Casas, L. A. Suzuki, & C. M. Alexander (Eds.), *Handbook of multicultural counseling* (pp. 199–217). Thousand Oaks, CA: Sage.

Kich, G. K. (1992). The development process of asserting a biracial, bicultural identity. In M. P. P. Root (Ed.), *Racially mixed people in America* (pp. 304–317). Newbury Park, CA: Sage.

Kivel, P. (1996). *Uprooting racism: How White people can work for racial justice.* Gabriola Island, BC: New Society.

Klein, J. (1980). *Jewish identity and self-esteem: Healing wounds through ethnotherapy.* New York: Institute on Pluralism and Group Identity.

Klor de Alva, J. J. (1988). Telling Hispanics apart: Latin sociocultural diversity. In E. Acosta-Belen & B. R. Sjostrom (Eds.), *The Hispanic experience in the United States* (pp. 107–136). New York: Praeger.

Knapp, S. (2001). *Fighting for freedom: Kindergarteners allowed.* Unpublished work sample, Oregon State University, Corvallis.

Kochman, T. (1981). *Black and White styles in conflict.* Chicago: University of Chicago Press.

Kohn, A. (2000). Burnt at the high stakes. *Journal of Teacher Education, 51* (4), 315–327.

Kroeber, A. L. (1948). *Anthropology: Race, language, culture, psychology, prehistory.* London: Harrap.

Kroeber, A. L., & Kluckhohn, C. (1952). *Culture: A critical review of concepts and definitions.* Cambridge, MA: Papers of the Peabody Museum No. 47.

Kuhn, T. S. (1970). *The structure of scientific revolutions.* Chicago: University of Chicago Press.

Kunjufu, J. (1984). *Countering the conspiracy to destroy Black boys.* Chicago: Afro-Am.

Ladson-Billings, G. (1994). *The dreamkeepers: Successful teachers of African American children.* San Francisco: Jossey-Bass.

Landau, J. (1982). Therapy with families in cultural transition. In M. McGoldrick, J. K. Pearce, & J. Giordan (Eds.), *Ethnicity and family therapy* (pp. 552–572). New York: Guilford Press.

Larsen, J. (1976, October). *Dysfunction in the evangelical family: Treatment considerations.* Paper presented at the American Association of Marriage and Family Therapists, Philadelphia.

LeCompte, M. D. (1994). Defining reality: Applying double description and chaos theory to the practice of practice. *Educational Theory, 44* (3), 277–298.

Lee, E. (1996). Asian American families: An overview. In M. McGoldrick, J. Giordan, & J. K. Pearce (Eds.), *Ethnicity and family therapy* (pp. 227–248). New York: Guilford Press.

Lewin, K. (1948). *Resolving social conflicts: Selected papers on group dynamics.* New York: Harper & Row.

Lewis, A. E. (2003). *Race in the schoolyard: Negotiating the color line in classrooms and communities.* New Brunswick, NJ: Rutgers University Press.

Linton, R. (1945). *The cultural background of personality.* New York: Appleton-Century-Crofts.

Liston, D. P., & Zeichner, K. M. (1996). *Culture and teaching.* Mahwah, NJ: Lawrence Erlbaum.

Lockwood, A. T., & Secada, W. G. (1999). *Transforming education for Hispanic youth: Exemplary practices, programs, and schools.* New York: Teachers College Press.

Lum, D. (1986). *Social work practice and People of Color: A process-stage approach.* Monterey, CA: Brooks/Cole.

MacDonald, C. D., & Sperry, L. L. (1995, February 15–19). *Predicting changes in preservice education students' ethnocentrism.* Paper presented at the National Association for Multicultural Education, Washington, DC.

Manson, S., & Trimble, J. (1982). American Indians and Alaska Native communities: Past efforts, future inquiries. In L. Snowden (Ed.), *Reaching the underserved: Mental health needs of neglected populations* (pp. 143–163). Beverly Hills, CA: Sage.

Marin, G. (1992). Issues in the measurement of acculturation among Hispanics. In K. F. Geisinger (Ed.), *Psychological testing of Hispanics* (pp. 235–252). Washington, DC: American Psychological Association.

Marin, G., & Marin, B. V. (1991). *Research with Hispanic populations.* Newbury Park, CA: Sage.

Marshall, P. L. (2002). *Cultural diversity in our schools.* Belmont, CA: Wadsworth.

McAdoo, H. P. (1985). Racial attitude and self-concept of young Black children over time. In H. P. McAdoo & J. L. McAdoo (Eds.), *Black children: Social, educational, and parental environments* (pp. 213–242). Newbury Park, CA: Sage.

McGoldrick, M. (1982). Normal families: An ethnic perspective. In F. Walsh (Ed.), *Normal family processes* (pp. 399–424). New York: Guilford Press.

McIntosh, P. (1989, July/August). White privilege: Unpacking the invisible knapsack. *Peace and Freedom,* 10–12.

Meier, D. (1995). *The power of their ideas: Lessons for America from a small school in Harlem.* Boston: Beacon Press.

Memmi, A. (1966). *The liberation of the Jew.* New York: Grossman.

Michaels, S. (1981). "Sharing time": Children's narrative styles and differential access to literacy. *Language in Society, 10,* 423–442.

Minuchin, S. (1974). *Families and family therapy.* Cambridge, MA: Harvard University Press.

Minuchin, S., Montalvo, B., Guerney, G., Rosman, B., & Schumer, F. (1967). *Families of the slums.* New York: Basic.

Monroe, S. (1997). Beyond Pocahontas: Authentic images of Native American female protagonists in children's literature. *The New Advocate, 10*(2), 149–159.

Moule, J. (1998). *My journey with preservice teachers: Reflecting on teacher characteristics that bridge multicultural education theory and classroom practice.* Unpublished doctoral dissertation, Oregon State University, Corvallis.

Moule, J. (2002, November). *Fighting for freedom: Kindergarteners allowed.* Paper presented at the National Association for Multicultural Education, Washington, DC.

Moule, J. (2003a). *Immersion for cultural competency and pedagogical strength in math and science* (Final Report for Eisenhower Professional Development Grant). Corvallis, OR: Oregon State University.

Moule, J. (2003b). A recent incident. Unpublished manuscript, Oregon State University, Corvallis.

Moule, J. (2004). Safe and growing out of the box. In J.J. Romo, P. Bradfield, & R. Serrano (Eds.), *Reclaiming democracy: Multicultural educators' journeys toward transformative teaching* (pp. 147–171). Upper Saddle River, NJ:Pearson Merrill Prentice Hall.

Moule, J., & Ingram, M. (2002, April). *Developing the cultural competency of White preservice and inservice teachers using socio-cultural poetry or "White girl what you got in your bag?"* Paper presented at the American Educational Research Association, New Orleans.

Moynihan, D. P. (1965). *The Negro family: The case for national action.* Washington, DC: Office of Policy Planning and Research, U.S. Department of Labor.

Murtadha-Watts, K. (1998). Teacher education in urban school-based, multiagency collaboratives. *Urban Education, 32* (5), 616–631.

Myers, H., & King, L. (1985). Mental health issues in the development of the Black American child. In G. Johnson-Powell, J. Yamamoto, A. Romero, & A. Morales (Eds.), *The psychosocial development of minority children* (pp. 275–306). New York: Brunner/Mazel.

Myers, H. F. (1982). Stress, ethnicity, and social class: A model for research with Black populations. In E. E. Jones & S. J. Korchin (Eds.), *Minority mental health* (pp. 118–148). New York: Praeger.

National Center for Educational Statistics (1996). *National assessment of educational progress.* Washington, D.C.: Institute of Educational Studies, U.S. Dept. of Education.

National Council of Teachers of English and the International Reading Association (1996). *Standards for the English language arts.* Urbana, IL: National Council of Teachers of English; Newark, DE: International Reading Association.

Nieto, S. (1996). *Affirming diversity : The sociopolitical context of multicultural education.* White Plains, NY: Longman.

Nobles, W. W. (1972). African philosophy: Foundations for Black psychology. In R. L. Jones (Ed.), *Black psychology* (pp. 18–32). New York: Harper & Row.

Noordhoff, K., & Kleinfeld, J. (1993). Preparing teachers for multicultural classrooms. *Teaching and Teacher Education, 9* (1), 27–39.

Norton, D. G. (1983). Black families life patterns, the development of self and cognitive development of Black children. In G. Johnson-Powell, J. Yamamoto, A. Romero, & A. Morales (Eds.), *The psychosocial development of minority children* (pp. 181–193). New York: Brunner/Mazel.

Oetting, E. R., & Beauvais, F. (1990). Orthogonal cultural identity theory: The cultural identification in minority adolescents. *International Journal of Addiction, 25,* 655–685.

Ogbu, J. U. (1978). *Minority education and caste: The American system in cross-cultural perspective.* New York: Academic Press.

Ogbu, J. U. (1992). Understanding cultural diversity and learning. *Educational Researcher, 21* (8), 5–14.

Orbe', L. V. (2004). *Racial identity, recognition of spouses' conflict resolution styles, and marital satisfaction in interracially married individuals.* Unpublished doctoral dissertaion, Columbia University, New York.

Oregon Department of Education. (2000). *1999–2000 summary of organization, students and staff in Oregon public schools* (SF00-07). Salem, OR: Author.

Oregon University System. (2001). *Cultural competence for teachers: A preliminary report on approaches in other states.* Eugene, OR: Oregon University System.

Ovando, C. (1990). Politics and pedagogy: The case of bilingual education. *Harvard Education Review, 60* (3), 341–356.

Paley, V. G. (1979). *White teacher.* Cambridge, MA: Harvard University Press.

Pang, V. (2001). *Multicultural education: A caring-centered, reflective approach.* New York: McGraw Hill.

Pang, V. O. (1994, December). Why do we need this class? Multicultural education for teachers. *Phi Delta Kappan,* 289–292.

Parnes, S. (1967). *Creative behavior guidebook.* New York: Scribner.

Perkins, M. (1994, March 17). Guess who's coming to church? Confronting Christians' fear of interracial marriage. *Christianity Today,* 30–33.

Petersen, P. B., Draguns, J. G., Lonner, W. J., & Trimble, J. E. (1989). *Counseling across culture.* Honolulu: University of Hawaii Press.

Pinderhughes, E. (1989). *Understanding race, ethnicity, and power: The key to efficacy in clinical practice.* New York: Free Press.

Pollard, K. M., & O'Hare, W. P. (1999). America's racial and ethnic minorities. *Population Bulletin, 54* (3), 3–48.

Ponterotto, J. G. (1988). Racial consciousness development among White counselor trainees: A stage model. *Journal of Multicultural Counseling and Development, 16,* 146–156.

Ponterotto, J. G., Casas, J. M., Suzuki, L. A., & Alexander, C. M. (1995). *Handbook of multicultural counseling.* Thousand Oaks, CA: Sage.

Poussaint, A. F. (1972). *Why Blacks kill Blacks.* New York: Emerson Hall.

Powell, G. J. (1973). The self-concept in White and Black children. In C. V. Willie, B. Kramer, & B. Brown (Eds.), *Racism and mental health* (pp. 299–318). Pittsburgh: University of Pittsburgh Press.

Proshansky, H., & Newton, P. (1968). The meaning and nature of Negro self-identity. In M. Deutsch, I. Katz, & A. Jensen (Eds.), *Social class, race and psychological development.* New York: Holt, Rinehart & Winston.

Reinharz, S., & Davidman, L. (1992). *Feminist methods in social research.* New York: Oxford University Press.

Rethinking Schools (1991). *Rethinking Columbus: Teaching about the 500th anniversary of Columbus's arrival in America.* Milwaukee, WI: Author.

Reynolds, C. R., & Kaiser, S. M. (1990). Test bias in psychological assessment. In T. B. Gutkin & C. R. Reynolds (Eds.), *The handbook of school psychology* (pp. 487–525). New York: Wiley.

Riche, M. F. (2000). America's diversity and growth: Signposts for the 21st century. *Population Bulletin, 55*(2), 3–38.

Rimm, S. B. (1997). An underachievement epidemic. *Educational Leadership, 54* (7), 18–22.

Rinaldi, A. (1999). *My heart is on the ground: The diary of Nannie Little Rose, a Sioux girl.* New York: Scholastic.

Rokeach, M. (1960). *Beliefs, attitudes, and values.* New York: Basic.

Romo, H. (1999). *Reaching out: Best practices for educating Mexican-origin children and youth.* Charleston, WV: Clearinghouse on Rural Education and Small Schools.

Rosenberg, M. (1979). *Conceiving the self.* New York: Basic.

Rosenthal, D. (1976). *Experimenter effects in behavioral research.* New York: Halsted Press.

Rosenthal, R., & Jacobson, L. (1968). *Pygmalion in the classroom: Teacher expectations and pupils' intellectual development.* New York: Holt, Rinehart & Winston.

Rowe, W., Behrens, J. T., & Leach, M. M. (1995). Racial/ethnic identity and social consciousness: Looking back and looking forward. In J. P. Ponterotto, J. M. Casas, L. A. Suzuki, & C. M. Alexander (Eds.), *Handbook of multicultural counseling* (pp. 218–235). Thousand Oaks, CA: Sage.

Ruiz, R. (1990). Official languages and language planning. In K. L. Adams & D. T. Brink (Eds.), *Perspectives on official English: The campaign for English as the official language of the USA* (pp. 11–24). Berlin: Mouton de Gruyter.

Saeki, C., & Borow, H. (1985). Counseling and psychotherapy: East and west. In P. B. Pedersen (Ed.), *Handbook of cross-cultural counseling and therapy.* Westport, CT: Greenwood Press.

Scanzoni, J. N. (1971). *The Black family in modern society.* Chicago: University of Chicago Press.

Scarr, S. (1993). Biological and cultural diversity: The legacy of Darwin for development. *Child Development, 64,* 1333–1353.

Schank, R. C. (1990). *Tell me a story: A new look at real and artificial memory.* New York: Scribner.

Seifer, R., Sameroff, A., Barrett, L., & Krafchuk, E. (1994). Infant temperament measured by multiple observations and mother report. *Child Development, 65,* 1478–1490.

Singer, D., & Seldin, R. (1994). *American Jewish yearbook.* New York: American Jewish Committee.

Sleeter, C. E. (2001). Preparing teachers for culturally diverse schools: Research and the overwhelming presence of Whiteness. *Journal of Teacher Education, 52* (2), 94–106.

Smolowe, J. (1993, November). Intermarried . . . with children. *Time, 142,* 64–65.

Snowden, L., & Todman, P. A. (1982). The psychological assessment of Blacks: New and needed developments. In E. E. Jones & S. J. Korchin (Eds.), *Minority mental health* (pp. 227–249). New York: Praeger.

Spencer, S., Steele, C., & Quinn, D. (1998). Stereotype threat and woman's math performance. *Journal of Experimental Social Psychology, 35,* 4–28.

Spenser, M. B., & Markstrom-Adams, C. (1990). Identity processes among racial and ethnic minority children in America. *Child Development, 61,* 290–310.

Stachowski, L. L., & Mahan, J. M. (1998). Cross-cultural field placements: Student teachers learning from schools and communities. *Theory into Practice, 37* (2), 155–162.

Stack, C. (1975). *All our kin: Strategies for survival in a Black community.* New York: Harper & Row.

Steele, C. (1992, April). Race and the schooling of Black Americans. *Atlantic Monthly,* 68–78.

Stonequist, E. V. (1961). *The marginal man: A study in personality and culture conflict.* New York: Russell & Russell.

Sue, D. W., Arredondo, A., & McDavis, R. J. (1992). Multicultural counseling competencies and standards: A call to the profession. *Journal of Counseling and Development, 70,* 477–486.

Sue, S., & Zane, N. (1987). The role of culture and cultural techniques in psychotherapy: A critique and reformulation. *American Psychologist, 42,* 37–45.

Sue, S. W., & Sue, D. (1990). *Counseling the culturally different: Theory and practice* (2nd ed.). New York: Wiley.

Sue, S. W., & Sue, D. (1999). *Counseling the culturally different: Theory and practice* (3rd ed.). New York: Wiley.

Sutton, C. E. T., & Broken Nose, M. A. (1996). American Indian families: An overview. In M. McGoldrick, J. Giordan, & J. K. Pearce (Eds.), *Ethnicity and family therapy* (pp. 31–44). New York: Guilford Press.

Suzuki, L. A., & Kugler, J. F. (1995). Intellectual and personality assessment: Multicultural perspectives. In J. P. Ponterotto, J. M. Casas, L. A. Suzuki, & C. M. Alexander (Eds.), *Handbook of multicultural counseling* (pp. 493–516). Thousand Oaks, CA: Sage.

Takaki, R. (1993). *A different mirror: A history of multicultural America.* Boston: Little, Brown.

Talbot, M. (2003, February). Searching for Sacagawea. *National Geographic.* 68–85.

Tashakkori, A., & Ochoa, S. H. (Eds.). (1999). *Education of Hispanics in the United States: Politics, policies, and outcomes.* New York: AMS Press.

Tatum, B. D. (1992a). *Assimilation blues: Black families in a White community.* Northampton, MA: Hazel-Maxwell.

Tatum, B. D. (1992b). Talking about race, learning about racism: The application of racial identity developmental theory in the classroom. *Harvard Education Review, 62* (1), 1–24.

Tatum, B. D. (1997). *"Why are all the Black kids sitting together in the cafeteria?" And other conversations about race.* New York: Basic.

Taylor, L. S., & Whittaker, C. R. (2003). *Bridging multiple worlds: Case studies of diverse educational communities.* Boston: Allyn & Bacon.

Thornton, M. C., Chatters, L. M., Taylor, R. J., & Allen, W. (1990). Sociodemographic and environmental correlates of racial socialization by Black parents. *Child Development, 61,* 401–409.

Tong, B. R. (1981). *On the confusion of psychopathology with culture: Iatrogenesis in the "treatment" of Chinese Americans.* Unpublished manuscript. The Wright Institute. Berkeley, CA.

Trawick-Smith, J. W. (1997). *Early childhood development: A multicultural perspective.* Upper Saddle River, NJ: Prentice Hall.

Trawick-Smith, J. W., & Lisi, P. (1994). Infusing multicultural perspectives in an early childhood development course: Effect on the knowledge and attitudes of inservice teachers. *Journal of Early Childhood Teacher Education, 15,* 8–12.

U.S. Department of Education. (1997). Washington, DC: Author.

Uba, L. (1994). *Asian Americans: Personality patterns, identity, and mental health.* New York: Guilford Press.

United States Bureau of the Census (2002). *Profile of selected social characteristics: 2000.* Washington, D.C.: Government Printing Office.

Valentine, C. A. (1971). Deficit, difference, and bicultural models of Afro-American behavior. *Harvard Educational Review, 41,* 135–157.

Vontress, C. E. (1981). Racial and ethnic barriers in counseling. In P. B. Pedersen, J. G. Draguns, W. L. Lonner, & J. E. Trimble (Eds.), *Counseling across cultures* (2nd ed., pp. 87–107). Honolulu: University of Hawaii Press.

Waldschmidt, E. D. (2002). Bilingual interns' barriers to becoming teachers: At what cost do we diversify the teaching force? *Bilingual Research Journal, 26* (3), 537–561.

Weinstein, G., & Mellen, D. (1997). Anti-Semitism curriculum design. In M. Adams, L. A. Bell, & P. Griffin (Eds.), *Teaching for diversity and social justice* (pp. 170–197). New York: Routledge.

White, J. (1972). Towards a Black psychology. In R. Jones (Ed.), *Black psychology* (pp. 43–50). New York: Harper & Row.

Wijeyesinghe, C. L., Griffin, P., & Love, B. (1997). Racism curriculum design. In M. Adams, L. A. Bell, & P. Griffin (Eds.), *Teaching for diversity and social justice* (pp. 82–109). New York: Routledge.

Williams, J. E., & Morland, J. K. (1976). *Race, Color and the young child.* Chapel Hill: University of North Carolina Press.

Williams, R. M. (1947). The reduction of intergroup tensions. *Social Science Council Bulletin, 59,* 119–127.

Wolkind, S., & Rutter, M. (1985). *Sociocultural factors in child and adolescent psychiatry.* Boston: Blackwell Scientific.

Wright, M. A. (1998). *I'm chocolate, you're vanilla: Raising healthy Black and biracial children in a race-conscious world.* San Francisco: Jossey-Bass.

Wylie, R. C. (1961). *The self-concept.* Lincoln: University of Nebraska Press.

Yamamoto, J., & Acosta, F. X. (1982). Treatment of Asian-Americans and Hispanic-Americans: Similarities and differences. *Journal of the Academy of Psychoanalysis 10,* 585–607.

Yeo, F. (1999). The barriers of diversity: Multicultural education and rural schools. *Multicultural Education, 6* (5), 2–7.

York, S. (1991). *Roots and wings: Affirming culture in early childhood programs.* St Paul, MN: Redleaf Press.

Index